Leisurely ISLAM

PRINCETON STUDIES IN MUSLIM POLITICS

Dale F. Eickelman and Augustus Richard Norton, series editors

A list of titles in this series can be found at the back of the book

Leisurely ISLAM

Negotiating Geography and Morality
in Shi'ite South Beirut

Lara Deeb & Mona Harb

PRINCETON UNIVERSITY PRESS

Princeton and Oxford

Copyright © 2013 by Princeton University Press
Published by Princeton University Press, 41 William Street, Princeton, New Jersey 08540
In the United Kingdom: Princeton University Press, 6 Oxford Street, Woodstock,
    Oxfordshire OX20 1TW

press.princeton.edu

Library of Congress Cataloging-in-Publication Data
  Deeb, Lara, 1974–
    Leisurely Islam : negotiating geography and morality in Shi'ite South Beirut / Lara Deeb
    and Mona Harb.
      pages cm — (Princeton studies in Muslim politics)
    Includes bibliographical references and index.
    ISBN 978-0-691-15365-0 (hardcover : alk. paper) — ISBN 978-0-691-15366-7 (pbk. : alk. paper)
    1. Leisure—Lebanon—Beirut. 2. Shiites—Lebanon—Beirut. 3. Recreation areas—Lebanon—Beirut.
    4. Leisure—Religious aspects—Islam. I. Harb, Mona. II. Title.
    BJ1498.D324 2013
    306.4′812095 6925—dc23   2012049867

British Library Cataloging-in-Publication Data is available

This book has been composed in Stempel Garamond

Printed on acid-free paper. ∞

Printed in the United States of America

10 9 8 7 6 5 4 3 2 1

Contents

List of Figures   vii

Preface and Acknowledgments   ix

Note on Language   xiii

INTRODUCTION: Exploring Leisure, Morality, and Geography
in South Beirut   1

1 New Leisure in South Beirut   35

2 Producing Islamic Fun: Hizbullah, Fadlallah, and the
Entrepreneurs   66

3 Mapping Leisure and Café Styles   102

4 Flexible Morality, Respectful Choices, Smaller Transgressions   135

5 Comforting Territory, New Urban Experiences, and the
Moral City   176

6 Good Taste, Leisure's Moral Spaces, and Sociopolitical
Change in Lebanon   208

Appendix: Quoted Figures and Characters   223

Notes   227

Glossary   261

References   263

Index   277

Figures

———

1.1 Fantasy World amusement park   36
2.1 Image from the LAA's Values campaign that reads "my family
    is my happiness"   70
2.2 Al-Saha Traditional Village restaurant   86
3.1 Map of location of Dahiya in Beirut   104
3.2 Map of the emergence and growth of leisure sites in
    south Beirut   105
3.3 Map of the geographic distribution of leisure sites in
    south Beirut   106
3.4 The main road in Sainte-Thérèse   107
3.5 Map of income distribution in south Beirut   108
3.6 Map analyzing leisure sites by size, functions, and price range 110
3.7 A diwaniyyeh interior in al-Saha Traditional Village restaurant 115
3.8 Ground floor of Bab al-Hara   117
3.9 Nasamat's garden seating area   120
3.10 Nasamat's garden entrance   121
3.11 Dining room at Swiss Time   123
3.12 Dining room at Aghadir   124
3.13 Coffee bar at Coda Café   125
3.14 Bab al-Hara's upstairs area   126
3.15 Dining room at Terrace   128
3.16 Photoshopped images of Italian monuments on
    Il Ponte's wall   131
3.17 Mural of a town, next to argileh storage in Il Ponte café   132
3.18 Lebanese heritage-style features, hung on the wall near
    contemporary faux-leather sofas in Il Ponte café   133
5.1 Signs on a major highway in Dahiya   177
5.2 A new highway in south Beirut   179

Preface and Acknowledgments

This book began with a conversation on a bench at the American University of Beirut in July 2002; it began with a friendship that grew into a research collaboration, and became a collaboration that nurtured that friendship. We had met earlier, in February 2000, while we were each doing fieldwork (and in fact, interviewing the same person back-to-back) on different topics related to south Beirut. But that conversation in summer 2002, which tacked between work and life, solidified what is certain to be a lifelong friendship and inspired this project, which we are now seeing to its conclusion.

Our collaboration began as an exploration of what we call the Shi'i Islamic milieu in Lebanon. Early research took us to Khiam in the South, the Bekaa Valley, and all around south Beirut. Our field research was violently interrupted by the 2006 Israeli war on Lebanon. Following that war, the café sector in the area became strikingly visible in new ways. We narrowed our focus to leisure, and even more specifically, the emerging ideas as well as practices of morality and space that are both producing and being produced by new leisure places in south Beirut. Looking back at our notes, our initial desires for our collaboration ranged from answering the question "Why is Hizbullah investing in entertainment projects?" to showing that the party is only one piece of the vibrancy of everyday life in south Beirut. In the end, we were inspired by Lebanese politics and specifically an advertising campaign positing a "culture of death" against those who "love life." We wanted to show the different ways that people can and do *enjoy themselves* in different parts of the city. We wanted to treat leisure as something that is, on the one hand, as disciplined as other aspects of life, and on the other hand, an arena for potential dissonance. We hope that the chapters that follow accomplish some of that.

The research and writing of this book have benefited from several generous sources of funding, for which we are grateful. These included funding from the University of California at Irvine, the American University of Beirut, Scripps College, a Wenner-Gren International Collaborative Research Grant, and an American Council of Learned Societies Collaborative Research Fellowship.

We are thankful to many individuals who shared their knowledge with us: Ali al-Daher from the Lebanese Arts Association, Ghassan Darwish from Hizbullah's Media Office, Abdul-Halim Fadlallah from the Consultative Center for Studies and Documentation, member of Parliament Ali Fayyad, and Ghobeyri's mayor Muhammad Sa'id al-Khansa. We are also grateful for the help of Sayyid Ja'far Fadallah (the son of the late Sayyid Muhammad Hussein Fadlallah) along with the representatives of Sayyid Khamenei and Sayyid Sistani's offices as well as the rapid email responses of the staff at Fadlallah's Web site. We thank all the café owners, managers, and land brokers we interviewed as well as the waiters (and few waitresses) with whom we had informal conversations. We particularly thank Adham Tabaja from al-Inmaa' Group and Jamal Makki from al-Saha Traditional Village.

The data for this book were collected with help from a fabulous team of research assistants. We warmly acknowledge Fatima Koumeyha, Lamia Moghnieh, Hazar al-Asadi, Tala A. Rahmeh, and Sara Aslam Dada. Nidal al-Azraq provided invaluable transcription assistance. We especially appreciate the outstanding work of Douaa Sheet on several research tasks and aid of Diala Dagher, who responded consistently to our numerous requests.

The maps in this book were conceived and designed by Ahmad Gharbieh. Working with him was a rewarding experience, and we thank him for helping us represent our data with such rigor and clarity, and teaching us how to think with mapping tools. We also thank Wissam Bou-Assi for her patience and dedication in executing these maps.

For reading and commenting helpfully on our work in various forms, we thank Lori Allen, Hiba Bou-Akar, Sherine Hafez, Howayda al-Harithy, Dina al-Kassim, Mazen Labban, Pardis Mahdavi, Samuli Schielke, and Chris Toensing. We are especially grateful to Esra Ozyurek, who turned her careful and pragmatic eye on the full manuscript. For useful comments and inspiring conversations, we thank Asad AbuKhalil, Kamran Ali, Talal Atrissi, Fadi Bardawil, Asef Bayat, Azza Charara-Beydoun, Teresa Caldeira, Ghassan Hage, James Holston, Zeina Maasri, Sofian Merabet, Maya Mikdashi, Richard Norton, Diane Riskedahl, Ananya Roy, Nezar Al-Sayyad, Nadya Sbaiti, Kirsten Scheid, Abdou-Maliq Simone, Susan Slyomovics, Fawwaz Traboulsi, Jessica Winegar, and too many lecture audiences to list.

At Princeton University Press, we appreciate Fred Appel's trust and editorial eye, and the diligence and patience of his assistant Sarah David, production editor Sara Lerner, copyeditor Cindy Milstein, and indexer Jan Williams, as well as the helpful comments of two anonymous reviewers. It should go without saying that all flaws remain our own.

For their friendship in Lebanon, we are ever grateful to Dia Abou-Mousleh, Mona Fawaz, Vienna Khansa, Haitham Khoury, Zeina Maasri, and Michel Sawaya (who also helpfully explained Lebanese real estate). Haitham in particular has been a generous (and always fun!) host for Lara in Beirut many times. In part, we owe the pleasure of working together to a mutual dear friend, Nadya Sbaiti, who prompted our conversation on an American University of Beirut bench years ago, accompanied us to a couple interviews, hung out in cafés, shared ideas, read pieces, kept us both sane separately and together, and always believed in this book.

There have also been myriad coffees, lunches, and dinners with our partners, Qutayba Abdullatif and Sami Atallah, in Beirut, San Diego, and Los Angeles. They were sometimes accosted with questions like "What does this décor make you think of? Do you like it? *Tayyib*, ["OK"] why? *Tayyib*, why not?" We thank them for tolerating our passion for ethnography—not always an easy task for the quantitatively inclined.

Mona thanks Sami for his unconditional love, amid the wails, smiles, laughter, yells, and billion requests of our beautiful little princess, Yasmine, and her high-maintenance big brother, Nadim. This book bears witness to the painstaking process that brought us together, from Hamra all the way to Manhattan and back. And Mona also thanks her parents, Sami and Salma, for their unfailing support and care.

Lara thanks Qutayba for the enduring (life's sunshine and love), the mundane (translations of Arabic slang yelled across the house), and everything we share that is beautifully enduring and mundane alike. She is grateful to her in-laws in Amman, where parts of this book were written, and her father-in-law for his interest in her work. And as always, Lara thanks her parents for their support and her relationship to Lebanon, and her brother, Hadi, for continuing to inspire, now with greater shared disciplinary language than ever, since he has defected to the world of anthropology.

There have been precious moments in our collaboration: the morning we sat in Mona's office at the American University of Beirut putting the finishing touches on our Wenner-Gren grant application and realized that we knew what we were talking about; the moment after a presentation in Berkeley, California, when we realized that we knew how to answer the questions asked by the audience; the moment in 2009 when we realized we had enough material to stop doing fieldwork; and the moment in 2010 sitting in a café on Makdisi Street when we realized we had just outlined our book, and to the surprise of other patrons, squealed like thirteen-year-olds at a Tiësto concert and hugged each other in delight. There have been innumerable emails, some of which simply exclaim, "I LOVE working with you!" and others that infectiously reinspire one of us to work on the project, and one particularly memorable interview when we had to restrain ourselves from laughing out loud when we were instructed that a woman's place is in the kitchen. There have also been near accidents, frustrations, and moments when we think it will never happen or aren't quite sure what the other is talking about, but those have paled in comparison to the pleasures of working together. We hope our readers enjoy the product of our joint labor as much as we have enjoyed making it.

Note on Language

––––––––––––––

Our interlocutors spoke mainly in Lebanese dialect, but also used Modern Standard Arabic, English, and French. We have used an extremely simplified system for transliterating Arabic, omitting all indication of long versus short vowels as well as any distinctions between *hard* and *soft* letters, and we do not specify which form of Arabic was spoken. We trust that specialist readers will be able to use the context to follow our transliteration. Proper nouns and place-names are rendered in their official or most common spellings in Lebanon (e.g., Nasrallah or Ain el-Mreisseh). When interviewees inserted English words into mainly Arabic statements, those English terms are indicated with underlining.

Leisurely ISLAM

Introduction

Exploring Leisure, Morality, and Geography in South Beirut

It was a typical Thursday around three in the afternoon in late summer about a year after Bab al-Hara opened.[1] We walked up a short flight of stone stairs and through a small outdoor seating area to the café entrance just above the level of the busy street. Two collection boxes for Shi'i charitable organizations flanked the main door—one for Al-Mabarrat, the organization affiliated with prominent religious leader Sayyid Muhammad Hussein Fadlallah, and the other for Hizbullah's Emdad Foundation. We stepped into a large room, its faux stone walls graced with antique objects and photographs from the popular Syrian television series that is the café's namesake. Two television screens were tuned to Hizbullah's Al-Manar station, with the volume set so low that it was barely audible. Toward the back of the room, beside a staircase leading to the first floor, a young couple was seated on one of the low couches arranged in a rectangle around a low wood and glass table. The couch was upholstered in the red-and-black-striped fabric common to these cafés. The wall behind them held an old clock, a sword, and a lantern, with a set of brass coffeepots resting on a narrow shelf below. The couple looked like they were twenty at most. Both wore jeans and sneakers, his accompanied by a black T-shirt with something printed on it, and hers by a long, loose purple blouse and brightly printed matching headscarf, pinned at the side to cover her neck but not her chin. His arm was draped lightly around her, and they appeared to be engaged in an intense conversation.

We walked up the stairs and were greeted by a sudden shift in décor.[2] Red, black, white, and zebra-striped leather chairs and sofas with metal legs were arranged around ceramic and metal tables, with checkerboard tops in the same colors under glass surfaces. Horizontal purple stripes along one wall framed a long poster of primarily red, black, and white computer graphic images ranging from a coffee cup and saucer to silhouettes of faces and bodies, with the English words "drink it" printed every so often. As it continued along the wall, the poster included enlarged photographs of groups of young people and more silhouettes, with the English phrase "I have something to tell you" accompanying them.

Besides our table, there were seven others with customers on this floor. A young man and woman, both wearing jeans and T-shirts, were drinking tall juices and having an animated conversation in one corner. Across the room sat another couple, drinking espresso. They looked a few years older, perhaps in their late twenties or early thirties, and were dressed more conservatively, he in slacks and a button-down shirt, and she in Islamic dress — a long, loose coatlike dress in navy blue with a blue and white printed headscarf. They seemed less familiar with one another; their conversation proceeded as though they were asking each another questions across the table. Scattered around the room were three tables of lone men sitting and smoking *argileh* (hookah); one seemed to be in his twenties, and the other two in their thirties or perhaps older. The coals for their argilehs were regularly replenished by men wearing two slightly different uniforms — one that resembled representations of Lebanese village dress during the Ottoman Empire, often seen on dolls or in folkloric performances, and the other that mimicked the outfits on the *Bab al-Hara* television series. One of the older men seemed quite familiar with the waitstaff and appeared at one point to be giving them instructions. Two tables were filled with groups of youths. Three young women and a young man pored over textbooks at one table, while three young men and two young women laughed and talked loudly at the other, making the most noise in the place.

We perused the menu, which was written in Arabic and frequently misspelled English, with a photo from the television series on the cover. The possibilities included a selection of coffee ranging from espresso to Arabic coffee to Nescafé, a variety of fresh fruit juices in various combinations, fresh fruit cocktails, sandwiches including *shawarma* (gyros) and *taouk* (grilled chicken) as well as *frisco* and other popular variations, a variety of *saj* (a thin bread folded over with a variety of fillings) options, and a selection of argilehs. Our young waitress was wearing tight black pants and a shiny pale-violet blouse in the latest fashion, with a sheer sparkly white and violet headscarf draped around her hair several times to provide coverage along with full makeup in intense colors. She took our order of fresh fruit cocktails and a chicken sandwich (which was delicious) to share, and stopped to flirt with one of the argileh smokers on her way downstairs to give the order to the kitchen. The other waiters were all young men wearing black shirts and pants with the café's logo on the shirt pocket. On this level, one television screen was set without sound to Al Jazeera Sports, and the other, also without sound, to a rerun of the popular Turkish telenovella *Noor*.

On a trip to the restroom on the ground floor, a glance over to the couple sitting near the stairs caught them kissing passionately. They remained the only downstairs customers. Our table afforded us a view out the window to the main street of Sainte-Thérèse below. A steady stream of passersby walked along the road, sometimes interrupting the flow of traffic to cross. Two blond women wearing business suits with skirts above their knees and pumps walked by quickly, followed by a shaykh in his robe and turban, a group of teenage boys eating sandwiches, a woman in Islamic dress holding a small child's hand, and a young woman in a green sleeveless sundress carrying a book bag; this young woman turned into the café and joined the study group seated in front of us.

By 4:00 p.m. the younger single man, both couples, and the loud group of youths had left. We were joined on the upper level by another large group, possibly a family. Two men pushed several tables together to create a space large enough for themselves as well as the three women, two children, and two babies with them. As they ordered a lot of food, two other men joined the older argileh smoker who knew the waitstaff. We asked our waitress who that argileh smoker was, and she explained that he was the owner of the café. Three argileh-smoking guys who sat together also joined the upstairs crowd, along with a table of two twenty-something women—one in a T-shirt, and the other in a sleeveless blouse—a table of two women in Islamic dress with a baby, and a table with a teenage couple, the young woman dressed to the nines in tight pants, a revealing strappy top, stilettos, full makeup, and straightened hair. The couple chose a corner table and sat on the same side next to each other.

Another trip down the stairs revealed that the original young couple had departed. Two men sat at a table to one side eating, and a conservatively dressed young couple with their son also shared a meal. A woman in a clingy hot-pink dress and heels, a woman in a slinky tank top, and a man in jeans and a fitted T-shirt stood in the center of the room deciding where to sit, and eventually settled into the low couch area beside the stairs. A staffperson, who had been walking around with cleaning supplies since our arrival, was mopping the floor.

An hour later the ground floor was dominated by male customers, with the exceptions of our research assistant Douaa and the group by the stairs; the group appeared to be on its second round of coffee drinks with argileh. At one table, a group of three men smoked argileh and drank coffee. Two of them appeared to be in their forties, dressed in business attire and having a work-related conversation. The third was younger, and wore jeans, a fitted T-shirt that said "Toronto" on it, and a Nike cap. He had a large tattoo of some kind of animal on his arm and bandages on his nose indicating recent cosmetic surgery. As two young women in knee-length dresses from the study group upstairs descended toward the exit and waited for a taxi, "Toronto" followed them with his eyes. Another young woman came down and walked into the restroom, and again he watched.

A man we had been introduced to as the manager arrived and greeted the table of three men on the ground floor. He is in his mid-forties, and on this occasion was wearing an off-white, button-down shirt with white collar and cuffs along with a shiny-pink necktie. One of the forty-something men took a call on his cell phone, speaking loudly in broken English, "We need sixty ton. . . . Yeah. . . . No, you have to call him. . . . Tell him you are from Monsieur Joseph [said with a French inflection]. . . . Yallah call him now." The young man rested a pair of sunglasses that appeared out of nowhere on top of his cap before greeting a young woman who walked in and headed upstairs. Meanwhile, the argileh table was joined by a fourth man dressed in jeans and T-shirt.

By now the manager was greeting almost everyone who entered the café, often indicating familiarity with them: "How are you, mademoiselle?" "Where have you been? *wayn hal ghaybeh*" "Welcome." The only people he didn't greet were young women who headed directly upstairs without a glance at him, including a group of five in their late teens or early twenties. One of them was wearing a casual sleeveless top and jeans, and the others were in tight pants that in one case revealed the details of her thong, long-sleeve stretchy shirts, and matching headscarves. They were followed by a blond woman in a miniskirt who scanned the upstairs tables quickly before heading back down toward the exit. As she left, the manager asked, "What, you didn't find them?" and she smiled and responded affirmatively as she walked out. A group of two fortyish couples entered and took a large, prominent table on the ground floor. The conservatively dressed man who had eaten on the ground floor previously with his wife and son returned with a much older couple—old enough to be his parents—and settled them into seats on the ground floor. He then walked over to chat with the table of two couples, and was joined there by the manager.

By 6:30 p.m., the upstairs was dominated by youths, with the exception of the owner, who still sat holding court with different passing male customers. The teenage couple left, after nursing their fruit juices for over two and a half hours. The study group was significantly reconfigured, with only one original member. There were also tables of five young women chatting and giggling loudly, a young man sitting alone who kept looking out the window, two young women with a young man, and a young woman in a rusty-orange, ribbed, low-cut tank top with two men of differing ages. The latter table was within earshot, and we heard the woman ordering coffees for herself and her companions as the younger one presented some kind of business deal having to do with the Arab Gulf to their older, white-haired companion. Downstairs people were mainly eating meals. The diners included the older couple, two forty-something men, a conservatively dressed couple with a teenage daughter with straightened hair, a black woman who did not wear a headscarf with a baby and a young preteen daughter who did, and a couple with two children who had their Sri Lankan domestic worker seated with them, and who the manager seemed to know quite well. Two couples with elegantly dressed, and subtly made-up women and men in business attire joined the table of two fortyish couples. A conservatively dressed young woman in a green headscarf walked in, and as she headed for the stairs, asked the manager if he had seen Sa'id. He replied that Sa'id was waiting for her upstairs. She joined the young man who had been looking out the window.

When the evening news came on Al-Manar, the manager turned up the volume on both televisions downstairs. The four couples had finished their food and ordered dessert, and were the only people paying attention to the news. The sound on the two televisions was not quite synchronized, so after a few minutes the manager turned the volume down on the television that was further from their table.

The downstairs crowd changed again around 8:00 p.m. to people who ordered mainly desserts and argileh. A mother and daughter sat underneath the stairs; the latter was wearing a fitted jogging suit and sneakers with straightened hair and flashy, long, silver earrings, and she was eating cake as her mother smoked argileh in a long, loose denim dress and a headscarf tied under her chin in a more "old-fashioned" style. When they walked over to the restroom together, the young woman asked her mom loudly in US-accented English, "Why does everyone stare?" One of those staring was a guy who appeared to be in his thirties sitting alone near the entrance, smoking argileh and texting on his phone constantly. About a half hour later, he was joined by a man who also ordered an argileh. Then another guy around the same age entered and greeted one of the waiters warmly, standing and chatting for a long time. A group of three men in their early thirties, one in jeans and pointy leather shoes, ordered only coffee.

Two women who appeared to be in their late twenties dressed in especially bright, tight, and revealing clothing, and speaking in Gulf Arab accents, walked into the café. This appeared to be their first visit to the place, because they looked around slowly and then walked down the stairs that led to the underground Turkish baths. As this was a men-only day for the baths, the manager ran down after them, smiling, and said, "Where are you going, mademoiselles? A little further and the alarm would have gone off! [He laughs]. *Tfaddalu*, welcome; be seated," he added, as he guided them back to the ground floor. As one of them chose a table and began pulling out a chair, the manager pointed up the stairs and said, smiling yet, "Tfaddalu, upstairs if you would like, tfaddalu," so they sat upstairs instead.

Immediately afterward a woman in her forties entered with two teenage girls, three preteen girls, two preteen boys, and two girls under five. The manager led them all the way to a table on the ground floor, shaking hands with the boys. He took their order, and a few minutes later large bowls of fruit salad drenched in vanilla ice cream and whipped cream, then sprinkled with strawberry syrup, honey, pistachios, and almonds were delivered to their table. Another group, one guy and two women in their late teens or early twenties, entered and tried to walk downstairs. The manager stopped them and explained about the bath, before choosing a table for them on the ground floor. Another man, the first person we saw wearing shorts, took a seat by himself directly in front of Al-Manar, now showing Qur'anic recitation, and ordered dinner. Soon after the manager changed the channel on both televisions to O TV, the channel affiliated with political leader Michel Aoun. Two young women, in their late teens or early twenties, sat beneath the stairs. One had curly hair and wore a tight black dress with leggings and heels, and the other had straightened hair, wore a patterned red-and-green dress, and sported copious eye makeup. A young man joined them after a few minutes.

Meanwhile, it grew crowded upstairs, where the space continued to be dominated by youths. The owner left, and the manager walked through periodically chatting with customers. There was a waitress and a waiter up here, and both were flirting with many of the young customers of the opposite sex.[3] After ordering coffees, the young woman in the orange tank top did not say another word; she just sat listening to her male companions. Other tables on this floor were occupied by a group of four young women in their early twenties dressed casually without headscarves, a casually dressed couple wearing jeans and pastel-colored T-shirts, two more couples, three groups of two young women each, four groups of two young men each, and two tables of mixed-gender groups of five to six people. There was a sense of constant turnaround as people left or were joined by new friends. At around 9:15 p.m., one of the young men said loudly, "Muhammad, put on Al-Manar, now the Sayyid will begin." The waiter handed the guy the remote control, and he said "Merci" and changed the channel, turning his chair to face the screen. As he did so, he asked us, "Sorry, does this bother you?" to which we of course replied that it did not. Once Hizbullah's secretary general Sayyid Hassan Nasrallah began speaking, many of the young men became attentive. The customer holding the remote control quickly flipped through all the other Lebanese channels to assess which ones were airing the speech before settling back on Al-Manar. About five minutes into the speech, two young women wearing headscarves walked downstairs, stopping before they left to ask Douaa where she had bought her shoes. Two other young women continued to crack jokes and argue loudly about a fortune-teller. A few minutes later several groups of men, ranging in age from late teens to late thirties, walked upstairs, apparently here primarily to watch Nasrallah's speech. It was 9:30 p.m.

The above vignette describes a typical weekday afternoon and evening in one of the new cafés in the southern suburb of Beirut or south Beirut, an area often maligned in the US press as "the Hizbullah stronghold" and known in Lebanon as Dahiya.[4] The Bab al-Hara café exemplifies many of the shifting features of leisure in south Beirut, and highlights many of the new ideas and practices of morality as well as geography that have emerged in this Shi'i-majority area of the city over the past decade. The café is located at the eastern edge of the area, close to the Maronite-majority neighborhood of Hadath where the Free Patriotic Movement political party, led by Michel Aoun and allied with Hizbullah, dominates. Bab al-Hara's architectural layout provides varying rooms and seating areas for different customers, with an eclectic décor that draws on at least two popular aesthetic styles, which we call contemporary and heritage. The menu offers a wide selection of food, beverages, and argileh flavors, but no alcohol, and wireless Internet access is available. The waitstaff and manager interact in familiar ways with a diverse, often carefully dressed customer base, and sometimes control patrons' movements, all under the watchful eye of the café owner. Patrons include people of different ages, styles, dress, and behavior; they study, flirt, chat, make out, laugh, hold business meetings, show off their clothes and accessories, eat and drink, and check out the other customers.

These are activities typical of any café in Beirut, but Bab al-Hara is decidedly not part of the circuit of hip leisure places frequented by the cosmopolitan young jet set featured in *New York Times* travel section depictions of the city. If we were to ask a typical American University of Beirut student who grew up in Achrafieh or Verdun how they decide where to go out, they would probably list factors like who is going, what they're in the mood for, where the place is located, what sort of transportation they have, what they can afford, and what the general atmosphere of a place is like. And chances are, they would not decide to spend their evening in Bab al-Hara, opting for a café or pub in Hamra or Gemmayze instead. So why is this café so popular? Who goes to Bab al-Hara, and why would they go to this café over another in Beirut when many Beirutis and Lebanese would scoff at such a choice?

To answer these questions, we need to first understand that many young residents of Dahiya are more or less pious Shi'i Muslims who would add a key idea to the list of factors affecting their decisions about where to go out: the legitimacy or appropriateness of the café in question—terms encompassing ideas about the reputation and morality of places, activities, and people. Bab al-Hara is one of the new cafés that have filled a particular niche produced by people who understand, however implicitly, the relationship between morality and geography when it comes to leisure choices and activities. These new cafés in south Beirut are often described as *shar'i* ("religiously legitimate"), *muhafiz* ("conservative"), or simply *munasib* ("appropriate") by both their clientele and owners. The term shar'i here refers to legitimacy in relation to Islamic precepts, though the precise details of some of those precepts remain debatable. The exceptions are alcohol and nonhalal meat, neither of which is available in any of Dahiya's cafés. There is also debate as to whether it even makes sense to apply the term shar'i to cafés, as some people believe that implies a formal religious approval that is beyond the bounds of jurisprudential purview. Conservative and appropriate refer to societal ideas about moral behavior, and the overlap and interchangeability among the three terms highlights the entanglement of social as well as religious ideas about what it means for a café to be a "good" or acceptable place. Also complicating this picture are the geographic and political aspects of "appropriate" cafés, as place has come to matter in crucial ways.

So what makes a café legitimate, conservative, or appropriate? There is little consensus on this question beyond the absence of alcohol and nonhalal meat.[5] Everyone ranging from religious authorities to devout Muslims to nonpious residents of Dahiya agrees on those two tenets, although few people actually remember the rule about meat unless they are reminded of it, which may also indicate that issues of halal versus nonhalal meat are taken for granted by many in ways that the absence of alcohol is not. Another essential element is the behavior of customers, but here again, where the lines are drawn varies widely, including among the pious. Most pious people agree that such cafés should not play loud music conducive to dancing nor tolerate overt physical contact between unrelated men and women, though again, which music is acceptable and how much physical contact is unacceptable are up for debate. More broadly, there is little agreement on what kind of behavior is appropriate, how people should dress, and where lines of absolute violation occur. Some of these moral boundaries are gendered, though not as strictly as they seem to be in contexts like Cairo (M. Peterson 2011). Complicating definitions of legitimacy further, a pious person may feel strongly that a legitimate café must not serve alcohol, but think that it is perfectly permissible to go to a café that does serve alcohol provided they themselves do not drink. For many people, figuring out whether a café is legitimate, conservative, or appropriate has to do with judgments about the "type" or "quality" of people who frequent it (*naw' al-nas*), encompassing a range of ideas about class, sect, piety, and politics.

Other potential customers assume that such cafés are only located in Hizbullah-friendly neighborhoods—an assumption they find comforting as it alleviates their fears of navigating hostile territory and fulfills their desires to frequent establishments that support the Resistance.[6] Similar fears and desires lead some people to avoid businesses in Beirut neighborhoods that are viewed as "anti-Resistance" along with those associated with the United States, like McDonald's. Finally, some people assess the appropriateness of a café based on its reputation and that of its owner.

But just being legitimate, conservative, or appropriate is not enough to attract customers. These characteristics combine with others, including the location and "class" of the establishment; cost of its menu items; a potential patron's class, tastes, religiosity, mood, politics, and ideas about morality; and factors like the time of year, with whom one is hanging out, access to transportation, the political situation, and ideas about the quality of particular cafés. Above all, people go out where they feel comfortable, as Hasan, a student in his early twenties put it, "Anywhere I am not comfortable is illegitimate." And indeed, "comfort" and the ability to feel at ease were among the most cited reasons for patronizing businesses. People often described feeling most comfortable around others who seemed to be like them—a feeling related to shared sensibilities about appropriate morals and social behavior, perceptions of class congruity, a sense of security linked to safety from physical or verbal harassment, and territorial belonging. In this book, we unravel these ideas about what makes people comfortable in particular places, what they consider to be appropriate cafés and activities, and how leisure is related to their ideas about morality, geography, and status in the city.

A decade ago, places like Bab al-Hara were nonexistent in south Beirut, or elsewhere in the city for that matter. While doing fieldwork in Dahiya separately for our dissertations in the late 1990s and early years of this century, we were hard pressed to locate a public place where we could sit comfortably, pull out a laptop and take field notes, or just sip a cup of coffee and wait in between interviews. The few Internet cafés that existed in this part of the city catered to young men playing computer games, and neither of us was brave enough to venture into those smoky masculine rooms. There were also a few informal coffee places—usually just a few plastic chairs set up outside a storefront—that were equally gender exclusive, with older men drinking Arabic coffee or tea and playing backgammon. Our field notes back then were typed on laptops at home or in cafés in Ras Beirut, near the American University of Beirut. By 2007, we were struck by the fact that not only were there now many places in Dahiya where we felt comfortable sitting, chilling, and working over coffee or fresh fruit cocktails but that we actually had myriad options too! Our summer 2008 walking survey of the southern suburb revealed that there were at least seventy-five cafés and restaurants in the area that had opened since 2000, and most of them had opened after the devastating 2006 war. While the project that has resulted in this book began as a broader exploration of the Islamic milieu that we describe in the following chapter, it has narrowed to focus on this specific aspect of that milieu: the newly vibrant leisure sector in south Beirut, complete with a plethora of innovative cafés and restaurants that cater to a predominantly young, fashionable, middle-class, and more or less pious clientele.

This relatively new leisure landscape has responded to, accompanied, and prompted desires for new forms of leisure. In recent years, debates about what kinds of leisure activities and places are appropriate have become quite common. We suggest that these cafés provide new spaces for leisure that are promoting flexibility in moral norms. The circumstances that both new spaces and desires for leisure provoke (for example, whether or not to hang out with a cousin who is drinking a beer) highlight tensions between religious and social notions about what is moral. A complex moral landscape emerges, facilitated by the existence of multiple religious authorities, a fraught sectarian political context, class mobility, and a generation that takes religion for granted but wants to have fun. We then argue that these negotiations of morality are crucial in influencing how people conceive and experience the city, especially when it comes to leisure. The key here is that morality and geography are dialectically interdependent and shape one another; neither can be understood fully in isolation. As people experiment with new ways of practicing and experiencing the city through leisure sites, their understandings of both geography and morality are reshaped.

The chapters that follow explore the relationships between morality, geography, and leisure in the politicized context of contemporary Lebanon. How do people negotiate morality in relation to different kinds of places, and geography in relation to morality? How do ideas about being moral shape people's spatial practices and urban experiences? How is the city navigated and inhabited according to varying moral conceptions? How does leisure reconfigure both moral understandings and urban geographies?

In chapter 1, we paint a rich picture of south Beirut and its Islamic milieu, which includes Hizbullah cultural sites as well as the cafés and restaurants that are our focus. We explain why there is a new emphasis on leisure for the Lebanese Shi'i community in the twenty-first century, elucidating the political, economic, religious, social, and urban changes that have taken place since 2000. Chapter 2 turns to the production of leisure by local entrepreneurs, and the efforts of both Hizbullah and religious authorities to control that production. These attempts to conceive and control leisure create a context where there are multiple authoritative definitions of what makes a place, behavior, or activity moral—a context that contributes to moral and geographic complexity in people's lives. Chapter 3 brings us into the new cafés that are the site for much of this moral and geographic complexity, mapping the cafés in Dahiya and describing their stylistic eclecticism.

The following two chapters are devoted to illustrating and analyzing how people negotiate leisure in relation to both morality and geography. Chapter 4 is an ethnographic exploration of moral complexity, focusing on the ways that more or less pious Shi'i Muslims employ moral flexibility in relation to specific leisure activities, including listening to songs, being around alcohol, attending weddings, and dating. We also examine how ideas about flexible morality are deeply gendered, and discuss discourses about "respect" in social interaction along with ideas about flirtation in new leisure sites. While chapter 4 concentrates on how leisure activities are negotiated, chapter 5 takes up the ways that pious Shi'i Muslims navigate and inhabit moral leisure places in different parts of the city. Different conceptions of moral and spatial orders yield a variety of spatial practices. These range from privileging staying within south Beirut to expanding one's urban experiences outside the area. We also look at how leisure facilitates these new subjective experiences of urban life, and how these experiences in turn simultaneously consolidate and challenge dominant power configurations. The final chapter turns to a discussion of taste in relation to class, sect, morality, and geography, before concluding by addressing some of the potential impacts of these new leisure practices. The remaining pages of this introduction set the stage for this exploration by providing some background on café culture in Lebanon and leisure in relation to Islam, laying the groundwork for our conversations about morality and geography, and introducing our methodology and interlocutors.

CAFÉS, LEISURE, AND ISLAM

Cafés are not new to Lebanon. Bab al-Hara and the other cafés in south Beirut represent both a continuation of and departure from the long-standing café culture in many parts of the Middle East. Ottoman records indicate that coffeehouses were introduced to Istanbul by two Syrian men around 1555 and spread throughout the empire (Hattox 1985). During Ottoman times, there were two types of coffee places: small local shops and grand coffeehouses. The latter were luxurious places that were known, especially in Syria and Iraq, for their gardenlike atmospheres that aimed to transport customers out of their urban and desert environments (ibid.). These were widely patronized by people of different classes, and were places for socializing, playing chess, backgammon, and other games, listening to storytellers, and sometimes consuming other drugs (hash and opium). By the mid-sixteenth century, such coffeehouses were common throughout the Ottoman Empire (Kirli 2004).[7]

Cafés were an integral part of downtown Beirut as it became increasingly urbanized and populated at the turn of the twentieth century. In this context, men who met to play cards or backgammon were the predominant patrons of the *maqha* or *qahwa* (or colloquially, *ahweh*).[8] These cafés were considered *sha'bi*—which translates literally as "popular" in a Marxist sense, and here means public or working-class—spaces, generally found in the squares and narrow alleyways of pre–civil war downtown Beirut as well as in residential neighborhoods and by the beach (Douaihy 2005).[9] The maqha served many social functions. It operated as a transitional space between rural and urban life, providing a conduit for migrants coming to work in the city to find jobs and meet one another, and serving as a "post office" for their families in the village (ibid.).[10] It also had a political function, serving as the place where leaders met with their client base.

Downtown Beirut's coffee shops became increasingly mixed gender beginning in the 1940s, reflecting the modernization of public spaces in the city center and influence of the French mandate (1920–43), during which the idea of eating out in restaurants and cafés became acceptable (Salamandra 2004). Two decades later, the practice of café leisure, and the gender and social mix of customers, changed significantly once again. The establishment of new commercial centers in the rapidly developing neighborhood of Hamra, the expansion of television, and the opening of movie theaters across the city drastically altered people's relationship to public space (Douaihy 2005). Ras Beirut became the capital's leisure center, especially its multisectarian, mixed-class Hamra neighborhood, where people went en masse seeking novel urban lifestyles.[11] A new type of café emerged, modeled on the Parisian *café trottoir*. This was the period during which Lebanon's reputation as a playground for Arabs and Europeans alike soared; its coastline was lauded as an "Arab Riviera" and its capital as the "Paris of the Middle East." Hamra's cafés were "modern public spaces" that "hosted different cultural and social activities and were open to all," including men and women of different religious groups (Sawalha 2010, 92). Their patrons were people who were comfortable crossing social boundaries and could afford to buy a relatively expensive espresso, although Arabic coffee remained a common option. Working-class men instead frequented the older form of coffeehouses, and working-class women tended to socialize in one another's homes (ibid.). Hamra was renowned for its café culture at this time, with places like Modca, Café de Paris, Horseshoe, Wimpy, and Dolce Vita gaining reputations as gathering spots for intellectuals and political activists.

The 1975–90 Lebanese civil war marked a major break in the leisure landscape of Beirut. All the downtown coffee shops closed. Neighborhood and beach cafés remained open, but with financial difficulties and a significant shift in customers. Older men spent time in spaces that became increasingly shabby. At the beginning of the twenty-first century, Chawqi Douaihy (2005) counted about 50 remaining coffee shops, including the café trottoirs in Hamra—less than half the approximately 120 that existed prior to the war. Many of Hamra's older cafés lost their hip aura during the war and were unable to make ends meet. Along with the neighborhood's cinemas, the cafés were gradually replaced by clothing stores, chains, discount shops, snack bars, and local fast-food places. A few local cafés persevered, including Café Younes, which adapted by opening a newer space, and a few new cafés opened, including Ristretto, which drew business from student residents of the apartments above it. Starbucks opened a plush two-story branch on Hamra in 2000, adding to the financial strain on local businesses. Modca closed its doors in 2003. Café de Paris, the last holdout from Hamra's prewar cafés, remained open through 2008, but was replaced in February 2009 by Crepaway, a local chain restaurant that continues to attract some of the older male Café de Paris crowd in the mornings.

Following the assassination of former prime minister Rafic Hariri in 2005 and the resulting political tensions in the country, security concerns affected people's mobility, and many confined their movements to their own neighborhoods. This led to the commercial revitalization of Hamra and several other neighborhoods, including Gemmayze, a residential area north of downtown that was gentrified and—to the dismay of many of its older residents—became a hip nightlife center. A plethora of new cafés and pubs (and in Gemmayze, clubs) opened. Hamra became the café epicenter of the city once again, with new places opening regularly, ranging from transnational corporate chains like Gloria Jeans (2009), Caribou (2010), and Coffee Bean and Tea Leaf (2011), to local businesses like Ka3kaya [sic] (2006), Laziz (2009), and Hamra Café (2010). The establishment of the cafés and restaurants in south Beirut that are our focus in this book—cafés like Bab al-Hara—reached its peak at around the same time as the Hamra and Gemmayze revitalizations.

What all these cafés have in common—Modca, Starbucks, and Bab al-Hara—is an emphasis on consumption as part of leisure or participation in commercial leisure—purchasing coffee, food, or argileh in order to spend time in a place as opposed to spending time in a public park (though those are scarce in Beirut) or visiting people in their homes.[12] It is today taken as a given that consumption, and specifically globalized forms and patterns of consumption, have permeated nearly everywhere on the planet, including the Muslim world.[13] Critical scholarship on consumption has put to rest assumptions that this reflects the "McDonaldization" of the world, or blind embrace of ideas and products. Instead, the global and the local come together to create conditions for consumption such that its meanings change in each context (Miller 1995; Pink 2009). Among these meanings are the construction and expression of identity, status, or affiliation, frequently in relation to politics, religion, and/or class. Meanings and practices of consumption—generally discussed in the literature as the consumption of products, whether international like Coca-Cola, or local and identity infused like Mecca Cola—are less clear when it comes to consuming leisure. In this book, we look at how consuming leisure is related to morality, identity, politics, and status in Beirut.

Leisure itself works as a marker of class status both in its display of the fact that one has free time to "spend" in leisurely pursuits and in relation to consumption. Thorston Veblen's ([1899] 1994) classic conceptualization of leisure highlighted this idea as "waste," arguing that the ability to waste time and money is the way in which a person demonstrates their wealth publicly, and thus establishes themselves as part of the wealthy class. Although the Qur'an and hadith present "an essentially positive view of leisure and recreation" (Martin and Mason 2004, 5), the notion of waste seems at first glance to conflict with Islamic values of modesty. Indeed, it does conflict with those contemporary interpretations and manifestations of Islamism that contend that fun is threatening to moral as well as political power regimes. Authorities actively shun fun in such contexts as potentially subversive. This is Asef Bayat's (2007) diagnosis, and it rings true for the Islamic Republic of Iran and the Kingdom of Saudi Arabia—in other words, for states where the dominant legal order is based on a strict interpretation of Islam. But this diagnosis does not apply to Lebanon, where there are myriad possibilities for Islam and leisure to come together, including the happy coexistence of fun and piety in the Shi'i community about which we write. Over the years we have heard some pious Muslims complain about waste in their community, most often in relation to youths wasting time playing video games or sitting in cafés smoking argileh. These critics view consumption, leisure, and displays of wealth or excess time warily, and see the spread of café culture in their community as a problem. This is a minority view, however, espoused by the few who believe that to truly be pious, one must always put community before oneself. We have heard far more arguments from pious individuals that stress the value of being able to breathe freely, relax, and enjoy oneself and one's time, sometimes suggesting that leisure is necessary to one's personal well-being and therefore a part of Islam.

Similarly, religious and political officials in the Shi'i Lebanese community find no fault with the display of wealth. For example, a representative of the late prominent Lebanese jurisprudent Fadallah explained to us, "It is not asked of humans to live poorly.... This is a personal choice...."

There are no taboos that prevent people from buying and wearing the most luxurious clothes, having the most luxurious cars, and living in luxurious houses, and so on. Why not?" When we pressed a Hizbullah official on the issue of whether material consumption, including leisure, is contrary to the party's Islamic values, he likewise corrected us:

> I think those are Catholic values, modesty and not showing wealth . . . as if we have to hide it. In the Shi'i ideology, it is not like that. Modesty has something to do with personal behavior, not material objects. Even the third Imam, Imam Hasan, some people said to him that his clothes were fancy. He said, "Yes that's right," and he opened his robe and showed them very shabby clothing underneath. He said to them, "These clothes are for me, and the others are for people." The shabby clothes were for him. And the outside ones were for other people . . . Imam Ali said, "Ascetism is not that you do not own anything but that nothing owns you."

This party official embraces material consumption, but highlights that modesty in relation to personal behavior remains an important religious value. That said, what constitutes behavioral modesty is itself up for debate. People do not simply "follow the rules" when it comes to leisure practices and choices. They sometimes not only ignore particular tenets but also disagree on what those tenets are in the first place. Dahiya's new commercial leisure sites—the new cafés and restaurants that today fill its streets—have catalyzed debate among the area's Shi'i residents, especially youths, about what it means to have fun in morally acceptable ways. To understand how Bab al-Hara and other cafés in the area differ from those in other Beirut neighborhoods, we need to understand morality and geography in Lebanon. We begin with the former.

MORALITY

One of the key concepts we draw on to illustrate youths' negotiations of leisure sites and practices is morality. While the ethnography that follows will paint the moral topography of leisure more colorfully, here we lay out the ways that we are using the concept of morality, the relationship between piety and morality, and what we mean by the phrase *multiple moral rubrics*. Both the terms morality and ethics convey a sense of right and wrong, or behavior understood as good or bad. Despite historical differences in scholars' use of the terms, much of the literature treats them as synonymous, at least implicitly.[14] One of the definitions we have found most useful for morality is "the forms and acts by which commitments are engaged and virtue accomplished—the practical judgments people make about how to live their lives wisely and well and, in the course of making them, do live their lives, albeit in the face of numerous constraints" (Lambek 2000, 315).[15] Building on this definition, we use the term morality in this book to underscore the idea of consciously trying to live a good life based on a code of conduct—a standard by which behavior is assessed to be good or bad. We prefer the term morality for our case because of its greater emphasis on socially constructed and determined values that are broadly applicable. For example, in common usage in the contemporary United States, an act like cheating on one's spouse is more likely to be described as immoral, as a violation of a generally accepted code of conduct for good behavior in society, whereas a doctor breaching confidentiality is more likely to be described as unethical, as a violation of a specific code of conduct for a specific set of people in society. In addition, the term morality is the better translation of *akhlaq*, the Arabic word most commonly used by our interlocutors to convey a sense of right and wrong.

The literature on morality within anthropology is simultaneously vast and narrow: vast in its origins in writing on social values (Durkheim 1965; Dumont 1977), and narrow in its recent configuration in studies of ethical self-formation (Mahmood 2005; Hirschkind 2006).[16] This recent configuration uses the language of ethics rather than morals to describe its object, as a legacy of the Aristotelian thinking on virtue ethics that it takes as foundational. Perhaps the best-known work that takes this approach is Saba Mahmood's (2005) *Politics of Piety*. Mahmood argues that women in the piety movement in Egypt actively cultivate virtuous dispositions through embodied practice. For instance, by vigilantly being aware of virtue in daily life, one may cultivate the desire to pray—a pious or ethical disposition. Mahmood's analysis describes a community for whom agency entails submission, and piety—or the attainment of greater piety—appears to be the ultimate desire. She provides a powerful and important critique of liberal assumptions about feminist agency and the universality of desires for "liberation." At the same time, this privileging of piety as a primary motivator, practice, and desire has a problematic effect. As Samuli Schielke (2009b) has noted, Mahmood's assertion promotes a desire for virtue over everyday life's competing motivations, including desires for other "good" or moral qualities not based on religious tenets.[17] Schielke's (ibid., S26) critique continues: "There is a risk—especially when morality and piety come together—of favouring the complete, the consistent, and the perfect in a way that does not do justice to the complex and often contradictory nature of everyday experience." Privileging piety and the cultivation of virtuous selves ignores the complexities of the social context in which such selves may be cultivated. When piety is taken up as the scaffolding for a more general claim about "Muslim ways of being," or moral and ethical behavior, our understandings of both morality and life in Muslim societies are oversimplified, and the complexities of daily negotiations of moral practice—including those of our interlocutors—are flattened.

This emphasis on contextual morality is not mutually exclusive from Mahmood's depiction of a moral subject who understands themselves to be in a process of becoming a better person. A person might not focus on self-improvement but still understand their morality as located on an axis of progress, even if active cultivation is not an immediate goal at the time. Many of our interlocutors fit this model, demonstrating "ethical subjectivity that is based on a coexistence of various motivations, aims and identity that can and often do conflict but do not constitute exclusive opposites" (ibid., S29) alongside a general sense—fluctuating in its prevalence at any given moment—that moral progress is possible as well as desirable. In other words, we are not suggesting that becoming a more pious person is not important to Shi'i youths but rather that it is one goal among many, and not necessarily the dominant one at any given time. In this book, we seek to add to a growing corpus of ethnographic work that indicates that piety and religiosity must be located in complex social fields.[18]

Schielke's work on Muslim youths in Egypt has provided a useful alternate analysis of how young Muslims negotiate complex and competing sets of moral norms. He highlights perspectives that discuss experiences of ambivalence and temporal specificity in relation to religion as well as the contradictory values that youth hold for their lives.[19] Yet in his analyses, young people maintain an "understanding of religion as a clear, exact set of commandments and prohibitions that leave little or no space for different interpretations or negotiation," even though they are not always working toward the perfect attainment of a moral self according to this criteria (ibid., S30). In other words, religious morals remain nonnegotiable, but other morals and values compete with religious ones for youths' attention and adherence.

In contrast, many pious Lebanese Shi'i youths think that despite the unchanging perfection of religious principles, human fallibility means that it is impossible to accurately understand those principles. Jurisprudents work to interpret them for daily life, but fallibility persists, complicated further by the mutability of everyday contexts. This means that interpretation is necessarily a continuous process, ever adapting to changing life conditions. Flexibility is built into the system. While some people take a particular jurisprudent's fatwas as fixed and stable rules through which a layperson can orient their own efforts to live morally, those fatwas can and do change, and others, especially youths, pick and choose the ones that fit their notions of what is going on rather than treating them as a rigid guide. The presence of multiple formal jurisprudents in the Shi'i community and their differing opinions facilitates flexibility in ways that may not exist in the Salafi Sunni context about which Schielke writes.[20] We do get a glimpse of this sort of flexibility, albeit more circumscribed than what we see in Lebanon, in Mahmood's (2005, 85) description of a religious lesson provided by one of her interlocutors, Hajja Faiza, in which she gives her students the interpretations of a number of jurists on any issue, teaching them "a mode of interpretative practice that foreground the importance of individual choice and the right of the Muslim to exercise this choice." Here we see a relationship between religious knowledge and moral practice much closer to that espoused by the Shi'i Muslims with whom we have spoken over the past decade. Mahmood attributes this stress on individual choice to a combination of liberal humanism and juristic tradition that teaches choice as a means to greater piety. In the Lebanese context, we also see the profound influence of the teachings of Fadlallah, a preeminent jurisprudent who emphasized individual responsibility for moral action as well as a long-standing consumerist sensibility that valorizes individual choice.

Like young Egyptian Muslims, our interlocutors understand both piety and the attainment of moral behavior as processes, locating themselves somewhere within them, and frequently, though not always, hoping to improve along these axes of valuation.[21] But they also understand many of the rules of the moral systems in which they live, including—with key exceptions like drinking alcohol—those based on religious values, as flexible and open to interpretation. The grounds on which the various competing registers for living a moral life are based are themselves in flux.[22] Many youths are "preoccupied with conducting themselves in the 'right way,'" where "being in 'the right way' is less a matter of adhering to principle than an ability to elaborate a narrative that holds together multiple discrepancies and contradictions in a clear sense of how one is situated in relationship to the lives of others" (Simone 2010, 145). Not only are youths in Dahiya living complex lives that require negotiating different and often competing sets of morals, they sometimes question and reinterpret the morality of various practices themselves as they stitch these personal narratives together. Rather than an increasingly moral subject defined according to the cultivation or attainment of virtues based on a religiously determined set of dispositions, here we see a moral subject constantly redefined in relation to multiple moral rubrics.

MULTIPLE MORAL RUBRICS

With the phrase moral rubrics, we bring Schielke's notion of "moral registers" together with an emphasis on "values" as described by Joel Robbins. The term registers conveys "modalities of moral speech and action," and highlights "the performative, situational, and playful ... character of norms" (Schielke 2009a, 166).[23] Within each register of moral discussion and action, certain values emerge as primary. The term rubrics allows us to

convey a stronger sense of a categorical guide or source of guidance dominated by the particular values that emerge as primary within each register.
Here we adapt Robbins's (2007, 295–96) "theory of value"—a theory he
puts forth to explain "why cultures allow choice in particular domains or
situations, and how such choices are felt to be moral ones by cultural actors."[24] Applied to the Urapmin context where he works, this theory suggests that multiple cultural logics, each with a different key value, lead to
social change and prompt people to "experience life as a continual process
of choosing between the conflicting values that structure [them]" (ibid.,
307). We appreciate the notion of multiple cultural logics with different key
values, but are hesitant about the idea that a single fundamental value may
underlie a cultural system. For this reason, we choose to use the term rubrics to simultaneously convey the constructed and always potentially
malleable nature of all these sets of moral ideas, discourses, norms, and
practices along with their normativity, as they frequently involve ideas that
people generally agree on, most of the time.

Moral rubrics, then, are the different sets of ideals and values that are
revealed as well as produced through discourses and actions in each of the
major registers, including the religious, social, and political-sectarian.[25] In
some cases they take the form of prohibitions, and in other cases the form
of what one "ought" to do. We identify three sets of moral rubrics. The
social rubric is based on values of social obligation, propriety, hierarchy,
manners, and reciprocity—values shared across Lebanese society. The
political-sectarian rubric reflects the conflation of sectarian identity and
political allegiance in Lebanon as well as ideas about the differential morality of Lebanon's political-sectarian communities. Differential morality here
encompasses understandings about difference in moral norms (e.g., Christians drink alcohol) *and* judgments about "other" groups that are related
to politics (e.g., not supporting the Resistance is morally wrong). For our
interlocutors, allegiance to the Resistance and to the political alliance led
by Hizbullah is a moral norm based on the political-sectarian rubric. Finally, the religious rubric is related to ideas about piety and religious commitment, or *iltizam*, and forms the dominant rubric at work for pious Shiʻi
Lebanese. It is based on a set of values that emerge from histories of interpretations of religious texts, with continual temporal manifestations
through jurisprudents and innovations related to individual judgment and
responsibility.

To take just the religious rubric here, praying, fasting, and giving alms to
charity are taken as "given" qualities of religious commitment that are not
worth mentioning because everyone agrees they are important.[26] Unrelated
to leisure, many people say that the *hijab* (headscarf) is part of iltizam for
women. When it comes to leisure activities and socializing, the one tenet
on which everyone we have spoken with agrees is that a *multazim/a* (reli-

giously committed or pious person) cannot drink alcohol. A close second was a vague statement about maintaining "boundaries" in interactions between unrelated men and women. There remained many gray areas of uncertainty within this rubric. Can a multazim/a dance the *dabkeh*, a traditional Lebanese folk dance thought to be more acceptable provided that men and women do not dance hand in hand, at a wedding? Can they dance to pop music in single-sex environments? Can they listen to pop songs? Can an unrelated man and woman shake hands? Can a multazim/a hang out at a place where other people are dancing if there is no alcohol? Can they hang out in a place with alcohol without drinking?

Uncertainty also exists as to the relationship of external appearance to assessments of morality according to religious rubric, though the majority of youths felt strongly that one could not judge people based on outward appearances. These youths' discussions usually centered on "hijab hypocrisy," but extended to men's clothing and facial hair as well. The younger the person, the more likely they were to suggest that appearance and religiosity do not necessarily line up; older individuals felt more strongly both that they do and they *should*. Batoul, a twenty-one-year-old college student, countered an older person in her group interview when the latter claimed that you could assess a person's morality based on dress by interjecting:

> I want to say something about that. Clothes don't reflect the person's personality. The way we think, we judge people based on their appearance. This is not right. I know people who don't wear hijab, and regardless if this is correct or not, they have morals, and their behavior is much much better than some people who wear hijab. . . . So let us not judge by appearance.

The vast majority of our interlocutors understood morality based on the religious rubric as a necessarily incomplete process, mirroring understandings of piety as a similar process where the end goal is ultimately unattainable. There was a perceptible tension between the idea, on the one hand, that religious commitment was a conscious process of coming to authenticated Islam and understanding why you do what you do (Deeb 2006), and on the other hand, the sense that a person could live within these processes of becoming a certain sort of person whether or not they spent much time thinking about it. The way this tension manifested for youths differently than an earlier generation was marked by young people's tendency to emphasize the significance of personal choice in behavior. That generational difference is taken up further in chapter 2 and informs the rest of this book. The idea that piety and morality were processes offered a space of imperfection, where contradictory impulses could be reconciled and ambivalence about rules of behavior could be cultivated. Perfection was both a passive goal and a murky one. Contradiction and ambivalence within the religious rubric in particular were facilitated by the focus on individual interpretation, the availability of multiple religious opinions in a marketplace of sorts, and the sheer diversity of Lebanon's small population.

Of course, the religious, the social, and the political-sectarian are not natural categories. They are, however, categories used by many of our interlocutors. We also find them a useful heuristic for teasing apart this moral landscape. On the one hand, these categories are coconstructed and overlap. One can argue that social obligation is also based on ideas of maintaining positive social relationships that can be traced to religion, or that political allegiance is deeply related to social obligation. Youths, for example, frequently contend that maintaining good social relations is part of *mu'amalat* and a value within the Islamic discursive tradition.[27]

On the other hand, clear distinctions between religious and social rubrics of morality in particular are seen in admonishments when people violate norms: a transgression within the religious rubric (say, drinking alcohol) is described as *haram*, using the normative theological value reference, while a transgression within the social rubric (say, failing to attend a relative's funeral) is described as *'ayb*, a commonly invoked word that means "shameful" and can be used to refer to a wide range of inappropriate behavior. What is *'ayb* is not necessarily haram and vice versa, as the former indicates a violation affecting one's relationship with other people, and the latter a violation affecting one's relationship with God. The concept of *'ayb* also captures the way that social rules for moral behavior are often implicit, unarticulated, assumed, and more difficult to unravel, as social norms or social taboos generally are. In contrast, religious rules usually have clear fatwas, and even when there is disagreement on the content of those fatwas or when fatwas clash, the disagreement is stated explicitly, making it possible to argue about the rules and take explicit stances on them more readily.

Many of the behaviors considered *'ayb* involve failing to participate properly in reciprocal social relations, like failing to visit a neighbor who is ill, attend a relative's wedding, or reciprocate or accept (depending on whose "turn" it is) a dinner invitation. In such cases, *'ayb* is invoked in gender-neutral ways. There is another dimension to the concept that specifically refers to gendered behavior that is considered shameful either because it marks women as sexually available or "loose" (*faltaneh*), or because it marks men as incapable. Here *'ayb* includes acts like a woman kissing her boyfriend in public, women smoking in public, and a man borrowing money from a woman. Gender difference also inflects the weighing of social obligations (*wajbat*) versus social propriety, where both men and women face social obligations, but women tend to feel the burdens of social propriety more intensely.

The fatwas of one religious authority in particular, Fadlallah, often high-light the tensions between the religious and social moral rubrics. For in-stance, he gave a fatwa that states that a mature young woman, even if she is a virgin, does not need the permission of her father or any guardian in her personal affairs, including marriage.[28] He then noted that the woman herself could in fact determine her maturity. This opinion clearly contra-dicted norms of social propriety in Lebanon, and Fadlallah's office re-ceived numerous complaints from outraged parents as a result. In response to this social upheaval, he moderated the statement, and in the email re-sponse to our question on the matter in 2010, his juristic office noted, "It is preferable (though not required) for a virgin young woman, even if she is mature, to ask the permission of her father, for the purpose of taking advice from her parents, and from their experience and desire for her best interests." Fadlallah was well aware of this discord between religion and social norms, or between moral rubrics, and felt that societal problems could be alleviated by society "catching up to" religion in terms of allot-ting sexual and other rights for women, because with social acceptance came social regulation.[29]

Such conflation or overlap between spheres is by no means unique to Lebanon. A similar example of the tension between the religious and social is seen in the depiction by Anne Meneley of Zabid's younger women, who are expected by their elders to take an active role in hospitality work during social events held at their homes. Meneley (1996) was surprised to find, on her return visit to Zabid after nine years, that these women prioritized a seminar on religious norms over their hospitality duties. When women who adhered to the hospitality norms criticized this, they framed their critique as one where the "Islamists" who promoted these new social norms were "lacking manners (*adab*), a term that connotes religious piety as well as social propriety" (ibid., 232). Here, as in the case we describe, the conflict was not only over religious versus social norms; it also was over what constituted religious norms in the first place, as visiting at key mo-ments in life and being generous to guests were considered part of one's pious duty, and understood as social values rooted in religion. Put simply, "Islamist" values were coming into conflict with what were understood as "Islamic" values (ibid., 233).

It is also important to remember that particular moral "rules" may shift rubric over time. In the 1970s and 1980s, wearing the headscarf was under-stood in Dahiya as a religious prescription, both a manifestation and marker of women's piety. By the turn of the twentieth century, the heads-carf had become part of normative female dress in the community. Young women today may wear it to express or enact their piety (or both), but they also may wear it simply because it is a fundamental element of clothing for women over a certain age in their community. What was once a clear marker of exceptional piety has become a form of normative dress, or a social norm to which women are expected to conform, in relation to assumptions about faith, but one that is also understood as not necessarily connected to faith.

What this all boils down to is that in many situations, there are multiple paths available through which one can make a moral choice—a choice understood to be good by accepted standards of behavior. Sometimes those paths converge, and sometimes they conflict. The social and religious converge when the notion that a woman should not smoke argileh in public because it represents "loose" sexual behavior complements ideas about maintaining one's health as well as Fadlallah's fatwa prohibiting all forms of smoking for everyone. They clash when Fadlallah's fatwa about an independent woman having the right to make her own decisions about temporary marriage contradicts the norm of social propriety that insists that a woman must be a virgin for her first regular marriage.

The political-sectarian rubric should not be discounted, especially in relation to the social. Because political-sectarianism is overlaid onto neighborhoods in the city, mobility is impacted by moral concerns about where one can and cannot go. Being a good Hizbullah supporter means privileging certain areas and avoiding others, and political values carry moral worth and potential judgment. The political and social may clash if a friend or colleague lives in an "enemy" neighborhood. One may face the choice between either spending time in that neighborhood and violating the political-sectarian rubric for morality, or offending a childhood friend or a newly made acquaintance, thereby violating the social rubric. When different tenets for moral behavior based on different rubrics clash with one another, those caught in the complex moral web that results often express feeling conflicted about their choices, experiencing guilt, or otherwise making a concerted effort to figure out the best way to navigate this terrain.

From this context of multiple moral rubrics, we argue that youth practices and discourses of morality are multiple as well as flexible, perhaps especially when it comes to ideas about leisure. This interpretive flexibility is also redefining ideas about leisure within these moral rubrics. Youths may even generate norms within the religious rubric by putting themselves into situations that necessitate regulation or insisting on reformulating prior regulations to facilitate their desires for a particular lifestyle. Thus we always mean flexible in this dual sense of the term: negotiations within clear-cut rules (e.g., I believe it is immoral and haram to sit in a pub, but I will go anyway without drinking), and negotiations of the rules themselves (e.g., I do not believe that sitting in a pub is immoral or haram). This does not mean that youths never have strong convictions about what is right or wrong but instead that those convictions sometimes change, and that their source is rarely a single authority. Most commonly, convictions about moral norms in all the rubrics are influenced by a combination of authoritative knowledge, habit, people in one's social worlds, and experiences. By no means is this a simple moral landscape; rather, these are constellations of ideas about what constitutes good versus bad behavior rife with contradiction and confusion. One key element through which these constellations of ideas and rubrics are materialized and inscribed is the city's geography.

GEOGRAPHY

Beirut is notorious as a sectarian city geographically divided into territorial enclaves affiliated with sectarian groups and their respective political movements. During the Lebanese civil war, space, sect, and politics came together as massive population displacements homogenized neighborhoods. These sectarian politics have had a critical effect on the city's leisure geographies.

When residents of Beirut decide where to spend their free time, ideas about the relationship between sect, politics, and space are often crucial factors. Dwellers recognize and classify spatial and visual cues associated with political-sectarian geographies, and navigate these politicized sectarian maps of urban neighborhoods with more or less ease, privileging certain places and avoiding others. The political-sectarian rubric for assessing morality is laid firmly on to ideas about place: "my" Muslim (or Christian) neighborhood is better, "cleaner," and more comfortable than "other" Christian (or Muslim) neighborhoods, which are bad, "dirty," and therefore threatening.

Following the civil war, city spaces gradually became less polarized. The famed "Green Line" that bifurcated the capital, separating Muslim west Beirut (Gharbiyyeh) from Christian east Beirut (Sharqiyyeh), became a major urban artery, crossed on a daily basis by many for work, study, or leisure. People ventured more easily into "other" neighborhoods. The few west Beirut neighborhoods that had retained some of their sectarian mix—especially the middle- and high-income areas of Ras el-Nabeh, Badaro, and Ras Beirut—became symbols of a postwar era of coexistence. The new Beirut Central District (BCD), including the rebuilt "downtown," also projected that possibility, albeit through capital and consumption.[30] Overall, between 1991 and 2005, political-sectarian geographies became less blatant and salient to residents. Despite this shift, place remained linked to political-sectarianism for several reasons. Beirut's small size, its residents' long-standing attachments to specific neighborhoods, its history of violence, and postwar reconstruction policies precluded radical shifts in the spatial order.

Throughout this history, moral assessments about place impacted and were complicated by the relationship between Dahiya and Beirut. Until the post-Liberation apex of Hizbullah's popularity in 2000, Dahiya was stigmatized by Beirut dwellers of *all* religious groups (including some wealthy Shi'i Muslim residents) as an Islamist ghetto of poor rural migrants who are ignorant about urban life, and as a space of anarchy, chaos, and illegality.[31] This relationship varied with the political shifts we detail in the next chapter.

The period of political tension—and specifically new Sunni-Shi'i politicized sectarian conflict—that followed the assassination of Hariri in 2005 led to the sudden, violent resurfacing of both old and novel boundary lines between and within Beirut's neighborhoods. Escalating insecurity led to the militarization of many areas of the city, with an increasing number of streets and neighborhoods closed off to protect politicians and government officials as well as high-end retail and business activities. Residents learned to navigate a new "city of security," using different competences and adding new variables onto their personal navigation maps.[32]

The Beirut-Dahiya boundary was solidified as specifically Sunni-Shi'i during this time, and the relationship of place to the political-sectarian moral rubric was reinforced. Despite the imperfect alignment of sect, politics, and place, ideas about morality in relation to place became a critical component of people's spatial practices and everyday lives. People increasingly differentiated others by sect, according to stereotypical interpretations of dress and other bodily signifiers. For instance, pious Shi'i women were believed to wear their hijab in a specific way and dress either in dark or bright (frequently described as garish) colors, especially green, while pious Shi'i men were believed to have a particular style that included collared shirts without neckties and large rings carved in silver with semiprecious or precious colored stones. Shi'i people were also assumed to speak in an accent related to their rural origins and be monoglot such that their speech was not sprinkled with English and especially French, with the latter associated closely with the Christian bourgeoisie. Similarly, Shi'i places were associated with a specific aesthetics. Of course, Shi'i individuals also classified others, especially Sunni Muslims, through stereotypical signifiers, including hijab style, other dress features, and accent.

The severity of this polarization erased other political possibilities as well as the fact that there were significant Christian partisans on both sides. Those who did not fit within the bifurcated lines of Sunni-Shi'i and Beirut-Dahiya were often silenced, to the extent that it frequently appeared that the entire country had chosen one side or the other. These divisions extended beyond the Beirut-Dahiya border and into Beirut's other neighborhoods, as partisans of the two groups generated spatial divisions wherever they were situated.

This overlap between political-sectarian moral judgments and place has had a significant impact on the leisure geography of the city. For pious people who want to enjoy their free time according to moral norms, navigating the city's possibilities for leisure is further complicated by the imperfect alignment of social and religious moral norms with moral space understood in political-sectarian terms. All three rubrics of morality—religious, social, and political-sectarian—are most easily maintained within Dahiya, where one can most readily assume that others' morality resembles one's own. Nevertheless, quite a few people perceive this choice as confinement and choose to venture outside their territory, inhabiting other spaces in the city that they view as abiding by at least some shared moral norms (for example, a café in "enemy territory" that does not serve alcohol).

SPACE, PLACE, AND MORALITY

The morality of ordinary people's everyday practices is inscribed in space. Simultaneously, space reconfigures ideas about (im)moral practices and people in relation to all three moral rubrics. Our discussion of moral rubrics and geography is built on this dialectical understanding of space, anchored in a Lefebvrian analysis.[33] It is also in conversation with scholarship that investigates space as reproduced through the power of moral authorities.[34] Space is constituted through and constitutive of social relations and material social practices. It defines categories of people and practices, generating systems of exclusion and inclusion related to classifications of good and bad behavior.[35] The term space refers to multiple sets of intertwined social spaces, and must be understood through these interrelations, temporalities, and scalar connections (Keith and Pile 1993; Massey 1993a).[36] In other words, space is not a passive flat surface for social, economic, and political action; it is dynamically and dialectically linked with people, places, objects, and events.

In this book, we use the term space to refer to the abstract space of the city, and the term place to refer to practiced or social space.[37] The leisure places we discuss—cafés and restaurants—are physical, mental, and social spaces. According to Henri Lefebvre's triadic model for understanding space, these cafés are conceived spaces because they are planned, designed, and managed by different groups of people, including political parties, religious organizations, and private entrepreneurs. They are also perceived spaces, because they are geographically located and distributed, and have specific forms. And they are lived spaces, because they are socially experienced by people, and generate informal collective practices and congeniality among customers.

This triadic model of space informs our discussion of moral leisure. We analyze conceived space by unraveling the political and economic forces that led different stakeholders to establish new cafés along with other leisure sites in Dahiya. We reveal perceived space by mapping café locations and spatial characteristics, and exploring the social and spatial practices of their patrons. And we look at lived space through the cafés' aesthetic styles and café goers' experiences. We are keenly aware of the inherent politics incorporated within these sociospatial dialectics. Social spaces are conceived, perceived, and lived as (im)moral in relation to power structures that influence their (re)production, including political allegiances and conflicts.

Our analysis privileges lived space, highlighting the everyday ways that people experience the city through leisure.[38] Through "communication components such as humor, noise, wit, amusement, play, sociability, solidarity, power, subversion, body language, behavioral arrangements, gossip and rumour," cafés provide a specific conviviality that people seek and enjoy (Graiouid 2007, 533). Cafés also blur the borderline between public and private spheres by domesticating public space, at times converting it into family space, a refuge, or a space that facilitates various acts of reciprocity. At the same time, they maintain a dynamic engagement with ideas of privacy, so that individuals maintain their voice within the collective arena of the café.

New forms of moral leisure in Dahiya highlight the area as a *casually lived* urban space as opposed to its all-too-common sensationalized image as a "Hizbullah stronghold." Looking at moral leisure places and practices also allows us to illuminate the class dimensions of the area along with its strong links to the neoliberal postwar city that privileges capital circulation, accumulation, and consumerism. In this way, we show how Dahiya—as south Beirut—is participating in the spatial production of the city through classed moral geographies that consolidate sectarian spatial fragmentation. Yet the area also provides possibilities for change through pious youths' contestations of these established boundaries. Dahiya's cafés operate as places that are simultaneously experienced through social interactions and controlled (with varying efficacy) by the dominant order. They are places where social space has the potential to be dynamically expressed, reinterpreted, and reinvented, if only for fleeting moments.

It is critical to consider sociospatial dialectics in order to account for the significance of moral rubrics in shaping the city's space. Morality must be added to the now-classic variables of gender, class, age, ethnicity, sect, and politics that govern spatial production in Beirut. The city is a rich urban laboratory that reveals how ideas about morality and geography operate in relation to one another. We argue that this productive relationship between morality and geography moves in both directions, and works to shape both sets of ideas and practices. Ideas about religious, social, and political-sectarian moral rubrics significantly shape and are shaped by conceptions, perceptions, and experiences of space.

RESEARCHING LEISURE IN DAHIYA

This book is based primarily on collaborative fieldwork conducted between 2007–9, including participant observation, surveys, and semistructured group and individual interviews. We also draw freely on each of our long-term research experience in Dahiya (Lara's since 1998, and Mona's since 1996) along with many conversations and informal interviews with long-standing interlocutors and friends in the area. Mona's teaching at the American University of Beirut has also informed our work through students' projects and thought-provoking class discussions. As a first for both of us, we completed some of the research for this book with the help of a wonderful team of assistants, who not only transcribed recorded interviews and scanned documents from libraries but also carried out our surveys of cafés and customers, and conducted a number of recorded group interviews.

Our participant observation took us to at least twenty cafés in Dahiya, many of them multiple times, and we draw on our field notes from those visits as well as the notes of our research assistants, who conducted participant observation in seven of these cafés at different times of day during varying days of the week. We chose those seven based on a survey of thirty-six cafés (approximately half the cafés in Dahiya at the time) conducted in July 2008 by Douaa Sheet and Fatima Koumeyha, who recorded information ranging from how many people the café held to who owned it to the price of an argileh. Data from that café survey also informed this book's four analytic maps, which were conceptualized and designed by Ahmad Gharbieh with the assistance of Wissam Bou-Assi. Douaa also conducted a photographic survey of the interiors of our seven focus cafés to assist us in remembering the details of their styles and décor during our writing (though we do not have photographs that include customers, out of respect for people's privacy and in keeping with owners' requests to avoid photographing people). Douaa and Fatima conducted a second survey of 405 customers across six cafés in Dahiya, collecting demographic data as well as information about how often they visited that particular café, how they originally learned about it, and how they rated its offerings, services, cost, and ambiance. With assistance from our quantitatively inclined spouses and Hazar Al-Asadi, we analyzed that survey data using SPSS statistical software (also a first for both of us). In addition, we draw on archival data collected by Diala Dagher, including fatwas on leisure-related activities and sites, newspaper articles, and magazine articles from *Baqiyat Allah*, a magazine published in Lebanon that espouses Sayyid Khamenei's perspectives, and consistently includes a number of articles about youths and youth issues.

We conducted semistructured interviews with six café owners, four café managers, the representatives of two jurisprudents (Fadlallah and Khamenei), a major Hizbullah-affiliated entrepreneur, and several party officials and politicians, including a mayor, two members of Parliament, and various media office representatives. Diala and Douaa assisted us with additional interviews with a third jurisprudent's representative (Sistani) and three land brokers (*semsar*).[39] We also formally interviewed several young women, and had numerous informal conversations about new leisure places and activities in the area with many women as well as some men in their thirties, forties, and fifties who we have known for years. Finally, with our research assistants, we conducted semistructured group interviews with fifty-two youths (age eighteen to twenty-nine; thirty women and twenty-two men) and eleven adults (age thirty-two to forty-nine; two women and nine men).[40] These group interviews were essentially directed conversations that included various combinations of two to four people, who may or may not have known each other previously.[41]

A NOTE ABOUT OUR INTERLOCUTORS

Interviewing young people made especial sense to us as our survey of café customers indicated that the vast majority of café goers in Dahiya are between eighteen and thirty-five years of age (over 80 percent). We found that group interviews were an excellent way to get a sense of how people talk about leisure in front of others. This was particularly important because our focus is primarily on what young people *say* that they do, which of course may or may not reflect what they in fact do. In this sense, our claims are about the ways they articulate decisions and ideas about leisure as much as, if not more than, about their actual leisure practices. We find their public declarations about moral behavior and spatial practices striking in their deviation from official discourses about morality in this community, and take it as quite significant that, as we will see, people are willing to publicly admit to many behaviors that are viewed as inappropriate or immoral. Indeed, we take this as an indicator of social, political, and spatial change. We are also interested in the ways in which people are intentionally grappling with the binds in which they find themselves, and see interpretive flexibility at work in these conscious articulations of different ideas of morality and space.

This interpretive flexibility is emerging in a space where over the past several decades, as we describe in chapter 1 and have detailed elsewhere (Deeb 2006; Harb 2010a), particular ideas and practices of piety have come to dominate public life plus take deep hold within personal life trajectories. Our customer survey found that almost all the patrons of cafés in Dahiya live in the area, suggesting that considerations of geography as well as the dominant ideas about morality in the southern suburb are important to the success of this leisure sector. As scholars, we are interested in understanding ideas about morality, geography, and leisure among Shi'i Muslims in Lebanese for whom faith is crucial, and who are centered as a community in south Beirut. We are not implying that all Shi'i Muslims or Lebanese agree with these ideas but rather that these ideas have become common in this part of the city.

As such, the majority of our interlocutors are Shi'i Muslims who both identify as such within the sectarian polity of Lebanon and view themselves as relatively pious people, though what this indicates varies widely. For the most part this means that they pray and fast, or try to, on a regular basis. Most—yet not all—women wore the hijab, although as we saw above, the extent to which that indicates piety is debated and debatable. Some people conformed to other indicators of piety, like not shaking hands with members of the opposite sex in greeting, and others ignored these tenets or disagreed with their validity in the first place. Few were in any way "evangelical" about their religious belief or practice; few cited verses from the Qur'an or tried to convince others (whether another participant in a group interview or one of us) of proper virtues and correct behaviors. Almost all the young men and many of the young women in our interviews have online lives, using the Internet to chat, maintain active Facebook pages, and otherwise engage in social networking.[42] Most people were what they described as 'adi or "normal," meaning that they neither refuse to socialize with the nonpious nor go out drinking and clubbing on a regular basis. But this definition of 'adi would certainly not be viewed as normal in Ras Beirut or Gemmayze, other neighborhoods in the city. Instead, it reflects the face of normativity in Dahiya in the wake of a Shi'i Islamic revival that we discuss in the next chapter. It is also a normativity that cannot be understood outside the context of sectarianism and ideas about resistance in Lebanon, as it includes a sense of opposition to and distinction from other Lebanese.

While the majority of Dahiya residents today conform to the basic outlines of political-sectarian, social, and religious morality that have emerged as hegemonic in the area over the past few decades, there are certainly many exceptions. The voices of only a few of those who do not fit in are included in this book, with the acknowledgment that there are many more, and that many of them find the practices and ideas of morality and social space that we depict here to be oppressive. A few of the nonconformists are loud and public, such as Lokman Slim, who owns the Hangar, an exhibition space in Dahiya, and who publicly critiques the hegemony of Hizbullah and the Islamic milieu in the area.[43] Most are not so vocal. Several are queer young people who have found communities and spaces where they feel comfortable in Ras Beirut, away from the questions and censure of their natal neighborhoods. A few are upper-middle-class youths who were raised in Dahiya, but sent to elite private high schools near the American University of Beirut and then to that university, so both their friends and favorite places are centered outside south Beirut. One of these young men explained to us that he spent his high school years deflecting "weird responses" from his classmates when they learned that he lived in Dahiya, but that he also never fit in there.

So there is Soha, a young woman we met during our search for a research assistant, who was quite religious as a child and teenager, but underwent a radical change in lifestyle during college, thereby instigating serious conflict with her religiously and politically connected Dahiya family, and prompting her to spend more and more time outside the neighborhood. There is Aziza, who Lara has known for years, who has remained a part of Dahiya's social fabric while building a life that extends outside it as much as possible. She tends to avoid many of the cafés we write about simply because when she goes out, she prefers to choose her companions, and can't escape running into extended family members and neighbors in Dahiya's new cafés. And there is Tala, Aziza's twenty-four-year-old assistant, whose family forced her to conform to a pious lifestyle as a child and wear a headscarf, and who today exemplifies "emo hijabi" style—a sort of Muslim goth meets *Flashdance* aesthetic. Tala walks a careful moral line in relation to both others' perceptions of her and her own understandings of as well as desires for her morality. Their voices may be quieter, but they remain in our minds as we write.

REGIONAL COMPARISONS

Lebanon is neither Egypt nor Iran. This seems like an obvious statement—something that should go without saying. But it is a statement that we feel the need to write, because so frequently they are the lenses through which work on Lebanon is viewed and the contexts for much of the secondary source literature we cite. And with good reason: both Egypt and Iran are much bigger and more important places, geopolitically and within scholarly communities. There are closer parallels between Lebanon and Turkey—another context for many of the secondary source comparisons on which we draw. These comparisons and contrasts are most striking in relation to three key topics: youths, café cultures, and of course, the so-called Arab Spring.

The chapters that follow provide a rather different picture than that depicted by recent work on Iranian youths (Khosravi 2008; Mahdavi 2009; Bayat 2007). The focus of these scholars on youths as transgressive has everything to do with the specificity of a context where Islamists in authority are "distinctly apprehensive of the expression of 'fun'" (Bayat 2007, 433). While moral norms do exist in Dahiya, as they do everywhere, they are asserted through social pressures rather than an apparatus of the state. Indeed, the lack of a state or party authority enforcing moral codes and norms has allowed a space to emerge where people—young and old alike—can fulfill simultaneous and noncontradictory desires for morality and fun. In his later work, Bayat (2010a, 18; 2010b) underscores these differences more clearly, noting that "the intensity of youths' activism depends, first, on the degree of social control imposed on them by the moral and political authorities." The contrast between the Iranian and Lebanese contexts is one where in the former, the state regime legislates moral issues and youths resist, and in the latter, there is little formal regulation of morality, multiple sectarian authorities compete, and youths instead are policing themselves for moral behavior.

Bayat's (2010b, 46) description of Egyptian youths is closer to what we see among our interlocutors, as they draw on what he called "accommodating innovation" as "a strategy that redefined and reinvented prevailing norms and traditional means to accommodate their youthful claims." But in this depiction, the youths' practices are bifurcated, such that they enjoy fun *and also* pray and fast. This seems to fit with Schielke's (2009a, 2009b) portrayals of situational morality among Egyptian youths as well. A similar scenario exists in Niger for young Muslims, who separate religious practices from other behavior (Masquelier 2010). In these contexts, there is a time and place for piety, and a time and place for other things. In Dahiya, we instead see a generation of youths who don't view their lives as necessarily bifurcated in this way, yet are striving to bring fun and faith together in ways they feel are more compatible—striving for a greater level of consistency in their lives across these dimensions. Understanding these youths' desires means viewing youths as "savvy cultural actors" who want to understand themselves as authentic selves.[44] For our interlocutors, that quest required engaging with ideas about morality as they navigated the complex urban spaces of Beirut.

The cafés we describe are a new component of that terrain. They are linked to both a long-standing café culture in Beirut more broadly and recent transnational café trends. But the new Dahiya cafés do not resemble the male-dominated coffee shops that have been part of many Beirut neighborhoods as well as urban neighborhoods across the region for centuries, and continue to play a major role in public life in many parts of the Middle East. Nor do they resemble the cafés of the intelligentsia in Hamra; nor are they franchises or imitations of transnational chain coffee shops priced too high for the majority of the population. They are more affordable than Cairo's new coffee shops and instead seem to share many of the stylistic elements of those in Istanbul.[45] South Beirut's cafés have become part of Lebanon's open-market *souq*, adding new moral and geographic options to it. One of their striking features is the relatively equal presence of men and women—a significant change from the exclusively male informal street hangouts and Internet gaming shops that previously dominated public leisure places in this part of the city. This is also different from the gendered world of coffee shops in Cairo, where men of all classes frequent "traditional ahwehs" to drink tea, smoke argileh, and play backgammon in a public space conducive to the construction of masculinity, while elite women and sometimes elite men spend time in new "feminized coffee shops" (M. Peterson 2011). This difference may also be related to the striking lack of gender segregation in public spaces in Lebanon (with the exception of places of worship) as compared with Egypt. There is no enforced segregation between family and *shabab* sections of most restaurants and cafés in Dahiya, nor is there a "morality police" like those in Saudi Arabia or Iran.[46] In Lebanon, mixed-gender socializing is neither unusual nor the exclusive domain of the elite, cosmopolitan, or Westernized.

Finally, regional comparisons also stop short of Lebanon when it comes to the effects of the Arab Spring on both our interlocutors and the country more broadly. Life in Lebanon goes on within an already-existing working democracy, albeit a severely flawed sectarian one. Not only is there no dictator against whom to revolt; divisions among Lebanon's political communities have been so deeply established over the course of the nation-state's modern history so as to preclude the stuff of united televised protests, most of the time. The country is also exceptionally tiny, highlighting the way that distances are as much political as they are physical. Politics in this small space are at once complex and mundane, and frequently seem utterly irrelevant to the massive social, political, and economic changes being wrought by people across the region in the face of violent repression by their governments as well as the ongoing US occupation of Iraq and Israeli occupation of Palestine. Sadly, many Lebanese are not particularly engaged in what is going on beyond their borders, aside from the occasional Facebook posts or solidarity demonstration. In Dahiya, most people, including youths, maintain their support for the Resistance against

Israeli aggression—a support that extends in spirit yet generally not in practice to solidarity with Palestine. They also seemed for the most part to support all the recent revolutions until Syria.

Initial apprehensions about the uprising next door have given way to skepticism and fear. Quite a few of our Shi'i interlocutors accept the official Hizbullah position supporting the Syrian regime, which the party has consistently presented as an ally against Israel and the United States. Even when they hesitate to buy the Hizbullah line, peoples' other concerns prevent solidarity with Lebanon's neighboring population, including fears of spillover violence, sectarian politics gone bad, and "Shi'a-hating Salafis." Indeed, as this book goes to press, regular armed clashes between supporters and opponents of the Syrian regime have escalated in north Lebanon. Less frequent incidents of violence have occurred in Beirut, Saida, and other areas of the country. Thus far, these events have not significantly disrupted daily life for most Lebanese. Leisure in particular continues to be lived at full force. Keeping this specificity of locale in mind, while remaining attuned to the patterns and connections that may emerge across the region, we turn now to chapter 1, where we present the context within which new leisure geographies have emerged in south Beirut, and describe how an Islamic milieu, the making of Dahiya, and a new generation of pious Shi'i Muslims have come together to produce an environment ripe for moral leisure.

New Leisure in South Beirut

In December 1999, seven months before the liberation of South Lebanon from Israeli occupation, an amusement park opened in Dahiya. It was located along its western edge, close to the Golf Club of Lebanon and several ritzy residential areas. Its Ferris wheel was shining new and could be spotted easily while driving on the highway that linked the airport to downtown Beirut. Mona was tempted to check it out with her 2.5-year-old son who had never been to an amusement park in Lebanon. Luna Park in the seaside Manara neighborhood of municipal Beirut was not clean enough for her taste, and its rides were old and rickety, and seemed unsafe. She called a friend who lived in the eastern neighborhood of Achrafieh, and they met with their kids at Fantasy World. Both of them were happily surprised with the park's accessibility from the highway, free parking, cleanliness, affordable prices, and wide variety of rides and attractions. They spent the afternoon comfortably on shaded benches watching their kids play. The amusement park was an island of entertainment, flanked by a highway to the west, a low-income settlement to the east, and high-end residential buildings to the north and south. Mona returned repeatedly with her son to Fantasy World, alone or with friends. In time, the rides lost their shine and the bright paint faded—but the place was always full of children of all ages, supervised by parents or domestic workers. A large restaurant with an open terrace, lush with trees and fountains, catered to families' needs, encouraging adults to spend time and money while their kids played nearby (see figure 1.1). A few months later, in early 2000, just blocks south of Fantasy World and also close to the highway, al-Saha restaurant opened its doors. The restaurant was housed in an immense yellow limestone structure that stood out from the surrounding built environment to such a degree that some passersby took to calling it "that castle thing." Al-Saha's owner was quickly overwhelmed by the demand it generated and

FIGURE 1.1 Fantasy World amusement park

could not keep up with the customer flow; we tell the story of the restaurant's expansion in the next chapter. The concomitant establishment of al-Saha and Fantasy World was a clear sign of new desires for leisure and entertainment in Dahiya.

These two major sites opened in an area of the city where businesses dedicated to leisure were scarce. They represent massive financial investments in leisure that foreshadowed and inspired the plethora of cafés that less than a decade later had filled south Beirut's streets. Before Fantasy World opened, people in Dahiya spent their free time at Beirut's Corniche, or eagerly awaited weekend trips to their villages in South Lebanon and the Bekaa. Lower-class men might hang out and smoke argileh on street corners, and teenage guys might play computer games in dim, smoky Internet shops. The wealthy visited downtown Beirut and cafés in upscale neighborhoods like Raouche, Manara, or Verdun. There were a few gyms in the area that met the sports and exercise needs of its residents, and several of them offered indoor pools used by women during the day and men in the evening. The need to enjoy oneself did not suddenly appear for people living in south Beirut, nor were desires for leisure and fun invisible in the pious Shi'i community before Fantasy World. There has, however, been a significant and palpable change in both how and where people have fun. Fantasy World and al-Saha are no longer exceptions; they are two among the many options that residents of Dahiya have when they decide how to spend their free time.

So why is this? Why has leisure been an arena of major social and spatial changes in south Beirut during the first decade of the twenty-first century? Where did both intensified desires for leisure and the conditions for the development of a leisure sector in Dahiya come from? The answers to these questions require a historical journey through this part of the city and the political, economic, urban, generational, and moral transformations that have impacted and been instigated by its residents, especially since 2000.[1] As we will see, the end of the Israeli occupation in 2000 marked a pivotal moment in the relationship of many Lebanese Shi'i Muslims to leisure. National and international politics in the following years eventually led to new separations between political communities, thereby altering relationships and spatial practices, including those related to fun. A recent history of economic and social mobility for Shi'i Lebanese came to fruition in the form of a consolidated consumerist class. A generation of youths who had been raised within an environment of religious revival and Hizbullah politics came of age. These factors have united to produce a vibrant leisure sector in Dahiya as well as a community of pious Shi'i Muslims who seek specific sorts of fun.

These multifaceted transformations have also resulted in what we call the *Islamic milieu* in Lebanon. Islamic milieu is our gloss for the Arabic phrases *al-hala al-islamiyya* or *al-saha al-islamiyya*.[2] These phrases have no fixed, a priori meaning. The synonyms that our interlocutors frequently use for *hala* and *saha* include *bi'a* and *jaww*, meaning "environment" and "ambiance," respectively. We choose to translate this loose concept that incorporates "state-environment-ambiance-arena" as the word milieu for several reasons. Whether referred to as the hala, saha, bi'a, or jaww, this concept simultaneously connotes the physical and symbolic spaces within which pious Shi'i Muslims live out a particular "state of being," the public sphere where its norms and values are debated as well as shaped, and the "state of being" itself with its continually shifting moral norms.[3] Pious Shi'i Muslims—those who consider themselves a part of the hala/saha/bi'a/jaww—are thus always participating in redefining the milieu. The milieu is continually reconstructed and reproduced by various actors, as opposed to being either an existential state or merely a context in which people live. The term milieu highlights this entanglement of physical spaces where ideas and norms are inscribed and negotiated, with the social environment constructed through those ideas and norms.

This chapter explains the history of the Islamic milieu, and describes its changing relationship to Dahiya and a new generation of pious Shi'i Muslims. Through this history, we will come to understand how political contingency, urbanization, economic mobility, and generational shifts have combined to produce an environment ripe for the development of leisure. We also consider transnational influences on leisure, and a general sense of the *infitah*, or "opening up," of Hizbullah and Dahiya as conditions for these new leisure desires and sites.[4] The most visible of these changes—and our starting point for this historical journey—is of course Hizbullah's popularity along with its incorporation into the social and spatial fabric of Dahiya and Lebanon.

HIZBULLAH IN DAHIYA AND LEBANON

From Inception to Liberation

Hizbullah is the most prominent face today of the multistranded Shiʻi mobilization that began in the late 1960s, and included a number of major actors with varying political perspectives, methods, and ideologies.[5] One of the earliest and most important of these individuals was the charismatic cleric Sayyid Musa al-Sadr, who came to South Lebanon from Iran in 1959, and established the Supreme Islamic Shiʻi Council in 1969 and Harakat al-Mahrumin (the Movement of the Deprived) in 1974, both of which were focused on winning rights for Shiʻi Muslims within the existing structures of the Lebanese state. With the onset of the Lebanese civil war in 1975, a militia branch of the Movement of the Deprived was founded, called Amal, an acronym for *afwaj al-muqawama al-lubnaniyya* (the Lebanese Resistance Brigades), which also means "hope" in Arabic.[6] Amal later developed into one of the Shiʻi Muslim political parties in Lebanon.[7] Al-Sadr disappeared while on a trip to Libya in 1978, thus attaining powerful status as a symbol of Shiʻi righteousness and unity for both Amal and Hizbullah.

Sayyid Muhammad Hussein Fadlallah, who moved to Lebanon in 1952 after training at the religious schools of Najaf in Iraq, was another key figure in the Shiʻi Islamic mobilization of the late 1960s. Until 1976, Fadlallah lived and preached in Nabʻa, a poor neighborhood in the eastern suburbs of Beirut. During a particularly violent series of events in the early years of the civil war, Nabʻa was occupied by the Maronite Christian Phalange militia, and many of its Shiʻi Muslim residents, including Fadlallah, fled to the southern suburb. There Fadlallah continued teaching and expanding his grassroots religious educational and development work, emerging in the early 1980s as one of the pivotal figures in the community. He is credited by many of our interlocutors as their inspiration, and by the mid-1990s had established himself as an important *marjaʻ al-taqlid* (henceforth marjaʻ or jurisprudent), or "source of emulation," in Lebanon—a status he continues to hold postmortem. This means that he was one of the jurisprudents to whom other Shiʻi Muslims could look for guidance in religious matters, as discussed further in chapter 3.

The context for these Islamically oriented mobilizations of the Lebanese Shiʻi community included the political and economic marginalization as well as disenfranchisement of Shiʻi Muslims in the Lebanese state since its inception, the perception that the Lebanese Left had failed to protect the Shiʻi community, the inspiration provided by the success of the 1979 Islamic Revolution in Iran, and the violence and instability of the Lebanese civil war (1975–90). Perhaps most crucial to the formation of Hizbullah in particular were two Israeli invasions of Lebanon, first in 1978 and then in 1982, when nearly a half-million people, mainly Shiʻi Muslims, were displaced from South Lebanon to Beirut and its suburbs. During the 1982 invasion, Israeli troops placed west Beirut under siege, and stood by as Christian militias massacred Palestinian civilians in the Sabra and Shatila refugee camps.[8] In 1985, the Israeli army withdrew partially, but continued to occupy the southern 10 percent of Lebanon using a proxy militia called the Southern Lebanese Army until May 2000.

Hizbullah was born in 1982 as a movement of armed resistance to the Israeli invasion and occupation, though the group did not formally declare its existence until February 1985.[9] Its Islamic Resistance (henceforth, the Resistance) eventually came to dominate the military resistance to Israel in the South, overshadowing Amal as well as leftist and other militia groups that were also fighting against the Israeli occupation. Tensions with Amal escalated to warfare in 1988, and ended with a Syria- and Iran-brokered agreement in 1989 that essentially conceded control of the southern suburb to Hizbullah. From its early days, Hizbullah was not merely a militia but instead a broader movement that built on the Islamic mobilization to develop social welfare networks and institutions in Shiʻi-majority areas of the country.

With the end of the Lebanese civil war in 1990, most militias either relinquished their weapons or hid them in basements and village storage sheds, and then transformed or retransformed themselves into political parties. With the blessing of most Lebanese, Hizbullah maintained its weapons in order to continue to fight the ongoing Israeli occupation in the South. The group also began transforming into a political party and participated in the first postwar elections in 1992, winning eight seats, the largest single bloc in the 128-member Parliament. Since that first election, Hizbullah has developed into a legitimate political party that works within the state, and participates in the same sorts of interparty wheeling and dealing that generally characterizes Lebanese politics.[10] It has continued to carry a major bloc in Parliament and numerous elected municipal positions throughout the country. In addition, its institutions have grown such that today Hizbullah manages one of the largest, most efficient social welfare networks in the country, and is allied with private entrepreneurs who share its moral and political stances. The party also administers a vast media network, including television, radio, and print media. And since the late 1990s, it has begun to focus on cultural activities, leisure, and tourism.

Hizbullah's popularity within Lebanon has shifted with political contingencies and events. Israeli attacks on Lebanese civilians and infrastructure—such as the 1996 Grapes of Wrath attack on Qana during which over one hundred civilians who had taken refuge in a UN bunker were killed—generally contributed to greater national support for the Resistance. The withdrawal of Israeli troops and Israel's proxy militia, the Southern Lebanese Army, from Lebanese territory on May 25, 2000, was understood by most Lebanese of all sects and parties as a victory for the Islamic Resistance, and fueled a high point in Hizbullah's popularity at the turn of the twenty-first century.

Liberation, as the Israeli withdrawal is referred to in Lebanon, also marks a key moment in the development of the leisure sector in Dahiya. For many Shi'i Muslims—especially those who supported Hizbullah, had family members fighting with the Resistance, or were from villages in the occupied South—the experience of war did not end in 1990. Reports on Hizbullah-affiliated radio and television stations shared detailed information about skirmishes in the occupied South, Resistance operations, and Israeli or Southern Lebanese Army attacks. Many people in Dahiya tuned in to these reports, and did not experience the 1990s as a time of calm in the way that their Lebanese compatriots did. For those who bore the brunt of the occupation and resistance to it, war ended in 2000. That was the moment when, in the words of many of our interlocutors, "we could breathe again." One woman continued, "People wanted to go out again, especially youths. People wanted to be out and about. It's natural, because we could breathe." As she suggested, one of the effects of this newfound sense of freedom and relief was renewed desires for leisure, entertainment, and fun.[11] Fun was no longer felt to be frivolous, as it often seemed when reports of martyrs lost were a constant part of the media and social landscape. Opportunities for leisure were emerging, as expatriate Shi'i Muslims started to return to Lebanon, riding on this moment of hope, and investing in the building and rebuilding of their community. The wave of expectation and anticipation that followed Liberation was short lived, however, and soon gave way to a new and newly ugly phase in Lebanese politics.

OLD WARS AND NEW SECTARIANISMS

Liberation was followed in the Lebanese political arena by calls for Hizbullah to disarm, having ostensibly fulfilled the goal of freeing Lebanon from occupation. Hizbullah's consistent refusals were based on the premise that conflict with Israel continued, due to the continued occupation of a fifteen-square-mile border region called the Shebaa Farms, persisting low-grade and occasional cross-border skirmishes, and the detention of many Lebanese in Israeli prisons.[12] The release of many of these detainees in January 2004 further fueled the demands to disarm Hizbullah.

In 2005, after the assassination of former prime minister Rafic Hariri, these tensions came to the foreground and, for the first time in Lebanese history, began to take the form of Sunni-Shi'i sectarian conflict. Hariri's Sunni Muslim party, the Future Movement, now led by his son Saad, took the lead in accusing Syria of involvement in the assassination while calling for an end to Syria's political, economic, and military presence in the country (a presence made possible at the invitation of Christian militia leaders in 1976). Hizbullah came to its ally's defense and organized a large demonstration to "thank Syria" for its service to Lebanon. That demonstration was held on March 8, 2005, and to this day the Hizbullah-led political alliance is known as the "March 8" movement. A few days later, on March 14, an even larger demonstration demanding Syrian withdrawal from Lebanon was held, hence the appellation "March 14" for those parties allied with the Future Movement. On March 17, Syrian troops began to withdraw from Lebanon; they had left by the end of April.

Following the Syrian withdrawal, Hizbullah expanded its role in the Lebanese government.[13] In elections held that spring, the party increased its parliamentary seats from 12 to 14, in a voting bloc with other parties that took 35 of the 128 seats.[14] Also in 2005, for the first time Hizbullah chose to participate in the cabinet, formally joining the government. Those elections saw Hizbullah master the political game in Lebanon, where candidates run as multiconfessional district slates rather than as individuals, which means that alliances are constantly being renegotiated with other politicians who may or may not back one another's various programs and ideologies.[15] For example, in the 2005 parliamentary contests, the Sunni Muslim on Hizbullah's slate in Sidon was Bahiyya al-Hariri, the sister of the assassinated prime minister. Six months after the elections, one of the quintessentially anti-Syrian figures in Lebanese politics, former general Aoun, leader of the Free Patriotic Movement political party and major stakeholder in the March 14 coalition, signed an agreement with Hizbullah, adding a major Christian political party to the March 8 Hizbullah-Amal alliance by switching sides.

Meanwhile, low-grade military conflict with Israel continued in the South. Until July 2006, this conflict was governed by a set of "rules of the game"—based on an agreement not to target civilians that was written after the Qana massacres in 1996.[16] According to these rules, a Hizbullah attack on an Israeli army post in the occupied Shebaa Farms, for example, would be answered by limited Israeli shelling of Hizbullah outposts and sonic booms over Beirut. Both sides, on occasion, broke the rules, though UN Interim Force in Lebanon observer reports about these violations found that Israel violated the Blue Line border between the countries ten times more frequently than Hizbullah did, in part because violations of Lebanese airspace counted, and Israeli planes continued to break the sound barrier over Beirut on an almost-daily basis. On July 12, 2006, in response to Hizbullah's capture of two Israeli soldiers, Israel unleashed the full force of its military.[17] Israeli warplanes, Apache and Blackhawk helicopters, tanks, and gunships battered Lebanon's cities and villages in an assault of a scale unseen since the 1982 Israeli invasion.[18]

While Lebanon and its population as a whole suffered tremendously during this attack, the brunt of civilian deaths and infrastructural destruction took place in the Shi'i-majority south of the country, the Bekaa Valley, and the southern suburb of Beirut. By August 14, when a tenuous ceasefire went into effect, 1,191 Lebanese had been killed, the majority of whom were civilians, and an estimated three billion dollars of infrastructural damage had been sustained.[19] Thousands were wounded, and nearly a million displaced from their homes—one-quarter of the country's population. Entire villages in South Lebanon were flattened during the attack, as were whole neighborhoods in south Beirut. Humanitarian and environmental crises continue, not least due to unexploded bomblets remaining from Israeli-dropped (and US-manufactured) cluster munitions.[20]

On the Lebanese side, Hizbullah fought the July 2006 war while the army stood by helplessly.[21] Political rhetoric during the war further escalated divisions in Lebanon, as Prime Minister Fuad Siniora of the Future Movement accused Hizbullah of being single-handedly responsible for starting the war by not coordinating the abduction of the Israeli soldiers with the government. He reinvoked long-standing national and international accusations that the party was acting as "a state within a state." Hizbullah and March 8 leaders responded by accusing the prime minister and March 14 alliance of betraying the nation and Resistance. Condoleeza Rice's visit to Siniora and her notorious statement qualifying the Israeli war on Lebanon as the "birth pangs of a new Middle East" sealed the divide.[22] Hizbullah accused the government and March 14 of conspiring against the Resistance, and allying with the United States and Israel to annihilate its forces. In a series of televised speeches watched by millions throughout the Arab world, Hizbullah's Nasrallah repeatedly defied Israel and challenged its assaults. He skyrocketed in popularity, achieving rock-star-like status as his image went up in taxis, cafés, and homes from Algiers to Cairo and Baghdad to Dakar. At the war's end, Hizbullah declared "Divine Victory" because Israel had not met its goal of eradicating it. The party asked the displaced to return to their homes and pledged that it would rebuild. On

August 14, 2006—the day the cease-fire went into effect—the reconstruction nongovernmental organization of Hizbullah, Jihad al-Binaa', aided by hundreds of volunteers, began conducting detailed surveys of the damage and prioritizing repairs. Nasrallah explained Hizbullah's reconstruction policy in televised speeches during which he pledged monetary compensation equivalent to one-year's rent to all who lost their homes, in addition to absorbing rebuilding costs.[23] Hizbullah also assigned to Jihad al-Binaa' the responsibility of rebuilding Bint Jbeil in South Lebanon and Haret Hreik in Dahiya—two symbolically significant areas that were razed to the ground by Israeli artillery, the former a key front in the war with Israel and the latter home to most of the party's institutions.[24]

Following the 2006 war, the political fracture between March 14 and March 8 widened into a chasm. The idea of the war as a victory became a rhetorical weapon. The series of political assassinations targeting March 14 leaders that had started with Hariri continued and further exacerbated the conflict, stirring up a general climate of insecurity, fear, and latent animosity among people from both camps.[25] Residents of Beirut and its suburbs entrenched themselves more deeply within their neighborhoods, distancing themselves from one another, and limiting their movement in and around the city. In October 2006, Hizbullah and its allies called for a national unity government giving them one-third plus one of the cabinet seats, which in the Lebanese parliamentary system constitutes a veto, because if one-third of the cabinet resigns, the government falls and must be reappointed. Prime Minister Siniora refused this demand, and the rhetoric continued to escalate until November, when all six Shi'i cabinet ministers resigned, leaving the executive branch of the government without representation from the largest political-sectarian community in the country.

Although the majority of Sunni parties in Lebanon were allied with March 14 and despite the proclivity of the US media to diagnose "age-old Sunni-Shi'i conflict" across the Middle East, the popularity of Hizbullah and March 8 "on the street" at that time belied this diagnosis. It is crucial to emphasize that the conflict in Lebanon has nothing to do with essential religious differences between Shi'i and Sunni Islam but rather is based on political and economic differences. Those political and economic differences are then laid on to political parties that have built themselves on sectarian identities. Sectarianism itself is not an a priori given in Lebanon (or anywhere else), and is instead a political and juridical reality that emerged through a complex history of the gradual alignment of politics with sectarian identities.[26] Building on its historical roots in the construction of Lebanon as a nation-state and the marginalization of Shi'i Muslims within that state, the contemporary manifestation of this conflict was catalyzed by Hariri's assassination and the July 2006 war. These events have led to a situation where, as noted in a report by the International Crisis

Group (2007), many Shiʻi Muslims who are not Hizbullah members and disagree with the party's religious ideologies feel a sense of belonging to a broader Hizbullah community that has come to stand for "the Shiʻa community." The contemporary sectarian conflict is also related to the polarization of Lebanon and the Middle East more generally along pro- and anti-US lines—a polarization that has been exacerbated since the 2003 US invasion of Iraq. In addition to the major issue of alliance, with the United States and Saudi Arabia on one side, and Syria and Iran on the other, March 14 and March 8 disagreed on issues of corruption, accountability, and political representation as well as the contentious issue of Hizbullah's arms, which were discussed in a series of failed "national dialogue meetings" held prior to the Shiʻi ministers' resignations.[27]

In December 2006, the March 8 alliance began a sit-in in downtown Beirut that lasted until the Doha agreement of May 2008. The sit-in paralyzed social and economic life in downtown, exerting sustained pressure on the government controlled by March 14 to resign. Two notable outcomes of the sit-in were that it highlighted the class dimensions of the conflict and rampant prejudice against Shiʻi Muslims in Lebanon. The area of the city where the sit-in took place had been the focus of Hariri's rebuilding of Beirut, replete with extremely expensive apartments and office space, designer stores, and pricey clubs where it is not unusual to find an entrance fee of several hundred dollars. The people maintaining the sit-in included many who were displaced or unemployed because of the 2006 war along with many who were unable to participate in the lifestyle represented by downtown's stores and clubs. The response to this contrast was striking, as racist and classist rhetoric toward Shiʻi Muslims flooded media outlets that supported March 14. Despite the fact that the sit-in included Christians affiliated with Aoun's National Patriotic Movement and Sleiman Frangieh's Marada party, and Druze affiliated with Wiʻam Wahhab's movement, the rhetoric singled out the Shiʻa and accused them of "invading" the capital city. One of the most dramatic examples of this rhetoric was a media campaign designed by the international advertising agency Saatchi and Saatchi for the March 14 group in cooperation with US Agency for International Development. The resulting billboards declared "I Love Life" in English and Arabic, essentially accusing March 8 of "loving death" in a double play on accusations that Hizbullah started the 2006 war and stereotypes about Shiʻi Muslims desiring martyrdom. March 8 responded, also in English and Arabic, by taking the "I Love Life" slogan and adding qualifiers like "with dignity" or "undictated" on billboards signed by "the Lebanese opposition" with a rainbow that included the colors of all the various political parties in the country.[28]

The economic aspects of the standoff materialized in a general strike called in January 2007 in response to the prime minister's proposal for a neoliberal economic reform plan that was to be presented to the Paris III conference as part of a request for foreign government donations to alleviate Lebanon's massive debt of over forty billion US dollars, mostly accumulated during the post–civil war reconstruction.[29] During the strike, small outbursts of violence between March 8 and March 14 supporters foreshadowed future escalation. Those outbursts reminded Lebanese that most, if not all, political parties in the country are armed. As tensions between the two sides simmered, the spate of political assassinations continued, adding to the general climate of fear. When President Emile Lahoud's term ended in November 2007, Nabih Berri, the head of Parliament and an Amal leader, repeatedly refused to call for the necessary parliamentary session to elect a new president on the grounds that the government was anticonstitutional because it remained without cabinet representation from the Shi'i community.

Aggravated by the political vacuum, tensions came to a head in May 2008. In response to government threats to shut down their private network of communication lines, Hizbullah and its allies took military control of Ras Beirut, a Sunni-majority area, for several days. Raids of Future Movement offices and March 14 neighborhoods revealed hidden weapons, and resulted in several people wounded and killed. Nasrallah justified Hizbullah's internal use of arms by claiming that it was the lesser of two evils — the alternative being civil war. Although March 14 also had armed fighters on the streets during this conflict, it quickly took advantage of Hizbullah's deployment of (far more organized) weapons and used this conflict to legitimize requests that the party be disarmed. By the time Hizbullah fighters withdrew and the army restored order, the political chasm had become an apparently irreparable split, with heightened sectarianism solidifying along Sunni-Shi'i lines. Qatar intervened and managed to bring the stakeholders together in Doha, brokering an agreement that included the election of Michel Suleiman as president, a new electoral law, and a distribution of ministerial posts that granted March 8 veto power.

Parliamentary elections were held in June 2009, and with the formation of a new government, an uneasy rapprochement was achieved. The resulting sense of relative stability led to huge numbers of tourists visiting Lebanon—many of them seeking the experiences described in a series of *New York Times* travel articles featuring the country, including one that named Beirut the top exotic travel destination for 2009. Real estate also began to boom, in stark contrast to the financial collapse of real estate markets across the world.[30]

Yet once again, relative stability was short lived. After months of rumblings and rumors, the UN Special Tribunal for Lebanon investigating Hariri's assassination released indictments in June 2011 and issued arrest warrants for four Hizbullah members.[31] In the buildup to this event, two

Hizbullah ministers and nine others had resigned en masse from the cabinet, causing the government's collapse by constitutional means. Telecommunications tycoon Najib Miqati was designated prime minister and tasked with forming a new government. Hizbullah refused the indictments, and the Lebanese state, with its new government, did not arrest the accused individuals by the tribunal's deadline. Nevertheless, the new government drew on reconstruction funds to pay the Lebanese contribution to the tribunal despite Hizbullah's opposition to it—another example of the party's political pragmatism. As we go to press, Lebanese politics remain volatile. Most recently, the uprisings in Syria led to the April 2013 resignation of Miqati.

This series of political events and the consolidation of Hizbullah's popularity among Shi'i Muslims represent one of the key factors in our answer to the question of why moral leisure has proliferated since 2000. The ability to "breathe" following Liberation and renewed interests in leisure combined with the subsequent political polarization and "fears of the other" to fuel desires for leisure closer to home, meaning within the southern suburb. Territorial enclaves were fortified, and mobility was limited, especially between 2006–8 when most Beirut dwellers remained within their neighborhoods to avoid the threats of explosions and violent demonstrations. At the same time, new political alliances, such as that between Hizbullah and the Free Patriotic Movement, brought people from different sects, regions, and backgrounds together, and sparked relationships across sectarian lines through collective political organizing and campaigning. The relative peace of this century, as compared to the years of civil war and Israeli occupation, allowed people to venture further from home, and young people often found themselves studying and working side by side with classmates and colleagues from other parts of the country and other worldviews. Fear in Lebanon is both buttressed and diminished by the small scale of the country and its capital—a scale that guarantees the close proximity of others, friend and foe alike. Yet political contingencies are only one factor in our answer to the question of why moral leisure has expanded recently. We now turn to another crucial component: economic mobility and the development of a middle-class Shi'i Muslim market in Lebanon, and its impact on the southern suburb of Beirut in relation to the city.

RESHAPING THE SUBURB

Dahiya: A Brief (Hi)Story

Dahiya, the Arabic word for suburb, is used in Lebanon to indicate a wide area to the south of Beirut that is notably not the capital's only suburb.

This area is approximately the same size as municipal Beirut and inhabited by well over a half-million people, mainly Shi'i Muslims. Its association with the term Dahiya has a complex urban, social, economic, and political history.

Since the French Mandate, French and Lebanese geographers and urban planners sought to reorganize the city's "misery belts"—suburbs inhabited by poor rural migrants and, after 1948, Palestinian refugees. They drew plans for housing units for the poor along with green suburbs for the middle classes, envisioning the ordered urban growth of the capital. This representation of the city—disseminated by planning professionals working for the public sector and urban scholars—distinguished city and suburbs both socially and spatially.[32] The city was portrayed as a center of urban modernity, high culture, and cosmopolitanism, while the suburbs were described as rural traditional villages, inhabited by poor squatters and refugees who did not appreciate urbanity. The media and local press confirmed this discursive distinction; so did politicians and other elites. Dwellers internalized them: city residents mocked the lifestyles and homes of those who lived in the suburbs. Administrative boundaries further consecrated this binary reading of the city. A municipality with boundaries that stopped at the suburbs' edges autonomously governed Beirut. Several local municipalities that depended administratively on the Mount Lebanon governorate in turn governed the suburbs, underscoring their inhabitant's rural origins.

The civil war completely altered realities on the ground. Downtown Beirut was destroyed and became a no-man's-land. The loss of the city center led to a decentralization of economic activities into other neighborhoods including those outside municipal Beirut. Waves of middle- and upper-income people fled the city, while others streamed in as a result of forced displacement or continued rural-urban migration. City and suburb spaces became polarized along sectarian lines, and sect was linked to politics such that people identified with a sectarian group were "naturally" associated with particular political parties or stances.

Depictions of city and suburbs shifted alongside these drastic, violent spatial transformations. In the early 1980s, the city separated into west (mostly Muslim) and east (mostly Christian) Beirut. The suburbs were also fragmented according to geographic location, sectarian identity, and sometimes ethnic identity. As they increasingly operated as self-sufficient territorial enclaves, suburbs were further excluded from the city. The common phrase *dawahi* Beirut (the Arabic plural of *dahiya*) was replaced by more specific terms (northern, eastern, and southern). "The southern suburb" (*al-dahiya al-janubiyya*) became the label used to refer to the area extending south of the capital toward the airport, homogenizing a variety of neighborhoods under a single umbrella term. By the late 1980s, the suffix al-janubiyya (southern) was abandoned, and by the mid-1990s, referring to al-Dahiya was sufficient to designate the area.[33] Everyone knew where "the suburb" was, and more important, whose suburb it was.

Hizbullah's domination over Dahiya happened violently in 1989, in one of the last episodes of the Lebanese civil war, during which the party fought its Shi'i counterpart, Amal, and expelled it from most of Dahiya's neighborhoods.[34] Hizbullah's appropriation of Dahiya led to fearful representations of its space: the southern suburb was named "Hizbullah-land" or "Dahiyat al-Khomeyni," in reference to the Iranian ayatollah who was the party's inspiration and spiritual guide until his death. Residents of other areas of Beirut became conscious of its boundaries and avoided entering its neighborhoods, driving by its edges rapidly. The Lebanese government and its city planners described Dahiya as a "Shi'i ghetto," a rebellious space defying state authority. Dahiya was represented as the site of crime, outlaws, and an unruly and grim existence. More than ever, the suburb and its dwellers were excluded from the city, singled out in their otherness, and portrayed in derogatory terms encompassing social, cultural, religious, economic, political, and spatial dimensions. They were poor, backward, illegal, fanatic, and anarchic. City dwellers were embarrassed by their existence at Beirut's doorstep and harbored not-so-secret wishes to eradicate them.

With the signing of the Taif agreement that ended the civil war in 1990 and Hizbullah's subsequent decision to join the Lebanese political system in 1992, Dahiya's relationship with Beirut progressively improved. Several elements contributed to this shift. Many were political. Beirut's downtown was being reconstructed by Solidere, a real estate company that was the brainchild of Hariri. The rebuilding of the city center symbolized the reconstruction of the state as it sought to exercise authority over its territory—under close Syrian scrutiny at the time. Public institutions (such as schools, dispensaries, and hospitals) were reinstated and/or rehabilitated in many Lebanese regions, including Beirut's suburbs. In 1998, municipal elections were held, yielding local government representation in all Lebanese towns and villages. Through reconstruction and the extension of the state, the Lebanese government, centered in Beirut, sought to modernize its urban and rural peripheries, with the declared aim of better administration and organization, which also implied improved monitoring and control.

Economic elements also contributed to the changing relationship between Beirut and Dahiya. The early 1990s were a time of economic boom. Large amounts of transnational capital were being invested in Beirut, benefiting all who agreed to respect one another's turf and not meddle in their respective transactions. This consensus was referred to as the "troika," in reference to the three poles of power ruling the political system: Sunni

Muslim, Shi'i Muslim, and Maronite Christian. Hariri reconstructed downtown using Gulf-based capital; Hizbullah consolidated its military resistance in the South, and attended to its constituency's needs through a network of institutions centered in Dahiya using Iranian and Shi'i diaspora capital (Deeb 2006). And while Hizbullah facilitated the evacuation of Shi'i squatters from downtown Beirut (negotiating on their behalf for minimal compensation) and did not oppose the creation of Solidere in Parliament, Hariri demonstrated a laissez-faire attitude vis-à-vis the production of what Hizbullah terms its "Resistance society" in Dahiya (Harb 2010a).

A short-lived normalization of the relationship between Dahiya and Beirut had begun, as the area became another administrative sector of the city, simply a geographic reference to a place; cabdrivers and administrators alike referred to it as Dahiya. The label was depoliticized and recuperated by public agencies that "banalized" its usage and placed it on street signs. This recuperation and semantic inversion of meaning was echoed in daily life. At the turn of the twenty-first century, more people than ever visited Dahiya's neighborhoods for work, services, shopping, or simply socializing. The suburb was less acutely othered, less exclusive, less stigmatized, and closer to the city and its residents. Political, economic, social, and cultural links were forged, partially challenging the binary dichotomy. This ephemeral normalization reached its peak in May 2000 with the widely celebrated Liberation of the South, which prompted many Lebanese to discover previously inaccessible or feared parts of their national territory, and establish stronger connections with their Shi'i compatriots.

The city-suburb dichotomy has been deeply affected this century by geopolitical changes ranging from the post–September 11, 2001, US "war on terror" to the installation of Bashar al-Assad at the head of the Syrian regime in October 2000 following his father's death. Growing political tensions between Hariri's alliance and Hizbullah reinvigorated the spatial opposition between Beirut and Dahiya, especially after Hariri's assassination. Discursively, this opposition started to appear in eerily familiar narratives distinguishing "backward, rural migrants" in the "poor, illegal, and lawless Shi'i suburb/ghetto" who "hated life and sent their kids to death," from "arrogant, egocentric oppressors" in the "corrupt, immoral, and self-righteous city" who "did not understand resistance toward a dignified existence free of occupation and injustice."

The Israeli war on Lebanon in July 2006 and its political aftermath fueled this growing hostility, which took on ever more violent, sectarian, and exclusionary terms. "Beirut is ours," "Beirut is a red line," proclaimed Hariri's advocates. Hizbullah labeled Dahiya "the rebel that never dies" and the "territory of the proud and the glorious." The March 8 sit-in in downtown Beirut was described by Beirutis as "Dahiya-fication" and an "invasion of our city," ignoring the multisectarian makeup of the protesters. Opinion pieces in newspapers rejected the migrants that were "ruralizing" Beirut, and were desolate over the transformation of its neat streets into picnic areas where people danced dabkeh, smoked argileh, and ate *kaak* and corn on the cob sold by vendors. The suburbs were accused of ruining the city's modernity and civilization. Jokes circulated about the incivility of Shiʻi Muslims and their inability to be urban. March 14 supporters were upset by participants' "Corniche-like" practices—a reference to the mixed public space along the coast, known as a hangout for the urban poor, who spend evenings there smoking argileh and enjoying their families, seated on the plastic chairs and tables they have brought with them.

The spatial climax of this conflict mirrored the political one, culminating in the May 2008 takeover of the city by Hizbullah fighters. The city's fear of the rebel suburb that grew as a monster at its doorstep materialized, and the separation between Dahiya and Beirut reached a new scale, comparable to that of the civil war. In the reentrenchment of sectarian communities in space that followed, residents of all areas began to stay closer to home once again. In Dahiya, those residents included a robust Shiʻi middle class that demanded places for leisure in their neighborhoods.

Growing Shiʻi Middle Classes

Shiʻi social and economic mobility had begun in the late 1960s, largely as a result of the Shehabist policies that strengthened state services, especially the establishment of the public Lebanese University and the Ministry of Social Affairs' centers for social services. The social dynamics of the war and postwar periods reinforced the economic changes in the Shiʻi community. The political party Amal joined the state in 1982 and initiated a steady distribution of services to its constituency through various public agencies as well as via networks of private entrepreneurs in what has been termed a "militia economy" (Picard 2000, 294). As of the mid-1980s, Hizbullah had begun establishing its own network of social organizations that distributed services directly to mainly Shiʻi recipients. Through different systems of public action—one grafted on the state, and one more self-sufficient—both parties managed to improve the living conditions of the majority of Shiʻi Muslims, who had been excluded from public services (Harb 2010a). These efforts were fortified by the social work of institutions affiliated with Fadlallah, such as al-Mabarrat, which built schools, orphanages, and hospitals across the country (Deeb 2006).

The urban middle class of Dahiya is thus partly the result of diligent efforts over the past three decades by the main stakeholders in the Islamic milieu. They succeeded in improving the social, economic, and urban status of the Shiʻi community. The majority-Shiʻi regions of South Lebanon and the Bekaa Valley that "used to be at the bottom end of the development hierarchy in terms of income and education status, extent of poverty or access to basic services," saw their social indicators improve in the early 1960s due to "the increased political weight and representation of the Shiʻi community, translating in[to] increased attention and influx of public aid, in addition to a growing volume of remittances and local investments by Shiʻi diaspora in Africa and the Gulf in their regions of origin in the South and the Bekaa" (Nasr 2003, 155).

In addition, Dahiya's urban middle class was empowered by the municipal elections that were reinstated in 1998, during which many Hizbullah members and prominent Dahiya families were elected.[35] Municipalities in Lebanon hold large prerogatives in local governance and development, and have a substantive margin of maneuver, although they face the challenges of limited human resources, a poorly decentralized fiscal system, and high dependency on the central administration. Despite these challenges, large urban municipalities manage rather well. Dahiya is subdivided into four municipalities, the largest of which is Ghobeyri. Under the mayorship of Hajj Abu Saʻid al-Khansa, one of Hizbullah's founders and politburo members, Ghobeyri has led major efforts in urban and economic development in Dahiya over the past fifteen years.[36] Such municipalities endowed Hizbullah with additional resources for their service delivery network, provided more efficient ways to distribute services, and created new opportunities for local and economic development (Harb 2009).

Our friend Marwan's story offers an example of social mobility within the Islamic milieu linked to Hizbullah and Amal's networks as well as consolidated power in Dahiya. Marwan lost two brothers during the civil war: one who fought for Hizbullah, and one for Amal. His family received some financial support from Hizbullah. Marwan had good contracting skills and attempted to start a business in the real estate sector. He used family owned land and some inherited money to buy and sell building materials. He was so successful that he soon was unable to stack all the materials within the lot. Rumor has it that he negotiated an agreement with the local Amal representative to squat on unused private land nearby and thereby expand his business. Additional rumors suggest that the local Hizbullah representative also supplied him with land. In any case, Marwan bought trucks and hired migrant workers, and quickly accumulated capital that helped him expand his business. He was able to help his family renovate their private house in a dense area of Dahiya, and build an additional floor on its roof for himself and his wife. As business improved, he left his parents' house and moved to a better neighborhood. Shortly thereafter, he saved enough money to buy land in the mountains and build a summer residence.

More recently, Marwan threw a fancy wedding for his daughter, a young headscarf-wearing woman who works in a major bank in Dahiya. Mona

attended the wedding, which was held at a hotel in Beirut's Christian suburbs and planned by an event management company—a common practice
among middle-class Beirutis. The staircase leading to the hall was lavishly
decorated with white orchids and lilies, with similar flowers arranged in
huge centerpieces on each table. After the approximately two hundred
guests were seated, the groom walked into the hall to the tune of Vangelis's
"Chariots of Fire," surrounded by young men in traditional attire dancing
and waving swords. The bride then entered, hidden in a white coach that
opened to reveal her elaborately embroidered white dress. The couple met
near an immense multilevel cake, intertwined their arms to drink apple
juice in fluted glasses, cut the cake together, and released two terrified
doves. Whitney Houston's "I Will Always Love You" then brought the
couple into a slow dance while a screen behind them displayed photos
of their lives since birth. The bride and groom—himself the son of a
prominent Hizbullah member—now live in one of Dahiya's expensive
neighborhoods.

The growth of a Shi'i middle class is also related to remittances from
transnational family networks, which contribute significantly to the incomes of resident Lebanese family members, facilitating opportunities for
improved social mobility.[37] This is not unique to Shi'i Lebanese; remittances have been vital to all sectarian groups and the Lebanese economy
more broadly.[38] Expatriates' remittances are estimated to constitute 22 percent of household incomes in Lebanon and 88 percent of their savings
(Hourani 2003). Our friend Aziza's immediate family illustrates class mobility within Dahiya related to remittances. While never poor, through the
1990s her family could be characterized as lower middle class or working
class. Her father owned a small business, selling tires and car parts with his
second son. Their shop was located on a side street in Dahiya, and was
destroyed several times in the civil war and again in 2006. Her oldest
brother, Ali, had quit college to flee Lebanon during the Hizbullah-Amal
street fighting during the civil war and was seeking asylum in Europe, and
Aziza had a college degree but did not work. In Europe, Ali first worked
as an agricultural day laborer for nine years, until he obtained residency
papers. He then found work with a telephone company, and began to send
home small amounts of money and damaged cars. The cars were repaired
and resold by her father, and Aziza used the money to start several businesses, all of which failed until finally, with a thirty thousand dollar lump
sum from Ali, she was able to begin a successful small business venture. Ali
then married a Lebanese woman whose own small business venture in
Europe became a financial success.

As these two businesses continued to grow, the family's situation began
to change visibly. Aziza's father's shop moved to a larger, more prominent
location on a major public thoroughfare in Dahiya, and he and Aziza set

her younger brother up with a small appliance store. The main bathroom in the family apartment was redone; the old blue tiles were replaced with "classier" beige and marble with elaborate gold-colored fixtures. The living room was refurnished in brocade and gilded fabrics and frames. The sitting room was reupholstered, air-conditioning units were purchased, and new kitchen and dining ware replaced the old. A few years later, the family hired a live-in domestic worker. Two additional cars soon followed, and the balcony was enclosed in glass. Finally, the family purchased a villa near the coast in the South, and are now saving money to fix and furnish it.

Aziza and Marwan are typical of the upwardly mobile Shi'i residents of Dahiya in benefiting from the Islamic milieu's institutions and/or transnational remittance flows. These factors have combined to provide many Shi'i Muslims with direct or indirect opportunities for economic and social mobility. In the wake of Liberation in 2000, private investments and real estate development schemes privileging middle- and high-end consumers multiplied in Dahiya. Several of these investors were return emigrants who moved back to Lebanon, often from the United States, bringing their business ideas with them. The owner of Sweet Café was one of these returnees; he had worked in construction, and then owned gas stations in Ohio and Michigan. He explained:

> I felt like doing something in Lebanon, especially after the war ended [in 2000]. Lebanon became stable. The investment environment improved; there was stability. We thought that people had the freedom to have fun; there was safety. So at the end of 2002 we did a study about what we could do in the country, what would work. We found that local entertainment projects have an audience. Also they are beautiful; they keep you in touch with people, and the income from this work is good. So we did this project and we worked on it for six months.

Hajj Abu Sa'id, the mayor of Ghobeyri who played a major role in the establishment of Fantasy World, confirmed the impact of Liberation on investment:

> During the [pre-2000] war [with Israel], we were focusing on the liberation movement. . . . Effort was going toward liberation; this is normal, this is like anywhere in the world. When Israel left, people started to think more about investment. Large investments began in Dahiya. Many tourist places opened, amusement parks, different types of restaurants, entertainment places, different types of cafés, and lots of gyms. This encouraged people to move toward these things.

From Abu Sa'id's perspective, the opening of leisure sites encouraged the development of leisure desires. Yet those sites were also opened in response to an already-existing though untapped market. When Fantasy World's owner described this new market, he situated himself as wealthy rather than middle class:

> There is a saying, "*al-rizq 'ind tazahum al-aqdaam*" [where there is movement/ chaos (literally of feet), there is fortune]. We, al-Dahiya . . . there is a huge number of people, six to seven hundred thousand. In the end, there is a class, not all Dahiya is poor. There is a class [*mustawa*] that has [economic] potential, and there is a middle class, and there is a lower class. . . . We are from the wealthy class.

Despite this characterization, most café owners are not in the wealthy owner class, and many run smaller cafés in partnership with several people as barely solvent businesses or experiments in addition to their "day jobs." The exceptions, like the owner of Fantasy World, rank among the wealthiest people in Lebanon. Most notorious among them was Salah Ezzedine. Known for his piety and close relationship with Hizbullah, he ran multiple businesses and sold investments with high returns to hundreds of people in a Ponzi scheme that allegedly reached at least a half-billion dollars before collapsing in 2009. Several of his scammed clients are believed to be prominent Hizbullah members. He was arrested by Hizbullah and turned over to the Lebanese justice system, which found him guilty of embezzlement and breaching financial laws. The Ezzedine scandal exposed the powerful capital circuits that underlie the Shi'i Islamic milieu.

Large investors and small-time café entrepreneurs alike are exploiting a middle-class market that is not limited to leisure. A prominent Hizbullah member described the economic power of the Shi'i middle classes to us: "We are a big powerful consumer movement that attracts big investors." Abu Sa'id's party-run municipality is also home to two huge consumer development projects. The French department store BHV and its associated supermarket Monoprix opened their doors in 1998 on the western side of Ghobeyri, just at its border with municipal Beirut, alongside a Burger King. More recently, a Saudi investor established the Beirut Mall in 2006 on the opposite side of Ghobeyri to the east, close to the Christian neighborhoods of Badaro, Chiyah, and Ain el-Rummaneh. Beirut Mall includes trendy US and European clothing stores, including Nine West, Vero Moda, and Mango, along with coffee shops and fast-food restaurants, including McDonald's, and a children's indoor theme park. These initiatives confirm the continued existence of a vibrant local middle class eager to consume and sustain its lifestyle.

Indeed, this points to another way in which Aziza and Marwan are also typical. As both their families obtained greater income, they initiated lifestyle changes ranging from renovating existing homes, to moving to more upscale neighborhoods, to wearing designer clothing and driving newer German luxury cars as well as US and Japanese SUVs, to roaming with their domestic workers in BHV and Beirut Mall. Consumption here is both a result of economic mobility and a sign of it.[39]

The middle class about which we write is at once an economic class related to the control of multiple forms of capital, and produced by local, national, and transnational networks related to flows of services, money, and education, *and* a culturally constructed social location and identity structured by economic as well as other forms of capital in relation to other groups in Lebanon.[40] In a recent conversation with a friend in Beirut about our project, Mona encountered surprise that there still was a middle class in the city. This friend assumed that the phrase middle class referred to people who lived in Ras Beirut, and whose cultural references were transnationally directed toward Europe and the United States—a class that many Beirutis believe has dwindled significantly in the wake of both emigration and economic hardship. The middle class in Dahiya is instead a class residing outside the city's municipal boundaries with cultural references that are equally transnational, but directed toward Africa, Iran, and the Arab world as much as toward Europe and the United States. Sherry Ortner (1998, 4) has demonstrated the ways in which class, race, and ethnicity are intertwined in the United States, such that race and ethnicity are "deeply 'classed.'" Similarly in Lebanon, class and sect are intertwined, such that neither category can be fully understood independent of the other. Indeed, in Lebanon, inclusion and exclusion in the middle class has a great deal to do with the dynamics of morality and geography that we take up in the coming chapters, and we specifically address the coimbrication of class and sect, along with taste, in chapter 6. Because class, sect, and space are linked, the emergence of a robust urban middle class in Dahiya has had profound effects on the southern suburb itself.

From Southern Suburb to South Beirut

The political and socioeconomic transformations of the past three decades increasingly linked Dahiya to the city, through a variety of physical, social, and economic connections. We refer to the southern suburb interchangeably as Dahiya and south Beirut in order to acknowledge the terms' various meanings while claiming the area as part of the city, despite the fact that residents and political groups from both sides—aided by sectarian politics, class positions, and constantly threatening geopolitics—continue to distinguish Dahiya from Beirut in their discourses and practices. Our claim that Dahiya is part of the city is supported by its new leisure sector.

Thus far, we have seen that leisure in Dahiya developed as the result of a combination of market-led investments in entertainment services with the postwar phase of Liberation that made people eager to enjoy their free time and gave them a sense that they had the "right" to have fun. As Hajj Abu Saʿid put it, "All societies evolve. In 1982, if I wore nice clothes, it would clash with the revolutionary phenomenon. . . . In the beginning, style didn't matter. We were in a revolution. It wasn't the time to select clothes and styles; we wanted to focus all our efforts on resistance. . . . Now things have changed. There is a space [*muttassaʿ*]." This is the space that allowed people to feel they could breathe, the space that allowed them to seek out new ways to have fun. It is also a space that links Dahiya to Beirut, through desires for leisure that take people across municipal boundaries and through leisure sites that cater to pious individuals who reside across the city. Yet there remains a missing factor in understanding the twenty-first century emergence of both the vibrant new leisure sector in Dahiya and particular forms of leisure desired by many of its residents. In order to fully understand these phenomena, we need to understand generational and moral change in south Beirut.

FROM VANGUARD TO NORMATIVELY PIOUS YOUTHS

A key reason for the surge in leisure in Dahiya—and the last major piece of our explanation for it—is generational change. The power of generational shifts in producing social change has been widely theorized from a number of perspectives.[41] In thinking about generations, we build on recent scholarship that has recentered Karl Mannheim's (1952, 291, 303) classic essay, "The Problem of Generations," and his discussion of a generation as a group of people sharing "a common location in the social and historical process" and participating "in the common destiny of this historical and social unit."[42] Generation here is produced and defined both through shared experiences and understandings of particular historical and cultural events, and through specific responses to those experiences and events.[43] In concert with these approaches, we understand generational categories to emerge in relation to specific cultural and political-economic contexts and via social processes. This does not mean that generations are automatically produced through shared historical experiences but rather that through specific social processes, particular groups of people begin to understand themselves and/or be understood as a generation. Nor does this mean that generations are unified; there is of course variation within them as well. The political, social, and urban transformations in the recent history of the Lebanese Shiʿi Muslim community have produced generational categories that are both articulated by our interlocutors and useful to our analysis of new leisure desires and sites in Dahiya.

Specifically, today's pious youths represent a significant generational shift away from what we call the *Islamic vanguard* generation. In terms of biological age categories, most vanguard members were born before 1970. The vanguard generation, more accurately, includes those whose efforts in the 1960s, 1970s, and 1980s led to the Lebanese Shi'i Islamic movement and its institutionalization. They are the agents of the political dynamics, class mobility, and urban transformations we describe above. Unlike today's youths, most of the vanguard generation people we have spoken with since the late 1990s trace their religious and political commitment to their late teens or early twenties, link it explicitly to education and consciousness-raising, and describe themselves as committing *despite* their family environment.[44] Not only did the vanguard build the Shi'i Islamic movement in Lebanon but it also raised today's youths. This vanguard consists of parents, teachers, school principals, reporters on Hizbullah-affiliated radio and television, Resistance fighters and engineers, volunteers in social welfare institutions, and the hosts of and attendees at Ramadan fund-raising *iftars* (Ramadan's daily fast-ending meal).[45] These people often had to fight against existing notions of morality held by their parents and grandparents—ideas cast by the rebelling Islamic vanguard generation as "traditional"—in order to enact their new understandings of authentic religious and political commitment, or iltizam. As thirty-nine-year-old Hanady put it, "The hijab was like tradition for them." Amani, who is the same age, responded in a way that clearly established both herself and her friend as members of the vanguard: "Yes, in the beginning it was traditional, but of course the next generation, their children, we committed fully after we learned a lot about our religion then [in the 1980s] because we did not know anything before." The vanguard is also a generation defined by its memory and experience of Lebanon without Hizbullah, the Shi'i community as marginalized and disenfranchised, and the labor that went into forming the Islamic Resistance. Finally, because it came of age during times of violence, whether the civil war or Israeli occupation, the vanguard generally was not afforded many opportunities for leisure and play.

The movement led by the vanguard resulted in the sedimentation, by the late 1990s, of a pious and moral lifestyle based on specific religious ideas and practices into commonsense knowledge and a new social norm for many people in Dahiya.[46] This sits in sharp contrast to the imposed "Islamification" that followed the Islamic Revolution in Iran, where Islamic practice was enforced and "a state of imposed normality makes transgression a norm" (Varzi 2006, 124). In Dahiya, we instead see a significant proportion of young people today who strive to be pious and live moral lives. Most of our young interlocutors traced the origin of their iltizam to young ages, either around *takleef*, age nine for girls and thirteen for boys, or to their midteen years, around age sixteen or seventeen, suggesting that it may be linked to stages of "growing up." This is not to say that all young people in Dahiya want to be pious and moral, nor that all young Shi'i Muslims who want to be pious and moral live in Dahiya. Rather, the social landscape of present-day south Beirut can be described as one where there is a critical mass of youths who understand piety and the religious rubric of morality to be key elements with which they are concerned as they strive to live lives that they understand as "good." This critical mass of youths coupled with their faith and genuine concern for their souls reflects one of the major successes of the vanguard generation's grassroots Islamic mobilization efforts, and attests to the *different* success of this mobilization as compared to Iran's Islamic revolution.

These Lebanese youths (who we refer to as more or less pious youths, or simply, youths or pious youths) were born between 1978 and 1990, and therefore were between eighteen and thirty in 2008 when we conducted most of our interviews.[47] The youth generation was raised after the key struggles of the vanguard had taken place, and came of age in a world where Hizbullah was already a popular and powerful political party. These young people may have attended schools affiliated with either Fadlallah or Hizbullah, and regardless, were certainly exposed to and often took for granted the hegemonic norms of public piety that accompanied the forms of authenticated Islam espoused by the vanguard. In other words, today's pious youths frequently take the status quo for granted in a way that the vanguard generation did and does not. Because this status quo is something that the vanguard generation struggled against social convention to produce, youths' presumptions about it are all the more striking.[48]

The notion of youth as a social category is not new in Lebanon, and shabab and sabaya have long been salient terms for young men and women, respectively.[49] What has changed in the pious Shi'i community is the additional meanings that have been placed on to ideas about age such that youths in the twenty-first century are understood to be experiencing and shaping the world in significantly different ways than the vanguard generation did when they were young. Hajjeh Um Ja'far, a woman in her early fifties, described the differences between her generation and today's young people to Lara in 2000: "When I became committed [to Islam] there was a lot of talk about us. Even within my family there was talk, you know, 'What's this iltizam?' While today, it's normal, a girl can put on the hijab and she doesn't have a problem." She went on to wonder whether what set her apart from her daughter was conviction (quoted in Deeb 2006, 226–27). Other mothers in the vanguard generation also expressed concern that their daughters were not adequately pious. Some suggested that this was related to the extent to which the community as a whole had reached a point where particular forms of pious comportment were a social norm. In other words, they were concerned because pious practice for youths had become normative and perhaps routinized in new ways, and because it was *not* constructed in opposition to the environment. Many parents feared that this very normativity would provoke an abandonment or insincerity of piety in their children.

Another vanguard member, who is today a Hizbullah party official, added the observation that today's youths are not content to have to sacrifice leisure for commitment, but unlike the vanguard, insist on having both. And some vanguard generation individuals find both the newfound wealth in the community and the consumption practices of youths disturbing. Jawad and Zayn, in their thirties and forties, respectively, described feeling uncomfortable around wealth and preferred to hang out with the poor. They typify an older vanguard generation model that remains common among volunteers in Dahiya's myriad charitable associations and among many party stalwarts.

Of course, not all youths disagree with the vanguard's assessment of their generation. Zaynab, Fatima, and Rola—all students in their early twenties—had a long conversation about "hijab hypocrisy"—young women who wear their hijabs "incorrectly," complaining about those who wore their scarves with clothing that was too revealing, or who laughed too loudly in public, walked sexily, or checked guys out in cafés.[50] They described this behavior as disrespectful and irresponsible, and disagreed with one another about whether the reason for this "phenomenon" was beginning to wear the headscarf at too young an age, wearing it to please a boyfriend, or the fact that "being *muhajjabeh* has become the new fashion."[51] Another young woman suggested that the hijab has become "like a passport" gaining a woman access to aspects of the Shi'i community, despite the fact that it comes with a great deal of discrimination in other parts of Beirut.

These concerns and self-assessments may not be entirely unfounded, and point to the difficulties in associating act with authentic intention in a context where religious rules have melded into social norms. Vanguard and youth generations alike view certain behaviors as both stemming from and indicative of piety, including unrelated men and women not shaking hands with one another and, for women, wearing the hijab. For the vanguard generation, these acts were clearly markers of public piety. For youths, however, because the normativity of such behavior called into question the concordance between public act and inner state, establishing any act as a marker of public piety took more effort. All but one of the young women who told us that her iltizam began at age nine when she put on the hijab took care to explain spontaneously either that her commitment had been a "true" and thoughtful "choice" (always using that term), despite her young age, or that she had "made a choice" to renew her commitment as a teenager. In other words, young women who started wearing the hijab at age nine, often as part of a school uniform, needed to work harder to establish the hijab as a choice, and thus as an authentic marker of public piety. This worked in reverse for the exceptions. Tala, a young woman who described being "forced" to wear the hijab by her family, explained that the incorrect way she wore it—incorrect both because she wore a scarf with tight clothing and because she went clubbing regularly—was the result of her lack of choice in the matter: "This is why I am like that." Soha gave the same explanation for why she changes her clothing to less conservative styles whenever she leaves her home neighborhood in Dahiya.

These parental concerns and peer critiques of the relationship between piety and public behavior point to the ways that Shi'i youths in south Beirut have begun to question moral boundaries—especially within the religious rubric of morality—related to ideas and practices of leisure. They do this through a combination of flexible moral ideas and spatial practices, as we discuss in chapters 4 and 5, respectively. Youth is an important category for leisure because through dynamics of generational change, these processes are deployed by and affect young people far more than others. In this sense, youth as a category is a part of the equation not because of an a priori association of leisure with age but instead because of the structural position of this particular set of people vis-à-vis political, economic, geographic, and social changes in Lebanon. While religious faith is certainly important to many young people in Dahiya today, and many do embrace a pious lifestyle, their definitions of that lifestyle differ from those of the vanguard generation. In addition to fostering an environment where norms of public piety and religious morality are taken for granted, the political and economic history depicted above have contributed to youths' self-differentiation from the vanguard in both identity and practice. The plethora of Shi'i social and political institutions established in the past few decades have ensured the existence of multiple sources of moral authority in the community, which facilitates youths' flexibility when it comes to moral norms. Youths' access to these opinions and sources of authority has been guaranteed by the technology—ranging from cell phones to the Internet—that infuses their world.

The world in which youths lived most of their lives was also a postwar world, one of relative security—however tentative at times—where people *could* go out and interact more frequently with others within as well as outside their community. They are the generation that came of age with the ability to breathe in the wake of the civil war and Israeli occupation. Even people at the older end of this spectrum who may have lived through the violence of the civil war as children spent their teenage years after it ended and lived their twenties after Liberation. This relative stability, combined with the economic changes and class mobility within their community, also meant that youths were more likely to be college students at institutions ranging from the public Lebanese University to the elite private American University of Beirut. Our primary interlocutors were not only young but also staunchly middle class.

In addition to the structural features of this generation that facilitate their particular relationship to leisure, age is relevant to their leisure desires in a specific way that is shared across Lebanon. Most youths residing in Beirut live with their parents until they get married. They have little, if any, privacy in their homes as they frequently share rooms with siblings or other family members. Given the late average year of marriage in Lebanon, many young people view this proximity to one's parents as a problem.[52] After university or work, they often do not return directly home but instead seek places where they can be on their own or with peers. The scarcity of public spaces in Beirut does not give them many options for this "transitional" time. Some go to the gym—if they can afford it—while others go to cafés or pubs. In that sense, new places of leisure in Dahiya are especially significant for pious youths because they provide them with possibilities for this in-between space that are both close to home and appropriate for their lifestyles.

Today's more or less pious Shi'i youths in south Beirut are educated, literate, expectant, and media savvy. They take certain religious norms as well as globalized mass media, satellite television, cellular phones, and the Internet for granted.[53] A generation that consists of quintessential individual consumers of leisure has been produced by a combination of assumptions about piety and morality, relative peace, technological savvy, education, and income. These youths feel entitled and able to debate ideas about leisure, morality, and space. As good consumers, they expect to be able to choose morality and leisure sites from within a set of options. Their flexibility when it comes to morality includes an acceptance of flexibility in others. They have also assimilated the idea that one can "work on" one's piety—a notion they share with the vanguard—into a longer time frame so that moral lifestyle choices may be gradually accumulated as one progresses (and sometimes regresses) along a "ladder of piety." The emergence of this generation provides a key missing link for understanding why desires for and sites of moral leisure have proliferated in Dahiya in the twenty-first century.

REVISITING THE "WHY NOW?" QUESTION

The elements discussed thus far have come together to produce a new landscape of moral leisure sites and practices in south Beirut—a landscape initiated by Fantasy World and al-Saha. Liberation in 2000 fueled both people's desires and market possibilities for leisure. The post-2005 escalation of internal political tensions and small violences in the country reentrenched sectarian communities in the city. And the concomitant political alliance between Hizbullah and key Christian opposition figure Aoun brought people from different sectarian communities together in a variety of public spaces in new ways. The significant expansion of an urban Shi'i middle class in Lebanon in the 1990s along with the post-2000 influx of return emigrant capital into the community added new investors and consumers to this mix. And a generation of more or less pious youths who take piety as normative while looking to consume multiple moral and geographic options in their leisure practices provides potent kindling. Together, these factors led to the formation of a new market, sparking the rapid development of leisure places in Dahiya in a relatively short period of time.

This cauldron of conditions was enhanced by two additional elements: transnational influences and the infitah (again, "opening up") of Hizbullah. The development of leisure places and desires that are concerned with morality in Dahiya parallels the emergence of leisure in a variety of urban Muslim-majority contexts. Neighborhoods in cities such as Tehran, Damascus, Istanbul, Cairo, and Amman have become lively sites for cafés and restaurants that cater to pious or practicing Muslim patrons. This phenomenon can be understood in relation to the growth of a broader transnational Muslim consumer market where faith and fun intersect.[54] While Beirut has long been a desirable tourist site for Arabs from the Gulf states, Europeans, and increasing numbers of North American and Asian visitors, south Beirut's leisure spaces aim to attract a different clientele.[55] In addition to their local and resident Lebanese customers, Dahiya's cafés and restaurants cater to pious Shi'i Lebanese expatriates and tourists from Iran as well as Gulf Arabs who shun municipal Beirut's sinful possibilities and prefer to relax in "moral" environments. Café owners as well as Hizbullah officials confirmed this deliberate effort to construct a market for moral leisure. Some of these owners coordinate with travel agents to put their cafés on tour itineraries for lunch or dinner, and several Hizbullah officials described plans to produce a map for what they called either "religious tourism" or "Resistance tourism."

While it is difficult to assess any causal relationships between this transnational market and the development of leisure in Dahiya, there are observable similarities across many dynamic urban Muslim-majority neighborhoods in the styles of new contemporary cafés, the ideas of morality that dominate them, and their mostly youthful patrons.[56] One can simultaneously sense the aesthetic echoes of cafés in old Damascus and the influence of US chains like Starbucks in many of Dahiya's new spaces—parallels we take up in greater depth in chapters 3 and 6. For many in the vanguard generation, Tehran represents a desirable model of contemporary urbanity, and Iran is a common destination for organized pilgrimage-tourism trips that combine visits to shrines with shopping and sightseeing. It is common for Shi'i Lebanese, as it is for all Lebanese, to have family members who have emigrated to the Americas, Africa, Australia, or Europe, or who work in Saudi Arabia, the United Arab Emirates, Qatar, or elsewhere in the Gulf. And as we will see in the next chapter, many of the entrepreneurs who have opened cafés in Dahiya have lived or traveled abroad, and cite transnational influences ranging from Dearborn to Tehran to Dubai.

Accompanying these transnational influences has been what many of our vanguard generation interlocutors described as the infitah of both Hizbullah and Dahiya since the late 1990s. This is the result of many of the changes described above, including the situation of relative political stability since 2000 (with the notable exception of 2006), considerably greater levels of economic capital in the area, and distinctions between the vanguard and youth generations. The infitah was also facilitated by the broadening of Hizbullah's rhetorical and electoral support base due to the increased sectarianization of Lebanese politics along Sunni-Shi'i lines and the sense that there are only two political options in the country.[57] With regard to Hizbullah specifically, the infitah can be seen in much of its cultural production, including films and video clips, as its language, music, design, and imagery have moved from militaristic to humanistic expressions. Party official Shaykh Ali spoke of this infitah with pride as he described a successful concert Hizbullah held with an orchestra that included as many Sunni and Christian members, respectively, as Shi'i ones.[58] Finally, the infitah characterizes the party's support of the leisure sector, where it may have begun consciously seeking ways to employ young constituents, and found in the development of leisure a solution that simultaneously generated jobs and appropriate entertainment for them. Talal Atrissi, a Lebanese sociologist who is sympathetic to Hizbullah and the Islamic milieu, suggested that this infitah is on a level atypical of Islamic movements, and that Hizbullah has demonstrated a significantly greater capacity to adapt to changing contexts throughout its history than have most other religiously based political parties.[59]

From the perspective of Hizbullah officials, both the party's infitah and what they perceive as an increase in serious social problems, such as drug abuse and trafficking as well as sex work in Dahiya, are the natural outcomes of the growth of their constituency and social base.[60] Through growth, they explain, the people who vote for, support, claim to affiliate with, or otherwise identify with the party will naturally encompass some who do not share all the party's moral tenets—tenets that are demanded and expected of official party members, but cannot be forced on other constituents. As Ali Fayyad, a professor at Lebanese University and a Hizbullah intellectual who later became a member of Parliament, observed, "In my opinion, there has been a shift from the idea of [political] party to the idea of group to the idea of society. Hizbullah is a party, and the group is a party with its constituents, but at the level of society it becomes a general social phenomenon." In other words, Hizbullah's successes—and really, the successes of the broader Shi'i Islamic mobilizations that it has claimed and inherited—have led to a necessary expansion of its community and the infitah that accompanied it. "I think this path [of Islamism] is a process. It starts with being extreme, and ends with being open and flexible. It starts from the party and moves to society," he continued.

Not all Hizbullah officials view this growth and the associated infitah positively. Increasing levels of and publicity about crime in poorer Dahiya neighborhoods led Hizbullah to abandon its policy of independence from state security and cooperate explicitly with the internal security forces to combat crime in "its neighborhoods."[61] Party members who work directly with youths expressed wariness about the spread of activities they perceive to "be unproductive, to waste youths' time, and expose them to uncontrolled behavior and activities (*ghayr madhbuta*) that are not in line with Shi'i Islamic values." Rather than criminality, such activities included prolonged Internet use, argileh smoking, and card playing, which are precisely the activities facilitated by the new cafés. This suggests that the relationship of Hizbullah and its dominant moral tenets to the new desires for and places of leisure in Dahiya is an uneasy one.

Other vanguard generation people understood this infitah differently. One café owner remarked to us in 2008 that people in Dahiya in general were more "open-minded" (*munfatihin*) than they used to be and that this was a reflection of what he called the "*labnani*" of the community—a term that connotes the act of "becoming Lebanese." He was referring to the commonly articulated idea, especially among middle- and upper-class Lebanese, that their "national" characteristics include an appreciation for fun, enjoyment, sitting around with one's friends, playing cards, joking, and otherwise passing time in leisurely ways. This stereotype infuses descriptions of how not only life but also "partying" went on during the civil war. It was a prominent aspect of pre–civil war representations of Beirut as "the Paris of the Middle East" and continues to pervade contemporary depictions of Beirut as a hedonistic tourist mecca in the region. Another café owner diagnosed the infitah similarly, suggesting that people "get bored" sitting at home and need "a place to breath" after work. She linked this desire to a contrast between life with and without war as well as a general sense of being "fed up" with Lebanese politics. "We got bored and disgusted with politics. We need to recover the days we lost. We lived during war, as did our families. Should our children live in war? Let us breathe a little bit." In this sense, Dahiya's infitah is related to both the span and intensity of the wars that its residents have disproportionately experienced. It is an escape, a liberation, brought on by a feeling that one has to make up for time lost and take advantage of the time one now has, because Lebanon's moments of calm are always fleeting.

Explanations for the infitah were accompanied by a range of descriptions about how life in south Beirut has changed in the twenty-first century. Not surprisingly, a commonly noted marker of these changes was observations about alterations in women's dress.[62] Just as the visibility of the headscarf marked the community's move toward particular forms of piety in earlier decades, comments about the greater variety in dress—and especially in clothing *among* women who wore the headscarf—indexed a shift to a more pluralist social environment where diversity *within* as well as between sectarian communities was accepted. These comments also confirmed that the hijab no longer marks space in Dahiya as it came closer to doing in the 1980s and 1990s. Any lingering assumptions that a hijab is an accurate index of a woman's piety and morality have been put to rest by the normalization of the scarf as part of women's clothing. Because appearances no longer reveal much about the morality of a particular space, amorphous ideas about behavior, manners, and respect have taken on greater importance.

With regard to changes in Dahiya specifically related to leisure sites, a woman in her thirties, at the cusp between generational formations, observed that it used to be shameful ('ayb) among conservative pious Muslims in Dahiya for a married couple to be seen together in public at a restaurant because people viewed that as a "date" and an indication of intimacy, as though they were announcing their intentions to go have sex afterward. That notion no longer exists. When al-Saha restaurant opened, it was subject to moral critique for facilitating social interactions between the sexes. But gradually, as people learned that the restaurant had a reputable owner, and that it served halal meat, did not serve alcohol, and played only quiet classical music, their suspicions were alleviated. As both al-Saha and Fantasy World, with its café and restaurant areas, grew in popularity, the idea of going out to eat and socialize became first acceptable, and then normalized in the community. In other words, part of the infitah included the development of the notion that this form of leisure is morally acceptable under certain conditions. The social environment itself was and continues to be transformed in a dialectical relationship with the establishment of leisure sites themselves.

The complex political, historical, urban, economic, and generational changes we have discussed, along with transnational influences as well as the infitah of Hizbullah and its constituency, have facilitated the emergence of both desires for and sites of leisure and fun in Dahiya. We now turn to the stakeholders who are responsible for producing south Beirut's new sites of leisure and try to control leisure, attempting to set its boundaries and limits.

2

Producing Islamic Fun: Hizbullah, Fadlallah, and the Entrepreneurs

———————————

> We have a business here. When we talk business, we need to talk
> about what the area can take. It is an Islamic area here, like from
> Hizbullah. If you want to have good business, you need to
> follow the requirements. If we have music and songs here, OK,
> there are people who would come, but the majority wouldn't
> come, and those are the ones who have money.
>
> —FADY, OWNER OF A CAFÉ IN SOUTH BEIRUT

Moral leisure is a sound business venture in south Beirut. Fady, a returnee
from the United States who opened a successful café in the area, understood this well. As he noted above, operating a café in Dahiya requires
abiding by the basic tenets of not serving alcohol or playing songs—and
failing to do that is simply a stupid business decision. Private entrepreneurs
recognized this quickly and established themselves as the main producers
of moral fun in south Beirut. Hizbullah's role in the leisure sector is less
powerful, despite party efforts to dominate cultural production as well as
control behavior in and outside cafés. Religious leaders have also shaped
leisure in the area.

In this chapter, we discuss these three types of major players—political,
religious, and economic—that are involved in producing and controlling
leisure sites. All three types of players are conceiving leisure spaces, and to
varying extents, feel responsible for ensuring that their customers abide by
particular moral norms. As the chapter concludes, we suggest that these
efforts to produce and control leisure create a situation of multiplicity,

where there are myriad possibilities for hanging out in south Beirut rather than a uniform leisure landscape.

THE POLITICAL: HIZBULLAH

Since the late 1990s, Hizbullah has devoted increasing attention and resources to developing, facilitating, and supporting cultural and entertainment activities inside as well as outside Dahiya. The party plays a wide variety of roles in creating leisure for the Islamic milieu, ranging from directly producing sites to co-opting existing sites to, most commonly, facilitating and supporting private entrepreneurs who abide by what are perceived to be appropriate moral standards.

DIRECT INTERVENTIONS

Hizbullah is directly involved in producing sites where culture and education are key components. Since its inception, the party has produced a wide range of media, including exhibitions, video clips, billboards, and media campaigns for special occasions like Martyrs' Day.[1] After Liberation in 2000, Hizbullah began investing greater resources in the cultural production of both the natural and built environments. In 2004, the party established an independent professional organization—the Lebanese Association for the Arts (al-Jam'iyya al-Lubnaniyya lil Funun, or LAA)—to be responsible for designing and implementing cultural projects commemorating the Resistance, centralizing previously dispersed efforts in this domain. The LAA marks the growing importance of what the party calls "culture" (*thaqafa*) as it brings together professionally trained artists, graphic designers, and architects in an institution that creates a variety of media and sites. Its projects address its constituents and a broader Lebanese public as well as an international audience—as demonstrated by its focus on multilingual and global-corporate graphic and architectural designs. Culture here is a holistic concept that includes ideas about politics, morality, nature, heritage, space, architecture, design, civic order, education, and taste. Its increasing significance for the party has accompanied the historical changes we detailed in the last chapter, including its infitah and the broadening of its constituencies.

The LAA's projects narrating the history and memory of the Resistance often combine ideology and education with leisure and tourism.[2] The projects are usually located in places important to the party: former detention centers (e.g., Khiam and Ansar), front lines during the wars with Israel (e.g., Mleeta and Maroun el-Rass), and sites throughout the mountains and valleys of the South and Bekaa Valley where Resistance and martyrdom operations occurred.[3] These sites reflect Hizbullah's efforts to organize its understandings of history, memory, nature, and culture, and shape them into landscape projects, asserting party understandings of these concepts as dominant within the Islamic milieu (Harb and Deeb 2011).

Party officials refer to these projects as components of "jihad tourism" (*siyaha jihadiyya*), "purposeful tourism" (*siyaha hadifa*), or "Resistance tourism" (*siyaha muqawama*). Tourism here is understood as geared toward "local" needs for entertainment. These projects also aim to provide an alternative form of entertainment for youths who are "straying" from the Islamic milieu's values and ideals. The LAA's director, Shaykh Ali Daher, complained to us during an interview about Mleeta, expressing serious concerns about what he called "the Bluetooth generation."

> This generation is the generation of *tarnikh*, of *tanbaleh* (slang, being a "couch potato," slothfulness, or inactivity) because of the type of entertainment available for them, the Internet, games, sitting, argileh.[4] We are working against this environment. We need something to help their minds, thoughts, and artistic taste. Something to make them alive and fresh, not lounging around at home or a café. Anything that requires effort, like the Resistance needed physical and mental effort. . . . I am not saying that we are against [the Internet and other technologies]; they have their positives and negatives. But unfortunately, in my opinion, they have emptied this generation. I mean, they have removed the brain, and put in its place fashion and trends and things that are entertaining, but unfortunately empty a person of his humanity. A person is willing to sit for three hours playing games, but he isn't willing to spend five minutes visiting his grandmother or doing an environmental activity. We are not asking him to pray; maybe he doesn't want to pray. But do something useful for humanity, not just for religion. Go and play sports, or paint. He should be a person active in his society. . . . We are not saying that these projects [Mleeta, Khiam, and Maroun el-Rass] are fighting this phenomenon, but we don't want to encourage it. Instead of sitting for three hours at the PlayStation, you can go walk for an hour in the forest and you'll feel refreshed, you'll wake up, you'll pay attention to your life, your education, your future. This is what I mean. These issues are the responsibility of education, schools, universities, and NGOs. We are participating through the language of art, through the language of entertainment.

In this statement, Shaykh Ali worries that the party's younger supporters' reliance on sedentary and passive entertainment has made them complacent toward what he casts as humanitarian, not religious, ideals. He views the Internet, gaming, argileh, and sitting in cafés as dangers that distance youths from morally and socially valuable activities like visiting one's elders, helping the environment, playing sports, or creating art. With these concerns in mind, Hizbullah members along with many others in the vanguard generation (which Shaykh Ali also represents) think that behaving morally in leisure is not only about things like avoiding alcohol but also about not wasting time. Not wasting time, from this perspective, does not necessarily require doing something for one's community, but includes doing something for oneself, like attending certain musical and theatrical performances.[5] This holistic understanding of leisure's relationship to other realms of life raises the stakes of controlling leisure significantly for the party as it faces a future with a generation of youths who takes the post-Islamic movement and post-Liberation world for granted.[6]

Shaykh Ali believes that a general decline in values has led to social problems such as divorce, selfishness, and drug addiction—problems common to both Dahiya and Beirut.[7] Against this background, the party initiated media campaigns geared toward raising awareness about "order" and "family values." Conceived by the LAA's Morals Committee, one campaign was titled "Values" (*qiyam*), and included both visual and substantive educational components, like billboards, television and radio shows hosting sociologists, lectures and workshops at schools, and Friday sermons. The campaigns slogans were "order is from faith" (*al-nizam min al-iman*) and "my family is my happiness" (*'a'ilati farhati*) (see figure 2.1).[8]

Hizbullah's direct interventions in the field of entertainment also include attempts to link to popular trends and youth activities. For example, it created a series of computer games, called *Special Forces*, in which the player is a Resistance fighter combating the Israeli or US enemy. While we don't actually know anyone who enjoys these games, presumably there is enough of a market for them to warrant their continued production, as yet another one was released in 2012.[9] In contrast to Shaykh Ali's desire to pull youths away from their computers, here the party is riding the technology wave that dominates youth practices. The party also demonstrated its ability to be hip by establishing a paintball facility, also named Special Forces and designed like a battlefield.[10] Not only do these forays into gaming and paintball reflect party efforts to hold youths' attention, they also suggest efforts to sustain interest in the militarized aspects of the Resistance through these leisure activities.

In addition, Hizbullah participates in or endorses other initiatives that project an image of the party as sympathetic to broader trends in entertainment and culture—a move that coincides with its infitah. The LAA prides itself on hosting monthly lectures with contemporary Lebanese artists, critics, and designers, such as Roger Assaf and Pierre Abou-Saab, known for their secular and leftist politics.[11] It also underscores the design influence of prominent Iranian artist Reza Abedini, who taught one of the LAA's employees at Tehran University. Abedini's influence largely explains the recent shifts in LAA graphic production toward modern aesthetics,

FIGURE 2.1 Image from the LAA's Values campaign that reads "my family is my happiness"

where references to locality are less stylized.[12] Indeed, some of the LAA's media campaigns influenced by Abedini's approach present Hizbullah to a national and international audience as a political party engaged in the critical reformulation of an Arab/Islamic artistic identity.

INDIRECT FACILITATIONS

Besides directly providing alternatives to mainstream entertainment through the work of the LAA, Hizbullah indirectly facilitates private investment in the "morally acceptable" leisure sector. Such facilitation is channeled primarily through south Beirut municipalities that are controlled by the party, because municipal councils are responsible for granting building permits for restaurants, cafés, and amusement parks.

In 1998, when municipal elections were held for the first time in thirty-five years, Hizbullah-backed lists won control of all four municipal councils in Dahiya. At this time, Hajj Abu Saʿid became the mayor of Ghobeyri, the largest and wealthiest municipality in south Beirut, and a few years later he was elected the leader of Dahiya's Municipality Federation.[13] Since then, he has promoted a wide range of social and economic activities, including leisure. Municipalities provide opportunities for Hizbullah to establish beneficial exchanges with an array of stakeholders, including entrepreneurs who need to obtain building permits and other legal papers.

Hajj Abu Saʿid told us about a Saudi entrepreneur who wanted to open a mall in Ghobeyri and inquired about the municipality's needs.

> He came to me in the beginning saying he wants to invest here. A Saudi man wants to open something in the middle of Dahiya![14] He said, "What do you want us to offer here, what would you like?" We said, "One thing, when you are done with the project . . ." at that time, he was still working on the permit, " . . . when you finish the project, in two years, we want a percentage of the employees you recruit to be from the area." When he finished the project, he called us and said, "We started, send us people!" When we have economic development, we have less unemployment and good social relations. When investments happen, foreign workers will leave the area, but locals will stay and take care of the project. These are positive issues.

The Beirut Mall opened in Ghobeyri in 2006. Because this foreign entrepreneur was himself a pious Muslim, the moral standards in the mall fit what one of the mall's employees called "his Saudi background." Alcohol is not provided in its restaurants and cafés, including in this branch of the Lebanese chain restaurant Bay Rock. In the supermarket on the lower level, however, alcohol and pork are sold in a separate glass-enclosed room with a separate cash register. This practice allows pious people to shop at the supermarket because the money for haram products circulates separately, and does not come into contact with them or, in their view, their money. This practice had already been put to good use a few years earlier in Monoprix, another supermarket in Ghobeyri that was later replaced by the TSC supermarket, which also adopted this arrangement.[15]

Most of the other private entrepreneurs who operate in Dahiya's leisure sector are Shiʿi Muslims, frequently residents of the area. Several of them lived abroad at some point, in the United States or Europe. The Ghobeyri municipality encouraged them to do business in Dahiya in order to promote local economic development and provide jobs. Early in his career, Hajj Abu Saʿid adopted an open-door policy through which he follows up promptly on people's requests and facilitates legal paperwork. During our visit to his office, we met one of the partners of the Inmaaʾ Group, Hajj Amin Chirri, who was a Hizbullah parliamentary representative at the time. The Inmaaʾ Group is the company that developed Fantasy World in 1999. Sitting next to Hajj Abu Saʿid, Hajj Amin praised the latter's contribution to the Fantasy World project, highlighting the mayor's multiple roles. He had participated in the choice of site as well as its design and planning, protected the project from undue interference, and enhanced the infrastructure around the project site. Hajj Amin explained,

> Abu Saʿid encouraged us to do the project, and gave us ideas about how it should cover the whole geographic area and should not be a small project. He helped with security work. He suggested that the location shouldn't be in inner Dahiya. No. We should attract people from outside to come to Dahiya, to have people interacting with each other. This is how we chose the location on the airport highway. It connects to the western side of Beirut. Nobody is paying attention to that! You can come from Achrafieh [eastern side of Beirut] in five minutes! Abu Saʿid also insisted that we have a large parking area—it's twenty-six hundred square meters, you know—to accommodate people's needs. He thought it would help attract people. He also did the infrastructural work and fixed the roads. He also promised to do the sidewalks; they helped make the street look good.

During this interview, Hajj Abu Saʿid was keen to note that Hizbullah ensured that the entertainment provided by these places would respond to the needs of the "general environment" in Dahiya in contrast to other areas of Beirut.

> In line with the general environment, we did not encourage places that offer alcohol. We did not encourage the style of casinos, like alcohol, gambling and things like that. . . . We did not encourage a pornographic environment [ajwaʾ al-ibahiyyeh]. This doesn't mean we don't have mixed-gender interactions [ikhtilat]; you do have ikhtilat.[16] Go to all of these places, you'll find people like in any other place in Lebanon, but not pornographic interaction [al-ikhtilat al-ibahi], or what we call specifically "sex tourism" [siyahat al-daʿara] . . . We were making sure that the area stays away from that. The goal of this entertainment is to respond to people's needs, not to satisfy their sexual instincts [gharaʾiz].

Given this, would Hajj Abu Saʿid describe these places as Islamic? The Ghobeyri mayor answered that "[these sites] are not Islamic in terms of economics and ownership, but al-hala al-islamiyya benefits from them, through its ability to control their working mechanisms and manage their services, legally though municipalities and socially through the party's organizations." He gave an example:

> We were able, for instance, to provide places even for very religious women, like swimming pools and gyms. We thought of people who are very conservative in

their interactions. We gave them privacy; we didn't take away their right to have access to entertainment. This is a remarkable development.

Note the "we" throughout Hajj Abu Sa'id's rhetoric. While, to our knowledge, neither Hizbullah nor the Ghobeyri municipality owns entertainment sites in Dahiya, the mayor talks about them with a strong sense of ownership.[17] This highlights the party's desire to present itself as responsible for the leisure sector and the benefits it provides for pious Shi'i Muslims. In addition, it confirms that Hizbullah wants to establish control over leisure sites. This is especially true of those that aim to teach moral and cultural ideas. In Dahiya, Ghobeyri led the party's cultural efforts through the construction of the Ghobeyri Cultural Center—a $5.1 million (not including the cost of the land) complex that provides spaces for sports, theater, exhibitions, and films. The LAA uses this center for its musical and theater performances as well as art exhibitions. Hajj Abu Sa'id underscored that "this [cultural investment] is a social choice because it is about how to direct the whole society. I can direct it to a rock party, or to jazz music, or to another thing! As they say, 'society accepts being led.' We are investing in culture."

NEIGHBORHOOD WATCHES

Besides intervening in and facilitating the leisure sector, the party wields its influence through a network of neighborhood committees for "enjoining right and forbidding wrong" (al-amr bil-ma'ruf wal nahi 'an al-munkar).[18] These committees do not exist in all neighborhoods, and appear to be organized on a street-by-street or block-by-block basis by residents (men and women) affiliated with Hizbullah. As explained to us by a party member we will call Hajj Abbas, the activities of these committees range from decorating their blocks during Ramadan and other holidays (in 2010, a popular Ramadan decoration was red Chinese lanterns) to notifying the party about "improper" activities taking place at local cafés. Once notified, he continued,

> So the news comes to us. What do we do? We go to the place. If we see something wrong, we warn them. We can close the place, and not with force. We are strong here not by force but by name. We tell the owner, we are talking to you from Hizbullah, and this is against what we do here and against our values.

Through information gathered from the concerned constituents who make up these neighborhood watch committees, the party is able to organize social and economic pressure in order to censor activities that fall outside its understandings of appropriate moral behavior. If a business does not reform (which generally means either refraining from serving alcohol or exerting greater control over mixed-gender interaction), Hizbullah will instigate a boycott, and put the café or restaurant out of business by damaging its reputation: "If a place doesn't follow the rules, we say that this place is 1, 2, 3, and we give it a bad name, and you wouldn't send your son or daughter there," Hajj Abbas concluded. If this doesn't work, the party will draw on its wide social networks and call on the owner's relatives to pressure the owner to close the business.[19]

Hajj Abbas also expressed pride in the party's efforts to censor Internet sites in cafés and satellite television in the area. Satellite distributors are pressured to limit access to "inappropriate" or "immoral" channels.[20] Café owners are pressured to either restrict or keep tabs on the Web sites that their customers visit.

> We tell [the owner], "This is your responsibility. If anything goes wrong, you know, there are children and young women there." You know he can check everything and see what is going on. Now you cannot stop things like chatting, for example. But there are things like photos. He can know what is going on in his place.

The neighborhood watch groups highlight Hizbullah's enmeshment in the social fabric of some Dahiya neighborhoods, at least from the perspective of party members. As a prominent woman in the party explained,

> Our society is helping a great deal with this. So today you find, as you mentioned, cafés, and these things are increasing a lot. And it is under our control, I mean, it's not outside our control. Even many of the owners of these projects make sure that we are in support of the project, because we have our organizations and centers, and people ask us, "Can we go to this place? Is there a problem with going to so-and-so's place?" It's not Hizbullah that's doing it. I'm saying that society, people, are demanding these projects, and are also asking our opinion of these projects.

LIMITED CULTURAL CONTROL

Both directly and indirectly, Hizbullah has been involved in producing a range of cultural projects addressing the Islamic milieu and its Shi'i constituents. The party's explicit investment in culture both provides alternative cultural options for people and promotes a particular lifestyle based on specific moral ideas accompanied by political allegiance to the Resistance along with notions of education and class mobility. The latter, combined with Hizbullah's additional emphases on history, heritage, public order, and taste, suggest slippage into more common usages of *muthaqqaf* in Lebanon to mean "cultured" in the sense of being a "cultivated" or "civilized" person. Hizbullah's use of culture thus explicitly elides categorical separation from both religion and politics.[21]

This holistic understanding of culture provides the basis for Hizbullah's post-2000 efforts at social reform in Dahiya.[22] Paradoxically, by opening up to the cultural sphere, the party has legitimized a realm of new possibilities and become one cultural stakeholder among many. The media-savvy postwar generation of Shi'i youths we spoke with were eager to consume culture without thinking so much about content. They simply wanted to have fun, albeit as we will see, within certain moral boundaries. For all Hajj Abu Sa'id's claims about leading society away from jazz and rock music, youths in Dahiya today may well choose to listen to jazz or rock and still vote for Hizbullah. And for all Hajj Abbas's claims about censorship, new leisure places in Dahiya provide opportunities for moral experimentation. Indeed, Shaykh Ali may have the best read on Dahiya's youths in his concerns about the "Bluetooth generation" and lucid skepticism about the potential of Hizbullah's cultural alternatives to affect youth leisure practices.

In other words, Hizbullah's efforts at controlling how people spend their free time are not as successful as the party would like to think. The exception may be alcohol. We have not located a restaurant or café in Dahiya that serves alcohol, which suggests that Hizbullah does prevent its distribution either formally or through neighborhood boycotts.[23] One café owner told us that guys who "looked like Hizbullah" (meaning they had short trimmed beards and wore shirts with no neckties) visited him and asked if his place served alcohol. He said, "They had their doubts because the café has a coffee bar where Italian soda syrup bottles are displayed and the bottles resemble alcoholic drinks." The owner told them that he does not sell alcohol, and since then, Hizbullah officials are regular customers at his café. On the other hand, it is unlikely that the party can control Internet and satellite television. Satellite channel availability—in all Lebanese neighborhoods—depends a great deal on the local distributor and their customer base. When Lara shared Hajj Abbas's pride about satellite censorship with her friend Aziza as they sat in her living room in Dahiya, Aziza laughed and flipped through the channels on her television, which were the exact ones available in Lara's apartment in Hamra. She related that previously there had been a Turkish channel that showed pornography late at night and that had been removed about a year earlier. It was also quite possible to access dating sites, pornography, and other clearly "inappropriate" Web sites from many of the cafés in Dahiya that provide Internet service. It is possible that if such browsing was noted by waitstaff, the customer would be asked to stop or leave, but we neither saw evidence of this nor heard stories about it.[24]

Despite the apparent conformity of leisure sites in Dahiya—including the ones in Ghobeyri—to key moral tenets, like limits on mixed-gender interactions or boycotts of US products, significant violations occur. Fantasy World includes an indoor restaurant where couples hide behind a column to enjoy greater intimacy. The Beirut Mall hosts a number of US food and clothing chains, including McDonald's, Dunkin' Donuts, Nine West, and Forever 21. For youths, such practices do not necessarily conflict with their ideas about morality. Indeed, for most of our pious young interlocutors, morality is a complex realm with multiple rubrics. The religious rubric for morality is shaped by youths' individual ideas about piety, which may be defined by their relationship to one or more religious jurisprudents. These jurisprudents also play a role in the production of leisure in Dahiya, and are the source for many key ideas about moral leisure practices and geographies in the community. We turn now to their assessments of leisure.

THE RELIGIOUS: JURISPRUDENTS AND ESPECIALLY FADLALLAH

Practicing Shi'i Muslims are supposed to choose a religious scholar who has attained the rank of jurisprudential reference (marja') and follow that person's interpretations on religious matters.[25] This is sometimes assumed to involve blind emulation, but emulation itself is something that people negotiate from situation to situation, frequently changing their marja' to suit the contingencies of the moment. These changes may occur for the sake of both serious and frivolous matters. For example, in her research on domestic workers in Dahiya, sociologist Ayat Noureddine (Fadlallah's daughter-in-law) found that people who do not usually follow Fadlallah will choose to follow him on his fatwa that all human beings are *taher* (pure or clean) so that they can hire Nepali domestic workers who are Buddhist.[26]

Despite various efforts to establish a single supreme jurisprudent, perhaps most famously that of Grand Ayatollah Ruhollah Khomeyni, historically there have been multiple living marja's who compete for followers, in part because there are financial stakes.[27] In Lebanon, the importance of following a marja', and indeed even knowledge of the term and institution, has increased considerably since the 1980s (Walbridge 2001b).

Lebanon's Main Jurisprudents

Since the deaths of Khomeyni in 1989 and Grand Ayatollah Abu'l Qasim Khu'i in 1992, there have been three major jurisprudents with significant followings in Lebanon: Grand Ayatollah Sayyid Ali Khamenei, Grand

Ayatollah Sayyid Ali al-Husayni Sistani, and the late Grand Ayatollah Sayyid Muhammad Hussein Fadlallah.[28] The perspectives and fatwas of all three are available to differing extents in Dahiya in a variety of media forms. Sermons, decisions, advice, and recommendations are distributed through books, pamphlets, audiotapes, and CDs, and are broadcast via Web sites, television, and radio.

It is difficult to assess the popularity in Lebanon of these three major jurisprudents relative to one another. In our ethnographic research experience, Fadlallah has been the most popular jurisprudent among educated middle-class residents of Dahiya, especially youths, since the late 1990s. He initially put himself forward as a possible marja' with the publication of his major *fiqh* books, after having served as Khu'i's representative in Lebanon for twenty-five years.[29] Although Fadlallah has been described in the United States as "the spiritual leader" of Hizbullah, this is not the case, and in fact, the conflation of these two sources of authority has had the effect of hiding the diversity of opinion that exists within the Lebanese Shi'i community. Fadlallah and Hizbullah often differed, most critically in their views about the relationship between spiritual and political authority. Specifically, they disagreed on the validity of Khomeyni's idea of *wilayat al-faqih*, or "guidance of the jurisprudent," the merging of religious and political authority into a single institution that was the basis for the Islamic state in Iran.

The role of the formal "spiritual leader" of Hizbullah has fallen, since Khomeyni's death, to Khamenei. He replaced Khomeyni as the head of the shura in Iran, and as such is the party's formal marja', although party members are free to follow a marja' of their choice, and anecdotal evidence from our interlocutors suggests that several follow Fadlallah in their personal matters. Despite this official sanction, it took Khamenei several years to develop a following in Lebanon. Initially, few Lebanese took him seriously as a jurisprudent because he was a scholar of much lesser rank than Khomeyni at the time of his appointment in Iran. Many people who had followed Khomeyni during his life either continued to follow him postmortem (which is permitted by some jurisprudents) or switched to Fadlallah. By 2008, however, Khamenei seemed to have grown in popularity, and several young people cited him as their marja' of choice. In some cases, this choice seemed to reflect the cache of following Hizbullah's formal marja' more than anything else. It was also related to the popularity among young women of a charismatic and attractive young sayyid, Sami Khadra, who conveys Khamenei's perspectives in his pamphlets and lectures. Polling data collected in 2009 also reflected higher support for Khamenei than expected among party rank-and-file members.[30]

Sistani, an Iranian living in Najaf, was widely acknowledged as the most popular marja' worldwide after Khu'i's death, and "inherited" the sponsorship of Khu'i's major foundations (Walbridge 2001a) as well as many of his followers in Lebanon and elsewhere. As such, state-affiliated Shi'i institutions in Lebanon, such as the Supreme Islamic Shi'i Council and most courts, follow Sistani. His visibility as a popular marja' in Dahiya increased after his international rise to prominence in the wake of the US invasion and occupation of Iraq.[31] In addition to the international and media visibility afforded to Sistani post-2003, there is another key factor that has affected his popularity on the ground in Dahiya: his accessibility.

All three jurisprudents have maintained offices in south Beirut since the 1990s. Yet Sistani's representative (unlike Khamenei's) is not Lebanese and is less connected to the social fabric than the shaykhs in the other juristic offices.[32] More crucially, his office is strict about providing only fatwas, and will not comment or discuss any matters that fall into the realm of "social issues" with followers. All three offices receive and answer questions asking about religious permissibility (halal) and prohibition (haram) for a wide range of issues, including proper prayer, marriage and divorce, inheritance distribution, working with food that may contain prohibited ingredients, performing autopsies, and appropriate clothing.[33] But, for example, when asked which sorts of songs it was permissible to listen to, Sistani's representative explained that that is not the sort of question that falls within his jurisdiction because it is "sociological." In contrast, the juristic offices of both Fadlallah and Khamenei provide advice to their followers on a broad range of matters, and engage in what might be thought of as "pastoral counseling." Young people especially may call the "advice sections" of these offices — which operate like telephone hotlines — and talk about their problems with the shaykhs, whether obtaining advice on how to handle a situation or simply venting to a sympathetic ear. Their queries range from relationships between the sexes to family tensions to how to discuss specific issues with people of other religions. Fadlallah's office in particular goes so far as to help students with papers they are writing on religion-related topics for school or university. Similarly, youths take advantage of Fadlallah's and Khamenei's Web sites to ask questions on a variety of topics.

We encountered this contrast in the three jurisprudents' willingness to deal with what they called "sociological" issues in our interviews about leisure in Dahiya. Sistani's representative would only provide answers to shari'a-related questions like "Is it permissible to dance with a member of the opposite sex to whom one is not married?" and did not discuss his thoughts (or Sistani's views) on the recent visibility of leisure in south Beirut. In contrast, both Khamenei's representative, Shaykh Muhammad Miqdad, and Fadlallah's representative, his son Sayyid Ja'far Fadlallah, were happy to share their views, which were strikingly similar. Both confirmed that there is no conflict between Islam and leisure. As Shaykh Muhammad put it, "Islam wants people to live with happiness, to forget sadness and concerns." Both also confirmed that the increase in leisure in Dahiya was due to a natural societal need for fun, though Shaykh Muhammad emphasized that "people needed places where they could breathe" after years of war while Sayyid Ja'far highlighted factors ranging from wives having less time to cook to a natural human need for relaxation. As he told us,

> As you know, there are human needs. . . . In the past, people used to eat at home and then go out in nature. Now things have changed. Sometimes a person wants to lighten the load of his household commitments—perhaps from a woman's perspective it is in relation to cooking. [The person] takes advantage of the situation [of having cafés], and at the same time, it is an opportunity for entertainment.

He continued, sharing a hadith while explaining it to us phrase by phrase,

> We have an Islamic scale, a hadith tells us, it gives a rule for the believer, it says, "It is necessary for the believer to have three hours" or three periods of time, here an hour refers to a period of time, and a person needs to divide this time, "an hour during which he collect his living," which means a person goes to work, "and an hour during which he calls to his God," this is to strengthen the relationship between a person and God, "and an hour that remains for himself and his desires outside of what is haram that will help the person to fulfill the other two hours." If the person's whole life is work and worship, he will live a kind of spiritual and psychological drought. And in addition, he will be unable to worship properly. Also he will not be able to live without relieving the pressures of work. Because of that, there is a need for a person to enjoy himself from time to time, of course within limits, without going too far in that direction, or his life will be nothing but fun.

When we got more specific and asked about their views on cafés in relation to leisure, Fadlallah and other jurisprudents only weighed in informally, suggesting standards of behavior rather than issuing fatwas about specific places. Fadlallah's juristic office's email response to our question about which cafés are appropriate stated that they are "those that do not offer forbidden meat and pork and alcohol, and also that are not related to the Israeli entity." He consistently emphasized that other than the clear rules on what is permissible and prohibited, into which fall things like alcohol, certain meats, and physical intimacy between unmarried people, everything else falls into the realm of personal interpretation and has more to do with societal values than religious prohibitions—in our terms, with the social rather than the religious rubric for morality.

While in this book we refer to the views of Khamenei and Sistani when appropriate, our primary focus is on the relationship of Fadlallah's perspectives and opinions to leisure, and negotiations of morality and geography. There are several reasons for this. First, Fadlallah has been a popular marja' in Dahiya since the late 1990s, and perhaps the most popular among middle-class youths, who make up a large percentage of café goers. Second, many of the fatwas that have facilitated everyday negotiations of morality and movement in the city in relation to leisure are his. In other words, his views have been the most consequential for shifting moral norms and spatial practices in the realm of leisure. Were we discussing, for example, new reproductive technologies, Khamenei's fatwas may in fact have the greatest social consequences (Clarke 2009). Third, Fadlallah was widely respected in Lebanon not only as a marja' for his Shi'i followers but also as a religious leader at the national level. People of all sectarian groups and political orientations paid attention to his sermons, and he played a prominent political role in the country at key moments, whether in his espousal of confessional coexistence or support of the Resistance. Fourth, Fadlallah is the only marja' who explicitly entered into the leisure sector through one of his affiliated institutions, discussed below. Fifth and finally, in the words of Lebanese University professor Talal Atrissi, "Fadlallah raised a generation."[34] Atrissi was referring to the vanguard generation. Yet this means that the youth of twenty-first-century Dahiya were raised in an environment where Fadlallah's views both explicitly and implicitly informed many of the social, moral, and geographic aspects of their lives—to such a degree that many young people echo Fadlallah's views on matters without realizing that they are doing so. In chapter 4, we present his and other views on key practices related to leisure, like listening to music. Here we confine ourselves to a discussion of some of the reasons for Fadlallah's popularity and some of the key ways in which he has influenced people's thinking about morality in Dahiya.

Fadlallah's Popularity and Malleability

Fadlallah's popularity was due in part to his clarity of language and pragmatism in his books and sermons. It was also due to the strong on-the-ground presence he maintained in the community during his life. He and his family lived modestly in a secure but surprisingly accessible building in Dahiya. By living among his followers and within society as opposed to apart from it, Fadlallah was able to retain an awareness of social realities and the problems that his followers confronted in their daily lives. He always had an open-door policy and met with followers regularly until his health deteriorated. His charitable associations played a role in his popularity as well, as he channeled the religious tithes he collected back into the

Shi'i community in Dahiya and across Lebanon through Al-Mabarrat Association's many education and health institutions as well as his Social Services Office.

Crucially, Fadlallah was also popular because he believed in the need for Islam to adapt to the contemporary world and thought that interpretation should work to facilitate young people's lifestyles whenever possible within the limitations of Islam. As Sayyid Ja'far told us in an interview in 2009, in Fadlallah,

> youths find that there is a marja' that provides, relative to others, a high level of conformity with their youthful needs and the requirements of life, so that they are finding that religion is able to help them balance between religious requirements, on the one hand, and the requirements of life, on the other.

To a certain extent, Fadlallah's role in facilitating youth lifestyles was intentional; he published a widely translated book in 1995 geared specifically at youth issues, and his juristic office prides itself on speedy Internet question turnaround time and the ability of its shaykhs to communicate with the young generation.[35]

Khamenei also seems to direct jurisprudence at youth issues, but with different effects. Our survey of *Baqiyat Allah* from 2001–7—a magazine published in Lebanon that disseminates Khamenei's fatwas and represents his perspectives—confirmed that many of the articles were about or directed at youths. The most common topics were the hijab, the Internet, and youth as a stage of life, followed by marriage, music and songs, Islam versus the West, family life, and male-female interactions. In general, the views expressed in the magazine reveal greater fears for and less trust of youths than Fadlallah does. For example, rather than suggest the positives and negatives of the Internet, the magazine assumes from the outset that it is dangerous, and requires constant regulation and monitoring.

Fadlallah also tends to be viewed as more open minded than others on a wide variety of issues, ranging from allowing people to play games (like cards) that could be seen as gambling provided money is not exchanged, to some of his stances related to gender and sexuality. He not only legalized birth control, for example, but also stated, "Women have the right not to have children even if this runs contrary to her husband's wishes" (Aziz 2001, 210). He also is less likely to rule against a practice based on the juristic principle of "necessary avoidance" of anything that could *potentially* lead to activities that are haram than are both Sistani and Khamenei.

Consider, for instance, one of Fadlallah's most controversial fatwas. In 2001, he stated that a mature young woman, even if she is a virgin, does not need the permission of her father or any guardian in her personal affairs, including marriage.[36] Maturity in this case means that a person is in control of herself and able to ensure her own interests.[37] This fatwa is used by some young women to claim maturity and take control of their sexual lives by entering into temporary marriages without anyone's permission or knowledge.[38] This is probably not what Fadlallah intended, as he also suggested to youths that they consult with their families about issues whenever possible. Shaykh Muhammad (from Khamenei's office) instead told us that virgins always require their father's permission before entering into any marriage, regular or temporary, and when we suggested to him that young people are ignoring this rule and using temporary marriage to date without parental knowledge, he continued, "We consider this a deviation from the path. This is an incorrect implementation of the shari'a rule." Sistani's view appears to be somewhere in between, as his representative noted that it is possible for a virgin to be independent in her affairs, but that she requires the consent of her father or guardian to attain this independence; in other words, unlike Fadlallah, Sistani does not think that a young woman can unilaterally assert her independence.

Our interviews with Shaykh Muhammad and Sayyid Ja'far illustrated the differences in Khamenei's and Fadlallah's perspectives on gender and sexuality in other ways as well. Shaykh Muhammad supplied a long, gendered litany of active and passive conjugations of Arabic verbs, along the lines of "the man desires, the woman is desired." Sayyid Ja'far instead stated simply: "It is clear that human beings need sex, men and women." And in stark contrast to Sayyid Ja'far's claim that one reason for the increase in cafés in Dahiya might be that women need a break from cooking, Shaykh Muhammad suggested to us that woman's "natural" place is "in the kitchen."

Another factor adding to Fadlallah's popularity was his consistent encouragement that his followers should use their judgment to interpret situations for themselves.[39] As Sayyid Ja'far explained, "It falls to religion to make a person aware of his responsibility (taklif) and tell him the limits according to the shari'a, . . . however, their application rests in the first place on him [the person]." In other words, Fadlallah emphasizes that in the end, moral behavior comes down to the individual and personal choice. Compare Khamenei's view on the matter, as explained by Shaykh Muhammad: "From my side I give him [any person] what I have, but from his side he needs to take responsibility. Let us assume that a person cannot prevent himself from doing haram. I'll tell him, 'This is not acceptable, it creates sin. God will punish you on the Day of Resurrection, and He will send you to hell.'"

At first glance these two stances seemed similar. They both stress the jurisprudent's responsibility to offer information about what is halal and haram, and the individual's responsibility to then choose to behave correctly (Shaykh Muhammad outlined the consequences of sin, while hell did

not come up as a topic in our interview with Sayyid Ja'far). As our interview with Sayyid Ja'far continued, though, a key difference appeared. He
observed that like other jurisprudents, Fadlallah advised people about what
is prohibited and permissible, and things like proscriptions on alcohol and
adultery fall into this realm. "But," he added,

> there is another level that is related to life in general, and that is the level of mor-
> als [akhlaq] or values [qiyam]. And this level rests on the choice of the indi-
> vidual himself, meaning that he chooses to participate or not participate, de-
> pending on his mood, his environment, his culture, and his perspective on his
> role in life. There are people who maybe don't like to go to certain places and
> people who don't like to go there at all. . . . As long as a person doesn't do any-
> thing prohibited in these places, then there is no problem with him going there.

While here Sayyid Ja'far is speaking specifically about cafés, the point is a
more general one about Fadlallah's approach to the implementation of particular rules, values, and morals in society. He acknowledges the existence
and power of multiple moral rubrics, while not using those terms. This
awareness highlights Fadlallah's empathy for the complexity of the moral
terrain his followers must navigate in their lives.

The relationship of people, especially youths, in Dahiya to Fadlallah's
opinions varies widely. While some may follow his advice to the letter,
many seem to have absorbed ideas from the broader social environment
that are traceable to his opinions, and others take up his ideas in ways that
do not reflect his original intentions. Put simply, Fadlallah's influence goes
beyond direct citation. It is also an influence related to the creation of an
environment where ideas about individual responsibility and using one's
own judgment have been accepted as normatively moral ideas even when
people cannot or do not cite him as their direct source. His opinions infuse
the practices of young people, whether they articulate this relationship or
not, and his emphasis on individual responsibility allows youths to experiment with different choices within a rather wide margin of maneuver.

Youths also indirectly pressure Fadlallah and other religious authorities
to rethink their opinions by asking questions. Because religious opinions
are often given spontaneously in response to specific queries, they are diverse, malleable, and change frequently.[40] The question asked may shape
the response, and numerous questions on a topic may lead a jurisprudent
to allot greater or renewed consideration to that topic. This is the case even
in relation to what one might consider unimportant issues, such as nail
polish. Many Shi'i religious scholars state that if a woman wants to pray
while wearing nail polish, she must complete her ablutions first and then
paint her nails.[41] Fadlallah's opinion on this matter shifted recently in direct
response to questions asked by young women who want to paint their nails

while also fulfilling their religious obligations. As of July 2008, his view was that if a woman left one nail (usually of the little finger or toe) of each hand and foot clear for water to pass over, she may complete ablutions while wearing nail polish.[42] By spring 2009, a young woman told us that his opinion on this had changed yet again. To check, we asked the question via his Web site, and indeed the response we received in April 2009 was that nail polish does not constitute a barrier and interfere with ablutions. One therefore may wash and pray while wearing it on all fingers and toes. In this way, young people may contribute to the flexibility of opinions by directing attention to specific matters or indirectly suggesting that a matter needs to be reconsidered if the marja' wants to facilitate their ability to live religiously appropriate but also youthful lives, as Fadlallah explicitly wished to do.

A JURISPRUDENTIAL VOID

Fadlallah passed away on July 4, 2010. His juristic office quickly posted a brief statement on his Web site announcing that "it is permissible for the emulators of the late Religious Authority, Sayyed Muhammad Hussein Fadlullah (ra), to continue to emulate him in a comprehensive manner." A few days later, on July 9, a second statement was posted, clarifying and justifying the first, and adding the phrase, "There are even some jurists who deem it permissible to start emulating by choosing a deceased Marjaa [sic]."[43]

While the idea that a person who has been following a marja' while he was alive may continue to do so after the marja' has died is not particularly unusual, and in fact was stated by Fadlallah and Sistani for people who wished to continue following Khomeyni postmortem, the second statement is quite radical. Even in the former case, people are encouraged to shift their allegiances to a living marja' so that they are both following dynamic fatwas related to the world in which they live and paying their *khums* and *zakat* to a living marja' who is able to appropriately distribute them. To suggest that someone who did not follow Fadlallah while he was alive may begin to do so now is almost shocking and indicates the significance of his death for the Lebanese Shi'i community.

Of course, Fadlallah's death creates a clear jurisprudential void, leaving only Khamenei and Sistani as living marja's who are significant to practicing Shi'i Muslims in Lebanon. The question of to whom his followers will turn is also related to political and economic calculations in the national and international arenas.[44] As of 2012, there is no one within his circle with the necessary knowledge and stature to take his place.[45] By issuing the unorthodox statement that people may continue to choose Fadlallah, the juristic office seems to be biding its time and hoping that it will be able to produce a scholar whose views are compatible with Fadlallah's to take his place within a few years. Until then, the void left by his passing will certainly be felt strongly, not only in the Lebanese political arena, but also for many pious youths who are trying to live lives that more closely approximate their everyday desires for fun without feeling like sinners. These youths may be one of the most important legacies of the late sayyid, and it remains to be seen how and whether their negotiations of leisure shift in his absence and with the realignment of jurisprudence that ensues.

AL-SAHA RESTAURANT

In addition to influencing ideas about appropriate leisure, Fadlallah has participated directly in producing the area's leisure sector. After Liberation, his al-Mabarrat charitable association decided to develop a major property on the airport road into a restaurant complex and raise funds through its profits. This was the brainchild of al-Mabarrat's head architect, Jamal Makki, who wanted to provide Dahiya's dwellers with a place to escape the area's urban density while contributing to Lebanon's tourism industry. He told Mona in 2005,

> Al-Mabarrat needed a financially productive project. I started thinking about a project that would fit the role given to Beirut. Tourism seemed like a good choice. But, how could you make a tourism project in a site that has no touristic assets? There is no sea and no mountains here [in Dahiya]! And we are in an area known for its ugliness and urban pollution. So I thought of creating a project turned inward that acts as a tourist attraction. I wanted something everybody would visit: Lebanese, Arabs, foreigners. I started thinking, What idea could mobilize a mosaic of different publics? Of course, it is nostalgia, history, heritage! Everybody feels good about remembering history and tradition.

In 2001, al-Saha Traditional Village opened its doors. Al-Saha is a large-scale restaurant complex spread over ten thousand square meters that can cater to a thousand customers daily, and includes—in addition to different indoor and outdoor restaurant seating areas—a motel, wedding hall, small souq, museums, playgrounds, poetry room, gardens, and library (see figure 2.2). As we discuss in the next chapter, it was designed to represent "Arabic and Islamic architecture." Flanked by a gas station also owned by al-Mabarrat, the building is impressive in scale and stands out in Dahiya's landscape. Al-Saha quickly became a major leisure landmark in the area and a destination for foreign tourists, especially Arabs and Iranians. It has also expanded internationally through the Assaha International Group, which has opened similar restaurants in Khartoum, Doha, and London.[46]

Al-Saha's opening marked a milestone for Dahiya's leisure scene. For the first time, pious people could go have a meal and spend their free time

FIGURE 2.2 Al-Saha Traditional Village restaurant

in a fancy restaurant in south Beirut, experiencing leisure comfortably. The restaurant was immediately successful. Al-Saha was where one saw fashionable young pious women, dressed trendily in heels and designer scarves, smoking argileh with female friends or in a mixed-gender group. It was where we saw couples having intimate lunches in isolated spaces, women socializing over brunch, men arguing about politics, and large families sharing a meal in the formal dining room. It was where a headscarf-wearing woman asked on her brother's behalf for Mona's phone number, after first interrogating her about her origins and current profession.

As al-Saha expanded, it attracted more and more customers. Despite its prices, which are relatively expensive for Dahiya, it remained cheaper than many restaurants in municipal Beirut, and people felt that their money was supporting a good cause. Al-Saha also made the Islamic milieu and Dahiya's residents visible to other Lebanese, especially in the years prior to 2005, during which a variety of customers visited the restaurant, including pious people who lived in Beirut. For its part, Hizbullah was not initially enthusiastic about al-Saha, and rumors circulated suggesting that the restaurant's food was not halal. These reservations soon gave way in the wake of al-Saha's popularity. Party institutions and members gradually became loyal customers, and at one point the restaurant complex included a stall where one could purchase a Photoshopped picture of oneself posing next to Nasrallah and other party paraphernalia.

In addition to providing one of the early paradigms for a space for moral leisure in Dahiya and inspiring, along with Fantasy World, many of the entrepreneurs we discuss below, al-Saha modeled moral leisure for pious Muslims as well as pioneered new ideas about permissible and prohibited behaviors so as to allow for a wider range of leisure-related activities. One recent example is that of eating lobster. According to one young Dahiya resident, when her father saw a display of lobster in al-Saha, he was shocked because it was considered by most (if not all) Shi'i jurisprudents haram to eat shellfish, lobster, or any "fish without scales." The display prompted him to call Fadlallah's juristic office, which confirmed that Fadlallah had recently issued a fatwa stating that no seafood was haram. We confirmed this ruling by asking the question via his Web site.[47] The response we received stated, "All forms of seafood that do not harm humans are permissible, though it is preferable to limit this to fish with scales."[48] Yet despite this preference, al-Saha served a variety of seafood, and in so doing, set a new standard for other south Beirut restaurants and for pious Muslims who ate at restaurants in other parts of the city.

While both Fadlallah and Hizbullah play significant roles in shaping leisure in Dahiya, their efforts cannot be fully understood without investigating the final key group of producers: the entrepreneurs. The private sector quickly identified Dahiya dwellers' demand for places to enjoy their free time and understood that many of them have the financial means to frequent commercial leisure sites. We now turn to these purveyors of fun in south Beirut.

THE ECONOMIC: ENTREPRENEURS

Leisure in south Beirut is predominantly a private sector phenomenon. Apart from al-Saha, all the cafés and restaurants we located in the area are owned and managed by private and independent entrepreneurs, often in partnership ventures. In this section, we profile several of these entrepreneurs, exploring how and when they decided to invest in leisure, how they manage their cafés, their efforts to control moral norms and appropriate behavior, and their assessments of the new phenomenon of moral leisure vis-à-vis the Islamic milieu, Hizbullah, and people's lifestyles. We begin with the Inmaa' Group—unique among the private entrepreneurs in terms of the scale of its investment in leisure.

THE INMAA' GROUP

The Inmaa' Group is a major contracting and development firm responsible for a series of amusement parks in Dahiya (Fantasy World and Family House) and across South Lebanon—Funny World in Saida, Family Park in Bint Jbeil, and Farah City in Nabatiyeh. Inmaa' has been in the contracting business for over two decades, building relatively affordable housing complexes in Dahiya. In the 1990s, it began catering to more affluent customers, with middle- and high-end buildings in more expensive Dahiya neighborhoods where zoning regulations promote larger apartments and lower population density. Inmaa' is known to have a close relationship with Hizbullah, as we saw firsthand during our interview with Ghobeyri mayor Hajj Abu Sa'id, who facilitated the Fantasy World project. When we went to Farah City in 2007, people referred to it as "Hizbullah's Luna Park," in a reference to the first amusement park in Lebanon, a much smaller place called Luna Park on Beirut's seaside Corniche.[49] Hajj Adham, CEO of the Inmaa' Group, clarified that association: "We are close to the party. But we don't have investors from the party. . . . [People say that] just because we are considered close to the party or have relatives in the party. So it is normal for people to say we are from the party." These kinship relations with Hizbullah members have facilitated the group's contracting work and growth over the years.

The Inmaa' Group's offices are housed in a prime-location building close to the airport highway. Hajj Adham, a large, easygoing man, received us in a spacious office expensively furnished with carpets, wooden tables and chairs, richly upholstered couches, and elaborate curtains. He is served by several secretaries and men who resemble bodyguards. Multiple phones sit on his desks, and television screens are arranged around the room. During our conversation, he did not hesitate to tell us that the group's capital investment for its four entertainment projects (as of 2008) amounted to some thirty million US dollars, and that it employs between seven and eight hundred people, depending on the season. He underscored the considerable finances required to operate, maintain, and develop parks of that scale, with monthly expenses averaging fifty to fifty-five thousand US dollars and sometimes reaching a hundred thousand US dollars. After the July 2006 war, Inmaa' bore significant losses, but according to Hajj Adham, thanks to its solid financial foundation, the group was able to recover. The Inmaa' Group's entertainment projects are owned by a shareholding company that includes several entrepreneurs. Between 15 to 20 percent of the annual profits are allocated for park maintenance and development. In some of the parks, Inmaa' rents space to other local businesses like the Baguette restaurant chain or international franchises, such as KFC and Krispy Kreme.

How did the Inmaa' Group decide to invest in the leisure sector in 1999 and open the first entertainment project in Dahiya? Hajj Adham's explanation focused on the financial sense it made to invest in entertainment because its returns are distributed steadily over time.

> There are two types of investments: temporary investment opportunities where the volume of profits is less than the permanent investment, but where profit is continuous and relatively independent from the economic situation. Currently, there's an increase in real estate development because of demand and supply. This increase will go on for few years, but will stop, whereas the other demand for [entertainment] projects will continue.

In addition to profits, Hajj Adham told us that Inmaa' wanted to create job opportunities and contribute to the socioeconomic progress of the community.

> The other point is, when we start to think business, we shouldn't always think with selfishness. In some cases, we could think selfishly. At the same time, people who have a message or goal need to create opportunities for others. I mean, he benefits, and so do others. When we have projects like that [entertainment], we usually have seven to eight hundred employees in our group. There, we benefit. The people with their families, you provide for them an important leisure place. At the same time, there is a large segment of employees that benefit. It has a ripple effect on society.

The successes and positive effects of Fantasy World and al-Saha sent a strong signal at the turn of the twenty-first century, and inspired others to follow in their footsteps.

Unsystematic Small Businesses and Partnerships

Over the span of a few years, smaller restaurants and cafés have multiplied in Dahiya's more affluent neighborhoods, supplying people with myriad options. The rapidity of the spread of cafés in the area, combined with general business practices in Lebanon, has contributed to a sense that many of these businesses are run in haphazard ways. This was the diagnosis of Fady, one of the café owners we interviewed. He was critical of the proliferation of leisure places, describing it as a "trend" that had not been carefully studied by many entrepreneurs and predicting the downfall of many of the new businesses at the first sign of crisis. Fady was a return emigrant who is the only person we interviewed who had prior experience in the restaurant business. He recalled how regulations in the United States prevent restaurants from opening within "less than three to five miles" from each other, as opposed to the tendency in Lebanon for similar businesses to cluster together in blocks. Complaining about the effects this has on other entrepreneurs, Fady said,

> Here, anyone who has forty or fifty thousand dollars, he'll find a place, do the décor, and open a café, and many of them will fail. They think cafés make money. They see [this place] and say, "I have fifty thousand dollars, I can open a café!" They need to have the experience and they need to do the right thing. It might be a kind of jealousy or they just don't think. They imitate each other. At the same time, they are hurting each other.

The story we were told about how another café was opened illustrates the limited planning involved in launching many local businesses. Nayla, the café's owner, was a young woman who taught at a university. After work, she frequently went to cafés to smoke argileh with her fiancé. As she told us in her interview, one evening as they drove around, they saw a "for rent" sign in an empty shop on the street where Bab el-Hara is located. "Without giving it much thought," Nayla convinced her fiancé to use their wedding savings to open a café. She continued,

> The owner asked for a year's rent in advance. We didn't have the money to pay for the whole year, so we agreed to pay him for six months. We paid the rent and began little by little. His [her fiancé's] cousin works in interior design, and his other cousin works in paint, which means we started as a *projet familial* [in French]. And I like decorating a lot—a lot. The idea came for entertainment, for ourselves and others. And I like doing business a lot.

In a follow-up phone conversation with Nayla in 2009, we learned that she had sold the café, and by 2011 it had closed altogether.[50]

Café business partnerships did not always involve family. Many were private partnerships between friends and acquaintances that ran other businesses individually and wanted to invest capital in the leisure sector because they thought it would yield good returns. Some of these partnerships took the form of shareholding companies like Inmaa'. But most of the owners we interviewed knew each other before going into business together, used their own savings, and did not take out bank loans.[51] They rented a ground-floor shop or the first floor of an apartment building for an extended period of five to ten years. Only two had conducted market research to evaluate need in the area; one of them told us, "People wanted good food and argileh at low prices." A third said that he studied the market on his own by observing what people liked in existing places.

> In al-Saha, they have *diwaniyyat* [or singular, *diwaniyyeh*; Arabic seating with low couches], [and] people like them, but they need reservations and are very

expensive. I made the place here with a lot of diwaniyyat, at no [extra] charge. They are very successful with customers. Some nights, I don't have enough seats for customers!

Similarly, only a few of the owners we interviewed paid to advertise their cafés, usually on Hizbullah's al-Nour radio station and al-Manar television station. Most owners relied instead on personal connections, proximity to workplace or home, and word of mouth. While this might be perceived as another symptom of the haphazard way that many cafés were opened, it may also reflect these entrepreneurs' knowledge about their customer base. In our survey of café customers, we found that 67 percent learned about the café they were sitting in at the time from their friends. Only 12 percent had heard about it via any form of advertising, and the remaining people had either heard about it in another context or seen it while passing by on the street.

Both the lack of systematic planning and the personal connections owners feel to their cafés manifested in the fact that most of the café owners we interviewed manage the places themselves. The few who did not hired managers with basic training or no restaurant experience at all, who then operated as employees under the owner rather than as professional restaurant managers.[52] We spoke with a few of these managers, and they all complained about their work conditions and especially the lack of autonomy they were granted to run the establishment.[53] In other words, they objected to the constant interference of café owners as they tried to go about their jobs. As Maher put it,

> People here don't understand that you can't be the owner and the manager, and that the owner should not interfere in the affairs of the restaurant, the décor, the menu, the kitchen, with the manager, with the staff. He only owns; he should sit back and delegate this stuff to professionals.

Another manager, Riyad, who had a degree in hotel management and had trained at a five-star hotel in Beirut, was also critical of how the new cafés and restaurants operate in Dahiya. He gave us a litany of complaints:

> Owners choose the location of the café or restaurant just like that; it's not based on a market study, and it's often about personal relations or place availability. Cafés and restaurants are not easily accessible by car and do not provide parking for customers. Most of them are in residential buildings, and this [layout] creates service problems between the kitchen and seating area. Also, the personnel are most often not properly trained and the service lacks quality. Also, menus are not conceived professionally and are randomly altered [by the owner].[54]

Despite the lack of planning and professional management that characterizes many of Dahiya's cafés and restaurants, a large number of these businesses seem to be thriving. Their owners frequently invested in the leisure
sector for financial reasons, and while they were hesitant to discuss the
details of their finances with us, many of their businesses have remained
open for several years.

FAMILY ENTERTAINMENT AND MORAL POLICING

In addition to financial motivations, some entrepreneurs justified their ventures into leisure by highlighting their contributions to the community's
socioeconomic development, in terms similar to those used by Hajj
Adham. There is an additional impetus guiding some investors' focus on
moral leisure in particular: "responding to families' needs."[55] As Hajj
Adham put it,

> Parents want their kids to enjoy themselves in an amusement park, which is the
> symbol of entertainment for children, but they do not have the patience to wait
> for their kids while they're playing. So the idea was to combine an amusement
> park with a restaurant, providing for the comfort of the families and the enjoy-
> ment of children.

Fantasy World caters to the whole family through different types of
restaurants with indoor and outdoor seating as well as snack bars. Some
amusement parks, like Family House in Dahiya and Farah Park in Nabatiyeh, also include a gym with a swimming pool that has sex-segregated
hours.[56] Not all entrepreneurs have the means to develop large-scale, func-
tionally diverse projects like Fantasy World, Family House, or al-Saha.
Cafés located within Dahiya's dense neighborhoods are usually on the
lower floors of apartment buildings and offer a variety of indoor seating,
but do not have the space to include playgrounds, gyms, or other
activities.

In addition to providing entertainment for family members of all
ages, addressing families' needs carries a moral message. Hajj Adham
continued,

> Other amusement parks in Beirut are not safe; their activities don't fit all age
> groups. People who go there are not well educated—ya'ni ["I mean"], those
> places don't provide comfort and safety. Your children could be harassed ver-
> bally or physically, or your wife could be subjected to offensive behavior.

He emphasized that the Inmaa' Group's amusement parks work hard
to establish "trust" with families and ensure the "safety" of children. They

conduct regular surveys to evaluate the "relationship" they want to build with families and especially mothers, who he considers "the most important visitor, with her children." To build this trust, Hajj Adham explained that it is essential to work on the "environment and morals" of the place.

> In the past, mothers were not able to take their children alone to amusement parks, because the environment inside these amusement parks was known [to be inappropriate]. Sometimes the ethics were incompatible—[there were] shabab [young men], teenagers, etc. Because of our [political] orientation and commitment to our traditions and society, we were affected. So we provided all the components to ensure a positive relationship between our projects and families, which we translated into our project's motto: "trust and peace of mind." If there is no security and peace of mind, she [a mother] will not come with her children. Because usually the father is busy; the mother comes with her children. She sits in the restaurant, and the children play in the amusement park. This is what led to this idea, because we are taking care of issues we are familiar with and that our families also need. This is what made this idea [family entertainment] succeed.

Hajj Adham emphasized the notion that the owner of a leisure site is responsible for supplying a morally appropriate environment. When we asked how they achieved such an environment, he answered,

> Of course, with time, people know who we are. So it comes from people. They know that our projects are shar'i, so they take this into consideration. Second, if an employee notices something abnormal, he'll come and tell the manager. Then the manager will solve the problem in a proper way.

And when "incidents" take place, he noted, the staff intervenes. "There are people, for example, a guy is sitting with a woman, he will kiss her or. . . . Everything is within the general rules, but sometimes it is a little too much. In a nice and proper way, [the manager] will ask them to stop."

Every café owner and manager we interviewed reiterated the idea that they were responsible for enforcing an appropriate moral environment in their establishments. But the definition of what constitutes inappropriate behavior varied from person to person. For instance, Walid, a manager, told us casually that it was normal for restaurants to control inappropriate behavior, and that this was common practice across Lebanon.

> The standards we have here for customers are the same as all places. They are not just for this area. We are not doing them just in Bab el-Hara. There is a particular policy for restaurants. For example, I don't allow someone to put his foot on the chair or come here with inappropriate clothes.

Walid's training in the service profession gave him a specific perspective on appropriate behavior that he extended to "all" businesses of a certain "class" in the country.

When we asked him, "Have you faced any situations involving inappropriate behavior in your restaurant?" he responded,

> Yes, and we had a problem. There was a guy who refused to leave; he didn't like the idea. He saw it as something personal against him. And a fight happened. You cannot come here with shorts and short clothing. It is not for religious reasons. For example, [it is like that] if I am sitting with my wife, my fiancée, or with my family in any place. We are not at the beach! Those rules are in all restaurants, not just in Dahiya. About music, we ask people to lower the volume when it's loud. We have soft music here. All of the five-star restaurants in Lebanon have soft music. We have soft music to please all people. It is not that Shiʿa don't listen to music. Everyone likes soft music.

And when we posed the question, "If there's a couple doing something inappropriate, do you interfere to stop them?" Walid replied in the affirmative again. "Yes," he said. "In general, if one of the female employees is at work, we send her to talk to them. They can have freedom to do whatever they want until they reach inappropriate behavior, like when they get too close to each other. But in general, we don't mind."

Walid's consistent emphasis on the universality of a code of appropriate conduct in restaurants was quite possibly related to his efforts to present Dahiya in a certain light to two researchers who were not from the area and were affiliated with Lebanon's most elite university. His stress on appropriate behavior more generally reflects ideas about class and taste, and reveals how Dahiya's leisure industry is reinforcing socioeconomic inequalities by excluding and marginalizing people who look nonconformist and/or inappropriate.

Walid also echoed the Inmaaʾ Group CEO's point about building trust with customers. He gave us the example of a father who knows him personally, and therefore drove his daughters and their friends, a total of thirteen teenage girls, to the café to watch a football game during the Euro Cup. Building trust mattered, "not just because we are in Dahiya, but in terms of business." At the same time, he dismissed the idea that cafés in general were places that parents could trust to look out for their children, noting, "There are people who come here in secret, behind the back of their families!" Trust here was about personal connections and relationships, and not about the type or location of a café.

Perhaps the most universally agreed on moral tenet that characterizes Dahiya's cafés and restaurants is the absence of alcohol. In municipal Beirut, some cafés without alcohol on their menus still serve beer "under the table," because beer exists in nonalcoholic form. One can order a "real" (e.g., alcoholic) beer, which is served in a glass so that others don't know that it contains alcohol. This avoids potential conflict with people who come to the café because it is known as an alcohol-free business, allowing the café to please both types of customers. We have not seen or heard about the clandestine availability of alcohol in Dahiya's cafés, and accounts from café owners indicate a strong propensity to avoid experimenting with this rule. It is a clear red line for them, both personally and for business reasons related to their reputations in an area where the majority consider alcohol consumption haram.

The owner of one of the trendier Dahiya cafés we visited used to work as a bartender, but made a "personal decision" not to sell alcohol in his business. "I don't drink and I don't work with alcohol." He added that selling alcohol might make him more money and that he could have opened a pub in Gemmayze, but that this decision makes him "happy and comfortable." Nayla shared with us a story about guys who came to her café with "their own stuff to drink," and when the waiter asked them to "remove it or leave the place," they grew angry. "I didn't care," she said, "It is better than me feeling bad. There are rules that we have to follow here. If you break them once, that's it. Just like home, there is respect for this place."

Despite the apparent universality of a ban on alcohol, there are specific conditions under which it is publicly consumed in Dahiya, in addition, of course, to drinking within some people's homes. Alcohol consumption is sometimes permitted in restaurants when it occurs behind closed doors if customers bring their own drinks. In one café, the owner told us about a large hall that could be rented where people can do "whatever they want." Both dance music and alcohol were permitted there because "it is a closed hall." Alcohol consumption also takes place at UMAM—the cultural center owned by a Shi'i opponent to Hizbullah—on opening nights and during cocktail parties. Again, this happens behind closed doors and is considered a private matter.

Another commonly cited behavior that required censorship was intimate interactions between men and women. One owner, Hussam, a return emigrant from the United States, argued that behavior needs to be controlled because his business was, as he put it in English, a "family restaurant" not a "youth restaurant" and therefore there were "constraints." He underscored the importance of maintaining a restaurant's reputation, its "name," and how business could be negatively affected if inappropriate behavior was known to occur there. Hussam echoed, from an owner's perspective, what we had heard about economic boycotts of Dahiya businesses that do not conform to moral rules. When asked, he gave us a more specific definition of inappropriate behavior: the display of "bad manners and behavior in public," specifically physical intimacy, like kissing, in front of families and children.

> This is something I am personally annoyed by and I refuse to have my children faced with such a sight. I don't accept it here. There are families, there are children, who come here. It's not necessarily a religious thing. These are things that do not conform to prevailing standards and good manners [dimn al-usul wal adab].

Hussam trained his staff to deal with such situations and shared an incident with us that one of his female employees described to him.

> This morning, she was telling me, "We had customers today, it was <u>hot, too much</u>, you know. . . . They were sitting inside, in the diwaniyyeh, and it was too much. I was embarrassed!" They [the employees] talked with them, "<u>Please</u>, stay respectful, there are families, there are children." Once, twice, the third time, khalas! ["it's over"].

In some cafés, patrolling mixed-gender interactions is complicated by interior design, reminding us that spaces can also affect behavior. Many include corners conducive to intimacy. One owner made the conscious decision not to provide seating behind columns to prevent private interactions. Fady—whose café includes a somewhat-secluded mezzanine space furnished with small tables for two—is careful to keep "checking on the customers to make sure nothing inappropriate is happening and send them a signal that they are not really alone."

Fady, whose quote opened this chapter, shares the view that it is crucial to monitor customer behavior. He also trains his employees to deal with public displays of affection that could disturb customers. As he described it:

> We have guys who come with their girlfriends. He puts his arm around her, and they talk. We don't mind that. Some people overdo it. It has happened here two or three times. You know, kissing; it is like they will jump on each other if we leave them alone! This is not a place for that.

He added that cafés are places where people meet and interact with those of the opposite sex, and that sometimes his staff interferes at the request of young female customers who are annoyed by young men's behavior.

> We always have guys [shabab] and young women [sabaya] here. Bluetooth is always active. But we cannot stop that. It is up to them. As long as they are sitting [on their own], it is something private, something secret. No one can see it.

But if there is someone bothering others, or guys are bothering young women, we cannot accept that. Sometimes young women come and complain about a group of guys.

Despite their concerns about mixed-gender interactions, both owners and managers celebrated the fact that Dahiya's leisure places have become important meeting spots for youths as well as businesspeople and families—a feature that is also lauded by café patrons. As Nayla explained,

Like people don't want to meet in someone's house. Young guys want to sit in a place together without bothering their mothers, so they meet here. Sometimes people meet for business. There was a group of men working with their cameras here. Another man was interested and wanted to buy a camera; he took their phone number, [and] they did business together.

Another owner told us,

I notice a lot of good things. This father and mother, they came in the other day with their daughter and her fiancé. They sat at different tables. They [the younger couple] got to know each other. A lot of people come to meet up with each other. To do business. One thing that caught my attention is how people host social events here now ['azayem]. People invite others more and more to cafés. This is new. They think, "My place is small, there's no electricity.[57] I don't want to bother my wife and deal with the stress of inviting people." They even invite their family, their brothers, their parents. . . . It could even be cheaper than hosting at home!

Leisure site owners in Dahiya project a neat image of an industry in which "appropriate behavior" seems to be smoothly enforced. Hizbullah and some area entrepreneurs would like to see the leisure sector operate according to certain rules of moral behavior, ironically more stridently than Fadlallah. Our observations in many of these places, however, reveal a less orderly picture where youth practices are more ambiguous and less conformist, as they contest political and religious authorities as well as the dominant moral and spatial order in Dahiya.

CONTROLLING LEISURE: WISHFUL THINKING

We began this chapter with Hizbullah's concerns vis-à-vis the "Bluetooth generation" and party's holistic approach to *thaqafa* as a way to attract "straying" youths. The party's worries about the Islamic milieu's cohesion are also revealed by the LAA's Family Values and Order media campaigns.

This focus on promoting appropriate values within its community is a symptom of Hizbullah's anxieties that while it remains the most popular political choice for Shi'i Muslims in Lebanon and the core of the Resistance, it may be losing ground as the primary moral authority for its supporters. This was diagnosed in chapter 1 by parliamentarian Ali Fayyad, who explained the perceived disruptions of moral and spatial order that leisure provokes as part of the party's infitah and a natural outcome of its growth. In his view, as the social base of the party expanded, Hizbullah had no choice but to become more open and flexible in relation to leisure. Otherwise, it risked losing its constituency, which in Lebanon quite literally translates into votes and political power.

The presence of pious young consumers as a market force has prompted major investment in leisure, and as we will see, begun to redefine morality and geography in relation to leisure practices. Despite the party's best efforts, Hizbullah does not have a monopoly on constructing the Islamic milieu. Hajj Adham, speaking as someone who is both involved in producing leisure in Dahiya and close to the party, confirmed the potential "threat" that leisure poses to the Shi'i community. He believes that business owners should control the leisure sector because they have a "responsibility" to both Hizbullah and society to maintain an appropriate environment. If owners are unable to exact this control, there will be negative consequences. The leisure sector in Dahiya, said Hajj Adham,

> has more negatives than positives. Not everywhere, in places that are planned and have control, and consider the general issues, they don't have negatives. Look, the population of teenagers here is quite big now. If you open a place for them and you don't supervise it in the proper way, you will have negative consequences in terms of behavior. . . . This control is not available everywhere. In the end, the party cannot supervise every small and big thing. . . . So as a society that supports Hizbullah, we are responsible for making sure things are right and proper on behalf of the party. And because of those who are unable to carry to this responsibility, things will get out of hand and affect society in a negative way.

Not all café owners in Dahiya are living up to this imposed responsibility.[58] While some avoid arranging their cafés in ways that encourage intimacy, others provide semiprivate spaces or totally enclosed rooms where "everything can happen." For the latter, morality is not a priority; business is.

Fadlallah, in turn, deals with the potential threat that leisure poses by emphasizing social regulation and norms over legal or jurisprudential solutions. In Sayyid Ja'far's words:

I think step by step, society is moving toward creating a kind of balance in behavior, and of course we cannot forget that there are deviant cases, because in relation to any social issue there are cases that are deviant. . . . We deal on the level of what is visible with this matter. Here it becomes important how open minded the jurisprudent is, how much he can see the issue in a way that is a little bit global, broader than the limited historical moment or limited social reality. . . . For that reason sometimes, people come and say to Sayyid Fadlallah, *wallah* this fatwa is making problems, and is going to lead to deviation, and like this. The sayyid instead sees the issue as long term; that eventually there will be increased social regulation of it. And it follows that the issue needs to take its normal time to resolve. But since the shari'a doesn't forbid it, the issue remains in the hands of the *mukallaf* [follower or person responsible for himself]. We set the limitations that we can and provide the guidance that we can, but society must slowly adapt to the situation. . . . So the role of the fatwa from the perspective of the sayyid does not stop only at the shari'a, as he always tries to find for a topic a sort of internal peace [*al-salam al-dakhili*] on the shari'a level and internal peace on the societal level.

This emphasis on seeking internal peace between jurisprudence and the contemporary social world can be understood to mediate several perspectives. On the one hand, it dovetails beautifully with Hizbullah's recent campaigns focusing on values. The Order campaign specifically highlighted the social rubric of morality in addition to the religious rubric, sometimes using plays on common aphorisms to combine the two (e.g., converting the saying "cleanliness is from God" to "order is from God"). On the other hand, seeking a rapprochement between jurisprudence and the contemporary world can also be understood to suggest that jurisprudence should *adapt* to the social world, and thereby facilitate the needs and desires of contemporary youths.

Cafés and restaurants in Dahiya are providing youths with many social and spatial opportunities close to home. They are also operating as sites of encounter between young people and owners who act as self-proclaimed paternalistic authorities, monitoring and regulating their behavior. But youths are not passive recipients and can be quite vocal in contesting authorities that interfere with their lifestyles choices. As Aziza, who grew up in a prominent Hizbullah family, told Lara in 2010, "The day the party tells me how to live my life, I will begin to fight against it."

While interviewing Riyad, the young restaurant manager, the conversation turned to Hizbullah's attempts to control moral norms in south Beirut. Riyad criticized the hypocrisy of one of his employers, who is affiliated with the party, for telling him that he cannot listen to pop music in his car, when Riyad has seen him gazing at women while completing his ablutions. He also emphasized that it is impossible to control behavior in an era of satellite television and the Internet. As our conversation continued, Riyad transformed from a manager explaining his work to one of Dahiya's youths, expressing typical desires to live according to his own morals, outside of what he perceives as Hizbullah's hypocritical and obsolete constraints. We asked him, "So do you think a music place can open in Dahiya?"

"Yes, it can open," he replied. "But I'll tell you something; it might be closed by Hizbullah."

"So there is pressure?"

"Yes, there is pressure," he responded, "but it is not fair. If you do something, why shouldn't I do it too? It's not all people, [just] some of them. Not all people are good or bad, and there are good people. But why are you stopping me from doing something you do yourself? *Fhimtini*? ["Did you understand me?"] I am telling you indirectly [smiling]."

"We heard that people would stop going to these places. They would boycott the place and say something bad about it."

"Yes, absolutely. For example, on my way to here, I like Tiesto [a pop artist]. I put his music in my car. I put songs in my car. I play music in the car, and I play Qur'an in the morning. I am free."

"Yes, it's your car . . ."

"It is my car!" exclaimed Riyad. "And *manti'ti* ["my area"]! No one can say anything to me about what I do here! Whoever he is!"

"Did anybody say anything to you about that," we asked, "about what you do?"

"Just the owner of the restaurant, the other one. There is no problem with al-Sayyid [one of the owners]. I went to a wedding with him [laughing]. The other one lectures me, 'Ya'ni, *inno* ["you know"].' I say, 'OK, when I see you, I'll turn it off. I don't have a problem.' Ya'ni, it is good that Manar doesn't show advertisements for soap! [laughing] We put NewTV on the television, [and] sometimes they put an advertisement for Dove, soap or shampoo *ma ba'rif* ["I don't know"], and he'll say, 'Remoooove it!! Remoooove it!! Don't leave any remote [remote control] with the customers!' Because there was a *mashhad* ["an (inappropriate) scene"]. OK, but people who come here, inno, no one here is under eighteen!"

"So how do you explain this, I don't understand?"

"No matter how you explain it, there's one analysis," replied Riyad. "Look at all the cafés that [are] open twenty-four hours here. And do you really think there is oversight on the IP addresses? *Ahlan bil* IP*yat* [literally, 'Welcome to the IPs,' a way of sarcastically highlighting that there is no control of IP addresses]. Of course not. Inno, 'adeh, tla'o minna ba'a! ["It's normal. Loosen up about it already!"]. Inno, in about two years, here we will be *kteer* ["very"] free, and *ahla, ahsan* ["nicer, better"]."

We questioned him a bit further, asking, "So you're seeing things moving toward more infitah?"

"Yes. Why? Because now there is an infitah, but it is hidden. As if somebody is holding it back. *Ba'den* ["later"], people will loosen up and get used to it. It is like when you have something unfamiliar. When you have something unfamiliar, all people see it. Now in a little while, it will be familiar, people will find it 'adeh, inno, *eh, shu hayda ya'ni* ["this is not a big deal"]."

While not all Shi'i youths are this skeptical of Hizbullah, most share Riyad's sense of the inevitability of social change in their community along with the role played by both technology and new leisure sites. The various efforts we have seen to produce and control leisure in Dahiya have contributed to a situation where there are multiple authoritative definitions of what makes a place, behavior, or activity moral. A new leisure landscape has emerged in south Beirut. What does it look like? What do the new cafés look like? What has the combination of new desires for morally appropriate leisure, the political context, new investments and markets, and producer efforts to control the leisure sector meant for cafés within this rapidly changing area of the capital? We take up these questions in relation to the distribution, characteristics, and interiors of Dahiya's new cafés and restaurants in the next chapter.

3

Mapping Leisure and Café Styles

Prior to 2000, Dahiya had a few pizza places scattered along some of its commercial streets that functioned like the local *man'oushe* and fast-food stands. There were also a couple restaurants by its western edge that mainly catered food as well as a few male-only traditional coffee shops. Mona regularly took her adviser and other professors to one of the restaurants, Kanana, during her PhD fieldwork in the late 1990s, as it was the only restaurant in Dahiya where one could get a decent meal. During most of these visits, the place was empty or occupied by few customers, but the open kitchen counter was always busy preparing take-out orders. Lara occasionally stopped at a juice stand near the Hizbullah media office, yet always took her drink to go as she never saw anyone actually sitting on one of the few stools it had in the corner.

With the introduction of the Internet in Lebanon, businesses providing access appeared across Beirut, including in Dahiya. Initially, Internet access was incorporated into the "amusement centers" where young men played pool and computer games. Eventually, some of these gaming centers began offering coffee, juices, and food—often picked up from a nearby bakery. They became small cybercafés, providing Wi-Fi along with wired desktop computers. Over time, they attracted an increasingly mixed clientele of youths. One of the first of these places to attract a mixed-gender crowd in Dahiya was Café. Yet. It initially opened in 2004 as an Internet café near a main intersection in the heart of south Beirut before being renovated into a café with a larger menu and Wi-Fi but no desktop computers, in keeping with the increasing trend for people across Lebanon to own laptops.

By the time Café. Yet opened, Fantasy World was already a popular family destination and al-Saha had expanded significantly. Following their leads and in response to the changing contexts we have described, at least one hundred "legitimate" cafés and restaurants have opened in Dahiya since 2000. The vast majority of their customers are between ages eighteen to thirty-five, and almost equally male and female. Most are employed, about a quarter are students; few are housewives or unemployed.[1] In this chapter, we provide a geographic analysis of the new leisure sites, mapping them onto Dahiya's streets and neighborhoods, and comparing their architectural design and aesthetic features.

LOCATING LEISURE IN DAHIYA

In 2008, we conducted a survey of thirty-six new cafés and restaurants in south Beirut, approximately half the restaurants and cafés in the area at the time.[2] All were privately owned, with the exception of al-Saha. Most were medium-size businesses, only two of which were owned by the same person, who had opened a newer café with a similar name prior to closing the original one (Sweet Land replaced Sweet Café). The few large-scale projects we surveyed included Bay Rock restaurant in the Beirut Mall and Everyday Café in Spinney's Supermarket—both at the northern boundary of Dahiya—and the two Inmaa' Group projects (Family House and Fantasy World). In 2011, all but one of the surveyed businesses were still operating, and many new ones had opened, following the same geographic patterns we had identified based on our 2008 data. Two of the new businesses were owned by the same partners (Nasamat and Swiss Time).

Our survey results confirmed our observation that the leisure sector in Dahiya expanded rapidly after Liberation. Of the surveyed businesses, 63.8 percent were established between 2006 and 2008, while 22.2 percent opened between 2003 and 2005, and 14 percent were functioning prior to 2002 (see figures 3.1 and 3.2).

The geographic distribution of the cafés indicates that they follow clear urban patterns (see figure 3.3). On the one hand, leisure sites are located on circulation axes and more precisely on two main arteries that were built relatively recently: the airport-Beirut Central District (BCD) highway built in 1996, and the Hadi Nasrallah highway built in 2002. Several cafés (about 14 percent of our sample) are located along the southern section of the airport-BCD highway, at the edges of low-density, high-end residential neighborhoods that were urbanized by the mid-1990s near the Golf Club of Lebanon. A larger number (36 percent) are concentrated along the midsection of Hadi Nasrallah highway, at the edges of dense middle-class, mixed-use neighborhoods, also urbanized by the mid-1990s. On the other hand, there are leisure sites located on Dahiya's peripheries. Two places sit near the municipal boundary with Beirut: a cluster of cafés (14 percent) is

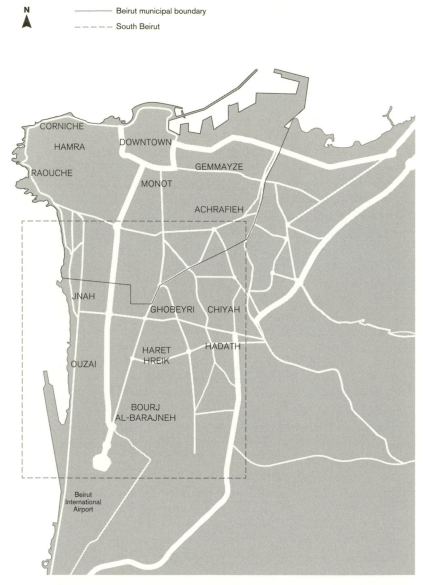

FIGURE 3.1 Map of location of Dahiya in Beirut. © Mona Harb, Ahmad Gharbieh, and Lara Deeb

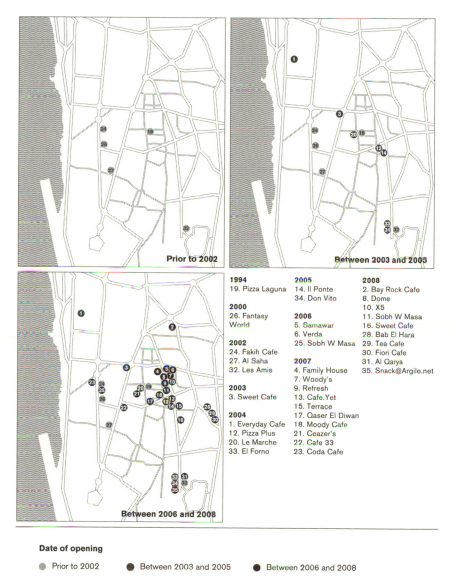

1994	2005	2008
19. Pizza Laguna	14. Il Ponte	2. Bay Rock Cafe
	34. Don Vito	8. Dome
2000		10. X5
26. Fantasy	**2006**	11. Sobh W Masa
World	5. Samawar	16. Sweet Cafe
	6. Verda	28. Bab El Hara
2002	25. Sobh W Masa	29. Tea Cafe
24. Fakih Cafe		30. Fiori Cafe
27. Al Saha	**2007**	31. Al Qarya
32. Les Amis	4. Family House	35. Snack@Argile.net
	7. Woody's	
2003	9. Refresh	
3. Sweet Cafe	13. Cafe.Yet	
	15. Terrace	
2004	17. Qaser El Diwan	
1. Everyday Cafe	18. Moody Cafe	
12. Pizza Plus	21. Ceazer's	
20. Le Marche	22. Cafe 33	
33. El Forno	23. Coda Cafe	

Date of opening

● Prior to 2002   ● Between 2003 and 2005   ● Between 2006 and 2008

FIGURE 3.2 Map of the emergence and growth of leisure sites in south Beirut (2000–8). © Mona Harb, Ahmad Gharbieh, and Lara Deeb

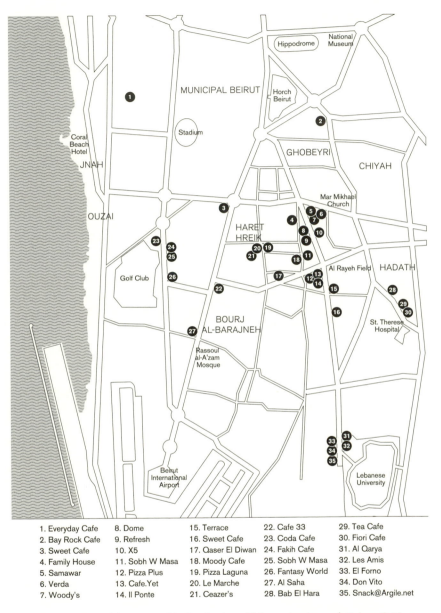

1. Everyday Cafe	8. Dome	15. Terrace	22. Cafe 33	29. Tea Cafe
2. Bay Rock Cafe	9. Refresh	16. Sweet Cafe	23. Coda Cafe	30. Fiori Cafe
3. Sweet Cafe	10. X5	17. Qaser El Diwan	24. Fakih Cafe	31. Al Qarya
4. Family House	11. Sobh W Masa	18. Moody Cafe	25. Sobh W Masa	32. Les Amis
5. Samawar	12. Pizza Plus	19. Pizza Laguna	26. Fantasy World	33. El Forno
6. Verda	13. Cafe.Yet	20. Le Marche	27. Al Saha	34. Don Vito
7. Woody's	14. Il Ponte	21. Ceazer's	28. Bab El Hara	35. Snack@Argile.net

FIGURE 3.3 Map of the geographic distribution of leisure sites in south Beirut. © Mona Harb, Ahmad Gharbieh, and Lara Deeb

FIGURE 3.4 The main road in Sainte-Thérèse

found in the newly established middle-class, mixed-use Sainte-Thérèse area near the Maronite neighborhood of Hadath, and another cluster (14 percent) near Lebanese University's western gate, mainly serving the student population (see figure 3.4). The rest are scattered along the old airport road and within the Haret Hreik neighborhood—two areas that have been urbanized since the 1960s and known as home to Dahiya's middle classes.

Comparing the geographic distribution of cafés with a map of low-income neighborhoods and land prices in Dahiya (see figure 3.5) confirms our observation that the leisure sector in south Beirut is closely associated with the middle-class market.[3] Land prices in the neighborhoods where leisure sites are located vary between what we categorized as middle-to-high and very high ranges for Dahiya. These prices are comparable to middle-range land costs in other neighborhoods, such as Ras el-Nabeh or Mar Mikhail, two older neighborhoods in municipal Beirut with rather-dated urban fabrics. None of the cafés and restaurants is near informal settlements or the Palestinian refugee camps within Dahiya; the only exceptions are located by Lebanese University, which is next to the Hay el-Sellom informal settlement. There, male-dominated traditional coffee shops (ahwehs) abut "fancier" cafés where young male and female students

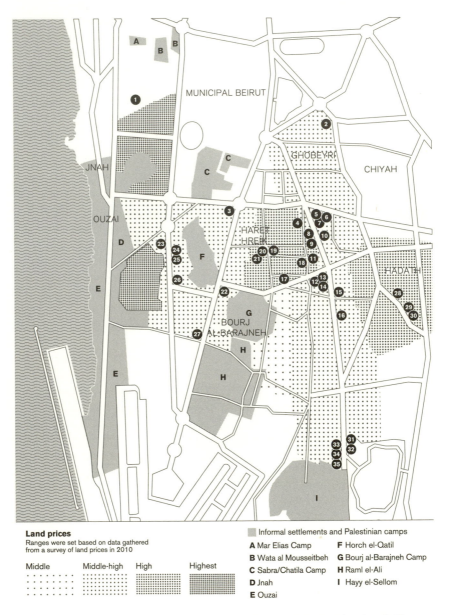

Land prices
Ranges were set based on data gathered
from a survey of land prices in 2010

Middle   Middle-high   High   Highest

▨ Informal settlements and Palestinian camps
A Mar Elias Camp   F Horch el-Qatil
B Wata al Mousseitbeh   G Bourj al-Barajneh Camp
C Sabra/Chatila Camp   H Raml el-Ali
D Jnah   I Hayy el-Sellom
E Ouzai

FIGURE 3.5 Map of income distribution in south Beirut. © Mona Harb, Ahmad Gharbieh, and Lara Deeb

meet. The two zones are clearly differentiated by their built environments. The ahwehs are housed in dilapidated low-rise buildings, with the extremely dense urban fabric of Hay el-Sellom towering behind them. The newer cafés are located in brightly painted high-rise buildings constructed with quality materials. In this part of Dahiya, class distinctions materialize in the built environment and its leisure options.[4] The effects of the distribution of cafés on Dahiya's sociospatial configuration are taken up in chapter 5. For now, suffice it to say that the expansion of south Beirut's leisure sector demonstrates the increasing sociospatial differentiation of the area since the civil war.

All but five of the surveyed cafés and restaurants are an integral part of the built environment. Those exceptions are immense, independent structures that seat over five hundred people, have open areas and parking lots, and are usually located on Dahiya's peripheries. The rest follow the more common Beirut pattern of occupying a lower floor of an apartment building, next to shops on the ground floor and/or first floor, one flight up. For those on the first floor, the ground floor often serves as a take-out station where passersby can purchase fruit juices, ice cream, and sandwiches. Thirty-nine percent of surveyed places could seat between a hundred and three hundred people, while the remaining 47 percent served between twenty and a hundred people at a time (see figure 3.6).

Most cafés provide diverse seating areas, accommodating various customer tastes and multiple activities. This diversity encourages a wide array of uses by different groups of people. In our visits, we frequently saw men smoking argileh and discussing business matters, women talking over coffee, mixed-gender groups of students working on their laptops, and couples conversing intimately behind columns or in secluded corners. These are neither male- nor female-dominated spaces, catering equally to single- and mixed-gender groups. The organization and design of café interiors encourages or discourages particular practices, and guides those interested in specific forms of sociality toward suitable seating areas. Some cafés provide an upper floor that is designed in a contemporary style to attract younger customers and "naturally" segregate their clientele into age zones.[5] Others place tables for two in darker corners or hidden parts of the café. Waiters also direct people, seating families and older customers in heritage-style or formally furnished sections, couples in secluded spaces, and youths in areas that are contemporary style.

Given the various stylistic possibilities provided by different cafés, people can choose which to frequent based on their needs and moods. Our survey of café customers showed significant relationships between gender and café choice, and between age and café choice.[6] Men preferred Coda Café to other places, and women preferred Sweet Café. Possible explana-

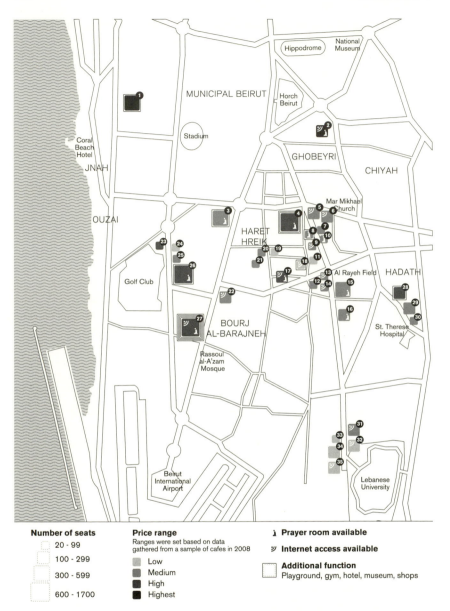

Number of seats
- 20 - 99
- 100 - 299
- 300 - 599
- 600 - 1700

Price range
Ranges were set based on data
gathered from a sample of cafes in 2008
- Low
- Medium
- High
- Highest

i **Prayer room available**

ッ **Internet access available**

☐ **Additional function**
Playground, gym, hotel, museum, shops

FIGURE 3.6 Map analyzing leisure sites by size, functions, and price range. © Mona
Harb, Ahmad Gharbieh, and Lara Deeb

tions for this difference are that Coda is on a main road at the edge of Dahiya that men might use more frequently in their commutes, and Sweet Café has a playground, making it a convenient hangout for women with small children. With regard to age, people between eighteen to twenty-five preferred Terrace and Fiori over Diwan and Bab al-Hara, while those between twenty-six and thirty-five preferred Bab al-Hara, and those over thirty-five preferred Diwan and Sweet Café and disliked Coda and Fiori. This seems related to differences of price and décor.

Some cafés took the idea of variety even further, and included playgrounds, computer games, dedicated Internet rooms, or—more originally—in the case of Bab al-Hara, a *hammam* (Turkish bath), sauna, and gym with an indoor pool in the building's basement, and in the case of al-Saha, a museum, souq, and poetry room.[7] Figure 3.6 illustrates this functional diversity, using symbols to note the availability of various services. Size clearly varies across geography, with a concentration of middle- and large-scale structures along main axes, and smaller places clustered within neighborhoods. Larger places tend to be more expensive, and provide a greater variety of services and spaces. Less than one-quarter of the cafés had a separate prayer room—far fewer than one might expect in this part of the city. Those that did ranged across all sizes and prices with the exception of the cheapest places. Only four places had a dedicated room for "families," underscoring the fact that mixed-gender social interaction in public spaces is not unusual in Dahiya and highlighting the similarity of norms across Beirut.

Approximately half the surveyed cafés provided Internet access or were in the process of obtaining it.[8] Internet availability varies across size, price range, and location, and tends to be found in places that deliberately cater to youths. Establishments that did not offer it were usually restaurants with full menus. One owner stated that he did not supply Wi-Fi because youths spend too much time surfing the Net and not enough money, and indeed we saw young people spend entire afternoons online with few drinks and no food on the table. Another criticized the behavior of youths online and said that he did not want to be associated with it.

With few exceptions, the surveyed cafés played instrumental arrangements of Arabic and Western pop melodies and classical music, set to low volume. On special occasions—during Ramadan, for instance—a café might bring in an 'oud player. Sometimes during our early morning visits, a café was quiet. At other times, sound came from flat-screen televisions that were positioned throughout the rooms. These televisions were often tuned to local or international news channels, and more rarely to the Rotana or MTV music channels, but usually at a low volume. During football (soccer) season, they were set to sports channels, and cafés became places where friends, male and female, gathered to root for their favorite teams.[9]

The surveyed businesses all serve halal food and only nonalcoholic beverages, in addition to a wide variety of tobacco flavors for argileh. Menu options typically included Lebanese mezza (appetizers) and shawarma, chicken kebob sandwiches, and saj. They also included international options like hamburgers, hot dogs, steak, and frequently Italian dishes like pizza and pasta as well as the more occasional Tex-Mex fajitas and nachos. Cafés served all sorts of hot and iced coffee drinks: espressos and lattes, instant coffee ("Nescafé"), Arabic/Turkish coffee, and "American" drip or "filter" coffee.[10] They offered selections of tea and herbal tea, soft drinks, and fresh fruit cocktails and juices. A few displayed coffee syrups and Italian soda flavorings in bottles lined up behind bars. A comparison of the prices of three commonly ordered items revealed consistency in the price of Turkish/Arabic coffee and grilled chicken sandwiches, but considerable variation in the price of an argileh. In 58 percent of the surveyed cafés, an argileh cost between 5,000 and 6,500 Lebanese pounds (LBP, or the equivalent of US$3.30–4.30) depending on the flavor. It was cheaper (4,000 LBP, or US$2.60) in nine places, mostly near the Lebanese University, and double the price in a few upscale restaurants—US$6.00 at al-Saha and US$7.30 at Bay Rock (a Lebanese chain) in the Beirut Mall. These items cost 30 to 50 percent less in Dahiya's cafés than in Beirut.[11]

Language and Reference Shifts

Our survey also looked at the language of café names and menus. Names were predominantly in European languages, with several in Italian (e.g., Fiori and Il Ponte), some in English (e.g., Family House and Sweet Café), and a few in French (e.g., Le Marché and Les Amis). This is in keeping with patterns across Lebanon, with one notable difference: the relative place of French in this hierarchy of European languages as compared to English.[12] Only seven of the thirty-six cafés have Arabic names (e.g., Bab al-Hara and Sobh wa Masa), and these were often transcribed on signage into the Latin alphabet in addition to, or sometimes in lieu of, Arabic orthography. Terrace, a café in the heart of Dahiya, was an interesting exception. Its name was displayed on its main sign only in Arabic script, transliterating a word generally pronounced with a French accent into Arabic text. A few café signs incorporated symbols that indicate Internet literacy and availability (e.g., Ceaser C@fe and Snack@argile.com). Café.Yet simultaneously plays on ideas about the Internet and bilingualism—the former when it is pronounced "café dot yet," and the latter when pronounced "kafeyat," converting "café" into an Arabic plural. Café names may also have personal or political significance. Café 33 was named after the thirty-three-day war in 2006, and X5 was named after its owner's favorite BMW car model.

Multilingual café signage is typical in Lebanon, where many people shift between Arabic and either English or French with ease, some speak primarily one of the latter, and some are fluent in all three languages. Proficiency in code-switching increases with education, though even Lebanon's worst public schools teach English or French, albeit not necessarily well, beginning at the elementary level.[13] A survey of twelve hundred Lebanese youths sampled proportionately by sect and region found that 41.3 percent were "in control of" written English, 43.1 percent of spoken English, 28.9 percent of written French, and 31.2 percent of spoken French (C. Harb 2010, 13). Signs across the country reflect this context in creative ways, transliterating words between alphabets and using playful translations.

Most surveyed café menus are written in both English and Arabic; nine had Arabic-only menus, and five had English-only ones, frequently transliterating rather than translating—for example, a grilled chicken sandwich would be listed as "taouk." They usually included multiple spelling mistakes, and sometimes transliterated Arabic into Roman letters using a system that developed with texting and instant messaging where numbers refer to Arabic sounds that do not exist in English (e.g., *2ashta, 3asal,* and *batata 7arra*).[14] This form of transliteration contrasts with more formal multilingual menus found in restaurants elsewhere, and highlights these cafés' newness and focus on youths. As compared to other parts of Lebanon, the lack of French on these cafés' menus is also striking, and along with the shift in café names, points to an ongoing transition from a French-dominated system to one where English is the preferred second (or primary, in some cases) language.[15] While some Lebanese associate this transition with a shift away from "Maronite Christian dominance" in politics and culture, it is also clearly related to the dominance of English as the global language for business and industry. In Dahiya, one hears far more English than in the 1990s, the result of social and economic mobility, and the post-Liberation return of emigrants from the United States and elsewhere. The prevalence of English in Dahiya's café signs and menus also may reflect a shift in stylistic reference away from France, which long dominated Lebanese ideas about what constituted high culture and leisure.[16] In south Beirut cafés, Italy represents coffee culture and Switzerland represents natural landscapes. We also see nods to the global corporate coffee shop exemplified by the US chain Starbucks. We now turn to these and other stylistic trends in café interiors.

PICTURING CAFÉ INTERIORS

South Beirut's cafés and restaurants display an extraordinary range and variety of aesthetic styles and themes. This eclecticism appears not only among cafés but within them as well. An "eastern" or *sharqi*-style seating area rich with antiquelike objects and artifacts evoking romanticized village life might be juxtaposed to a modernist arrangement of bright colors and sleek furniture. A solemnly furnished space reminiscent of a living room, with dark wood elements, crystal chandeliers, and extensive drapery, may open on to a terrace ornamented with fake greenery and other natural references. In this section, we tease apart the four dominant styles that together constitute the overwhelmingly eclectic aesthetic sensibility that characterizes most of Dahiya's cafés and restaurants.[17] For heuristic purposes, we separate these styles into heritage, nature-garden, formal dining, and contemporary—keeping in mind that these themes often work together to produce different sorts of effects and environments.

Heritage Style

Sweet Café's décor was dominated by the repetition of three arches side by side. An old window rested on one wall, and wooden details around the room looked as though they had been taken from old houses. The walls were painted to approximate old stone, using texture as well as color. The ceiling was low, and painted so that the walls seemed to extend into the sky—pale blue with clouds, and a small bird here and there. Dim lighting shone from lanterns with low-wattage lightbulbs. A large worn Qur'an sat on a wooden stand to one side, and Qur'anic verses hung on the walls, some hand carved in wood. The walls also held sepia photos of Beirut from the prewar years, enlarged black-and-white photos of people dressed in Ottoman fashion, and the occasional antique mirror, interrupted by television screens set to al-Manar and a few air-conditioning units. In the center of the room, wooden chairs with burgundy leather seats surrounded wooden tables; the sides of the room were furnished with low couches upholstered in a red-and-black-striped fabric. Artificial plants filled the edges and corners, and an old gramophone sat along one wall.

This café exemplifies heritage style complemented by elements of nature-garden style. Heritage style encompasses themes of village life, earlier lifestyles, and values that are often understood by people as "traditional" (taqlidi) in a positive sense.[18] It packages idealized versions of tradition and heritage into nostalgic and romanticized longing for olden times, and specifically for the simpler life of the village. This utopian vision is expressed architecturally through stone or faux-finished stonelike walls, wood, and wrought iron, and in earth and muted tones. The national specificity of this village is frequently claimed through the juxtaposition of three arches next to one another—a feature typical of old Beirut houses and nineteenth-century Mount Lebanon mansions that has become one of the symbols of "Lebanese" architecture.[19] Old or antique objects hang on the walls, or sit on shelves, and evoke village practices like serving Arabic coffee in a copper pot, preserving food for winter, baking saj bread, or grinding spices with a mortar and pestle. Furniture arrangements suggest non-

FIGURE 3.7 A diwaniyyeh interior in al-Saha Traditional Village restaurant

urban lifestyles, though not necessarily that of a Lebanese village. Low couches upholstered in a ubiquitous red-and-black-striped fabric are arranged around tables, accompanied by carpets on the floors and walls, and occasionally a tentlike drape hanging from a ceiling fixture. These sitting areas are redolent of ideas about being "Eastern" or "Arab," and resemble the sorts of couches one sees in Bedouin tourist tents in Jordan and elsewhere, down to the fabric. Owners and café patrons alike refer to them as diwaniyyat (see figure 3.7).

In Dahiya, the earliest and now-classic example of this decorative style is found in al-Saha, where the scale in which the traditional was reinterpreted has created a hyperreality. Al-Saha's architecture attempts to recreate the idealized space of the village through a plethora of elements that appeal to visitors' collective memory along with their associated representations of Arabic and Islamic heritage. The facades are covered with carved yellow limestone and wood-framed windows; white plastered domes spring from its crenulated roofs; and a high turret flanks one corner, enhancing its fortress-like aspect. A multitude of architectural details (corbels, balconies, and canopies) from different historical periods and geographic areas are mixed together.[20]

Al-Saha's architect, Hajj Jamal Makki, explained to Mona that the interior was also designed as a "traditional village." The "challenge," he said, was to "translate the concepts of history and tradition into elements that materialize their meanings to people." His intention was to make customers feel as though they are in a village within the city. Hajj Jamal was inspired by Lebanese writer Anis Freiha's well-known novel *Isma' ya Rida* (Listen Rida), which praises genuine village values over a corrupt urban lifestyle. He borrowed extensively from Freiha's book to design al-Saha's spaces, in addition to bringing in his own interpretations of heritage.[21] He translated the houses of two of the book's characters, Abu-Ahmad and Abu-Khalil, into dining rooms, created a "village spring" (*'ayn*) in the middle of a "village *saha*" ("open space"), and added a souq. Along with his brother (who he described as fond of "heritage things"), Hajj Jamal also designed a wax museum that displays craft production using life-size figures as well as water, sound, and light effects.[22] The ideas about heritage conveyed by al-Saha's architecture and exhibits are intended to promote learning about identity. As Hajj Jamal put it, "Heritage is profusely displayed here to force itself on the users so they learn about their origins and their identity while they are being entertained."

Al-Saha has been a great success. It has become a landmark and leisure destination for people from across Lebanon as well as foreign tourists and businesspeople. It has also been a key inspiration for south Beirut's burgeoning café scene. There are many other examples of the heritage style in these cafés, including at Bab al-Hara and Terrace. Bab al-Hara highlights the importance of media in cultivating an appreciation for heritage, as the romance of an earlier era swept the region when the Syrian *Bab al-Hara* television series captured the attention of Arabic-speaking audiences, including in Lebanon, each Ramadan from 2006 to 2010. Indeed, the design and décor of its namesake café, featured in this book's opening vignette, is directly inspired by the telenovella. Figure 3.8 shows one corner of Bab al-Hara's ground floor, subtly decked out with flags for the World Cup. Bab al-Hara also highlights the slippery nature of the past that is captured in these rooms—Ottoman, Bedouin, and village elements are freely mixed on its walls and in its furnishings.

Such heritage themes in architecture and décor are common across the Middle East, and appear in restaurants and cafés from Damascus to Istanbul, Tehran to Amman.[23] In Amman, for example, the past two decades saw a veritable boom in large-scale restaurants, like Kan Zaman, that evoke village themes, and more recently smaller cafés with similar décor elements have opened in the "old downtown" area. Jordanians sometimes explain these places as "modeled on Damascus," which boasts a heritage restaurant scene within the old city. Mahmoud and Rabi', two of our interviewees who appreciated what they called "traditional Arabic décor," remarked that before al-Saha opened, they used to drive to Damascus "to sit in places like that, like Damascus Gate. We didn't have them here before." Some of

FIGURE 3.8 Ground floor of Bab al-Hara

Mona's non-Lebanese students also drew comparisons to Damascene restaurants and cafés along the Syrian-Lebanese border when they visited
Dahiya's cafés for the first time.

This style—in combination with the nature elements we discuss below—
is also typical of Lebanese and Middle Eastern restaurants in the United
States, such as Victory, a restaurant (now closed) in Anaheim, California,
that had elaborate village scenes and painted architectural detail gracing the
walls of its interior dining room (Victory also shared with Dahiya cafés
diverse menu options). During our first visit to Sweet Café, Mona noted
that she hadn't seen anything quite like its décor in Lebanon before. Lara
responded, "That makes sense because I feel like I'm in a Lebanese restaurant in Dearborn or Anaheim!" And indeed, Sweet Café's owner had returned to Lebanon a few years earlier from Michigan. The other return
emigrant we interviewed, the owner of Terrace, also favored heritage style.
In the US context, this can be read as typical of diaspora nostalgia, or how
ethnic restaurants are marketed and designed in relation to North American multiculturalism. In Lebanon, there are other relationships at work,
and the village represents an earlier time as much as, if not more than, a
different place.

Explanations for the appeal of escaping to an earlier time in these leisure
sites often suggest that a village aesthetic functions as a foil for customers'

constructions of their own identities as urban.[24] In other words, by consuming the village, one firmly establishes oneself as urban and modern. Mona Abaza (2006) similarly suggests that the popularity of heritage objects and furnishings in Cairo is a way to assert "ethnic chic" as a form of upwardly mobile taste in competition with Western imports. Another common explanation, one more consistent with the narratives of café owners we interviewed, is the idea that heritage elements are appealing because they evoke nostalgia for a time and/or place that was or is better than one's present circumstances. Here the values placed on the urban-rural divide are reversed. Place and time are conflated in an idealization of village life as serene and relaxed as opposed to the city's chaos. In the village, one can lead a good moral life in keeping with so-called family values, whereas the city corrupts with its vice and anomie.[25]

In Lebanon, the village is valorized more than the city. Sune Haugbolle (2010, 87) argues that since the early 1990s, "nostalgia has been a widespread sentiment in Lebanon." He points to the plethora of cafés and shops across Beirut with names like Kan Zaman (Once upon a Time) and Baladi (My Country/Homeland), popularity of the *artisanat* (craft markets), and surge in heritage organizations, antique shops, and *baladi* (village) products. Haugbolle suggests that by focusing on aspects of heritage that were shared across Lebanon, people were able to escape the divisions created by civil war. "The logic of this approach was that, whereas they might disagree vehemently over the causes of the civil war, members of all sects and parties eat hummus, listen to Fairuz and dance the dabke" (ibid., 89). Christopher Stone (2008) locates nostalgia for the Lebanese village further back in history, arguing that it was related to urbanization. He shows how nostalgia for the Christian Lebanese mountain village in the Rahbani brothers' musical theater came—through their dominance of the Baalbek festival—to represent Lebanese heritage more broadly. Likewise, the novelist who inspired al-Saha's architect is associated with a Maronite Christian historical narrative of Mount Lebanon and its village life that gives Christian Lebanese "a stronger capacity to claim both governmental and sovereign belonging" as well as "assume a governmental position vis-à-vis Muslim Lebanese" (Hage 1996, 471). Al-Saha's reference to Freiha contests this hegemonic position and allows the Shi'i community to participate in the production of national heritage. Ironically, the Christian-village specificity of the Rahbani project and the Freiha novel has successfully produced a multisectarian nostalgia for a generic Lebanese village, seen across Beirut. The new Hamra Café boasts traditional Arabic coffee cups and argileh on its advertising, and several cafés in Achrafieh are replete with artisanat objects and designed with multiple references to heritage architecture, including triple arches, corbels, and wrought iron balustrades.

While all these meanings resonate with the heritage style of Dahiya's cafés, the village also carries meanings specific to this part of Beirut. Nostalgia and the prevalence of heritage-style elements may be related to the violent loss of access to village life experienced by many Shi'i residents of this area during the long years of Israeli occupation of the South and Bekaa Valley. Shi'i Muslims from these regions still nurture strong relations with their home villages. Like other Lebanese, they visit their villages regularly on weekends and holidays, adding to the flood of cars jamming roads into Beirut every Sunday evening. Moreover, by drawing on generic village objects and design details, Dahiya's cafés subvert the notion that the quintessential Lebanese village is a Christian mountain village. By claiming the village, they claim membership in the Lebanese nation for the area's mostly Shi'i residents.[26] Hajj Jamal did this deliberately, when he explained that al-Saha shows that "we can provide [Lebanese] heritage too!" Claims on and nostalgia for village life in café design are closely associated with a second stylistic theme common to many south Beirut cafés: nature.

NATURE-GARDEN STYLE

To enter Nasamat (Breezes), you walk though its parking lot to an entryway. Stepping in, you find yourself between a large green space surrounded by young trees and an extensive seating area with wicker chairs and plastic tables under umbrellas. Passing over a wooden arched bridge and next to a replica of a well, you come to the stone path that leads to the door. To the side, a playground, shaded by nearby high-rise apartment buildings, entertains young children. Inside is a space decorated in an understated version of heritage style, with simple beige stone walls hung with a few pictures and objects, including television screens, tuned to al-Manar on this particular visit as it is election season. Most of the room contains wicker chairs surrounding wooden tables, save for one side that instead has diwaniyyeh seating, once again covered in that popular red-and-black fabric (see figures 3.9 and 3.10).

Nasamat is one of the few cafés in Dahiya that was built as a stand-alone structure on an empty lot and can therefore provide ample outdoor space for patrons.[27] What sets such cafés apart is this outdoor space, generally used for a garden that interrupts the dense urban environment and noisy city traffic. It is both a metaphor for beauty and calm, and a literal oasis of green among Dahiya's tall buildings. In these gardens, the café owner becomes a landscape designer. The owner chooses trees, flowers, and shrubs, adds pergolas, wooden bridges, and ponds, and often adds water through wells, canals, and waterwheels. They hire workers to shape natural rock and stone, or create plaster replicas of common garden elements, and build

FIGURE 3.9 Nasamat's garden seating area

walls and paths that weave through the greenery. Furnishings are usually made of bamboo or wicker and wood, though glass tables and metal or plastic chairs make occasional appearances.

Nature-garden style is not restricted to places that are able to provide large, open-air landscaped spaces. Many cafés in Dahiya include it through symbolic and figurative elements, such as arrangements of artificial flowers and plants, the occasional live plant, and paintings or photographs of snow-capped and forested mountains. Like Sweet Café's sky ceilings, Il Ponte's staircase walls were painted in a trompe l'oeil of a picturesque "Italian" town full of flowers and trellises, overlooking sailboats on a river, thereby bringing the Italian countryside into the café interior.

Sometimes nature-garden style represents the relationship of Dahiya dwellers to their homes—whether evoking the village, or an urban rooftop or balcony garden—especially when nature is present in a controlled form. Here nostalgia for the village manifests as a longing for fruit from one's trees or vegetables from one's garden.[28] Losing access to the village means losing access to food grown on one's own land. The village also represents a space of calm tranquility because it is associated with the outdoors and spending time in green spaces. This too is a romanticization of the Lebanese village experience, which can be quite loud, with car horns and televi-

FIGURE 3.10 Nasamat's garden entrance

sion sets competing with baying donkeys and roosters, and which has its own forms of social interaction that may be as hectic as those of the city.

The emphasis on nature can be quite distinct from heritage style as well. Some cafés overtly associate natural spaces with Switzerland, envisioning the Alps as the ideal clean space of nature in contrast to the pollution characteristic of Lebanon. Framed photos of snow-capped mountains and edelweiss hang on Swiss Time's walls, with the café's name also suggesting Switzerland as the perfect escape from Dahiya. Shaykh Ali referred explicitly to the Alps as a space of idealized purity when he shared his early vision of the Mleeta project with us. At that time, several years before Mleeta opened, he showed us pictures of "Swiss bungalows" that resembled log cabins as inspiration for the design of its hotel area. While all of Beirut is devoid of green space, Dahiya's urban density and the inaccessibility of its short coastline due to illegal settlements make it feel as though it is especially lacking in natural spaces—a feeling that was echoed by many of our interviewees. Some cafés try to respond to that need by creating an urban oasis.

Nature may also represent a longing for paradise, both mundane and divine. As Christopher Houston (2001, 83) points out in his analysis of the emphasis on nature in an Istanbul café, "There is nothing particularly 'Islamic' about this simulacrum of nature." He instead highlights a "global dialectic . . . in which the felt need for *'nature'* as a refuge, a getaway, is understood not as a reaction to the global destruction of a sense of home but as an aspect of its reconstruction" (ibid.). For some pious Shi'i Muslims, reconstructing this relationship to nature takes on connotations of the divine. There is a relationship between a particular sort of environmentalism and contemporary forms of religious ideology in Dahiya. Hizbullah scouts are taught to maintain trails and respect the natural landscape. The party's Resistance museum at Mleeta highlights the relationships of its fighters to the environment (Harb and Deeb 2011). A pious woman might teach her children that God is visible in every tomato. And women's Islamic charitable associations take poor children to rivers in the South to teach them to love what one woman described to Lara in 2001 as "the nature that God gave us."

The relaxed ambiance of the garden is sometimes combined with a large interior dining room with a more decorous ambiance, often referred to by waiters and owners as the "restaurant." We gloss the principal style of these rooms, also reflected in a few smaller cafés, as "formal dining style."

Formal Dining Style

Swiss Time is a large stand-alone café with an exterior garden. Its interior is divided into two sections. The more intimate enclave has walls half paneled in dark wood and a few windows draped in brown curtains that admit dim natural light. Low wicker sofas in beige and brown with bright red cushions encourage lounging. During our visits, mixed-gender couples were frequently sitting closely together in this secluded space, enjoying its privacy. Two large aquariums without any fish sit on wooden cabinets and define the enclave's entrance, preventing direct visual contact with the larger outer hall. The hall is grander in style and design. About fifteen large round and square dark wood tables with heavy marble tops and high-backed carved wooden chairs filled the space. A few of the tables were made of dark gray wicker and seem to have been brought in from the garden area as needed. The overall impression in the hall was sober and formal. The waiter confirmed this as he explained to us, "This is the restaurant area. It is more formal [*rasmi*]. You can hold special events

FIGURE 3.11 Dining room at Swiss Time

['*azayem*] here. We serve nice food. A lot of people hold their events here" (see figure 3.11).

Several cafés include these formal dining halls. While some, like Swiss Time, maintained a simpler style, others, like Aghadir or Fantasy World, included patterned fabrics for furniture and curtains, marble fountains, stone walls, wooden details, and gypsum-textured ceilings as well as fancy chandeliers. Curtains concealed natural light, and indirect lighting created a dim and restrained atmosphere. Objects that one would find in a home— vases of artificial flowers, gold-framed still life or landscape paintings, ceramics, and antiques—evoked an expensive living or dining room (see figure 3.12). The customers we saw in these formal-dining-style halls were mainly older groups of men or couples, and families.

In middle- and upper-class Lebanese households that can afford both, the living room, as opposed to the sitting room or den, is a formal space, designed for entertaining and honoring guests while displaying one's social status and wealth. It is only used on special occasions and otherwise sealed off from the rest of the house. Often, the woman of the house is in charge of the décor. Sofas and wooden chairs in antique styles are upholstered in cream, gold, beige, red, and green fabrics with gold details. Matching curtains are heavy and multilayered. Copper or crystal chandeliers hang from ceilings designed with floral or geometric gypsum motifs. Substantial

FIGURE 3.12 Dining room at Aghadir

gilded frames surround paintings and perhaps Qur'anic verses. Vases, antique objects, and crystal bowls sit on side tables. Paralleling the purpose of these living rooms, formal-dining-style restaurants are places where people invite others out to dinner or host receptions. The décor and ambiance simultaneously convey comfort, formality, and grandeur, providing an alternative space to the home in which one can suitably honor one's guests.

While formal-dining-style spaces are part of south Beirut's leisure boom, they are less common than the heritage and nature styles, and rarely frequented by youths. The next and final style is also less common, although it is growing in popularity in Dahiya, especially in response to the youth market.

Contemporary Style

Coda Café, the only twenty-four-hour café we know of in the area, typifies contemporary style. Coda is coowned by a former Il Ponte employee and return emigrant from Italy. As with Il Ponte, Italian references are present, but in more subdued ways. A wooden coffee bar with dark brown leather stools dominates the entrance. Behind it are displayed bottles of coffee syrups and Italian soda flavorings, looking deceptively like alcohol (see

FIGURE 3.13 Coffee bar at Coda Café

figure 3.13). The café's furnishings include leather sofas as well as dark wood tables and chairs, in a color scheme of browns, tans, and a soft red. The exception is a small raised seating section in the back with orange beaded fringe curtains—an area that one of the owners called "the VIP room." A huge painting on one wall picks up the reds and browns of the décor. It is reminiscent of a Jackson Pollock piece, and may well be a copy of one, as the owner found it at a place that specializes in replicating work by famous artists.

Contemporary café spaces feature furniture in leather, glass, steel, and sometimes plastic. The strong lines and angles are accompanied by bright primary colors, and occasionally zebra and leopard skin patterned prints. The walls are striped or covered in photographs that resemble stylized advertising copy, often incorporating English words (see figure 3.14). These cafés frequently have a coffee bar, spongy couches that are conducive to lounging, and English-only menus. Typically, these places provide free Wi-Fi access along with the standard argileh, coffee, and food items.

There is also variation within the contemporary style. Fiori is a small café on the opposite side of Dahiya, owned by Nayla, the young woman mentioned earlier who loves interior design. Walking into it, we were struck by the intensity of the pink, pistachio, and lavender of its walls and leather chairs.[29] Nayla chose these bright colors in response to the dark

FIGURE 3.14 Bab al-Hara's upstairs area

mood of Beirut politics in May 2008. She insisted that "these colors cannot be in a house. When someone wants to come to a café, he wants to see something different, not like what he has at home. The idea behind these colors is to go beyond the routine."

Despite stylistic difference, people use contemporary spaces in ways similar to the heritage or nature-garden styles. You find people of all ages in all these cafés, though there are proportionately more youths in those featuring the contemporary style. The coffee and food items on offer are also similar, and contemporary style spaces are just as full of argileh smoke as are other café spaces. This can be explained partly by the resurgence of argileh's popularity among youths across the Middle East beginning in the 1990s—a resurgence that paralleled its newfound trendiness in the United States and France.[30]

These contemporary-style interiors explicitly refer to the cafés' inclusion in a transnationally connected world that includes corporate chains, Facebook page listings, and Internet lists of restaurants in local areas including Dahiya. Through this inclusion, south Beirut's contemporary cafés are carving out a new stylistic niche. They are quite different from the "modern French-style cafés" that predominated in Hamra prior to the civil war and continue to inspire businesses across Lebanon. Such French-style cafés tend to be smaller, maintain a stronger interaction with the street, and serve upscale coffees, wines, and food (e.g., Mie Dorée or Paul). They also are perceived to be "intellectual" spaces where regulars may have impromptu discussions, and the walls function as a rotating art gallery or visual display of the place's history. Dahiya's contemporary style more closely resembles the global-corporate coffee shop typified by Starbucks or Gloria Jean's.[31] Global corporate coffee shops usually provide several distinct seating areas, with larger couches, and tend to be more detached from city life outside. They often serve brewed "American" coffee drinks along with Italian coffees in dozens of flavors and varieties as well as pre-made food for a clientele of youths, students, and foreigners. Their interior spaces are generic and do not convey a particular historical narrative. Yet Dahiya's cafés are not nearly as impersonal as this model.

Contemporary-style cafés in Dahiya represent neither the French-style café model nor the global-corporate coffee shop one. Many of them incorporate contemporary style as one element among many, catering intentionally to a variety of customers. Bab al-Hara's ground floor mixes heritage and formal dining styles while its upstairs affords a sleek modernist space. Café.Yet is mostly contemporary, even though there is a small side room upstairs decorated with low couches, village antiques, and fabric draped from the ceiling to simulate a Bedouin tent. At first glance, Terrace seems to feature heritage style, with diwaniyyeh seating in darkly stained wood carved with animal and plant designs against a wall of sandblasted beige stone adorned with false windows framed in the same dark wood, gold-framed paintings featuring Bedouin Arabs in traditional dress, and replicas of ancient mosaics. Yet this same diwaniyyeh area incorporated contemporary elements, like its wooden ceiling beams and red leather seats, and its wicker furniture evokes the garden spaces of other cafés (see figure 3.15). As a whole, south Beirut's new cafés seem to be creating a new genre of coffee shop that mixes an idea of global culture with a specific locality.

ECLECTICISM AS STYLE

Leisure sites in Dahiya often mix and match multiple aspects of these styles, imbuing them with a consistent sense of eclecticism. A pastiche of elements is common within each style as well, such as an Islamic mosaic adjacent to a clay pot used in villages in the Chouf mountains to pound za'tar or zebra-striped chairs near a wall plastered with an image of happy young people skiing. This eclecticism extends to the multiple services that cafés often provide and variety on their menus. At Café.Yet, for example, the English-only menu offers coffees, fresh fruit cocktails, juice drinks including virgin versions of popular alcoholic drinks like daiquiris (one of which claimed to include "rum syrup"), a variety of argileh flavors, and saj

FIGURE 3.15 Dining room at Terrace

sandwiches. Other cafés may have a wider variety of food choices, but the
general focus on coffees, juices, and argileh is consistent. Unlike upscale
coffee shops in Cairo that deliberately restrict their menus to European
and North American possibilities, thereby distinguishing their patrons
from other Egyptians (de Koning 2006), these places do not set themselves
apart via their menus and instead offer several options to their clientele.

This eclecticism is not new to Lebanon, but the ways in which Dahiya's
cafés demonstrate it in their interior spaces may be novel. Lebanon's constitution as a nation is dependent on a deliberate claim to multiple identities — not only in relation to sect, but also in relation to language, ethnicity,
and external point of reference. The Arabic-English-French argot spoken
by many Lebanese, and degree to which it crosses class lines and is a concern for educators, parents, and leftist activists alike, is a case in point.[32]
Ideas about Lebanese national folklore are nothing if not eclectic, bringing
together assumptions about myriad civilizations and eras. The Rahbani
performances discussed above have been replaced at the Baalbek Festival
by the Caracalla folk dance troupe. Meant to represent "Lebanese culture"
and described as such by people from all the country's communities, Caracalla is a dizzying mix of styles, colors, music, clothing and dance steps — a
smorgasbord-like construction of folk culture that is understood to be

Lebanese. There are a few cafés in other parts of the city and country that mix and match ideas as well as objects from various eras and places in their décor. But none do so to the extent of places in south Beirut. An aesthetic of eclecticism is pronounced in this area of the city.

This style also can be seen in some Dahiya homes, where different furniture types mix with decorative objects that—in Aziza's mother's sitting room—include an antique vase, a wooden carved elephant, Dutch china dolls, plastic vases of fake flowers, and silver-framed photos of children and grandchildren. Aziza hates this mixture, calling it 'aj'a ("clutter"), and occasionally tries unsuccessfully to impose a simpler and more streamlined design in the room. In her view, the clutter signifies "Dahiya," which she associates with being of lower status than other parts of Beirut. By distancing herself from this aesthetic style, she is claiming mobility away from her mother's tastes and Dahiya. She avoids south Beirut cafés because she both finds them similarly cluttered and fears she'll run into too many people she knows there. Her mother disagrees with this assessment of her own knick-knacks, and instead views them with pride as a mark of her cosmopolitan and transnational connections. This is also the perspective she has on many of Dahiya's new cafés. We take up these associations of class and status with taste further in chapter 6.

There are number of explanations for the greater prominence of eclecticism in café interiors and offerings in south Beirut than elsewhere in the city. Café culture in Dahiya is newer, and combines an array of ideas encountered in (or imagined about) the city, village, and/or transnational contexts. South Beirut's cafés draw from and add to earlier forms of heritage style found across Lebanon, spaces for formal dining inspired by home interiors, landscaped outdoor spaces evoking nature's tranquility, and new forms of modernist sensibility related to global-corporate coffee chains.[33] By the time these cafés emerged, it was commonplace for middle-class consumption to include objects, styles, ideas, and foods from around the world.[34] Their pastiche is a mark of contemporary globalization. In addition, consumer desires did not find expression in a leisure sector in Dahiya until recently, allowing entrepreneurs to simultaneously work from a blank slate and respond to diverse demands. Eclecticism of style might thus be intentional—a design meant to be inclusive—as when owners deliberately cater to what they perceive to be the needs and desires of different age groups of customers in the same establishment. Customer comments sometimes confirm this idea, as when Hanady, who is almost forty, and appreciates the heritage and garden styles, explained,

> You want to try to improve the place by creating artificial beauty to give people the feeling that they are sitting in a natural place. People like to go to the moun-

tains, to green places. These things are not available here [in Dahiya]. The heritage places also, they recall history, heritage, like al-Saha and Sweet Land.... They use Eastern things, which we enjoy.

When café owners choose to mix the heritage and garden-nature styles, or include these styles that appeal to older customers alongside the contemporary, which is assumed to attract youths, they are hedging their bets. This is both a business decision and a commentary on the diverse uses as well as customers for whom these spaces are designed.

It is important not to underestimate pragmatism in café design and the way that it might lead unintentionally to an eclectic style. Owners often design a café themselves without seeking professional expertise.[35] They act as contractors and devise the interiors with the skilled laborers they have hired, based on their combined ideas about style and technical know-how.[36] Furthermore, an owner may incrementally develop their café, adding to it, redesigning original spaces, and adapting rooms for new functions. In our repeated visits to cafés, we saw many such changes. In the predominantly contemporary-style Café. Yet, a small room was sectioned off from the main space and decorated in heritage style after the owner decided that he wanted to provide customers with an "Eastern ambiance" as well. Fantasy World also undergoes regular "makeovers" to offer something "new" to its clientele, with the latest addition being a large hall catering to formal dining customers, rich with marble and wood. Alterations vary with finances, time, and energy as well as the vagaries of what is available in stores at any given moment. The red-and-black-striped fabric that is ubiquitous on diwaniyyeh couches in many south Beirut cafés, or the wicker chairs and tables in their gardens, may well have been affordable and plentiful when these spaces were designed.

In the end, eclecticism should be understood as reflecting the diversity of experience in Dahiya. This includes the broad range of transnational networks that Shiʿi Lebanese have forged over the past decades—networks that include both the United States and Iran in ways that belie simplistic understandings of the community vis-à-vis an interconnected world as well as other Arab countries, Europe, Australia, and West Africa. Eclecticism suggests an aesthetic shaped by the multiple experiences and transnational and historical references of Dahiya's residents, including class mobility, return emigration, loss of home villages, and identification with ideas about being Lebanese, Arab, and Muslim as well as citizens of an increasingly globalized world. At the same time, there remain reminders that one is in Dahiya. In addition to the area's specific manifestation of eclecticism, all the cafés we visited had donation boxes for local charitable associations, including the blue-and-yellow ones of al-Emdad, Hizbullah's social welfare organization. These are usually found along with other decorative

FIGURE 3.16 Photoshopped images of Italian monuments on Il Ponte's wall

objects on a low table at the entrance or near the cash register. We only saw a framed photo of Nasrallah in one of the cafés we visited, sitting next to a copper coffee pot and Qur'an.

South Beirut's eclecticism was perhaps best epitomized in Il Ponte (see figures 3.16, 3.17, and 3.18). One of the first cafés to open in the area, Il Ponte sits at a busy intersection in what is referred to as "the inside" of Dahiya. The cover of its English-only menu boasts an embossed stylized image of a mixed-gender couple sitting face-to-face over coffee. Below the image, the name of the café reads "Il Ponte Italian coffee shop." Professionally designed, the interior space provides a few tables and chairs on the ground floor along with a larger area one flight up. The wooden coffee bar is prominently placed facing the entrance and displays flavored syrup bottles on the back wall, alongside an Italian flag and a hat in Italian colors. The wall to the left is decorated with a large-scale Photoshopped poster of four Vincent van Gogh paintings, reflected by a rectangular mirror on the opposite wall, above which sits a wood-framed Qur'anic verse. On the way to the stairs, you pass a refrigerator displaying fresh fruits and ice cream, a second "Pepsi" refrigerator filled with soft drinks, a crepe-making area, and a large popcorn maker. The landing wall is a mural of a tranquil town overlooking a river and green hills, painted in soft pastel colors by a local

FIGURE 3.17 Mural of a town, next to argileh storage in Il Ponte café

artist. Arriving upstairs, you see dozens of argileh on the floor. The upstairs space is bordered by glass windows and offers several seating areas.
Some are low couches, in red-and-blue leather, arranged around low glass
tables. Others are metallic chairs surrounding small dining tables on which
sailing symbols, like a ship's helm, are printed. The wall is covered with
large images of famous Italian monuments, Photoshopped to include their
names in bold letters. Several black wrought iron balustrades, and green-
and-red wooden window shutters covered with a red-tiled small canopy—
another symbol of Lebanese architecture—hang on the same wall. Tiny

FIGURE 3.18 Lebanese heritage-style features, hung on the wall near contemporary faux-leather sofas in Il Ponte café

black-and-white photos of Italian monuments are scattered around the room.

In its juxtaposition of heritage, nature-garden, and contemporary styles in close proximity in a small space, Il Ponte produces a heightened sense of eclecticism. It also casually mixes a range of transnational references with local ones, emphasizing how normal this multiplicity is in Lebanon and Dahiya. Van Gogh and Italian history easily and "naturally" coexist with Lebanese architectural symbols and religious iconography, while Italian coffee and pizza are served with fresh fruit cocktails and argileh. Perhaps the mural of the picturesque European town on a river most eloquently conveys the ordinariness of this global-local convergence for café culture in Dahiya through its display of an idealized, imagined Western semiurban landscape—a display that quietly inverts Orientalist imaginings of a rural Eastern fantasy.

When people, including Aziza, associate this stylistic hodgepodge with Dahiya, they are not referring only to aesthetics, décor, and architectural design. The Jeita Country Club, which caters to wealthy Christian Lebanese, bears a striking resemblance to Swiss Time, a Dahiya restaurant, but is not depicted by most people in the same terms. These assessments reflect assumptions about Dahiya's residents, and have as much to do with ideas about where the cafés are, who hangs out in them, and how they hang out as they do with their actual appearance. The next chapters take up these threads, beginning with notions about morality in south Beirut's leisure scene.

4

FLEXIBLE MORALITY, RESPECTFUL CHOICES,
SMALLER TRANSGRESSIONS

———————————

It is good to look and then select, everything is available
and clear, all we need to do is select. When you go to a store,
you select what is good/appropriate for you [*illi binasbik*].

—RABI', AGE TWENTY-EIGHT

Rabi' is not talking about shopping for clothing or a new stereo system. He is describing how he relates to the manifold options available to him when he goes out. The combination of new cafés in Dahiya and new desires for leisure that may take people beyond its borders have prompted greater public negotiation of moral norms for common café activities. Decisions have to be made about where one wants to hang out or be seen—decisions that often have to do with perceptions about a café's reputation and respectability. Those perceptions, in turn, rest on a set of criteria that includes the presence or absence of alcohol, type of music played, and appearance and behavior of the customers. Also important to these calculations are the café's location in the city and ideas about security, politics, and social space—ideas that we take up in depth in the next chapter. Pragmatic concerns like transportation and expense also factor in, as do the time of year, with whom one is hanging out on a particular evening, and the vagaries of mood.[1]

Cafés are places where people are essentially forced to take a stance on the morality of specific activities, not only by choosing whether to partake, but also by passively accepting others' participation in their presence. Because many of the moral "rules" about the sorts of things one can do in a café—like listen to music or smoke argileh—are not clear-cut, cafés require people to navigate complex moral terrain in order to have fun while feeling good about themselves. In this chapter, we take up a number of these debatable activities in order to show how more or less pious Shi'i Muslims, especially youths, employ moral flexibility in their discourses and practices of leisure. In some cases, people negotiate among different rubrics of morality, while in others they choose to ignore particular tenets or disagree about the accuracy of a rule in the first place. We begin with the presence of songs and alcohol in cafés, which leads us to consider situations of compromise where people must strike balances between what they perceive as religious rules versus social obligations. We then turn to youths' ideas about individual choice in morality, adding an analysis of how those ideas are gendered. This leads to a discussion of another major criterion by which cafés are judged: the behavior of the customers. Ideas about appropriate social interaction are infused with a discourse of "respect" for oneself, others, and the environment, and are focused mainly on comportment between the sexes. The chapter concludes by considering flirtation, and how our interlocutors perceive the possibilities for picking people up in cafés as well as their experiences doing so.

SINFUL CAFÉ OFFERINGS

> I do listen to songs. I don't consider myself 100 percent [religiously] committed, but you know, normal. Since I was young I have prayed, fasted, gone on ʿumra. But I do have some things that are red lines that I don't cross, you know, great sins [kabaʾir, or singular, kabira] that we don't do. Like alcohol, for example. I would never go to a place where there is alcohol, and I would never drink.
>
> —AMER, AGE TWENTY-THREE

MUSIC AND SONGS

Music is not officially regulated in Lebanon (as it is in Iran, for example), and youths' ideas about the acceptability of certain forms of music and singing vary widely. Most people in the vanguard generation, jurisprudents, and Hizbullah deem haram (prohibited) any music conducive to dancing, or that "excites the sexual instincts."[2] And most pious young people understand this to be the dominant view.[3] Beyond this limit, however, there is a great deal of variation and variability in the perspectives of moral authorities. Interpretations about music's permissibility have fluctuated throughout the history of Islamic jurisprudence. There are hierarchies of music and song ranked according to acceptability by jurisprudents, with hadith that support differing views about the details of the hierarchy. Many religious scholars place as much importance, if not more, on the context and accompanying behaviors as on the music itself. For example, eleventh-century scholar Imam al-Ghazali stressed both context and the effects of music on one's life and behavior. Popular contemporary Egyptian Shaykh Yusef Qaradawi similarly underscores context and associated behavior. This means that how restrictive an opinion is depends on that person's understanding of appropriate behavior rather than on judgments about music itself.[4]

Sayyid Ja'far reminded us that in the 1970s and 1980s, the vanguard considered music completely prohibited.

> I remember one of the Islamic radio stations, for example, at the beginning of any program, they started with the name of the station and then silence, silence! And then the greeting and name of the program, and they would begin. This is how it was in the past. Now, no. There are new opinions about music.

Quite typically, Fadlallah's opinions are the least restrictive, and his juristic office receives scores of questions about music and songs. Since at least 2000, his view has been:

> It is fine to play all musical compositions that do not excite the sexual instincts, with any available musical instruments, and it is also acceptable to teach and to learn how to play any instrument and to listen to them, and also to buy, sell and acquire them.[5]

Sistani takes a more conservative route, adding to the basic prohibition on music that excites the sexual instincts any music played for groups that are engaged in amusement or play (al-lahu wa al-la'b) (Moh'd al-Hakim 2004, 325).[6] Khamenei seems to be the most restrictive, having recently stated, "Although music is halal (permissible), promoting and teaching it is not compatible with the highest values of the sacred regime of the Islamic Republic" (quoted in Dehghan 2010). This view appears to have less to do with religious interpretation than with the Iranian regime's political project as well as efforts to channel Iranian youths toward socially and economically "productive" activities. Similarly, in the "Fatawa al-Qa'id" section of the August 2002 issue of *Baqiyat Allah*, Khamenei stated that any music that takes a human being into a state of euphoria is haram, and that one should only listen to cassette tapes registered and approved by the Islamic Council. This response demonstrates how out of touch he is with his followers in Lebanon, since they are unlikely either to check with the Islamic Council in Iran (to which he is presumably referring) or, in 2002, listen to cassette tapes.

Despite Khamenei's opinions and role as the formal marja' for Hizbul-lah, the party has broadened its musical horizons over time.[7] Party-related anthems (*anashid*) have existed since the mid-1980s, but they did not begin to include string instruments until the early 1990s (Atrissi 2008). After 2000, Hizbullah began to deliberately cultivate musicians and use "West-ern" instruments, including electric guitars and drums. The LAA's all-male Sun of Freedom Orchestra has been performing live in free concerts since 2008.[8] Shaykh Ali suggested to us that the idea that all Western musical instruments are haram is an inaccurate assumption. Instead, he explained, what matters is the context, so that instruments used in *lahu* (frivolous amusement) are forbidden, as is music that "mimics" the music associated with lahu. Yet he continued, "When you are performing a good national poem, or a poem about the mother or father, even if you use the same in-struments that known [lahu] singers use, because this is for a good purpose, the issue of religious prohibition can be removed."

Here Shaykh Ali highlighted both the role of individual interpretation and importance of context in determining the acceptability of music and songs. He also noted Hizbullah's inability to control music even when popular singers (male and female) sing Nasrallah's speeches to danceable melodies (a genre that rose in popularity after the 2006 war): "We tell them what we think, and it is their business. If they sell them, we cannot say no, we cannot force them."[9] He explained that any desires to censor music are complicated by the variation in fatwas along with the fact that "some ju-risprudents argue that there are no haram or halal songs. They say, 'people can judge.'"

Fadlallah is one of these jurisprudents. He emphasizes that the content of lyrics matters. As Sayyid Ja'far put it, "If the content is sound/correct, then it is halal, but if the content is wrong, then it is haram." In keeping with Fadlallah's insistence on the capacity and responsibility of the indi-vidual, he suggests that listeners pay attention to their responses to a song and judge it accordingly, avoiding those that affect them in a forbidden way (i.e., turn them on). Even in love songs—where Fadlallah draws a line be-tween permissible songs that inspire *shawq* (longing or desire) and forbid-den ones that fuel *ghara'iz* (sexual instincts)—it is left to the listener to determine which sort of response they are experiencing. This differs sig-nificantly from Khamenei's view, which is linked to the Iranian state's of-ficial censorship, and that of Sistani, who takes the cautious path of neces-sary avoidance and rules all songs haram, with the exception of those in wedding processions (*zaffeh*).[10]

Given this variation in official opinion, it is no surprise that pious Mus-lims, especially youths, hold a wide variety of views on music and songs.[11] Until recently, musical choices were a private matter, affecting practices at home, in the car, or through an MP3 player. With new options for leisure, music has become a public issue as well as a key criterion by which people judge social spaces and publicly negotiate their own morality. In the past, taxis were the most common spaces where someone might encounter songs they believed to be immoral. We heard stories, especially from people over age thirty, about asking drivers to change the radio station or lower the volume, and complaints about those who refused to do so. Youths were less likely to make such requests, expressing a reluctance to impose their personal moral tenets on others. In Nada's words, "You can't make him turn down the music; he is free in his car."

Of the fifty-five young people with whom we conducted formal interviews, 29 percent said that they don't listen to songs and avoid cafés that play them. For three of these people, this was a new restriction, part of their efforts to "develop" their piety—in one case through a major lifestyle change that included ceasing to dance at weddings and "wear shorts in the street." Eighteen percent said that they don't listen to songs on their own but would go to cafés that play them, explaining that they could direct their attention away from the songs or sit in a quieter part of the café. Another 31 percent said that they listen to songs both on their own and in cafés. The remaining youths were divided among those who preferred to avoid songs but wouldn't leave a café if unacceptable music began after they had sat down (6 percent), those who determined acceptability based on the lyrics (7 percent), those who felt that the music's volume mattered (6 percent), and a few young women who listened to songs in secret and expressed feeling guilty for doing so (3 percent).

It was more common for young men to listen to songs only in cafés than young women, while the latter were more likely to enjoy songs both publicly and privately, and were also the rare interlocutors who admitted to listening privately in secret. Whether women in fact were the only ones to listen surreptitiously or men were less likely to admit to clandestine behavior, this begins to suggest gender differences in how behavior is judged by others or in concerns about those potential judgments. The greater congruence between women's public and private behavior (i.e., more women who listen publicly also listen privately) indicates two additional gender differences. First, women may be more flexible about moral evaluations of songs, and second, women who believe songs are haram may take greater care than men to avoid being seen in places that play them.

Young people who listen to songs both privately and publicly are divided between those who think this is a morally acceptable practice and others who view it as a minor transgression. Amer—the young engineering student whose quote is the epigraph to this section—falls into the latter category. He listens to songs and thinks this is a minor infraction as compared to drinking alcohol.[12] Riyad, on the other hand, used to listen to Lebanese pop singer Wael Kfouri on the telephone with his "pious and very [religiously] committed" fiancée, and neither felt that this was wrong. Listening to songs exemplifies both aspects of moral flexibility that we outlined in the introduction: flexible practice within clear-cut rules, and the flexibility of the rules themselves. There can be a great deal of flexibility as to whether or not it is even immoral to listen to songs as well as flexibility over how well one abides by that prescription if one believes it to exist. Such flexibility may emerge between people or within the same individual.

Pious Muslims frequently echoed Fadlallah's criteria for assessing a song's content. Again and again, we heard about the importance of the degree and quality of response to a song as the criterion by which it should be judged. Concerns about a song's influence on a person can be understood in relation to the role aural media plays in creating sensory knowledge, and cultivating particular dispositions or inclinations in the listener.[13] From this perspective, listening to songs is a fraught activity because listening actively to blasphemy may move a person further away from God.

Some people had set personal measures for assessing songs' effects, like Mahmoud, who revealed, "I don't listen to women's voices [singing] because it influences me." Others, especially youths, evaluated content and disagreed among themselves as to the acceptability of specific examples. Some limited "good content" to songs with nationalist themes, including some Fairuz songs along with party anthems and folk tunes, while others extended acceptability to "classics" like Umm Kulthum's "Laylit Hubb" or the entire Fairuz repertoire, including her love songs.[14] Young men sometimes validated their avoidance of certain genres by critiquing their "quality" and poking fun at what they described as "silly" lyrics. Hussein, a student in his early twenties, explained, "The reason I don't like music is not religious, it is because I feel the words are meaningless and trivial [*bala ta'mi*, literally, "without a taste," and *tafiha*]." He shifted into a mocking falsetto, "I love you, you love me," then paused and continued, "I like Fairuz because the words are rich with meaning." Hadi, a young businessman, shared this perspective. He enjoys Na'eem al-Sheikh's songs with lyrics about bad luck and social issues, "with words like 'I am going to the sea to complain about my misery's secrets.' . . . But to listen to a love song, like 'I cannot sleep, and I sing to her from under the window' [also said in a mocking tone], absolutely not." Many of Na'eem al-Sheikh's songs address religious and national themes, with lyrics that are broadly acceptable to a pious audience (including a song titled "*Araq*, I Don't Drink *Araq*").[15] Yet his lyrics are generally set to rapid rhythms, some based on Lebanese dabkeh beats and others closer to contemporary Arabic dance music— commonly referred to as "tistik tistik" or "tistik dam dam" rhythms. His music is definitely danceable, and informal YouTube videos of his performances include made-up young women in tight sleeveless minidresses dancing alongside men—behavior that Hadi, along with most of our pious Shiʿi interlocutors, would find immoral.

This and other apparent contradictions—like some young people's extension of permissibility to all songs including those of seductive Lebanese pop star Haifa Wehbe—were often resolved with the argument that a person can avoid an immoral response through mental concentration. While the idea that one should assess the potential effects of a song is clearly related to Fadlallah's views, the suggestion that it is possible to control those responses is an innovation added by youths. Lara's earlier encounters with the idea that people can control their responses conformed more closely to Fadlallah's position. For example, in 2002 a vanguard generation woman with whom she was sharing a taxi tried in vain to convince the driver to turn off the Arabic pop music emanating loudly from the radio. The woman then pulled a notebook out of her purse and began writing in it attentively. When Lara interrupted her to ask her what she was doing, she explained that she was making a to-do list in an effort to tune out the music. More recently, Rana and Rima, both Red Cross volunteers in their early thirties, spent part of an interview in 2008 discussing the difficulties they had with taxi drivers who refused to turn off the radio, with Rana sharing her "strategy" of writing poetry to "distract" herself from the lyrics in those situations. In all these cases, the women would have preferred to avoid the songs and exerted effort toward shifting their responses only when they found that they had no other choice.

Youths, on the other hand, express greater confidence in their abilities to listen to music "morally," "shut out" inappropriate music, or control its effects on them. Zayna, a twenty-three-year-old American University of Beirut student, observed, "I am *muhajjaba* (a woman who wears the Islamic headscarf), but I have no problem listening to music. It's not a big deal. I consider music to be a form of stress relief for me, so I have no problem going to a café that plays music." For Zayna, music's effects are positive, related to stress reduction rather than to the potential for immoral feelings. Batoul related that her university's cafeteria played pop songs and that exposure to them wouldn't necessarily influence her negatively, exclaiming, "I don't have to sing along!" Yusef articulated a similar sentiment as he told a story about how he had recently prayed in a song-filled café.

> A while ago, we were in a place that has songs. For me it's normal. I don't pay attention to it. There was a guy with us who asked me, "How can you pray when there are songs?" I told him, "Believe me, I don't pay any attention to it." He asked me again, "How did you just go and pray here?" I replied, "I didn't pay attention to it. I can pray; this is a religious duty, I have to pray. The songs

are on, but I am not paying attention." At any moment, a person can ignore
something, just like I can avoid looking around me; my mind was busy with
something else.

About half the pious youths with whom we spoke shared Yusef's idea
that an individual can control their response to songs. Yusef's story also
points to the commensurability of spaces allotted for prayer with pop
music in cafés. Like their young customers, the managers and owners of
cafés in Dahiya interpret the acceptability of music flexibly, usually making
decisions about what kind of music to play based on assumptions about
what will attract the most business. For the most part, this means that cafés
play music without lyrics (often Fairuz melodies, 'oud, or classical European or Arabic music), reflecting their managers' or owners' assumptions
about the majority of their patrons. This is especially true of cafés located
in the heart of Dahiya. The main exception is Café. Yet, one of the first cafés
in the area to cater specifically to youths. On weekend evenings at Café.
Yet, instrumental arrangements of Fairuz melodies give way to various
Buddha Bar mixes.

Cafés located at Dahiya's edges often deliberately target a more diverse
clientele in terms of both levels of piety and sectarian group. For example,
at Fiori, a café situated between Dahiya and the Christian-majority neighborhood of Sainte-Thérèse, the owner explained that she turns on MTV if
the current patrons appear to her like they would enjoy it, but that she
would then change the channel if customers who look more "religious"
entered. During our visits, the televisions were frequently set to Melody (a
music video channel) with the volume turned up. Fiori also plays loud Arabic pop music for private parties held upstairs in an open loft area, allowing
the songs to drift audibly throughout the café. Coda Café, located along
the airport highway at Dahiya's other edge, hosts singers and bands on
weekend nights, and plays American and British pop music.

Given the diversity of entertainment environments within and beyond
Dahiya, choosing where to go out often involves taking morality into account. Sometimes this requires assessing and/or violating the religious rubric, and sometimes it involves managing competing and conflicting moral
possibilities. Before turning to some of these moral negotiations, we discuss a second common criterion used to evaluate the morality of cafés: the
presence of alcohol.

ALCOHOL

As Amer noted above, drinking alcohol is viewed by many as a significant
infraction, although most jurists do not refer to it as *kabira*, as Amer did,
instead reserving that category for acts like murder or usury. Nevertheless,

the prohibition on drinking alcohol is one of the most unambiguous rules within the religious rubric of morality for pious Muslims, and is a norm that serves to distinguish the pious from the nonpious as well as Muslims from Christians in Lebanon. There is no disagreement on this prohibition in the Lebanese Shi'i community, despite room for interpretation of the various Qur'anic verses on the topic.[16] This is a moral rule that is essentially taken for granted, and those who violate it do so with the knowledge and belief that they are engaging in sinful behavior.

As we saw in chapter 2, Hizbullah claims to uphold the no alcohol rule for its members and community. The party does not tolerate alcohol consumption among its members or close supporters, and social pressure is exerted to prevent drinking. In one case, the wife and daughter of a man who occasionally drank whiskey in his home pressured him heavily to stop because one of his in-laws was a prominent party member. In addition to pouring all his whiskey down the drain and haranguing him about it constantly, they made the forceful (and eventually convincing) argument that if anyone knew that someone in the politician's family drank, his reputation and career would be ruined.

Given this environment and the absolute prohibition on alcohol by all jurisprudents, consuming alcohol was the most significant "red line" (khat ahmar) for more or less pious youths. With rare exceptions—a few people we have known for years, and one café owner who used to be a bartender— none of the self-identified practicing or more or less pious Muslims we spoke with admitted to drinking (although of course this does not mean that none of them drink). Even the exceptions were telling, as in one case when a pious friend took a sip of one of our glasses of wine and immediately experienced a reaction that resembled a panic attack.

Nonetheless, for many youths, the question of what sort of relationship a nondrinker can have to a place where alcohol is being consumed and/or sold remained a much more flexible matter.[17] In other words, will you buy things from places that sell alcohol or sit with friends in a place that serves it? Only 13 percent of our young interlocutors refused to purchase anything from a place that sells alcohol. This is relatively low compared to our experience with vanguard generation people who tend to inquire about the separation of cash registers if alcohol is present in a store. This generational difference suggests that youths are less worried about permissible financial transactions than they are about being in the presence of others' sinful behavior.

Approximately half our young interlocutors stated that they would categorically refuse to enter a place with alcohol and leave if they discovered it after entering, and the other half said that they would go but simply not drink themselves. Of the latter group, several young people differentiated between cafés that serve beer and "bars with whiskey," and several explained that they would ask their friends not to drink, highlighting the visibility and proximity of alcohol and drunkenness as factors in their decisions. It is also important to note that people who firmly stated that they would not enter places that serve alcohol often told stories later in our interviews about times when they had in fact hung out in pubs and cafés that serve it. The higher moral stakes of alcohol consumption led to greater incongruities between people's initial statements about their behavior and their stories about "exceptional" situations. Obviously, in order to have any relationship whatsoever to a café that serves alcohol, one has to leave Dahiya, and we discuss that "border crossing" in greater depth in the following chapter. Here we look more closely at the kinds of situations that may prompt such border crossing in the first place.

CONFLICT AND COMPROMISE

The best thing is to know how to deal with the people you are sitting with. I know each group, and I deal with them as they are. Sometimes I have friends come over who are [religiously] committed and don't listen to music. If a song comes on television, I switch [channels]. If we are watching a film and a song comes on, I put it on mute. And I have friends who listen to songs. When they come to my house and a song starts I let it play. You have to know how to deal with people.

— AMER

MANAGING FRIENDS AND FAMILY

"I had no choice." This was one of the most common phrases we heard when people told stories about times when they had deliberately violated a religious rule. These moral compromises most frequently transpired when the prohibition of alcohol came into direct conflict with the social rubric of morality, and specifically with morals based on valuing good social relations. While most people believed that maintaining good social relations was a crucial aspect of living a moral life, youths tended to prioritize this value. This was the premise underlying flexible approaches to being around alcohol. As long as one did not drink, there was room to disagree about the consequences of being near others' sinful behavior. Some young people also reminded one another in our group interviews that treating others well is itself a value taught by Islam and not "merely" a social norm. These reminders drew attention to the common separation between values understood as religious versus social within this community, while also acknowledging the dominant emphasis on prioritizing the religious rubric for moral behavior, as taught by the vanguard and jurisprudents.

Members of the vanguard generation were far less likely to concede religious precepts for social norms or economic interests. They were also less inclined to view social obligations as critical components of their conceptions of themselves as good people and generally privileged the religious rubric as the primary moral standard in their lives. Examples from our research include a television cameraperson who consistently refused to film news clips in locations where songs or alcohol were present despite complaints from colleagues, and several bank employees who absolutely refused to attend workplace social events where there was alcohol despite the negative consequences for their career advancement. As Amani, a bank employee in her early forties, put it, "There are red lines that are impossible to cross."

This generational difference in the willingness to cross red lines in compromise surfaced in an interview that included two friends and colleagues who work together in media: Rabiʿ, who is in his late twenties, and Mahmoud, almost ten years older. We asked them whether they would go to places that serve alcohol with their friends. Rabiʿ began, "In principle no. . . . But frankly, it has happened with me. Once we were invited out and there were Christians there, and they wanted to drink."

"What did you do?" we asked.

"I generally try to avoid going with them to cafés and restaurants," Rabiʿ replied,

> so that I don't embarrass them [*ahrujhum*] and they don't embarrass me [*yihrijuni*]. That time, I waited a short while and then left quietly, and it wasn't noticed. I didn't hurt anyone's feelings. There was another time we were invited to a birthday party and the plan was to have it at their home. We accepted, and later they changed the place to a nightclub. The idea here is clear; it was too much to accept. Of course, you can say no with your pride and without worrying about it [laughing]. It doesn't need much thought.

Mahmoud chimed in, "On this point, I don't want to go to a place and be embarrassed [*inhirij*]. If I am sitting at a table, and someone ordered alcohol and wants to drink, I'll leave."

"You don't do what Rabiʿ did?"

"No, I'll leave immediately."

"Even if it upsets the people with you?"

"*Yistiflu*! ["Let them do what they want!" or "Tough, they can deal!"]. Just as he has the freedom to drink alcohol, I have the freedom to leave— even if this is a relative of mine," Mahmoud exclaimed, continuing,

My uncle [father's brother], for example, drinks alcohol. We were at my sister's wedding, and he wanted to trick us, to hide it; he mixed it with Pepsi. I heard that my uncle did this, and I went to him, [and said,] "If you please" [*iza bitrid*]. Of course, he may have thought that I wasn't respectful enough to him, but I explained to him, "This is cheating, and this is a wedding, and we don't want to have sins here." So if I were with someone [drinking], I would leave.... I am not going to stay at the same table. I want to show him that he should respect me and respect my presence. OK, he drinks, but respect me! How should I respect him when he doesn't respect me?

While both Rabiʿ and Mahmoud avoid being around alcohol, there is a striking difference in their attitudes and approaches to situations where friends or family members are drinking. Rabiʿ is worried about not hurting his friends' feelings and does what he can to maintain good relationships with them, although going to a nightclub is plainly beyond his limits. Mahmoud, on the other hand, privileges his religious values over his social relationships. He goes so far as to explicitly correct the behavior of his father's brother, who according to social norms is due his respect. Respect is in fact a key idiom in Mahmoud's response, as he prioritizes a claim for respect for his religious values over respect for social values supporting patriarchal age hierarchies.

Also telling is their different uses of conjugations of the Arabic root *haraja* to connote embarrassment. This is the term that most often accompanies explanations for both why people prefer to avoid alcohol and why it is difficult to do so. Its range of meaning includes concerns about jeopardizing a person's position, offending or being offended, and saving face. Rabiʿ uses the term reciprocally, indicating his desire to avoid awkward situations where the moral contrast between he and his friends will be highlighted—situations where both parties may feel uncomfortable with his refusal to imbibe. A number of social norms are at work here, including ideals about hospitality, reciprocity, and sharing food and drink. Underlying these ideals lurk an awareness of the prohibition of alcohol along with assumptions about possible judgments where one or the other may "lose face." If Rabiʿ emphasizes his belief that drinking is immoral, what would that say about his opinions of his friends? For their part, they may feel that his refusal to drink with them indicates a lack of social graces and reflects negatively on their skills as hosts. The situation is further complicated by the facts that these friends are Christian, and thereby do not share Rabiʿ's religious rubric for morality, and that they are all Lebanese, living in a society with a history of intersectarian coexistence. Rabiʿ's general evasion of these situations and his reciprocal use of haraja illustrate the value he places on social relationships as well as the efforts he exerts to avoid damaging them. Mahmoud, in contrast, uses the term unidirectionally, to denote his own experience of potential embarrassment or loss of face in a situation where he would be exposed to others' drinking. The tone of their responses also conveyed this difference, with Rabi' sounding almost apologetic, and Mahmoud expressing annoyance at the lack of respect he perceived for his position. This is captured in his exclamation yistiflu!—an expression that implies distancing, whether through dismissal of or frustration with another's view.

This discrepancy was typical of our conversations, as most youths expressed much greater concern for social norms and relationships than did people in their thirties and above. Life stage provides a partial explanation. There is a greater probability that older individuals will have already established enduring groups of similarly pious friends, be engaged or married with children, and have bigger job worries and less free time. Age may also bring with it social confidence or a honed ability to traverse complex social terrain. At the same time, some of this generational difference has to do with youths' greater flexibility toward the religious rubric for morality. One might expect this flexibility of older individuals, as they are more likely to suffer economic consequences for moral intransigence because their jobs bring about many of the situations where they may encounter problematic behavior. Because of the social distances between areas of Beirut, college students from Dahiya, especially those who attended Islamic high schools, may find themselves spending significant time with people who have very different beliefs for the first time in their lives. They often make friends at university who are surprised to learn about their lifestyles. While moral inflexibility may have social consequences for students, and some young people shared stories about losing friendships due to their adherence to religious principles, they are unlikely to have economic effects.[18]

For example, Ali explained, "Sometimes my Christian friends ask me to go out and have a beer."

"What do you tell them?" we asked.

"I say I have to study. Or they ask me out to a nightclub, [and] I tell them I can't, I'm busy. I don't show them that I don't want to hang out, but I get away in a different way."

Muhammad interjected, "But that's wrong, you're lying to them."

"No, it's not, because I'm not saying that I'm better. It's haram to say I'm better than him or he is worse than me."

Muhammad and Ali's disagreement hinges on whether it is better to lie in order to politely escape a problematic invitation, or be direct and tell one's friends that they are wrong to go to such places. Ali thinks that the polite way out is the more moral one, because to be direct would be to suggest that you are better than other people, which is also wrong. Muhammad's view instead reflects the moral duty one has to be both honest with others and share your values with them. For a few young men with whom we spoke, sharing values in this way was linked to a project of social reform, though for most it was simply about educating one's friends about personal moral boundaries in order to prevent awkward social situations in the future. And Muhammad himself often compromises on his moral principles in order to have fun, demonstrating the malleability of a single individual's responses to the presence of transgressive behavior. For instance, on a trip to a ski resort in Faraya, he and his friends intentionally went to a restaurant with a live singer. As he described it, "And the singer started with the blasphemy [*kufur*], and we sat down like everything is normal, you know it happens, people dance, eat, drink, smoke, it's not like I can change their ways, that's their lifestyle. I can't change it."

The frequency of multisectarian social and work contexts is a hallmark of Lebanon's pluralism, and points to the long-standing enmeshment of sectarian groups as well as regular interactions among people with varying ideas about morality.[19] Crucially, many of the values in the social rubric—including the importance of maintaining good social relationships, hierarchies of respect, and reciprocity—are shared across Lebanese communities and generations. Among pious Shi'i Muslims, the generational difference manifested in terms of how people *prioritized* religious versus social moral rubrics when they came into conflict, and which values they chose to violate. While youths were more likely to hang out in places that facilitate haram activities "out of respect for my friends," they also had a variety of strategies for dealing with friends and family members who drink. These included going along with the crowd, trying a place once to see what it was like, indirectly swaying a decision about where to hang out by complaining about other aspects of a place like noise or ambiance, directly explaining beliefs to friends, sitting at a table without alcohol on it while others drank nearby, leaving a place immediately, and refusing an invitation from the outset. Even those who underscored their avoidance of alcohol often shared "one time when it happened," at a party or with a group of friends from out of town. As our conversations continued, those stories usually multiplied, presenting patterns of compromise that their authors didn't necessarily articulate.

For some youths, compromise depended on either the extent to which a social event was viewed as an obligation or the distance that the other person had traveled. "It is different when it is an issue of politeness, if my friend has come from Khiam [a village in the South] to see me, it is different. Then I stay," explained Hadi, who said that under other circumstances, he wouldn't spend time around either alcohol or songs. The significance of distance is also revealed by how frequently people compromise when friends or family visit from outside Lebanon. Long histories of Lebanese emigration to North and South America, Europe, Australia, and West Africa as well as temporary labor migration to the Arab Gulf states ensure that most young Lebanese find themselves in this situation on a regular basis. Those living "outside" [*mughtaribin*] often visit during summers, and those living "at home" are expected (and expect themselves) to "host" them by being available to hang out plus share their knowledge of the newest cafés and restaurants, including those that serve alcohol. Amer, for example, who said that he would "never" hang out in the vicinity of alcohol, also told us that when expat friends visited he intentionally took them to places that serve it. He explained that these friends might not enjoy places in Dahiya and continued, "Sometimes people visit for five days. You need to show them more than one place. You cannot take them just to Dahiya. They'll get bored."[20]

Another common compromise-provoking situation was the "good-bye party" marking the departure of a friend or family member to their country of residence or work. Jihad and his fiancée Zayna, both American University of Beirut students, told us about one such evening. Zayna began, "One time we went, they wanted to watch a football match."

"It was the European Cup," Jihad interjected, as Zayna continued, "We went with his brothers, to a place, a café. He told us it would be outdoors. But when we got there, there was beer on the other tables."

"The environment was not appropriate," Jihad picked up the story, "like, loud songs, and they serve drinks. My brother was leaving the next day [for Dubai]. What I'm saying is that I try not to go to such places, but because they were all there, I gave up and went. It happens, but not every day."

Zayna explained, "I was very upset at the time. But his brother was leaving, and I said, 'It's OK, I didn't know there would be drinks.' I said to Jihad, 'Let's not return here,' and we agreed not to go back. Whatever happens, we will not go back there."

"For the football, the atmosphere was nice," Jihad concluded, "but the drinking and alcohol weren't, but *yallah*, we let it go."

Of course not all young people are flexible, and it is possible that those who were willing to speak with us leaned toward more malleable moral positions. With the exception of one group interview in which three young men held unusually conservative convictions and even tried to convert our research assistant, our interlocutors were critical of peers they perceived as extremists. Amer, whose friends quite typically include non-Muslims, nonpious people, and pious Muslims who are stricter than he is about their behavior, complained,

My friends at university, they know that I listen to music. If there is a place with songs I go, I don't mind it, and they are still my friends, though if I ask them to go with me they won't. But there are some [religiously] committed people, if they approach you and notice that you are listening to songs or your cell phone plays music, they look at you like you are disgusting or wrong; they run from you. Either you are like them or not.

Our group interviews were also sometimes forums for vociferous disagreement. Ahmad, Qasim, and Rami, friends in their early twenties who met in their university engineering classes, had an argument during which their constant interruptions of one another make it difficult to discern their exact statements on the recording. Rami consistently took the stance that "merely by going to that kind of place, you are doing haram," Ahmad was more moderate and allowed that social obligations could lead a person to hang out in places with songs, while Qasim extended this view to include socializing in general, saying that one can "walk along a path of piety" and still be around minor infractions in order to hang out with friends or maintain relationships. Qasim also insisted, over Rami's vocal protests and attempts to interject Qur'anic verses, that one can easily hang out in a place with loud pop music without having an immoral response by controlling one's mental focus. As Amer noted above, these variations in ideas about morality sometimes lead to social exclusion, reminding us that some people within the Islamic milieu—more commonly but not exclusively in the vanguard generation—uphold social hierarchies in which people are distinguished by their perceived levels of piety.

There may also be gender differences in flexibility, especially in relation to moral choices that are publicly visible, like one's choice of café. For instance, while both Jihad and Zayna preferred to avoid alcohol, Zayna was more adamant than Jihad about this restriction. In the same interview, Mariam took an even stronger position, saying that she always refused to enter places with alcohol "because the person drinking and the person sitting are participating in the same haram." Shortly before the interview, she had been planning to go to a good-bye party, but when she arrived and saw drinking and dancing inside, she left immediately.

I was ready to say good-bye to them, but I turned around and left. I cannot accept that. So I made [a friend] drive me home. Yeah, I was upset because I was ready to go and say good-bye to my friends and hang out with them, it has been a while since I saw them. But I did not upset God. If they are mad, it is OK, no problem.

While it is difficult to establish a significant pattern of gender differences in our interviews, young women were more likely to engage in secret behaviors. This may be related to the visibility of women's identification with a pious lifestyle through their clothing, especially the hijab. A pious woman in a headscarf sitting in a place with alcohol is more likely to turn heads and raise accusations of hypocrisy in the minds of others than a pious man doing the same thing, in part because the man's commitment is not as visible.[21] This is also related to greater community and family concern for women's morality—a gendering of moral judgment and surveillance common to Lebanese society beyond the Shi'i community.

Young women were also more likely to express negative emotional reactions to haram activities than young men. Zahra listens to songs on her own, but feels deeply guilty in public places where music is played. Her friends from school are less pious than she is and go out clubbing regularly. She once went to a ski resort with them and was so upset when they began dancing that she began to cry. When asked why, she explained,

> Because it wasn't my environment. I didn't expect it to be disgusting like that. There were songs and dancing. I couldn't take it. I looked around and who are these people? I am not disrespecting them, but I am different from them. I affect them and they affect me, and if I keep going to places like that, my commitment will become less, because you are affected by the environment around you.

Beyond the possible gender differences in emotional expression suggested here, Zahra highlights one reason for the angst prompted by spending time around transgressive behavior. Some youths believe that exposure to haram will negatively affect their own religious commitment. For them, balancing their piety with their social lives was fraught. Even Amer, who seems to navigate competing moral rubrics with relative dexterity, suffered the consequences of taking his expat friends out. "It is impossible for me to relax in any place that has alcohol," he said, "I feel something bothering me; I feel like I am doing something wrong; I feel guilty. . . . When I do that I stay worried for like three days."

Because alcohol is believed by many to be a significant infraction, these negotiations weigh on the minds of youths like Amer. When different rules for behavior based on different values clashed, those caught in the middle expressed feeling conflicted about their choices, experiencing guilt, or otherwise making a concerted effort to deal with this moral complexity. The desire to choose the best path is not merely a desire to make one's life easier; rather, it is a desire to choose the path that will lead to the most moral result, taking into consideration ideas about both religious tenets and social values. To further illustrate the clash between these two moral rubrics, we turn to one of the situations where this happened most overtly: weddings.

Contending with Wedding Invitations

Leisure often involves invitations to events and outings. Because weddings hold especial importance for social relationships, the stakes of successfully negotiating their invitations are high. For this reason, weddings are the type of social event that best exemplifies the difficulties that the more or less pious face within this complex moral context.

Many activities that some people deem haram take place at weddings. Of these, alcohol presents less of a problem for the pious because they are less likely to have family members who would publicly serve it, and such a thing would rarely, if ever, happen these days in south Beirut or most Shi'i villages. Dancing and songs, however, continue to create dilemmas for those who believe they are haram. Some families hold sex-segregated weddings, others play only classical or instrumental music, and still others only dabkeh, a Lebanese folk dance thought to be more acceptable provided that men and women do not dance hand in hand. Yet with the shift toward greater public piety in Dahiya in the 1980s and 1990s, even dabkeh at weddings or *mawlids* came under scrutiny.[22] At an all-women's mawlid that Lara attended in 2000, the conservative singer scolded women who got up to dance dabkeh, upsetting members of the local Islamic women's organization that had sponsored the event. In 2008, we asked a waiter in Dahiya if we could bring our own music to a private wedding party in the room that his restaurant reserved for special events. He told us that only classical music would be acceptable because it would be audible in the rest of the restaurant even with the doors closed, and "it has to be shar'i." He followed us out, explaining apologetically, "In this area, we can't do it, no weddings with music and dabkeh."

When confronted with an invitation to a potentially problematic wedding, most people attended anyway because they "had no choice." Some reframed the situation by downplaying the importance of the moral rule that was contravened, or worked to find a solution that would allow them to simultaneously uphold their social and religious values. Only two of our interlocutors absolutely refused to attend weddings. One was a young woman who rather unusually has chosen to wear an 'abaya, a full black cloak covering her head and body.[23] She didn't attend her own brother's wedding. "I said to him, 'I love you, my brother, but I cannot go,' because it was in a restaurant where I can't go, with music and songs. I am wearing an 'abaya; I don't feel that I am able to do this thing." Others echoed the idea that a woman wearing an 'abaya should not attend weddings, again foregrounding assumptions about the relationship between a woman's dress and her piety along with its associated behavioral restrictions. As Hadi noted, "Sometimes you will even see a woman wearing an 'abaya there, and then when the wedding starts she'll leave. But if you are wearing an ʿabaya, why did you come in the first place? Sometimes you ask yourself, 'What does this wedding mean for a woman wearing an ʿabaya?' Maybe the wedding is her cousin's."

Rami, the young man who took the most extreme position in the disagreement described above, was the other person who unconditionally refused to attend weddings. In that argument, he gave the example of declining an invitation to a childhood friend's wedding because there would be a DJ. "He invited me, I didn't ask him to go. I said to him, 'I can't do that.'" Qasim frowned at this, and disapprovingly related a story about acquaintances who spent only five minutes at their own brother's wedding. "Look how far it will go; it's their brother, and they won't sit there for his sake!" He himself goes to friends' weddings no matter what and just goes for a walk outside if the environment overwhelms him.

Many pious youths who avoid songs drew on the strategy that Qasim found distasteful, arriving early at weddings so that they could depart before the music and dancing commenced. This allowed them to make an appearance and fulfill their social obligations without violating their morals. Hadi commented, "When I was invited to my friend's sister's wedding, I had to go. First he is from the neighborhood, and also they invited me four times."

"They don't know that you don't listen to songs?" we asked.

"Yes, they do, but people invite you. So in the end I had to go. I went early, like ten minutes earlier, just to show myself. I sat, and they played classical music. They served food; I ate till I was full. I talked to the DJ and told him, 'Before you start the music, tell me.' So before he started the songs I left."

Hadi's story also highlights the intensity of social pressure around weddings, such that declining an invitation makes a significant statement. For Zayna, a close friendship was important enough for her to stay at a wedding with songs and alcohol despite her intense discomfort.

> There was an engagement party for one of my friends. I was muhajjaba already then, but I couldn't not go. Inno, they are among my closest friends. And they were serving drinks. I had no choice; I went. I didn't stay too late. And I tried to sit somewhere that didn't have drinks on the table. I did my duty [wajbat] toward my friend. It was her engagement; I couldn't abandon her.

We asked her how she felt during the party, and she replied, "I was very uneasy [mdayʾa], but I tried my best to look comfortable even though I was uncomfortable. And I stayed far away, like if this table had drinks, I would choose that one [points further away]."

Family members may exert control over weddings that they are hosting (and paying for). One young woman told us about a conflict between the

bride and her mother at a wedding she had attended at al-Saha. Because
al-Saha follows Fadlallah's fatwas, mixed-gender weddings with dabkeh
music are allowed, but women are not permitted to dance in front of men
(essentially preventing women from dancing altogether in that context).
Several times during this wedding, female friends of the bride began dancing and the music would stop. Finally the muhajjaba bride, in defiance of
her more pious mother, stood up and began dancing as well. When the
music stopped yet again, guests began urging the DJ to allow the bride to
dance at her own wedding. The restaurant did not make an exception.

Such control over events may also work in the opposite direction, with
family members pressuring more pious youths to include activities that
they generally try to avoid. Zaynab was struggling with this issue when we
interviewed her along with two of her friends. She tries to avoid mixed
weddings if there is any dancing at all, even dabkeh, because she doesn't
dance in front of guys, but in her words, also doesn't "like to sit at the table
like an idiot." She explained the exceptions to her efforts:

> Unless it's in the family and I can't [avoid it]. For example, I am having an en-
> gagement party soon. I want to have music for dabkeh, not for anything else,
> but it is going to have to be mixed gender. I know that this is haram, but this is
> a compromise solution [with her parents].

Her friend and classmate Fatima chimed in, "For me, it depends on the
person. . . . I try as much as I can to avoid going to mixed-gender weddings.
But for Zaynab, she is my friend. I have to be there."

"Do you dance if there are guys there?" we inquired.

> Zaynab is not having dancing; she is having dabkeh. But I also have my cousin's
> wedding and I have to go. So I will have to control myself not to dance. If I have
> to, I'll stand there without dancing. You know, I am waiting for the day I get
> married. Maybe he will be more [religiously] committed then me, so I can avoid
> this. They'll know that I am with someone who is against going to mixed-gender
> weddings. Now I can go because I am single. But I want to reach the point
> where people know that I cannot go, so they can't force me to. Right now, if I
> have to go, I'll go, but not to parties and things like that, unless the person is
> very close to me.

Zaynab is explicitly compromising her own ideas about morality and
putting her friend in a compromising position due to pressure from family
members—who also consider themselves pious, and would never tolerate
pop music or alcohol—to have a mixed-gender engagement party. Fatima
says that her commitment requires work on her part, and expresses frustration that her family and social circle aren't supporting her efforts ade-

quately. When she suggests that such social support would come more readily if she were married to a more religiously committed man, she presents us with another way that gender factors into these negotiations. Rather than her hijab signaling piety and carrying with it a set of assumptions about how she should behave, in Fatima's case, only a precept that she views as stronger—namely, respect for her husband's piety—can relieve her of the social obligation of attending weddings. Such limitations on how freely people can navigate this complex moral terrain emphasize the gendered limits of moral flexibility.

"TO EACH *HIS* OWN": THE GENDERING OF MORAL CHOICE

> I like Tiesto. I have some [of his music] with me in the car. I put music on in the car, and I listen to Qur'an in the morning. I am free [to do so]. It is my car and it is my space. No one can question me.
>
> —RIYAD, TWENTY-SOMETHING-YEAR-OLD CAFÉ MANAGER

INDIVIDUAL MORAL CHOICES

In addition to attesting to the tensions between ideas about religious rules, social propriety, and social obligation, our interviews revealed the diversity of youths' opinions on these matters, and their acceptance, for the most part, of that diversity among their friends and peers. Again and again, among friends, peers, spouses, and strangers, young people disclosed that they listen to songs or go to places that serve alcohol. And while certainly some do feel pressured to cease these activities, most reported that the prevailing understanding is that moral behavior is something every individual determined and developed in their own way. As long as the dominant red lines were not crossed, there remained space for negotiation, movement, moods, and even day-to-day changes without accusations of hypocrisy or immorality.

Such a "to each his own" or "live and let live" attitude was considerably stronger among youths than among people over thirty.[24] Youths were hesitant to ask people around them to change their behaviors, often noting that they "had no right" to do so or some other variation of "You cannot make people do what you want." As Muhammad put it, "I'm not saying that you should be a shaykh; if you want or don't want to listen to music it is up to you."[25] Yusef noted more generally, "We don't impose religion on personal relationships, because in the end this is a friendship." "I don't care about my friends' beliefs, my relationship with God is independent/by itself/

separate [la hala], and my relationship with my friends is independent, and my relationship with society is also independent," agreed Abbas.

In addition to acknowledging the flexibility of both behavior and interpretation, this attitude implicitly reflects Fadlallah's views on individual responsibility for moral behavior. Moral flexibility facilitates a certain amount of leniency on the part of many young people with regard to their own choices as well as those of their friends. They frequently cautioned against judging others, stressing the importance of being tolerant and open to others' perspectives and lifestyles. But for some, this tolerance was linked to the belief that God would be the ultimate judge, so that although people could "do whatever they want," there would be consequences in the next life. This more closely approximated the views of jurisprudents, including Fadlallah, whose emphasis on individual responsibility includes accountability for consequences. Youths' ideas about those consequences, however, still depended on how bad a person thought a particular activity was. Listening to songs may or may not be immoral, but if it leads you to transgress further (say, to make out with a girl to whom you are not married), it becomes a problem. Nonetheless, it is essentially *your* problem.

Some youths linked their individualistic understandings of morality to the idea that piety is a process. As Fatima observed, "No one is an angel, and no one can say, 'That's it, this is me, and I cannot change.'" In this way, moral flexibility could be accompanied by an emphasis on the importance of "working on oneself" to become the kind of person who makes "better" choices. Yet unlike many in the vanguard, this was viewed by most youths as something that they could worry about later in life, expressing a hope to "someday be religiously committed enough" to avoid certain cafés and activities.[26] As Layla remarked, comparing herself with the friend seated next to her, "I don't have a problem being in a place that has alcohol. I may change later, *inshallah* ["God willing"]. . . . Her commitment is stronger than mine; there are levels I haven't reached yet." Rather than a rigid process of climbing a ladder of faith, this conception of processual piety is exactly what allows space for ambivalence and contradiction.

Regardless of whether or not they stressed the importance of self-improvement, most of our young interlocutors understood behaving morally as an individual choice. In Rabi''s words from this chapter's epigraph, "All we need to do is select." Choice here is facilitated by the existence of different juristic opinions, so that youths today may search for the interpretations and fatwas that most closely reflect their own desires and ideas. It is also facilitated by the access to religious information that youths enjoy.[27] Rabi' linked this process to shopping—an apt analogy that confirms our sense of the connection between ideas about individual moral responsibility and a consumerist sensibility among youths.

In order to truly choose the moral path, many youths believe that they need to "be convinced" of the values underlying any rule, whether from the religious or social rubric. The popularity of this idea that one must be convinced of a practice *before* doing it suggests the hegemony of what Deeb (2006) has described elsewhere as an emphasis on "authenticated" religious belief and practice. Rather than doing something because one is taught to do it, or because it is the way things have been done in the past, a person in this context should ideally learn about the reasoning behind a particular tenet, and then embrace it in both intention and practice.[28] The dominance of a "conviction-first" perspective among youths represents another "success" of the Shi'i Islamic mobilization in Lebanon—one that may be an unintended (and not always welcomed) consequence of the sedimentation of Fadlallah's ideas about individualism into "common sense."[29] The importance of intention prior to practice also partially explains young people's hesitancy to "correct" others' behavior, as forcing change might create a situation where there is discord between a person's inner and outer states, calling into question the authenticity of the behavioral change.

For some youths, focusing on the significance of prior intention creates room for ambivalence or skepticism, and allows them the flexibility to enjoy a wider range of leisure activities as long as their intentions are morally sound. And while people's convictions are variable and minds do change, they frequently change from one intractable stance to another. As opposed to living with moral uncertainty, people tend to seek stable ground within this terrain of malleable morality. We rarely heard statements like "I don't know if listening to pop music is haram or not"; people instead tend to have a position on the matter. Another effect of highlighting conviction and choice is that there appears to be little rhyme or reason to the patterns of what any individual considers appropriate moral behavior. For example, Zaynab thinks that weddings violate the shari'a and only attends them out of familial social obligation, but she has no problem spending time in cafés that serve beer if there is no visible bar. On the other hand, her friend Rola will not step foot in a place that serves alcohol, but is happy to attend dry weddings, and listens to songs both publicly and privately, but does not dance. Behaviors can also be based on unrelated ideas (e.g., about health) that indirectly support a moral position, as in Maisa's reasoning: "I'm scared to drink, not because it's haram or anything, but because you can become an alcoholic from one sip."

The predominance of a "to each his own" perspective among youths does not mean that figuring out how to live a moral life is easy, nor that discussions are devoid of critique. As we saw above, youths often feel guilty about their choices. For someone who wants to be a good person according to multiple values and standards, the notion that individuals are responsible for both moral action and assessments about morality greatly raises the stakes of everyday decisions. Flexibility should not be mistaken for moral relativism, and the blame is the flip side of responsibility. It may open new spaces for censure, as casting leisure activities as decisions subject solely to individual intention places blame squarely on the shoulders of the person engaging in the activity.

Reproach is more likely to fall on the shoulders of young women than young men in part because their hijabs publicly announce claims to religious commitment, placing a greater burden on them to uphold those claims. Social propriety also limits choices for young women, sometimes in ways that clash with ideas about egalitarian moral standards rooted in religious interpretation. Some young women find religious rules "liberating" from social norms, as we noted in our brief exploration of temporary marriage in the introduction. Others, like Fatima, are looking to marriage to facilitate their avoidance of problematic social obligations. Most commonly, however, social propriety and religious rules combine to create a context in which to each *her* own remains an unattainable ideal.

GENDER, APPEARANCE, AND JUDGMENT

Women's presence in Dahiya's new cafés is not in question here. Women's presence in cafés does not signify something particularly new for Lebanese gender relations, as women's café going seems to in other Arab contexts.[30] Beirut is strikingly mixed gender in its socializing and public spaces compared to Cairo, Amman, and other regional capitals. In Dahiya's cafés, we see an eclecticism of gendered use that parallels the eclecticism of décor. A single café may include tables of men smoking argileh, couples on dates, women chatting over coffee, and mixed-gender groups of students. In addition, in our survey of café customers we did not find any significant relationship between gender and time of day prior to 9:00 p.m.; until that hour, men and women were equally represented in cafés.

What is at stake is instead the appearance and behavior of those women. Vanguard generation mothers and teachers commonly instruct girls to "respect the hijab," meaning to publicly and privately behave in ways befitting a pious person. This reflects the coexistence of ideas about cultivating virtues through practice with ideals of authenticated Islam—a coexistence necessary to the idea of an Islamic dress code in schools. Obviously not all young women in Dahiya wear the hijab, but the proportion that do has dramatically increased since the 1980s. Some muhajjaba young women willfully defy these lessons, especially if they feel that it was not their choice to wear the hijab in the first place.

Young women's different ideas about hijab are revealed in the "emo hijab" style.[31] Lara first met self-identified emo hijabis in 2008, young headscarf-wearing women whose dress cited a range of influences from goth to *Flashdance*. The transnational phenomenon emerged as a fashion in Dahiya in the mid-2000s, when emo-style accessories and black nail polish became relatively trendy.[32] Some emo hijabis deliberately dissociate themselves from ideas about "respecting the hijab," while others view their stylistic choices as a form of respectable dress and behave accordingly. Tala fit in the former category. She had begun covering her hair because her family threatened to cut off financial support if she did not change her dress and behavior. When Lara met her, she was wearing a tight black long-sleeve shirt and pants along with a ruffled off-the-shoulder plaid vest. Her hot-pink cotton head wrap barely covered her hair, and the lacy-black scarf loosely draped over it revealed her neck. Black stilettos and a black leather bracelet with metal studs completed her outfit. Tala views herself as an outsider to Dahiya's moral norms, and explicitly linked her dress to rebellion against her headscarf; emo hijab was still hijab, so it met her family's expectations, but it was not "proper hijab," and therefore expressed her personal ambivalence about the religious rubric. As she put it, "This is not hijab, it shouldn't be used. This is a style. But because I didn't like the hijab on my own, but I was forced to wear it, I am like this. . . . If I was convinced of it, I wouldn't wear it like this, I would dress the way religion asks."

Hala's friend Dana was dressed similarly in tight jeans and a tight white shirt with a plaid bustier jacket, with a lacy-black length of fabric wound in a complicated manner over a plain black cotton scarf that covered her hair and neck, and rhinestone-studded black stiletto sandals. Dana identified as religiously committed, prayed regularly, and spent most of her free time in Dahiya's cafés. She viewed her style as a fashion choice that fit within the rules of propriety for young women and strove to behave in similarly moral ways while out with her fiancé, a young man from a well-connected Dahiya family with ties to Hizbullah.

In addition to how one wears the hijab, a key issue is whether a woman wearing a headscarf may sit in a café that serves alcohol. In one group interview, Layla, in her mid-twenties, found herself at odds with a vanguard generation man on this matter. She was adamant that it doesn't affect her if others around her are consuming alcohol and regularly hangs out with her boyfriend in cafés that serve it, saying, "I don't have a problem with that. I know it is haram, but it's his business. This is how I feel now. I don't know if I am going to stay like this or not."

Mahmoud took issue with her views in a patronizing tone: "This may lead to embarrassing situations that are bad for the hijab and what you are representing. He may say something wrong to you after he gets drunk."

"As long as we don't reach that point," retorted Layla, "I don't have a problem with it."

"Should we wait for bad things to happen to run from them, or as educated people, should we avoid these situations to protect ourselves?" Mahmoud replied.

"I believe that each person is responsible for his own issues; you have
your religion, and I have mine. It might be a beer; he is not going to get
drunk. I will drink Pepsi. It doesn't bother me! It's his business. As long as
we are sitting in an appropriate way, then I have no problem."

Faced with Layla's intransigence, Mahmoud finally resorted to suggesting that she would "grow out of it" when she became more religiously
committed and scolded her for "disrespecting" the hijab:

> When we became more multazim, we cannot do things for others that are
> against our religion. Just as we respect him and his religious practices, he should
> respect our religion and our hijab. . . . [W]hen a woman with the hijab is sitting
> at a table with alcohol, the first thing they'll say is, "Look what women with the
> hijab are doing." We shouldn't let anyone disrespect the hijab.

Despite the gender and age differences between them, Layla maintained
her stance until the interview facilitator changed the subject, and ignored
Mahmoud's attempts to dismiss her views as naive.

Other youths, both male and female, shared Mahmoud's position that
women's dress and behavior should correspond. They thought that the
"more Islamic" features that one's body exhibits, the stricter one should
be—and hence Hadi's surprise above at the appearance of a woman wearing an ʿabaya at a wedding with songs. He assumed her presence must stem
from social obligation, and did not allow for the possibility that she might
believe songs are acceptable or that she can control her responses to them.
Alia reflected thoughtfully on the signifying role of the ʿabaya in relation
to assumptions about women's behavior. "For example, if a woman is
wearing an ʿabaya, with all my respect to those who wear them, you notice
when her behavior has flaws. There is no one who does not make mistakes,
but with women wearing ʿabayas you notice that people take note of what
they do."

As she continued, Alia demonstrated her awareness of a double standard
in judging the behavior of pious men and women. "Generally speaking,
even if guys are multazim, no one blames them for anything in today's
society. This is what I have noticed. You see a multazim as though he is just
like any other person, but with a style that leans a little bit toward Islam.
The rest of it remains obscured."

Her friend Nada disagreed, suggesting that people do judge men by
their appearances. "For example, if a guy's appearance is too spiky or if he
is wearing ripped pants, people don't look at him the way they look at a
person who is calm and sensible and isn't checking anyone out."

Alia responded that all men, multazim or not, no matter what their appearance, behave immorally by checking out women. Nada was not convinced, saying, "Still, if I see a guy acting like that, I will ask myself, 'That guy is multazim? Is that the behavior of a guy who is multazim?' We still talk; it's not that we talk about girls and we don't talk about guys." While Alia and Nada agreed that there are standards of appropriate behavior for religiously committed men, Nada insists that both men and women are judged by their appearances, while Alia holds that men can more easily hide their religious commitment, and therefore avoid judgments based on assumptions about the relationship between piety and behavior.

Smoking argileh in cafés confirms and complicates both Alia's and Nada's views, since it is an activity where social propriety heavily influences gendered and generational judgments about morality. In Cairo, the presence of argileh marks the traditional café as a male-only domain and it is not available in the new coffee shops (M. Peterson 2011). But in Dahiya, like much of Beirut, argileh has become widespread across cafés and restaurants.

Women Smoking Argileh

Argileh smoking, perhaps the most common café activity in Lebanon, is instructive for considering the gendered dimensions of ideas about morality. Almost all the young men and over half the young women we spoke with and saw as we hung out in cafés in Dahiya (and elsewhere in Beirut) smoked argileh. Older men usually smoke as well, sometimes gathering in cafés at around 5:00 p.m. for something akin to an "argileh happy hour." Women over thirty-five generally do not smoke in public, preferring to do so in the privacy of their homes, or those of friends or relatives. Generational differences in both argileh smoking and opinions about it are common across Lebanese communities. Argileh has become more popular among Lebanese youths since the mid-1990s—part of a transnational trend that includes the increase in numbers and popularity of hookah bars near colleges and universities in the United States and Europe.[33] In Lebanon, ideas about argileh are intertwined with issues of taste and class, and we take up those aspects of the practice in chapter 6.

When we asked the representatives of Fadlallah and Khamenei about smoking argileh, their responses revealed differences of opinion on both argileh and gender. Fadlallah has given a fatwa that prohibits smoking in all forms for both men and women, "because it is harmful and causes serious damage to one's health according to the experts, to the extent of dangerous and fatal illnesses."[34] Sayyid Ja'far went further, telling us that he finds it absurd that people should require a fatwa on the matter. "It should be enough for a person to think about the issue and study its harmfulness

in order to stop. It is unbelievable that a person needs a juristic prohibition
to stop smoking!" In contrast, as of 2011, Khamenei had not prohibited
smoking, and Shaykh Muhammad paused between puffs on his cigarette
to tell us that he advised people on the type of argileh tobacco he believed
was less harmful.[35] He then surprised us by continuing, unprompted, to
insist, "I don't like argileh for women! It may reach the level of haram
when women smoke in cafés." This shaykh's focus on gendered social propriety, rather than the gender-neutral health consequences of smoking, is
typical of vanguard generation views.

Firas, in his late thirties, explained, "The argileh, for me personally, I
don't feel it is right to see a woman smoking argileh. . . . Maybe I can accept
a woman smoking a cigarette, but the argileh, not at all." Many of our older
interlocutors agreed. Some, like forty-year-old Hanady, took it a step
further.

> It is very wrong for a woman or girl to sit and smoke argileh in a public place.
> I am against women smoking cigarettes in public places! What, then, if it is an
> argileh? What happens, she becomes like a guy sitting there. I am against it. It is
> not acceptable. It is not acceptable customarily ['urfan] or morally
> [akhlaqiyyan].

In keeping with Hanady's perspective, many women we know who smoke
(and many in Lebanon do) continue to hide their cigarettes from their
fathers well into their thirties and forties. Some of these same women will
smoke argileh in public because it is considered a communal social activity, underscoring disagreement as to which form of smoking is more
acceptable.

Other than Shaykh Muhammad, no one described women's smoking as
haram. Instead they portrayed it as violating custom, or simply as 'ayb. As
a reminder, 'ayb is a term used to refer to a wide range of inappropriate
behavior often related to the social rubric of morality, and what is 'ayb is
not necessarily haram. While older people commonly think it is 'ayb for
women to smoke anything in public, perhaps because it signifies having
"given in to temptation," many of our older interlocutors were especially
concerned about the recent phenomenon of young women smoking argileh
in cafés. Every vanguard generation parent we spoke with saw it as evidence of the moral decline of youths and society. "What kind of society
raises a generation like this?" one father exclaimed. In casting argileh as a
generational problem, these parents stood in ironic agreement with parents
across the country and political spectrum. Notably, argileh smoking was
not viewed as "more 'ayb" for women wearing hijab than for those who
didn't, underscoring again the social propriety roots of this moral guideline. The sole exception was a young woman who had recently stopped

smoking argileh in public because she felt that it was disrespectful to her hijab. One might expect pious people to invoke Fadlallah's fatwa prohibiting smoking, but most do not—quite likely because they and/or everyone they know smokes. Smoking (argileh, cigarettes, or cigars) is the norm in Lebanon, and until recently it was difficult, if not impossible, to find non-smoking spaces to hang out.[36] To our knowledge, as of 2011 there were no such spaces in Dahiya.

When pressed to explain why smoking argileh was especially 'ayb for young women given its gender-neutral health consequences, people consistently returned to the idea of its appearance. *"Ka manzar, mish zabta"* ("As a look, it isn't right") was the typical response. One interpretation of this problematic appearance refers to a common though usually unarticulated visual association between argileh smoking and fellatio. The polite way to pass an argileh is to form a loop with the hose, passing the loop rather than the phallic mouthpiece. This association hovered under the surface of Shaykh Muhammad's comparison of cigarettes to argileh. "Cigarettes are less of a problem [for women], but argileh, she is using the hose [*narbish*] like this [gestures with his hand]. . . . If she wants to smoke argileh, she can smoke it in her house." His discomfort is focused on women's public handling of the argileh apparatus itself—a discomfort perhaps shared by others in the vanguard generation. This explains the vociferous negative reactions to the *appearance* of younger women smoking argileh as opposed to the idea of women smoking tobacco more generally. Sometimes this critique took the form of flirtation, as when a young man teased the young woman in charge of renting laptops to customers at a café about her constant argileh smoking. "You know what my dream is?" he asked. "What is your dream?" she replied. "To see you without that [argileh] in your mouth!" "Impossible!" she retorted, giggling. Interpreted thus, argileh provides support for the idea that social propriety is most likely to trump religious rules when it comes to ideas about female sexuality (Deeb 2010; Clarke 2009). Concerns about public argileh smoking also relate to the social surveillance of women's behavior through *haki al-nas* ("gossip").

Gossip

Social pressure may be exerted through gossip about young women who publicly break with moral convention. During one summer, Lara had several opportunities to speak at length with Tala, her friend Aziza's twenty-four-year-old emo hijabi office assistant. Tala fasts and prays, follows Fadlallah as her marja' "because he is the easiest one," and also enjoys going clubbing with her friends in Jounieh, a Christian town north of Beirut, far from the eyes of the pious. "We go and stay late, and it isn't anyone's business. Look, I am not hiding in the corner or doing something shameful for me. I live my life as I want, in front of everyone, and I am not harming anyone." She has tried alcohol, but didn't like its taste, so doesn't drink. Despite pressuring her to wear the hijab, Tala's family also facilitates her leisure life by avoiding direct questions concerning her whereabouts. It helps that they like her Shi'i boyfriend, who shares her perspectives on moral behavior, and seem to believe that he will help her settle down. Yet Tala's insistence on her right to choose her lifestyle comes with a keen awareness that she is the object of haki. "The eye is always on me. They say, 'She did this and that.'"

Other young women, like Soha, who is not pious in the least, may lie to their parents, fight with them about lifestyle choices, or otherwise defy their wishes. In Soha's view, her family's opposition to her behavior has more to do with gossip than religious belief. "They are saying you stayed out late at night." Such concerns about reputation affect young women across Lebanon, especially in urban areas where there is little privacy as to one's comings and goings. For example, a young woman from a nonreligious Christian family once arrived home at 6:00 a.m. from an evening out clubbing to find her mother on the balcony yelling, "What is this? The prostitutes arrived home earlier than my daughter!" Notably, both Tala and Soha's sense of reputation's importance is produced by comments from their families. None of the youths we spoke with expressed significant worries about reputation themselves, yet almost all our older interlocutors did, particularly when talking about their own daughters.[37]

Tala and Soha have to leave Dahiya to go clubbing, and it is their *imagined* behavior during these outings—based on assumptions about their dress, the time they get home, and people outside Dahiya—that fuels gossip about them.[38] The flip side of these assumptions relates to notions of how people *should* interact with one another within Dahiya's cafés. Ideas about moral ways to socialize are another criterion by which people choose where to spend their time.

SINFUL SOCIAL INTERACTIONS

Ihtirim halak! ["respect yourself!]

—A COMMON ADMONISHMENT

RESPECTFULNESS

Many of our interviewees cited "people's behavior" as a key factor in their decisions about which cafés to patronize. Ghenwa went so far as to suggest that other customers are her primary criterion; she frequents cafés regardless of the presence of alcohol and songs provided that she is happy with their clientele.

The most commonly used words to explain what counted as appropriate behavior were respect or respectful (*ihtiram* or *muhtaram*)—respect for oneself, others, and the place where one is sitting. Similarly, when asked how they behave in cafés, almost everyone said simply "with respect." As Qasim put it, speaking about his own behavior, "Of course a person pays attention—for example, not to yell or speak too loudly. . . . You just pay attention in public places. You want to respect the place, ya'ni, you're sitting in public; you want to respect the people around you."[39] Most people were unable to articulate exactly what they meant by respect, highlighting the norms of social propriety at work here and the relationship of what is considered respectful to a wide range of values, including those pertaining to the religious rubric and class. Negatively assessed behaviors were usually described as 'ayb or *bala zo'* ("tasteless" or "without manners"). Our young interlocutors generally said that they would ignore such behavior around them in cafés, while several vanguard interviewees called for greater disciplining by waitstaff.

For some, bad manners and inappropriate behavior were indexed by the volume of people's voices, implying that everything from loud laughter to joking audibly to talking on the phone so that others could hear was bala zo' or *zanakha* ("an annoyance"), and should not happen in respectable places. Some people gendered this rule by citing religious tenets that hold that women should not draw attention to themselves (*laft nazar*), criticizing women laughing loudly in public or flirting with waitstaff. Older people additionally thought of women smoking argileh as laft nazar.[40] Some young women applied ideas about tasteless behavior and attention seeking to young men, noting that guys that *ya'mlu harakat* ("act in attention-seeking ways") and check out girls in cafés are behaving immorally. Many people also drew on class-based ideas about good manners and applied these notions of propriety to both sexes.

Another common way our interlocutors described disrespectful or tasteless behavior drew on euphemistic or direct references to improper heterosexual displays of physical intimacy, including touching, hugging, holding hands, and making out. As they put it, "*Ma byihtirmu halon iddam an-nas* ["they don't respect themselves in front of others"]" or "*Ma byit-sarrafu dumn al-usul* ["they don't behave according to the rules"]." Defining the rules for acceptable male-female interaction was less specific; people often resorted to phrases like, "They should maintain the shar'i distance between them." There was substantial disagreement as to what this meant, with some suggesting that couples should sit across from one another, and others contending that sitting close together was fine as long as it was not "excessive." People also disagreed about the limits of appropriate physical contact for couples that were engaged or married. A generational disparity was evident here as well, again typified by an argument between Mahmoud and Layla.

Mahmoud began, saying,

> Sometimes I see a man and woman walking in the street, and he is hugging her, for example. There are people who automatically say, "This is his wife." Why? Because they mean to give them the benefit of the doubt. But here he is the one who is bala zo', because this street has its own sanctity. If a female and a male are walking in the street, they have to respect people.

We asked him, "What if they were in a café?"

"Even inside a café," he insisted. "For example, if he's holding her hand. If she is your fiancée or your wife, wait until you go home and hold it! This is a violation of the shari'a."

Layla interrupted, "If two people are sitting next to each other, a man and a woman, we don't know if she is his fiancée or his wife. So what if he holds her hand or plays with her hair?"

"It is affecting me," Mahmoud replied.

"Why?" she asked.

"Because I am at this place," he said, "because it is supposed to be respectable."

"And you consider this disrespectful?" Layla pressed.

"It affects public life."

Layla's tone grew more annoyed as she argued, "Maybe this is their way of expressing their feelings."

"Their way at home, not among people."

"Maybe they want to express themselves at that moment."

"No, I don't want to be in this environment."

Mahmoud shifted into a falsetto, as though mimicking a teenaged girl, and mocked her, saying, "*Yaay shu romanci*! ["ooo, how romantic!"]." His voice shifted again, this time to sarcasm. "What, should I get up and get a rose for him to give her?"

At this point, Layla was fed up and spoke sharply, "No, don't get him a rose! The point is, it's none of our business. Why should I have an opinion about what they do? *Yistiflu*. As long as they are still within limits."

Mahmoud concluded the exchange by trying to placate her with this explanation: "I think that if a guy loves a girl, they understand each other through the language of the eyes, and that's enough. When they go home, they can do whatever they want."

Quite typically of his generation, Mahmoud suggests that norms of propriety combine with religious rules to call for keeping "romance," even with one's wife or fiancée, within the private sphere. Later in our conversation he complained, "Shabab w sabaya [young men and women] take advantage of shar'i cafés. They plan a time to meet there, sit next to each other, and talk, and things happen." Layla, on the other hand, thinks that as long as the couple is within the "shar'i limits"—meaning that they are behaving in ways that are permissible within their relationship to one another—acts like holding hands in public are perfectly acceptable. Crucially, she points out that no one can assess whether or not a couple is in a permissible relationship (i.e., regularly or temporarily married, or engaged with a marriage contract) without prior knowledge of the people involved. Also quite typically of her generation, she stresses the notion of to each their own, asserting that judging the couple's behavior is a matter for God and "none of our business." Because there is no way to know whether a couple is doing something halal or haram (especially given the possibility that a secret temporary marriage may exist), youths' negative assessments of public displays of affection generally stem from their ideas about social propriety rather than religious rules.[41]

During our visits to cafés across Dahiya, we saw a good deal of male-female interaction that many of our interlocutors of all ages would view as moral only for couples in a permissible relationship. Couples often sat close together, and sometimes made out in not-quite-private nooks and crannies. Many youths confirmed that such behavior was commonplace in cafés in the area, usually denying their own participation. Some, like Hadi, objected to public displays of affection on the grounds that they tempted him to also act immorally.

> When I go out with my fiancée, for example, she is halal for me. If we are sitting there, and everyone sitting there is respecting themselves, smoking argileh and drinking coffee, I am not going to kiss her. I can wait until I go home and then kiss her. Ya'ni, I am forced to do what others are doing in the social environment around me. But if I go out with my fiancée and I find that there are people sitting in the corner like this [inappropriately], people lying on the couch there, in the end I want to do like them, I want to be absorbed into the ambiance also. And in the end she is halal to me. . . . I mean, if someone kisses his wife in public, he isn't doing anything wrong, but in the end, it's not seen as moral.

Youths' critiques of public displays of affection, stories they told in our interviews, and our own observations in cafés across Dahiya attest to the fact that cafés are providing new public spaces where young people can hang out with girlfriends, boyfriends, lovers, fiancées, or spouses. In addition, youths sometimes "see" and "begin talking with" new lovers and partners in cafés, adding another layer of complexity to moral valuations of male-female interactions.

MORAL FLIRTATIONS

Flirtation is an inevitable part of the café experience. Young people check each other out, ask each other out, use Bluetooth technology to pass their phone numbers around, and often meet not only new lovers and spouses but also new friends. We heard about many married couples that met this way as well as stories about former and more casual relationships. Many of our attempts to ask direct questions about meeting people for intimate heterosexual relationships (i.e., picking people up) were hindered by the secrecy maintained around dating and sexuality along with the reluctance of young women in particular to talk about it.[42] Endogamy within sectarian groups is relatively high in Lebanon, in relation to factors including class, education, and the political alliances of the moment. Among pious Shiʿi Muslims, couples may meet in a wide variety of contexts, including school, university, and work, in cafés or other public leisure sites, and through friends or family. "Introductions" to potential spouses were and continue to be common, with older female relatives often taking on the role of matchmaker for children, nieces, and nephews. It is commonplace for an older woman to approach a younger one and ask her about her marital status, family, and village of origin in order to assess the potential for a match.

Our research assistant, a young woman in her twenties, was frequently approached by people interested in making her acquaintance as she helped us conduct a survey or took additional notes on a café. At Terrace on one occasion, she was approached three times: a young man sent her no less than seven requests to connect their cell phones via Bluetooth so that they could exchange messages and images, looking over and smiling at her each time; a woman with two small children asked her if she was single, explaining that she was the "kind of young woman" in whom her son would be interested; and a group of young men called her over to their table to tell her that they wanted to include their ages and phone numbers on the survey "especially for her."

Families differ on the acceptability of dating, with some trusting their daughters to behave properly while out in public with young men and ignoring the potential for gossip, and others insisting that the couple get to know one another within the family home, either under watchful eyes, or with a parent or sibling popping into the room at irregular intervals. While some parents prefer to learn about a potential spouse for their daughter after she has already ascertained her interest, most require the young man to visit them and obtain their permission to "talk with" or get to know her prior to any one-on-one interactions. As one parent noted, "If he wants to see her, to talk to her, he can come to our house. In front of my eyes and my wife's eyes. Unless there is an engagement or a marriage contract."

Some young women also noted that it was easier to avoid gossip by getting to know someone at home, so that in case the relationship does not lead to an engagement, you do not have to deal with the gossip of people who have seen you together.

Many pious families move quickly toward an engagement and sign the marriage contract at that time (*katb kitab*). During the long engagement period that usually follows, the young couple is free to date and hang out together in public or private. The two are also able to engage in intimate behavior permissibly, as they are considered legally—but not socially—married. Young women are still expected to preserve their virginity for after the formal wedding celebration that marks the advent of their social marriage, and many simply do "everything but" vaginal intercourse with their partners. Other parents hesitate to perform katb kitab for a long engagement because if the engagement fails their daughter is considered legally, though again not socially, a divorcee. They may prefer to allow the couple to get to know one another first (with strict limits on physical contact) and save the marriage contract for closer to the actual wedding. Some young people use a practice called *zawaj mu'aqqat* ("temporary marriage") to date, which is a contracted relationship between a man and woman, without any witnesses, limited to a specified period of time and in accordance with a specified dowry, either symbolic or substantial, provided for the woman at the end of the contract. They generally do so without telling their families and sometimes not even their friends, however, due to the continued stigma associated with the practice and the intense opposition of most vanguard generation parents to the idea of their daughters contracting such marriages.[43]

Not only are young women expected to maintain their virginity until their wedding night (an expectation shared by all Lebanese sectarian groups) but their reputation also is a key factor in their marriageability. A sexual double standard was a common feature in young men's contradictory statements about the acceptability of temporary marriage for young women (who are assumed to be virgins). Quite typically, a young man would say, "It's OK if it is a way to get to know a girl, but with the intent of marrying her, if you are engaged or something like that." Yet when we then asked him whether he would contract a regular marriage with someone to whom he had been temporarily married, he would reply, "No, I wouldn't do that."[44] Young men also drew on stereotypes about gender roles, suggesting that sex would naturally decrease a man's affection for a woman but increase the woman's affections for the man. As Tala observed, "There are guys who don't care if the girl did sex before, and there are guys who are attached to tradition, they need to see blood when they make sex for the first time. . . . But even if they are open minded, their families don't know about it."

The stakes of lessened marriageability are particularly high in Lebanon due to its unusually skewed female-to-male population ratio.[45] Many Lebanese women across the country feel a great deal of anxiety about their marriage prospects—anxieties that surface in phenomena like elevated per capita rates of cosmetic surgery. Concerns about reputation and marriage prospects converge in the lack of objection, among many of our young female interlocutors, to meeting young men in cafés as long as their intentions are sound. These women usually insisted that they were only interested in serious marriage possibilities and that "his goal must be respectable"—meaning that a man's intent in approaching her was to get to know her as a potential spouse. For this reason, many young women told us that they would never go out with someone who had not publicly declared his intentions to her family because, as Lamia put it, "How would I know if he is serious? Some guys do that for fun. I don't want to have a bad reputation."

Partly because cafés are pickup sites, youths treat them as catwalks, taking the opportunity to display their taste, piety, status, politics, and bodies. Young men wear tight T-shirts and jeans with visible brand names and smell of expensive colognes. Large single-stoned rings that contain a protective "hijab" (a slip of paper on which a Qur'anic verse is written) signal their piety or identification with the Shi'i community; cell phone ringtones set to a speech by Nasrallah or a Hizbullah anthem signal political affiliation or allegiance. Young women told us that they perceive these signs of association with Hizbullah and the Resistance quite positively, despite their awareness that young men may exaggerate their proximity to the party just to score points with them. For their part, except for those in full Islamic dress, bodies are on display. Women who don't wear headscarves often wear revealing low-cut and sleeveless tops over tight jeans or slacks; those who are muhajjaba choose long, but frequently formfitting clothing instead. Scarves generally were tied in the latest style, which in 2008 included lifting one's hair into a high bun at the back of the head and allowing the scarf to fall over it in a sort of bouffant. A carefully placed tag might reveal a European fashion-house insignia. In typical Lebanese style, nearly all women wore heels and makeup, with variations in how heavily the cosmetics were applied. In other words, with the exception of a greater proportion of young women wearing headscarves, youths in cafés in Dahiya dress like Lebanese youths elsewhere in the city. Most of them dress to be noticed, itself a violation of the religious rubric, which forbids publicly attracting attention from the opposite sex.

When a young man approached, a young woman usually assessed his intentions by evaluating his questions or informing him immediately that if he is interested, he should "come visit [her] at home," indirectly suggesting that he publicly declare his interest by asking her parents for permission to see her. Most vanguard men and women see no problem with couples meeting in respectable cafés provided that the courtship takes place in accordance with social norms and ends in marriage. Café owners also noted the popularity of their businesses as dens for budding relationships. At the same time, the vanguard generation tends to think that a great deal of the flirtatious behavior they observe in Dahiya's cafés crosses the line into immorality with the "looks exchanged, the smiles, and winking."

Some young men also spoke about the importance of good intentions, and some went so far as to suggest that it would be better to approach a young woman indirectly from the outset. Hadi explained,

> For example, I am sitting here right now at our table, and there across from me, there is a guy sitting with two girls. . . . Let's say I looked at that girl [gestures] and I liked her. I'll meet her in a morally appropriate and respectful way [tari'a akhla'iyyeh wa muhtarameh]. Not like what we see on television where the guy is signaling to her with his hands and winking, or something like that. No, if they have a guy with them, I'll go talk to him, say, "Excuse me, can I speak to you for a minute on the side?" and, "I saw this girl you are with and she appealed to me, and I would like to talk to her and visit her at home and go out with her."

Hadi was one of the more propriety-conscious young men we interviewed. He had met his current girlfriend in a café and was dating her with her parents' blessing. Before that relationship, he had met a young woman who asked to see him behind her parents' backs. He refused and went to visit her parents. "I said no, I won't see you outside the house; my intentions are good. Now if I just wanted to have a girlfriend, that's something else." He laughed ironically. "But I learned not to go to her house again, because I went, and her family wasn't comfortable with it, because she was young." Despite her parents' refusal, Hadi stopped by the store where this young woman worked to see her several times before deciding that they were incompatible.

Almost all the young men we interviewed were comfortable approaching young women directly in cafés. Prior to his engagement to a young woman that he met through her relatives, Ja'far used to simply walk up to women in whom he was interested, ask them if they were engaged, and if they weren't, frankly tell them he wanted to get to know them. Others agreed that it was easiest to be direct about one's intentions, noting the nuances between passing someone a phone number or bluntly asking to meet—fi majal nata'arraf? ("can we get to know each other?"), which implies dating or sometimes temporary marriage—versus asking politely and more formally whether it would be possible to talk to one another. Young women, like Diala, were sensitive to these distinctions.

Once I was in a restaurant with my aunt, and the waiter was passing by us a lot, and then he went and talked to my aunt. Many times people get married this way. If the guy has good intentions, he can ask me. He can say, "I saw you here, can I have your home address," or "I am serious and I want to continue with this." Other guys, they just want to have fun. He'll ask for your phone number or just bother you.

Not only were young women cautious about accepting propositions outright, they also emphasized that following the guy's initial approach, the ball was fully in their court. As Amina explained, "What happens depends on what the girl wants, on whether she gives the guy an opportunity. There are girls who like a guy and want to meet him, and there are girls, even if a guy comes to meet them in a respectful way, they yell at him/shame him [bahdalu]." Or as Mariam put it, "If I have the intention to get to know him, I will show him that."

Despite young women's general insistence that they were only interested in meeting potential marriage partners, the prevalence of couples who date casually—based on the many firsthand stories related by young men and secondhand stories related by young women as well as information from parents and juristic offices—shows that quite a few young women do in fact accept men's advances for more casual relationships. Young men's stories and our observations also indicate that young women are not merely passive recipients of advances but also may initiate contact by "exchanging looks" with young men or directly flirting with them. Our research suggests that there are quite a few young women and men who frequent cafés specifically in order to pick people up—something none of the young women we spoke to would admit directly.

The advent of Bluetooth technology has facilitated many introductions in recent years, though it does not appear to be as common a strategy in Lebanon as it is in societies where public interaction between men and women is legally restricted (i.e., Saudi Arabia and Iran).[46] Soha explained how Bluetooth works to us, "I can open my Bluetooth, and a guy opens his, and one of us asks if we can meet. He might ask, 'Where are you sitting,' and I'll say, 'I am raising my hand now.'" Unlike Soha, who does not identify as pious, most young women emphasize that they only used Bluetooth "for fun." Some opened their phones carefully underneath café tables so that no one could see them. Others openly laughed with their friends about incoming messages from young men, but then erased the messages and phone numbers without responding (at least not publicly). As Zayna put it, "If I were [the kind of] girl who wanted to enjoy this silliness, I'd phone [a guy who sent her his number via Bluetooth], but I erase the numbers."

One of our group interviews included a married couple that had met a few years earlier via Bluetooth in Il Ponte. Bilal, who was thirty-two when we interviewed him, started narrating, "Our story begins with a Bluetooth interaction, and I met her, talked to her, and gave her my number, then I told her that I'd like to get to know her more. . . . I mean I didn't know her for a long time before I went to her house, maybe a bit less then a month, then less than two months later we got engaged for seven or eight months before we married. . . . So that is how I met my wife, in five minutes I met her, she was sitting right in front of me and by mistake something happened with the Bluetooth."

We interrupted here, prompting laughter with our next question, "What do you mean by mistake! We want to hear the full version!"

His wife, Ghenwa, teased, "Which version?" as Bilal continued,

"She had her Bluetooth on, and I sent . . . I don't remember what I sent at that time."

"What, you've forgotten?" cut in Ghenwa, still teasing.

"A picture or something, *wallah*, I don't remember exactly."

"There was my phone and my friend's phone," explained Ghenwa, "and we opened Bluetooth and like that . . ."

"And I had put my number as my [Bluetooth] name."

"Yeah, he had put his number, and then it happened like he told you."

Bilal added, "And I hadn't intended to go to the café that day; usually every day I would go with my friend at 2:00 p.m. I get off work early, and we would go and smoke argileh and then go home. But that day I got off at 6:00 p.m. and I didn't want to go. I went to pick him up from work, and he said, 'Let's go just for five minutes, half an hour, something like that.' I told him, 'Really I can't, I am really tired and my head hurts and I can't go out.' So it really was a coincidence, because usually we don't go there in the evening, but this time we did."

"Coincidentally."

"Maybe there is no such thing as chance in religion," he commented, "but it happened."

"No, there is chance," Ghenwa insisted.

"Fate."

We interrupted again, this time asking Ghenwa to tell us more about her perspective and whether she had used Bluetooth to meet people before.

She replied, "No. Bluetooth was still a new trend so we were excited about using it. It's possible that we played with it at home first and tried sending each other things, but that's it."

We asked, "So this is the first time it happened in a café?"

"In a café? Yes, this was the first time. Me and [my friend], we both had it open and we were playing around, sending stuff back and forth to each other, and it happened."

"So how was his approach? How did you react?"

Bilal interjected, "At first she was going to hit me!"

She protested, "I was not! How can I explain this, I wasn't really paying attention to the situation, you know? It wasn't until later that I noticed, and it wasn't until we were about to leave that Bilal came and talked to me and said, 'I would like to talk to you and get to know you better.' And by that time he had already sent me his number through Bluetooth, and that is how it happened. So I gave him a missed call, and he called me, and we talked for a little while, and that's it."

We pushed them a bit further, asking, "He just said he thought you were going to hit him. What exactly happened?"

Bilal jumped in again, "In the beginning, yeah, I said, *'ba'ad iznik'* ["with your permission"])." Ghenwa started laughing again as he continued, "She stood up to leave, and I said, 'With your permission,' but I was still sitting down."

"I said, 'At least stand up!'"

"And she said, 'Like this? *Hayk!? Bisir hayk!?* Are you really asking me like this!?' So I said, 'Excuse me,' and she continued walking down the stairs, so I ran after her and told her my number. I told her I sent her my number via Bluetooth, but she said that she didn't see it, but she did actually see it of course."

Ghenwa was still laughing. "Yeah, I had seen it."

"She had memorized it by then!" Bilal teased, "So I gave it to her again and I didn't imagine that she would call, but she did."

"Yes and you know, I just called randomly [*da'ayt hayk*], I didn't call with any specific intention, I don't know why I did. I mean, I noticed the number and I even remembered it, and I said, 'OK, why don't I call?' Maybe I was bored, I don't know. I felt, I don't know, I sensed that he was good, something made me sense that he was nice. There is something about a man's look that makes his character apparent. And just like that it happened, on the phone."

As Bilal and Ghenwa's story demonstrates, cafés have provided new public spaces where pious Shi'i Muslims may make the acquaintance of people they might not otherwise meet. Also striking about their tale as well as other stories about people meeting partners in cafés is the way that they both assumed the other was an appropriate prospect. Those assumptions are based in part on appearance and comportment, as Ghenwa noted. But they are also based on the fact that they met in a café located in a particular area of Beirut, where the majority of the patrons are assumed to share social, religious, and political characteristics.

It is difficult to overemphasize the importance of moral evaluations of activities ranging from heterosexual physical contact to being in the proximity of alcohol to listening to music. Put bluntly, "The kind of people who go there and what they do" are primary criteria by which people judge places. These are also criteria within which people negotiate their own practices and make choices not only about where to go but also about what to do in their leisure time. As we have seen, those choices often involve compromises among differing rubrics of morality as individuals weigh a variety of options. Surveillance and concerns about others' perceptions are the flip side of the security and validation that comes from being within one's community. At the same time, ideas about moral behavior may indicate assumptions about the relationship between people and place in the city. In the next chapter, we explore how spatial understandings and practices both shape and are shaped by flexible morality.

Comforting Territory, New Urban
Experiences, and the Moral City

Over the past few years, most of Mona's students at the American University of Beirut were utterly unaware of Dahiya's new leisure sites until she asked them to conduct fieldwork in a south Beirut café for her class. For these students—mainly upper-middle and upper-class Sunni, Druze, Maronite, and Shiʻi Lebanese living in upscale areas of Beirut—Dahiya is scary; it is an area they only bypass en route to or from the airport. Few (mainly Shiʻi) students had even heard of al-Saha, and those who had knew about it because they had been invited to a wedding there, or gone with a friend or family member.

During the first class field trip to a Dahiya café, students' typical reactions included surprise at the area's scale, relief at its resemblance to other neighborhoods, and appreciation for its vibrancy. "It feels like a whole city!" and "I really like how life here is in the streets!" are common exclamations. When they arrive at the café, students happily and with palpable relief observe that it isn't *really* different from places they go in Beirut, is "clean," and is "not shaʻbi"—meaning that it is not a working-class space but rather one that appears somewhat middle class. They are reassured by their sense that they can relate to some of the people sitting in the café and the general ambiance. After that first visit, they often ask Mona, "So what's different, besides the fact that these places don't serve alcohol?"

Despite these observations and reactions, most of these students were not interested in returning to cafés in south Beirut because they did not feel "comfortable" there. Some said that they might take a cousin or friend visiting from abroad in order "to show them Dahiya." Like many Beirutis, they associated "seeing Dahiya" with a sense of curiosity related to gazing at the exotic "Shiʻi other."[1] Others instead reacted like Beirut's leftist intellectuals, foreign students, and Lebanese expatriates. For them, Dahiya's

FIGURE 5.1 Signs on a major highway in Dahiya, showing portrait of martyr Imad
Mughniyyeh, and behind it, a charity box for Hizbullah's nongovernmental organization
al-Imdad

cafés—especially al-Saha and, for youths, Café.Yet—provide an easy way
to visit the often-romanticized Resistance community.[2]

Two of the signs that visually materialize this Resistance community in
urban space and remind people of its sacrifices are the martyr images that
hang on poles along several main streets in Dahiya as well as the practice
of naming streets after martyrs. For instance, the Hadi Nasrallah highway
that cuts through Dahiya is named after Nasrallah's son, who died in a
Resistance operation in 1997. This is not a characteristic unique to south
Beirut as martyrs' images are common in other Beirut neighborhoods too.[3]

Whether exoticized, romanticized, or simply dismissed altogether, most Beirut residents erase or incompletely acknowledge south Beirut as part of the city's leisure geography. Avoidance initially based in fear and political-sectarian judgment gives way to avoidance rooted in ideas about class and taste, which we take up further in the next chapter. Similar erasure and incomplete acknowledgment characterizes the relationship of Dahiya dwellers to Beirut. With few exceptions, our interlocutors did not include Beirut in their leisure geographies, categorizing the city as an uncomfortable, unsafe, and immoral space. The key exception to this was the seaside Corniche, the wide, paved path that winds along the shore at the city's edge.[4]

Yet Dahiya is well connected physically to the city through an efficient transportation infrastructure that is currently being expanded with additional tunnels, bypasses, and highways. With respect to the urban fabric, perhaps the most noteworthy difference between Beirut and Dahiya is the absence of colonial heritage buildings in the latter. The quality of the built environment is also poorer in south Beirut, largely deteriorated from wars, high density, and a lack of public maintenance. Nonetheless, Dahiya is not that different from other Beirut neighborhoods, especially working-class ones, in terms of both population density and the morphology of the built environment. The new high-end residential developments in south Beirut resemble new affluent areas elsewhere in the city in style and construction materials (see figure 5.2).[5] On the morphological level of city streets, blocks, and lots, Dahiya cannot be distinguished from municipal Beirut on a map. In that sense, south Beirut is no different from the Bourj Hammoud and Dora suburbs/neighborhoods to the north of the city, or Furn el-Chebbak and Ain el-Rummaneh to the east. They are all physically and formally part and parcel of the Beirut agglomeration.[6]

On the social and economic levels, the relationship between Dahiya and Beirut is not always reciprocal or balanced. Social exchanges, however, are part of the everyday lives of most residents, who often have family, friends, colleagues, or partners in one or the other place. Some extended families have members who reside in both places and regularly visit one another's neighborhoods. Those living in Dahiya might send their kids to school and university in Beirut, shop and eat in Hamra or Verdun, and enjoy their free time at the Corniche, at the movies, or in trendy Gemmayze. Those living in Beirut might go to Dahiya to complete paperwork at the Ministry of Labor, repair their cars in Ghobeyri or Ouzai, or buy cheap furniture in Ouzai or cheap clothing at Souk Mouawad. Some people have lived in south Beirut since birth and do not want to move, and other choose to live there for its proximity to Beirut with relatively lower real estate prices.[7] Overall, movement between Beirut and Dahiya is far more frequent, intense, and dense than most people acknowledge.

FIGURE 5.2 A new highway in Haret Hreik, with new buildings on both sides, show-casing the middle-income neighborhoods in Dahiya

Beirut's sectarian politics have a critical effect on people's mobility and their leisure choices. Leisure geographies are linked to these politics and the accompanying assumptions about safety, comfort, and morality.[8] People recognize and classify signs associated with political-sectarian geographies, and make choices in their spatial practices accordingly. These navigations are further complicated by the imperfect alignment of the social and religious moral rubrics with moral space understood in political-sectarian terms.

In this chapter, we argue that new moral leisure geographies are changing pious people's spatial experiences both within Dahiya and between Dahiya and Beirut. We begin with those who feel more comfortable remaining within their neighborhoods, and how this preference confines and territorially limits their spatial and leisure experiences. We then examine the urban experiences of those who prefer to venture outside the familiar to inhabit other city spaces that share their moral norms. For these people, especially youths, new moral leisure geographies provide opportunities to experience the city through leisure and develop new sets of urban competences. This helps them develop their own leisure maps in ways that fit their evolving social, religious, and political-sectarian moral rubrics. The chapter then shows how moral leisure facilitates new urban experiences in Dahiya and Beirut by promoting street life as well as public interactions. Finally, we end with reflections about how the city is being reshaped by the spatial practices of youths living moral leisure. Despite the stigmatization that dominates people's perceptions of one another and their associated territories, the relationship between Beirut and south Beirut may well become more permeable due to spatial practices in relation to moral leisure.

INHABITING THE COMFORTABLE: "STAYING INSIDE"

> Why go outside [*barra*]? I have everything here [in Dahiya]. I can
> live an excellent life, go to the best cafés, dress in the best clothes,
> and I am in my own neighborhood, and I have everything. So why
> go outside?
>
> —JAʿFAR, A STUDENT IN HIS EARLY TWENTIES

The idea that Jaʿfar expresses—that one can have everything without leaving south Beirut—is relatively new and highlights Dahiya's transformation from a marginalized suburb to a vibrant urban area with its own leisure sector. The recent availability of cafés in Dahiya has even led some youths, like twenty-year-old Ali, to lose interest in Beirut.

> We used to go to Beirut and spend the whole evening looking for a place to sit where we could feel comfortable. Sometimes we couldn't find one and we used to go back home! Now we have many places and cafés here, and they are the same as Beirut and near our homes. I am living here, and I am happy here.

As Ali notes, the convenience of proximity and accessibility prompt many Dahiya residents to stay in the area. Amira, for example, told us that she always shops and hangs out in Dahiya because her friends live nearby, and because the cafés and clothes are cheaper than elsewhere in the city. But convenience is not enough to explain the desire of most of our interlocutors to stay within south Beirut when other areas of the city are only a ten- or fifteen-minute drive away. To understand the ramifications of the political-sectarian division of urban space in Lebanon, we have to look to our interlocutors' discourses about comfort, security, and belonging.

THE COMFORT OF *ENTRE-SOI*

Many young people prefer to stay within their neighborhoods because they seek the comfort of entre-soi—the security and validation that stems from being among one's peers and community.[9] They openly avoid Beirut, venturing beyond Dahiya's borders only for specific purposes. Such youths have restricted leisure geographies and a strong sense of boundaries that differentiate a worrisome "outside" (barra) from a reassuring "inside" (*juwwa*). Many of our interlocutors used the common word barra to convey leaving Dahiya—a term that carries connotations ranging from outdoors to external to foreign. Hasan invented a more specific phrase: "When my friends ask me, 'Where were you?' I tell them, 'I was in the nation outside [*bilad barra*].' I mean the place outside Tayyoune [the northern boundary of Dahiya]. Outside this limit, I feel like a stranger [*gharib*]." For Hasan, everything outside Dahiya is foreign, and Dahiya is the center of his world, his personal capital city. Some youths go so far as to erase Beirut entirely from their leisure maps and use barra to refer to their home villages, often in the South or Bekaa Valley.

Several pious young people who viewed Dahiya as the geographic center of their lives understood Beirut to be not merely external to it but also the stigmatized periphery. They associated barra with immorality and promiscuity, and linked these characteristics most frequently to districts known for their nightlife (e.g., downtown, Monot, or Gemmayze) and Christian-majority east Beirut. The idea that certain areas of the city were immoral cut across age and gender. Forty-year-old Abdallah told us, "When I want to go out, outside Dahiya, I need to know where I am going. If I want to go to downtown, I am going to see people from all walks of life [*shi bi rass, shi bala rass*]. There's alcohol, there is loud music, songs, behavior that doesn't relate to my piety in any way."

Inside Dahiya, many pious youths and older people alike feel comfortable because they know that the dominant moral order is that of the Islamic milieu, with which they largely identify. "In my area, there is nothing that contradicts my beliefs. People who are not pious are obliged to live the way I live. I don't follow their lifestyle, they follow mine," explained Muhannad, who is a student at the elite Lebanese American University in Hamra. Danya, an engineer in her mid-twenties, further clarified this perspective:

> I am pious. I cannot go open a café in Manara or Ain el-Mreisseh or Verdun [Beirut neighborhoods], and tell them, "Alcohol is not allowed," or open a gym

and say, "No songs here." I cannot do that. People will not accept that. It doesn't work. For example, [in Beirut] I can't have [female] waiters who wear hijab, [male] waiters who don't shake hands [with women]; you can't, you can't! In Dahiya, the environment imposes itself. There are other sects living here, there are Christians, but they can't open a place and say, "We will sell alcoholic drinks here." They will lose money. They can't; they need to remain within the bounds of the environment they are in or it won't work.

Abdallah, Muhannad, and Danya all underscore the idea that each political-sectarian group is a moral group that is allotted its own territory, and entitled to control the moral environment within that territory. Internalized knowledge about the Islamic milieu's norms combines with confidence that place and morality are normatively aligned to provide pious people the certainty that cafés in Dahiya will meet their moral expectations. This reassures those who prefer to avoid the process of finding out whether a business serves alcohol or not. In Beirut, this information is usually not indicated clearly outside the café, which may put people who refuse to sit in places that serve alcohol in the potentially embarrassing situation of having to leave after sitting down and reading the menu.

Other people with whom we spoke focused more on the comfort and reassurance of being entre-soi that accompanied staying inside Dahiya. For twenty-year-old Rola, this meant feeling freer closer to home. She described feeling vulnerable outside Dahiya because it was "too exposed." Rola continued, "In Dahiya, I feel like I am in my area, my neighborhood. I do go out a lot to Beirut; my university was in Raouche so I know it well. I also go to downtown, but I feel more constrained there. Here I feel freer in my movements." Abdallah works outside Dahiya, and declared that his heart "warms up" when he approaches home. Amer elaborated, portraying Dahiya's spaces explicitly as home and its residents as kin.

> You know the saying "The person who leaves his home becomes less worthy"? It's like that, the people here in Dahiya, they are all from your home. I can be coming from far away, but when I go inside this place [a café in Dahiya], or a place like Dahiya, a place like me, I feel comfortable, I feel like I am in my home, as if I opened the door of my living room and went in!

The sense of familiarity, belonging, and kinship that Amer and Abdallah highlighted along with Rola's emphasis on freedom of movement and the sense of shared morality described above are all characteristics of what Ghassan Hage (1997) describes as "feeling at home."[10] For many of our interlocutors, the desire to stay inside Dahiya was fueled by a desire to feel at home in these terms. As they articulate this desire by representing Dahiya as inside and Beirut as outside, they invert the original relationship of suburb to city. Dahiya is idealized as the center, a space of home, community, and belonging, while Beirut is represented as a separate external space associated with immorality. Home here is not only about comfort and entre-soi but also may imply physical safety.

THE SECURITY OF POLITICAL-SECTARIAN COMMUNITY

For several pious young people, a reluctance to leave Dahiya arose from efforts to avoid potential problems related to sectarian politics. Twenty-year-old Rami explained, "I go there, to Beirut, and they stare at me, they point at me, they say, 'Look this is a Shi'a!' They know from my beard. This happened to me several times." Rami not only feels unwelcome in Beirut but also highlights the naturalized association of sect with community and place. He is by no means exceptional, and articulates a sentiment that we heard in different contexts from men and women of all ages. Young men's concerns about leaving Dahiya were sometimes conveyed with explicit references to violence. "Today, everyone feels more comfortable in his own neighborhood. It's not like I am scared, but you don't know when someone might start shooting at you!" twenty-year-old Muhammad exclaimed, laughing.

Young women were more apt to express worry about their safety, and several had stopped going to Beirut after Hariri's assassination in 2005. In a group interview with three nineteen-year-old premed students, Lina brought up this topic, saying, "After [2005], you avoided going to Beirut; you don't want to get into a strange situation, to get into trouble. As a girl wearing hijab, you feel uncomfortable in Raouche or downtown on your own. You feel different from the majority of people there." Her friend Sahar concurred:

> Yeah, before Hariri's assassination, we used to go to Beirut and feel like we are in Dahiya; there were lots of people down there. Now we have to think beforehand. Politics divided people. Before, I didn't used to think about which places to go there. Now I need to think about where to go. I don't want to get into trouble or feel uncomfortable.

Like many young women, Lina and Sahar assume that they are more easily identifiable by their headscarves, despite the fact that there are plenty of women living outside Dahiya who also wear them. They also feel uncomfortable based on their knowledge of the political divisions separating them from many residents of other neighborhoods. Zayna, an American University of Beirut student, was especially critical of the reemergence of political-sectarianism in 2005, asserting, "People are now, I don't know, *khalas*, it's like he's Sunni, Shi'i, Druze. At university, we had friends. When Hariri was killed, they stopped talking to us, as if we killed Hariri! These are very ugly ideas!"

Political-sectarian differentiations between inside and outside Dahiya have translated into a reinforced sense of territorial boundaries, exemplified by Rami's worry that he will get into trouble when he leaves Dahiya. His response is to avoid Beirut when he is on his own, only going when surrounded by friends. "If I am there on my own, and someone says something bad about me or my community, I will respond, of course, I won't let them bad-mouth us, and I'll get into trouble! With friends, I feel more comfortable," he shared. Then he added, "When we go to Beirut, especially after the July [2006] war, we tell our parents and our friends, in case something happens [laughing]! In Beirut, I am the Shi'a who killed Rafic Hariri!" Rami's joke and Zayna's anger about assumptions that "the Shi'a" assassinated Hariri refer to the politicized investigation into his death and accusations that Hizbullah members were involved. The experiences of young people from Dahiya who venture to Beirut and feel threatened or self-conscious reflect the tensions that have thrown a new wedge into Sunni-Shi'a relations in Lebanon since 2005.

The extent to which this wedge is in fact new is revealed by the experiences and geographies of older pious people in relation to leisure activities. Several told us that since 2005, they have only gone out in Dahiya or South Lebanon, yet that in the past they used to frequent a wide range of places not only across Beirut but also across the country, especially in the mountains. Forty-year-old Said observed that "the security situation affected our outings a good deal. A lot of people, even I, used to go frequently to Raouche, to Manara, to Broummana."[11] He continued, "Even friends of mine who are not pious stopped going. They used to go to downtown, to Jounieh [a city in the north], to Jbeil [also in the north]. Now I prefer to go to a café nearby. A lot of people who used to go for leisure outside Dahiya now only go out inside Dahiya." Forty-one-year-old Zayn added, "Since 2005, our regular trips to the mountain have stopped. If I go with my wife who wears hijab I worry about potential problems, or that I seem hostile to a particular party, or that the area is affiliated with a particular party."

These experiences of estrangement from formerly familiar parts of the country are shared by youths, like Amer, who worried during a trip with friends to the Druze-majority mountains that things might degenerate into a fight because of how people stared at them. "In all honesty, if I go to the mountains, I feel like I am not in Lebanon, not in my country. I feel like I am in a strange place, like I do not fit in, like I am wrong," he told us. Political-sectarian difference has impacted not only urban geographies but national ones too, narrowing the areas of the country where pious Shiʻi Muslims feel that they belong.

BELONGING AND PRIDE

People who preferred to stay within Dahiya for their leisure outings identi-fied strongly with it as a political-sectarian moral space.[12] Amira expressed this idea, underscoring a keen emotional connection to the Islamic milieu along with its people and places.

> Honestly, these days in Lebanon, with the circumstances and sectarianism, I don't feel comfortable in environments that are not related to my sect. Yaʻni, honestly, I'll tell you, I am Shiʻi, you tell me to go live in Tariq al-Jadidah [a Sunni neighborhood assumed to be politically affiliated with Hariri]; you can't.[13] It's not that people aren't respectful. No, on the contrary. But if someone says something, somebody will shoot. You'll get upset. We are in times when things are polarized. If you don't follow your leader, you can't, ʻan jadd ["seri-ously"]. And then, there, you feel, as an environment, excuse me yaʻni, during fasting, during prayer, during Ramadan, you are among your people, during iftar, during the call to prayer, nobody is in the street, subhan allah ["praise be to God"], hayk ["like this"], I feel it's impossible for me to live outside my sect, mustahil ["impossible," said emphatically]!

Amira links her comfort to a number of the themes we have discussed, including political-sectarian tensions, territories, and moral norms. She also takes great care to indicate that this is the situation for everyone. In her view, Lebanese have been polarized behind political-sectarian leaders and parties, and their hostility to those perceived as outsiders is not due to disrespect or ill manners but rather to a naturalized sense of political-sectarian belonging that limits specific communities to specific spaces.

Some people viewed this sense of belonging and the concomitant choice of staying inside Dahiya as a political act. They expressed pride in south Beirut's moral environment and the ability of its residents to sustain the Resistance cause against all odds. For them, Dahiya is a space that is mor-ally superior to the city according to all three moral rubrics—a space that should be defended against negative stereotypes via this comprehensive morality. Mahmoud mounted such a defense by questioning how depriva-tion is assessed, suggesting that the dominance of particular religious and social moral norms in Dahiya make it a better place than Beirut:

> They say that people in Dahiya are deprived. [But] pious people in Beirut are deprived compared to those in Dahiya! In Beirut, there are no places that don't serve alcohol. In Dahiya, I feel comfortable going into places. They have cred-

ibility [*amana*]. For example, in other places, they bring a bottle of the water to the table and charge me for it without me ordering it. Here, the waiter asks me, "Do you want water?" This is a moral behavior that abides by religious standards.

Mahmoud's argument against stereotypes rests on challenging what is valued in the first place and highlighting morality's role in determining what makes a place "good."

Others, like Mariam, instead challenged stereotypical representations of Dahiya by asserting that it has become more like Beirut. Her "we've caught up now" defense accepts and inverts the civilizational measure used by those who denigrate Dahiya.

> Before, they used to say, "Dahiya is backward," and unacceptable things, "*yiii*, Dahiya, look at this person, she's so Dahiya," if she's wearing bright colors. Like they have stereotypes. Now I am happy that we have improved; we have cafés, we are independent, we don't have to go outside Dahiya, we don't have to go to places to prove we can go out. No, we have cafés. We are like other places. We are civilized. And more beautiful than outside. Now people from outside want to come see what we have. I am so happy we have this environment!

Rather than suggest that Dahiya is different but better than Beirut, Mariam emphasizes the similarities between the two spaces, especially in relation to ideas about taste, class, and the availability of leisure. In her narrative, a lower-class taste indicator—wearing bright colors—has given way to the upward mobility demonstrated by the availability of beautiful cafés—a change she views with pride. Ja'far also expressed pride that Dahiya now provides the same sorts of commodities and leisure possibilities as other places, even making it an attraction for foreigners.

> Dahiya has everything now. Clothing stores that are very fancy, especially after the [Beirut] Mall opened. Cafés, restaurants. My friend visited from Germany. I took him to a restaurant here to eat Lebanese food. He was very happy. Another Italian friend of mine is visiting. He wants to eat Lebanese food, and he knows about Bab el-Hara; he wants to try the *hammam*. I am very happy in Dahiya and I feel that it has everything.

As Ja'far continued, it became clear that he was not only proud that Dahiya provided fancier clothing and food options than it had in the past but also proud of his community's resilience.

> And after the [2006] war, I am proud to be from Dahiya. Inno, we got hit, and returned better than before. We have people, doctors at the university, and peo-

ple *ktir* <u>open mind</u> ["very open minded"], people who made something of themselves, and they are from Dahiya. It's very wrong when people say they are lesser people.

Similarly, Amani argued that south Beirut's cafés demonstrate that "Dahiya's residents, they are not less than others. They have the reason and intellect to organize themselves. Nobody is better than anyone else." She also linked this explicitly to politics, noting, "This demonstrates the culture of life we have despite the difficult circumstances, despite the destruction Dahiya went through; now it has risen from its ashes, like the Phoenix." By referring to the culture of life and the Phoenix, Amani is directly appropriating a political slogan and image from the anti-Hizbullah March 14 political alliance. In doing so, she simultaneously asserts pride in Dahiya's resilience and suggests that Dahiya is not so different from Beirut after all.

Like Ja'far and Amani, our interlocutors were deeply affected by the 2006 war. Many had to flee the area to escape the daily deadly bombardment, and returned to find their homes, or those of their relatives and friends, damaged or destroyed. They saw their neighborhoods reduced to rubble and witnessed Hizbullah taking the lead to rebuild the area. Just as 2005 marked a moment of reentrenchment of political-sectarianism in urban and national space, 2006 marked a moment where Dahiya dwellers experienced intense reattachment and love for their home neighborhoods. As Mahmoud put it, "I don't only feel comfortable in Dahiya. I adore Dahiya! After the 2006 war, when I walked in Dahiya, *wallah al-'azim* ["I swear to God"], I felt the destroyed buildings. Sometimes I cried, but I cried out of pride; those rocks are pride and dignity, and we don't know their value!" Twenty-six-year-old Layla realized how much Dahiya meant to her when she was forced to leave during the 2006 war. She said, "I didn't like Dahiya much before the war. I didn't. I used to like other environments. But the moment I left, I started loving it, like one loves her village."

Such attachments to and pride in Dahiya led some young people, like Mariam, to get angry with those who wanted to leave the area for leisure.

Why? Why go outside Dahiya? We can find everything we want in Dahiya. Especially after the war, they made an effort to make everything we need available to us here in Dahiya. Why is Hamra better than Dahiya? Why should we go to the [other] places? Inno, <u>wow, prestige</u> [sarcastically], *aklass* ["classier"], and I don't know why, here they made better places! And now my friends who live outside, they ask me when are we going to this café I heard about?

In her tirade, Mariam highlights the persistence of ideas about Dahiya as lower class than other Beirut neighborhoods despite the plethora and variety of cafés and restaurants that now line its streets. She also connects the desire to leave the neighborhood to other class markers like language, by sarcastically invoking the English phrase "wow, prestige" to answer her question "Why go outside Dahiya?" "Wow, prestige" replicates the response she imagines people who want to leave Dahiya would give to her question. It also refers to both the tendency to use English words and leaving Dahiya as markers of class mobility. The term aklass conveys classier by applying an Arabic grammatical formation to the English word class. Using aklass may reflect Mariam's judgments about those who leave Dahiya and/or betray her own multilingual speech practices, which reflect her status as an undergraduate student at the American University of Beirut.

Some older pious people, like Hanady, thirty-nine, also rejected interaction with areas outside Dahiya and associated boundary crossing with betrayal.

> It's not only the security situation. Even if it's calm. . . . After 2006, people in Dahiya became more, it's going to sound harsh, they have a territorial bias toward their area ['indun ta'assub la manta'itun]. I am one of them. After 2008, I don't buy a thing from outside Dahiya! I won't go to cafés outside Dahiya! Never! I don't go out outside Dahiya! I am biased, I am territorially biased, toward Dahiya! We have self-sufficiency, why go outside?

The majority of our interlocutors, including most pious youths, expressed feelings of pride in and belonging to Dahiya as well as a clear preference for spending their leisure time inside the area, among people and within an environment they trusted based on a sense of political-sectarian connection. But this was by no means a universal sentiment. We now turn to dissenting opinions about leisure within Dahiya, and to those who contested the idea of being restricted to a particular community and space, and wanted to pass beyond their neighborhood's borders to experience other parts of the city and country.

EXPERIENCING THE CITY: "GOING OUTSIDE"

CRITIQUING TERRITORIAL CONFINEMENT

One rationale for challenging the idea that it was better to stay within Dahiya had to do with the constraints of being limited to one area of the metropolis. Even Hanady, who proclaimed her "territorial bias" toward Dahiya, complained that entre-soi also felt claustrophobic, which intimates that her refusal to leave south Beirut hinges on the post-2005 political context. As she put it,

> When I go to the cafés [in Dahiya], I never feel completely relaxed/happy [*mun-shariha*]. No, I feel it's artificial. It is confined; there are no views. The location doesn't make you feel like you "changed atmosphere" [*ghayyarti jaw*, a phrase connoting de-stressing]. It is too confining. I feel the atmosphere is boring—maybe because I know most of the people who go there. This bothers me a lot. I know many people in the places we go. You feel constrained. I try to act indifferent, but it still annoys me.

Rather than focusing on the boredom of social routine, younger pious women were more likely to describe feeling inhibited in Dahiya—an effect of the gender differences in behavioral expectations discussed in the last chapter and the possibilities for surveillance by people who might know you in places close to home. Twenty-year-old Zaynab explained this, noting, "Outside is free, I feel free to laugh out loud without attracting attention in Beirut, whereas in Dahiya, people will notice and stare. Dahiya is a shar'i place, a place of religious commitment. I need to pay more attention to the way I dress, to my behavior." For a few young women, escape meant leaving Lebanon altogether, whether on pilgrimage trips to Iran or shorter visits to Damascus.[14] Diala, for example, used to visit the famous Souq al-Hamadiyya in the Syrian capital on a regular basis because there she felt free to laugh loudly and eat ice cream on the street—activities that she worried would lead to negative gossip about her if she were recognized.

Other youths, male and female, found remaining in Dahiya limiting in other ways. A few concentrated on what they depicted as the lesser quality of the area's leisure places; they preferred to go to Beirut and especially its seaside cafés. Hussein initially focused on ideas about quality and class, but quickly shifted his narrative to suggest that the only difference was proximity to the sea.

> I don't like staying inside [Dahiya] because there are no classy places to go. Restaurants are too working class [sha'bi], and I don't like how they are directly on the street. I can feel people staring. Inno, they are nice, but the problem is the scenery. I like to go to places in Beirut where I can smoke argileh and look at the sea. It's a great view. I go to cafés here, and it's the same thing, same quality, same prices and all, but you don't have the view.[15] I feel relaxed there. It's important.

Even youths who generally preferred to stay close to home mentioned that remaining in Dahiya was limiting. They made an effort to go to Beirut for specific events or activities, including academic conferences or lectures, political talks, and leisure activities such as exhibitions, theater performances, and movies. A group of pious students in their early twenties who

attend universities in Hamra discussed this in one of our interviews. We
asked them whether they go outside Dahiya for leisure.

Jihad replied, "We have to go outside. Why should we stay confined in
our ghetto [*mutaqawqa'in*]? One time I said to my friend, 'I am going to
Verdun,' and he said, 'Oof, you're going to Beirut. I haven't been there in
seven years [laughs]!' This is too much!"

Mariam responded to him, "But it's not about ghettoization [*taqawqu'*],
it's just about proximity. Why should I go far if everything is close to me
and it makes feel comfortable [to stay nearby]?"

"Me, I go outside Dahiya a lot," added Zayna. "I get bored staying in
Dahiya. I divide up my week. One day I go to Hamra, one day to Verdun,
one day to Mar Elias. I like it like this. I go around a lot. But I prefer Dahiya. I feel more comfortable."

In this exchange, Jihad uses a term—mutaqawqa'in—derived from
taqawqu', a word commonly used by Lebanese politicians to describe the
extreme ghettoization or isolation of political-sectarian communities from
one another.[16] He felt that people who stayed inside Dahiya and detached
themselves for extended periods of time from other parts of the city were
unnecessarily exaggerating the effects of the political situation for silly reasons. His fiancée, Zayna, agreed with him indirectly by describing her multiple leisure destinations. Her personal map of the city incorporated several
different west Beirut neighborhoods, in stark contrast to the personal geographies of most of our interlocutors, which tended to be more restricted
to Dahiya's imagined boundaries. Among pious youths, there was a great
deal of variation in both their knowledge of the city and desire to learn
more about it.

Developing Urban Competences

The way that Zayna portrayed her movements across the city indicates an
ease of mobility acquired through urban experience—a central component
of which is leisure—facilitated by her self-confidence. Ja'far, who lived in
Dahiya while studying and working in Beirut, also spoke casually about
his regular border crossing, normalizing his mobility. "I am international!"
he laughed. "I have many friends abroad, and I am open to everyone. But
I have limits. I go to Hamra; my dentist is there. I don't feel wrong, 'adeh."

Zayna and Ja'far have advanced urban "competences"—skills that people
acquire through their experiences in/of the city that allow them to make
sense of the city's multiple and complex codes as well as negotiate those codes
across and within neighborhoods.[17] Urban competence varies with age, gender, income, and—in Lebanon—political-sectarian identification and ideas
about morality. Twenty-something Dima, for instance, has limited urban

competences, but seems to be interested in developing them, as indicated by her desire to leave Dahiya—a desire rooted in complaints about its urban density and her perception that it is dirtier than elsewhere.

> I don't have a problem with other neighborhoods. I don't say, "*Barrat* Dahiya" ["outside Dahiya"]. I go to places, but I don't know streets well. But I am not that attached to Dahiya. I am not, <u>wow</u>, Dahiya. I never used the term Dahiya before [going to] university. When people asked me where I live, I said, "Ja-mous, Chiyah," and they answered me, "Oh, here, with us, in Dahiya?" Dahiya . . . people in it are very bad; some people are good. I went to a school in Ain el-Rummaneh [nearby Christian neighborhood]. People there, it's another world. They speak about different things. It's something else. The street is so clean. Here, people dirty the street, throw garbage on the street, [and] they say, "Everybody does it."

Dima, like several of the youths we interviewed, is still learning how to access other neighborhoods in order to expand her map of the city, while more or less maintaining the different rubrics that constitute her moral ideas. So is Amira, who is familiar with only one Beirut neighborhood, Mar Elias, and is comfortable there because its class dimensions remind her of Dahiya. She is uneasy in upscale areas of the city, which she qualifies as "completely different worlds." Young people like Amira or Dima can gradually claim these "different worlds" along with their alien streets by learning about their broader environment and developing the urban competences they need to navigate the city.

Not all pious youths are interested in diverse urban and leisure experiences. Those who share the views of Lina, Amer, and Mariam are quite comfortable with their confined leisure geographies. Others seek opportunities to push the boundaries of their comfort zones and experience how the city operates. They may learn how leisure in the city relates to their concerns about morality through a variety of experiences in different neighborhoods. While learning these competences, their leisure geographies will be in flux, varying between the extremes of a confined territory and an expanded urban network, a circumscribed encounter and an intense experience of the city.

And like Zayna and Ja'far, several of our interlocutors already had wide urban geographies and a solid set of competences that allowed them to feel confident outside their political-sectarian enclave. These people tended to be in their late twenties and were often college graduates who had accumulated some professional experience. Their dispositions allowed them to feel comfortable expressing their identities and claiming moral identity as a right. These characteristics in turn allowed them to patronize a wide range of cafés across Beirut, and interact comfortably with "other" people and places. Jaʿfar exemplified this in ways that highlight Lebanese ideals of sectarian coexistence.

> Yes, there is some difference [between Beirut and Dahiya people] . . . free *aktar hinneh* ["they (Beirutis) have more freedom"]. But I deal with that maybe because I have more self-confidence. I am like that, pious. I have conviction. I am not wrong. We talk, and I argue my point. You think like this, I think like that. We are different, but not against each other. We are friends.

Not only did self-confidence foster the extension of social, professional, and economic networks and urban experiences for youths; it also allowed them to filter those experiences through sets of shifting personal and socially mediated guidelines. Those guidelines frequently defined limits to their urban mobility based on their ideas about morality.

GUIDED URBAN EXPERIENCES

Jaʿfar's outgoing personality facilitated his dynamic interactions with the city. His urban experiences illustrate the ways that new leisure geographies in Beirut and south Beirut are being produced through as well as by ideas about morality, with its overlapping religious, social, and political-sectarian rubrics. Jaʿfar often meets people on the Internet—young women and men with whom he chats regularly. Sometimes, if friendships develop, they meet in the physical world. He gave us an example about how he controlled those meeting spaces so that they did not violate his moral norms. He was planning to meet Christian friends he knew through chatting and carefully chose a café located at the northeastern edge of Dahiya where it intersects with a Christian-majority neighborhood. His reasoning for picking this place included the knowledge that the café did not serve alcohol and was patronized by Christians. Such knowledge is a key determinant of his leisure geographies as they incorporate new additions. Jaʿfar has delimited a clear set of guidelines for choosing leisure sites, prioritizing the religious rubric of morality.[18]

> First it should not serve alcohol. Second, based on reputation, if bad guys go there, or couples go there, or there's music. In Dahiya, these things are controlled [*madbuta*]. Outside Dahiya, I mostly go to House of Donuts in Sodeco [now closed] and Tayyouneh. In Raouche, in Hamra, we go to Barbar, there's nothing else there.[19]

Other pious youths have developed different sets of personal guidelines to categorize city spaces and places as morally acceptable or unacceptable.

These vary according to their understandings of their own piety, prioritizations of the various moral rubrics, and more or less flexible understandings of moral norms. They also may vary over time as their ideas and circumstances shift. These guidelines influence—but do not determine—behavior, and contribute to the variation and flexibility of youths' understandings of morality. Along with other criteria ranging from a desire to be polite to the time of day to how much money is in one's pocket, these guidelines influence youths' leisure maps in terms of both extension (number of destinations) and intensity (repeat visits to the same destination). The diversity of views on moral issues discussed in chapter 4 appear in young people's diverse guidelines for which cafés and neighborhoods they will frequent.

Sometimes these guidelines reflect a desire to avoid places where people might be ignorant of pious youths' moral norms. "I cannot go to Verdun or downtown," said Danya, for example. She continued,

> I cannot go there! They just don't have any shar'i atmosphere—unless you go for curiosity or if you are going to Biel for an exhibition. Even exhibitions, the ones in Dahiya are preferable. Also, in Dahiya, people will give you space to walk; in Biel, they will come close to you. Even clothing places in Beirut, Hamra, or Verdun, the guy comes and tries clothes on you directly, hovers around you. They don't do this in Dahiya; they turn away.

As Danya's discomfort shows, and as we saw in the last chapter, gender matters to both people's personal guidelines and how they are perceived by others, or think they are perceived. Gender also impacts young women's guidelines for when one can patronize particular places. Some will go to places in Beirut during the day, but avoid them at night. Danya, who goes "to the sea" in Beirut regularly, will only go during the day because "at night, there are things that happen, you can't go, you know. In the evening, you go with your family to places where you can guarantee nothing wrong will happen, like Terrace, Fantasy World. No one likes to go to a restaurant if an hour later someone gets drunk and starts [behaving badly]." Other young women included Hamra in their "daytime-only" guideline. The gendered desire to avoid leisure places at night does not apply only to Beirut, although night may be understood to begin earlier further from home. In Dahiya, prior to 9:00 p.m. women and men were equally represented in cafés; at that point in the evening, cafés are progressively patronized by all-male and mixed-gender groups, so that by 10:00 p.m. there are few all-female groups, if any, remaining.

Some pious young men think that young women should be accompanied when going to certain places in the city—a rule that young women often contest. Twenty-three-year-old Lamia's male friends told her that it was "forbidden" for her to go walk on the Corniche with her girlfriends, warning that guys there could *zannikh ʿalayhum*—meaning tease them in a harassing way or flirt obnoxiously with them. Lamia vehemently disagreed with this suggested guideline.

> We don't accept this. It's the girl who allows a guy to tease/harass/annoy her [*zannikh ʿalayha*] and she is the one who can stop him. We are in a public place. When we go to the beach, we might go sit on the sand by the sea. A guy may oppose this idea. But we are not doing anything wrong! When we go there, we choose an empty section next to the beach. We play and enjoy our time. We don't go against our religion or our morals. All we do is change atmosphere/de-stress. We have a good time and then we leave. We abide by the [moral] constraints [*dawabit*]!

Political-sectarianism also affects guidelines. Most commonly, pious young Shiʿi Muslims avoid talking politics when they are in Beirut. Danya usually goes out in Dahiya, but she—unusually among our interlocutors—lives in Beirut. The convenience of going out closer to home takes her to cafés in Hamra occasionally. She explained, "Out of respect, it is not appropriate to be in a café [in Beirut] that is used by all kinds of people and sit in an ignorant way. We are educated people; they are not my enemies. I respect their opinion. I usually try not to have political conversations there." Batoul also engages in self-censorship. She is a student at a university located in the Sunni-stronghold Tariq al-Jadidah and goes out with her Sunni friends to cafés in Beirut. She carefully avoids discussing politics or religion in order to maintain those friendships. For Danya and Batoul, the guideline about censoring political discussion extended from the social rubric for morality; they prioritized relationships over expressing their political views.

Others may self-censor in order to avoid attracting unwanted attention. Muhannad is especially careful if he happens to overhear a political conversation. As he put it, "There are some places in Beirut where it's difficult to discuss politics. When you are in a place in Beirut that supports someone and you support someone else, you can't talk politics. That's how the country is." Lara experiences this hesitation to be identified as an outsider every time she hangs out in Hamra with her longtime friend Aziza, who lives in Dahiya yet prefers to spend her leisure time outside the area. In Hamra's cafés, Aziza lowers her voice to a whisper whenever she says anything about politics or current events in Lebanon. She even whispers when she mentions the names of Dahiya neighborhoods, or religious or political leaders, including that of her uncle, a Hizbullah politician who is not particularly well known outside the community. She also instructed Lara, whenever she forgot this rule, to lower her voice or wait until later to continue a conversation—sometimes with a significant amount of urgency.

MAPPING THE MORAL CITY

When they are outside Dahiya, pious youths' knowledge about leisure places is not always well developed. Those in their late teens and early twenties—who are often only beginning their explorations and are still constructing their groups of friends—frequently find themselves in places that violate their moral standards. As they gain experience, they build "literacy" about the city's moral leisure geographies and grow better able to avoid uncomfortable situations. Hasan, for example, who is twenty, does not go out a lot and rarely ventures beyond Dahiya. When he is invited to Beirut, he accepts the invitation, and tries to adapt to the café or restaurant. He asks friends to alter plans when he notices "something" (like alcohol on the menu) prior to entering an establishment. But sometimes he doesn't notice "something wrong" until they are already seated. In those cases, he is not comfortable expressing his unease and will resort to communicating it indirectly by ordering only water, which he hopes will send a message to his friends, and prompt them to leave or choose a different place next time they hang out. As Hasan learns more about the city, he will be able to map a geography of leisure that is appropriate for him and suggest locations to meet friends in the future.

Danya, a pious Beiruti, developed this sort of urban literacy over time. She is married now, but explained that when she was younger, she neither knew which places served alcohol nor had the courage to walk out of places that were morally unacceptable to her.

> At [the] university, I didn't know all the places well yet and I was still a beginner in my religious commitment. So we used to go to a place, and I would be surprised to find alcohol. I was ashamed to leave then. I had friends who were not pious and from another religion who said to me, "What's the problem? We are not drinking!" Then I had to go to those places because I didn't have experience, I didn't know better. Now I know which place is like this, and which place is like that.

Several of our young interlocutors were still in the process of figuring out where to experience appropriate leisure in Beirut. But knowledge of moral leisure geographies is not enough. Mariam, an American University of Beirut student who knows Beirut, described the relationship of knowledge about leisure sites to the complex social negotiations that take place around differing ideas about morality. The anger she expressed above at those who seek to leave Dahiya for leisure may reflect how often she feels like she has to concede her desire to stay in Dahiya in order to hang out with nonpious friends who live near Hamra. She goes to Hamra cafés with them provided they choose places without alcohol, "because they're not going to go all the way to Dahiya even if it makes me more comfortable!"

Knowledge of moral leisure geographies combines with people's personal guidelines and ideas about moral norms in various rubrics to create multiple shifting possibilities along with strategies for experiencing leisure in different areas of the city. Together, these elements generate a map of leisure possibilities. Just as we saw a great deal of variation in people's maps of the moral city, some, like Ja'far and Muhannad, take care to never leave their outings to chance, and have clearly drawn maps of moral leisure in Beirut. Others, like Hadi and Jawad, enjoy trying new places and are confident that they will leave a place that they find unacceptable. Nada falls somewhere in between. Her map of moral leisure is wide and incorporates Beirut because she used to live there and is accustomed to being outside Dahiya. She relies on her social networks and only goes out with people who share her values. She also assesses places before going out and includes in her repertoire several downtown cafés (including some that serve alcohol) where she can sit outside. She distinguished between downtown and a nearby neighborhood known for its club scene: "You know the neighborhoods, and you can tell if a place is good or not. I do not go to Monot, for instance!"

Moral leisure sites within and outside Dahiya have allowed pious Shi'i youths to navigate and inhabit the city in new ways. Youths' leisure geographies are thus a good indicator of how the city is increasingly experienced through mappings that include or exclude neighborhoods, incorporate or bypass sites, and favor or circumvent routes.[20] These mappings are not set in stone or benchmarked against strict rules but instead are changeable. They generate novel categories of lived spaces in the city, shaped by ideas about the (im)morality of place. The city is demarcated into demonized sections that are dismissed and idealized sections that are privileged, including and excluding certain people accordingly.[21] Through these demarcations, these mappings produce a range of spatial practices that fragment and segregate the city into (im)moral places and neighborhoods. Particular city streets, blocks, and neighborhoods are appropriated and marked by pious youths' presence and interactions as they hang out, wait for each other on street corners, enter and leave cafés, window-shop, laugh, and flirt. Through bodies marked as pious—especially female bodies—living leisurely moments, the everyday spaces of the city are transformed.

Clearly ideas about morality shape spatial practice. It is critical to underscore that space also shapes moral norms. For example, Lamia goes to a seaside café that plays music in the evening, but she sits on the patio where the music is buffered by the sound of the waves. The way that this café's space is conceived allows Lamia to use the place morally. Here, space itself generates the possibility of a moral spatial practice and urban experience. Social interaction can facilitate the relationship between space and morality. In a Beirut ice cream parlor, Diala confidently asked a waiter to lower the music's volume and the waiter complied "because he saw [she] wears hijab." By changing the shop's features, the waiter allowed it to become apt for moral spatial practice. In both these cases, conceived space was easily modified to accommodate for different moral norms.

Lamia told us another story that highlights how social and spatial practices come together to reconceive an immoral space.

> In my university, lecture halls in the science building, they're like a cinema. They're very big, and all the tables are next to each other in rows, so if you want to go inside, you have to pass very close to the guys. This doesn't work for us. When we want to sit down, we ask them, "Please, can you exit the row [to let us in]?" Even if they're in the middle, they need to go out for us to enter. It's impossible for us to walk in and let this *contact* [in French] take place. Once, we were a bit late, the professor was about to start, and we told a guy, he was sitting in the middle, "Please stand on the table, we will pass and then you can sit down." So he said, "Oooooh, you are pious people?" They think that it's because we're pious. But if you think about it, it's not only because I wear hijab. For any girl, *mish zabta* ["it doesn't work"], morally I mean. Many guys, Christians even, they get out and let us enter, respectfully, without us even asking, because for them, it's a moral duty.

By asking young men to inhabit space in a different way to allow young women to pass by without any bodily contact, Lamia and her friends are reconceiving both space and spatial practice to make them conform to their moral norms. As students with the right to access the university's lecture halls, they felt empowered to ask their peers to temporarily change how they occupy space so that they were equally able to occupy it. Crucially, Lamia does not understand the moral norms at stake solely as religious ones, but instead views them as falling within a social rubric of morality that highlights respectful interactions between men and women.

The city's leisure geographies provide far fewer opportunities to make such requests, especially in private spaces. Pious youths cannot ask Beirut businesses that serve alcohol or play dance music to abide by their standards. They also cannot easily avoid salespeople who may have different ideas about appropriate contact or crowds at exhibitions or events. They try to inhabit public space in ways that make them feel comfortable, and are especially able to do so on the Corniche. Indeed, the extensive use of the Corniche by visibly pious people has led some Beirut residents to complain that it has become a Dahiya space. These observers often neglect to note the variety of people who frequent the Corniche, singling out pious Shi'i Muslims in ways that highlight the negative stereotyping of and discrimination against Dahiya's residents.[22]

The fear that space will be occupied by "Dahiya's people" is one of the reasons behind the continued closure of Beirut's main public park (Horch Beirut), which is situated at municipal Beirut's southern border close to Dahiya's northern sections. This pine-tree-filled area is the largest park in a city notorious for its congestion and lack of public green space. In 1995, France gave the Lebanese government the resources to rehabilitate the park, which had burned during the civil war. New pine trees were planted, and the area was landscaped. It remained closed for a few years to protect the vegetation and allow the trees time to grow. In 1999, a small section was opened for public use. As we go to press fourteen years later, most of Horch Beirut remains closed to the public. The Beirut municipality, which oversees the park, claims that it lacks the human resources to manage it. Many people do not find this excuse convincing, as the municipality has significant financial resources yet is making no efforts to overcome the problem.[23] There are also relevant political circumstances: the Sunni Muslim mayor of Beirut has been systematically elected with Hariri support since the end of the civil war.[24] After his term in office ended, in a private conversation in 2007, one of these mayors gave one of Mona's former students two reasons to justify the park's continued closure: "to protect Beirut dwellers from the potential danger of sectarian violence," as Horch Beirut lies adjacent to the Shi'i Ghobeyri and Sunni Tariq al-Jadidah neighborhoods; and more tellingly, he worried, "the park will be invaded by all the Shi'a of Dahiya, who will ruin it."

By mapping the city into good and bad leisure places informed by the stereotypes as well as power configurations exemplified by the Horch Beirut case, pious youths understand urban space according to "anchor zones" they use to navigate neighborhoods and expand their urban networks. As we heard in many of the narratives above, youths elaborate tactics and competences to enter, belong to, adjust, and alter their mappings of the moral city. Their maps are always in process, in part because younger individuals are still learning to inscribe their ideas about morality onto spaces and places. Another factor may be youths' greater openness to experimentation. The generational shifts we have outlined are also relevant, as members of the vanguard generation tend to have more solidified ideas about other places and people. Pious youths, on the other hand, both take moral norms for granted within their community and view them with greater overall flexibility, allowing them to experiment as they explore the city's possibilities.

LIVING MORAL LEISURE IN THE CITY

The new moral leisure landscape has geographic impacts on both Dahiya and Beirut.[25] The last section of this chapter explores how cafés and restaurants are reconfiguring Dahiya's sociospatial structures and the Dahiya-Beirut relationship. South Beirut's new cafés promote street life and public interactions, contributing to more vibrant urban dynamics. These dynamics take on another dimension when they occur where different sectarian territories connect, in border zones that facilitate greater negotiations of morality and geography.

New Urban Dynamics in South Beirut

While café culture has been important to some Beirut neighborhoods for a century, it is crucial to keep in mind that it is a recent addition to Dahiya and the pious Shiʻi community. As Saʻid reminded us, "Cafés in these times are the new leisure space that makes people happy. The café is a place for letting go, breathing, entertainment, meetings, interactions, inviting friends out." Young men and women alike enjoy the variety provided by the area's cafés, and they value discovering new places. Layla compared discovering a café to making a new acquaintance. "It's like, you know, the more you meet people, the more you see new areas, the more your culture is renewed and enriched. A new café is like a new person!" In today's Dahiya, moral leisure sites offer plenty of opportunities to meet new people, hang out with old friends, plan social events, study, chat in person or online, vent, gossip, spend time alone away from family, and relax.[26] Couples told stories about meeting in cafés. Customers befriended waitstaff or other customers, expanding their social networks. Some used cafés for business, selling merchandise or meeting with clients. For Hadi, cafés are the only place he can meet a female friend to talk and vent. "If I need my [female] friend to talk about something, I cannot go to her house, she cannot come to my house," he explained. "Where can I see her? In the entrance of the building?! Of course not. I invite her to a café."

In addition to being centers of social life, cafés enable people's interaction with their neighborhoods, reshaping those neighborhoods' dynamics. People who walk to the café occupy the street and public space in new ways, as flaneurs seeking leisure in urban space, experiencing the street and surrounding buildings and activities. People who come by car to the café affect the neighborhood by disrupting traffic and urban life, whether on a main or side street. New social and spatial practices emerge on streets outside cafés as well as on their patios. People hang out at entrances—beginning or continuing a conversation, blocking passersby, and often speaking at easily overhead volumes so that conversations incorporate newcomers and are regularly reinvigorated. Some cafés provide take-out service on the street level, encouraging people to wait and converse with other customers and staff. Those that serve food from nearby snack bars and restaurants force waitstaff to interact with people working in neighboring businesses who also frequently bring ongoing discussions into the café.[27] In all these ways, cafés encourage a more *urban* experience of the city by fostering street life, pedestrian culture, and a sense of neighborhood.[28]

Cafés also allow people to claim spaces and inhabit them in ways that blur the boundaries between public and private, particularly with their multiple interior and exterior spatial arrangements. Our interlocutors found this eclecticism appealing, as it enabled them to appropriate café spaces, mark them with their preferences, and dwell in them for extended periods of time. Because customers are usually visible to the street, this impacts public space outside the café and therefore urban space more broadly, and can affect people's ideas about the relationships of space and morality.

While men and women both use and claim café spaces, the ways in which they inhabit and personalize them varies. For the older men we interviewed, cafés provided an opportunity to claim personal territory that they felt unable to assert at home. Abdallah views cafés as important venues for changing his mood and breaking daily routine.

> The café can be considered an outlet/breathing space [*mutanafass*]. What I appreciate is that I go there to escape from the environment, to let go. At home, you live a routine. You look at your wife, your kids, television, *ma fi shi* ["there's nothing"]. You go, smoke an argileh, drink tea, change atmosphere/de-stress [*ghayyir jaw*], with other guys, you talk about an issue, work on a project, you use the time productively, you kill time.

Zayn underscored cafés' valuable role in the specific context of Lebanon: "Cafés reduce one's stress and anxiety. Because of war, people are more anxious and need to go out more to reduce this stress. Having more cafés encourages people to go out more, and it helps them." For Zayn and several other men in their late thirties and forties, the value of cafés materialized in their status as "regulars"; not only did they have preferred cafés, but also preferred tables and orders that waiters were able to anticipate.

Younger men also cultivated relationships with cafés, laughing and exchanging advice with owners, staff, and other customers. They especially appreciated what they perceived as the openness of owners and staff to their suggestions about service and seating arrangements, which led them to feel like cafés were a space over which they could exert a certain amount of control. Ahmad, Qasim, and Rami, all in their early twenties, have scheduled weekday times during which they hang out over argileh and food in cafés near their university. They patronize several different places to avoid boredom, and are sometimes joined by other friends who know where and when to find them. Like older men, younger ones explained that going to cafés helped them relax and highlighted their various forms of sociality. Ahmad appreciated being able to discuss problems with friends, thus getting their support and advice. Qasim added that cafés broadened his social world, letting him know "what is going on outside, and to hear things, see things, see new people, and be entertained." For many young men, cafés become second homes—places they inhabit with comfort and familiarity.

Gendered norms of respectable comportment make it more difficult for women to develop relationships with café owners and waitstaff, who are usually male. Despite this, we saw quite a few joking and familiar interactions between female café customers and male staff. Students study or hang out, mothers bring their young children, and older women use cafés as surrogate homes for hosting social events. Hanady, who above expressed both a territorial bias toward Dahiya and claustrophobia from seeing the same faces repeatedly, also underscored the new cafés' social value for working women and mothers.

> Cafés have positive sides. Sometimes, cafés allow you to host people, to treat someone like a guest. Last time I went, I invited my friend out for lunch for her birthday. I didn't want to buy her a gift. Working women today, they don't have time, but they still need to fulfill social duties. [A café] is a nice place. It solves the problem. My sisters and I, we use cafés a lot to invite people out, have birthday parties for kids. It's good. You make use of it.

Women in their thirties and forties are often responsible for maintaining relationships via reciprocal social invitations. Many shared Hanady's view that cafés have solved the problem of hosting events, and invite friends and family members out to meals in south Beirut's establishments. This signifies broader changing patterns of socializing and social obligation in the area, as noted by café owners in chapter 3.[29] Amani linked this new café function to desires for more diverse entertainment options and the need to host large groups of people, particularly during Ramadan's festive evenings.[30]

> People go out a lot during Ramadan. They spend their evenings out. Night becomes day, day becomes night. The rooms in these places allow people to meet

and enjoy each other's company. It ensures better social interactions, celebrations; we can't host the same number of people inside our houses. It's good to have more places, because we can change, according to our moods. We enjoy trying new places, discovering new things.

These transformations in everyday life and leisure are inscribed in the built environment. Public space is reconfigured through the different ways that diverse café patrons occupy it at various times of day, creating opportunities to negotiate or contest modes of urban life. These contestations are more salient in cafés situated between sectarian groups—for instance, in Sainte-Thérèse, where people's ideas about moral behavior in public space vary widely.[31]

Claiming Rights for Moral Leisure in Beirut

Dahiya's new moral leisure sector raises a series of questions about the place of moral leisure in Beirut more broadly. Danya and Muhannad discussed the limitations of the relationship between geography and morality. She began, saying,

> My problem is that in Lebanon, as pious people, the only shar'i places are in Dahiya. We don't have an outlet to the sea, and the sea would be the best site to have shar'i places. The South is too far. As pious people, we are confined. We can't go to those nice places in the mountains, in Aley, Bhamdoun; it's all alcohol and dancing. It's not just about pious people but also about conservative people. A lot of families from all sects can't go to those places with dancing, singing, women with no clothes!

Muhannad replied,

> Yes, but I don't think we can control where shar'i places open. Lebanon is divided, not only geographically but also its people. There is interaction but it is divided. You can't say to a Christian for whom alcohol is halal, "I want a café without alcohol." The geographic location limits you.

Muhannad exemplifies the to each his own position we described earlier, extending it to Lebanon's diverse political-sectarian spaces. The vast majority of pious people we spoke with did not challenge the dominance of "immoral" leisure in other parts of Beirut or Lebanon, recognizing those areas as belonging to other groups with different dominant values. Rather than challenge the city's political-sectarian divisions, they confirm them through their geographic practices, avoiding other territories and staying inside their own. While they may complain about feeling confined, or pass moral judgment on others in ways that conflate the religious and political-sectarian rubrics of morality, in the end they surrender to spatial segregation as a status quo situation over which they have no control.

Occasionally, however, we heard discussions—like this one among three young women—that suggest that some pious youths want to push that status quo. Zaynab began the conversation.

> I want to tell you something. There's only one café open for pious people in Raouche [a seaside west Beirut neighborhood], and it is very, very, very modest and very small. It feels vulgar. Young kids go there. The quality is very low. We don't go there. Why should it be of that class? Because it is for pious people?!

Fatima agreed with her, asking, "Why are all the pious places in Dahiya? Inno, we are cursed with staying in Dahiya because we want to be pious? *Tayyib*, where to go? I go out every day. Should I go to Dahiya every day? *Tayyib*, once, twice, three times, twenty times . . . and then?"

Rola tried to explain, "The country is like that. For example, downtown has a specific reputation. If you put a pious place there, it won't work. It has its people. . . ."

"I disagree with you," interrupted Fatima. "If al-Saha opens in downtown, it will do very well!"

Zaynab chimed back in, highlighting downtown's relationship to tourism:

> But tourism is not for the pious. Tourism allows everything. People who think about opening a pious place are close to pious people; their wife or their daughter is pious. And these people are mostly in Dahiya. This is demographics. Someone in downtown will not think about the pious. He will think about making money.

"Do you think there's a need for places in downtown, though?" we inquired.

"Yes, there's a social need," Zaynab replied.

Once again, Rola told us why it wouldn't work. "But they will lose financially. It might work during the day, but at night, people will find it boring."

"But I am pious," exclaimed Fatima, "and I want to stay out late in the evening [*baddi es-har*]!"

"As a pious person, I cannot stay out late in the evening," countered Rola.

"Even for the conservative families, not just the pious ones, downtown has a bad reputation," continued Zaynab.

My father is not pious; he's secular. When I tell him I want to go out with my friends in the evening to al-Saha, it's different from if I say I am going with my friends to <u>downtown</u>. With my uncle, who's a communist, it's the same. But I think, each neighborhood, even if it is fancy, needs to have a place for us, not for pious people, but for conservative people. And I think the place will succeed.

"Yes," Fatima agreed, "My brother will stop going to places with alcohol if al-Saha opens in <u>downtown</u>. A lot of people will be happy to be in pious places."

"They can make a lot of money," Zaynab added. "A lot of Gulf pious people will be happy to have those places in <u>downtown</u>. There's a big tourist need."

Rola made a final effort to describe why this was impossible or at least unlikely, noting, "What I was saying is that <u>downtown</u> itself has another character...."

"But we have to change that!" interrupted Zaynab again, conclusively ending the conversation.

This dialogue reveals how the new moral leisure landscape in Dahiya is not merely responding to the needs of pious youths but also empowering some of them to become more vocal in claiming the right to have moral leisure options in Beirut. Zaynab wants "every neighborhood" in the city to accommodate the needs of people whose lifestyle abides by particular moral norms. She justifies her claims by referring to the social rubric of morality, which she assumes will be shared among a wide spectrum of Lebanese and tourists. She and Fatima refute Rola's efforts to "explain" why that is a hopeless desire. They argue that the tourism sector could be imagined to include moral leisure options, that pious people are entitled to have fun, even at night, that there may be a transnational market for pious entertainment, and in the end, that pious people might have the power to change the city.

Lefebvre consistently reminds us that while the lived spaces of the city are full of promise for change, they are quickly recuperated by the dominant order. He invites us to be conscious of the insidiousness of that process and hence live spaces in ways that challenge it, allowing the right to the city to thrive. This is not an easy task. Leisure places are not spaces of absolute freedom but rather operate as a mechanism of social control, where youth activities are supervised and contained. Zaynab and Fatima represent those who seek to make the city their own, to reinvent it according to their own desires and notions of morality. Rola and Muhannad, on the other hand, represent those who allow the dominant order to prevent the possibility of change by passively accepting the status quo. While Zaynab and Fatima's position is atypical, it shows how Dahiya's youths mark an increasingly vocal generation pushing the boundaries for spatial change in *both* Dahiya and Beirut. While in chapter 4, we saw how youths are contesting moral norms related to leisure, here we see their potential to use their ideas about moral norms to challenge spatial practices in and spatial experiences of the city.

By fostering desires for particular forms of leisure and demonstrating the financial success of sites that uphold specific moral norms, Dahiya's new leisure sector may be initiating avenues for urban change. Private investment continues to rise in businesses at the area's edges, often bringing in transnational capital.[32] Real estate prices are soaring in response, generating a surge in high-end housing and commercial developments in south Beirut's few remaining empty areas. Furthermore, the market is slowly but surely expanding toward Beirut as an increasing number of appropriate cafés are opening in neighborhoods along the sea and in Hamra (e.g., Tasty in Hamra and Dardachat in Ain el-Mreisseh). These cafés are large, located in prime locations, and provide the valet parking typical of Beirut businesses. At first glance, their only distinguishing features are that they do not serve alcohol and the majority of their patrons smoke argileh.

Ka3kaya [*sic*], for example, is located on a major street in Hamra that is lined with cafés and bars, and known among college students for pub-crawling. It is the only place along that strip that serves argileh but not alcohol. Ka3kaya attracts an eclectic crowd, including pious people, foreign tourists, and American University of Beirut and Lebanese American University students. The entrance overflows with wooden tables and chairs, often occupied by older men smoking argileh while watching passersby on the busy street. Inside, the décor is eclectic, leaning toward heritage style. The café has a mezzanine floor that attracts couples and mixed-gender groups of youths. On one Sunday evening, loud pop music blanketed the noise from two groups of men playing backgammon, a group of older men discussing business, two young women wearing hijab conversing over coffee, several families dining, five mixed-gender couples, and several European tourists. What seems to distinguish Ka3kaya and other Hamra cafés that do not serve alcohol from Dahiya's cafés is that they appear to be more permissive of behavior considered inappropriate in Dahiya, such as playing games and loud pop music.

These market-driven changes underscore the class component of the new moral leisure sector. South Beirut's cafés are establishing new hierarchies within the Shiʻi political-sectarian community, and revealing class distinctions among and within Dahiya's neighborhoods, altering urban dynamics in the process. Moral leisure sites cater to those who can afford to go out and consume, and the emergence of this sector is linked, as we described in chapter 2, to the development of the area's middle class. These cafés reproduce the spatial understandings of the middle and upper classes within the Islamic milieu, and their conceptions of a hygienic, ordered space that excludes lower-income groups.[33] Customers generally appreciated whatever moral enforcement café owners and staff provided, as it highlighted their comfort being entre-soi in not only the political-sectarian and moral senses but also in relation to class, where "disorderly behavior" was not permitted.

Real estate investment often accompanies the emergence of leisure in a neighborhood in ways that confirm greater class demarcations and exacerbate the unequal distribution of urban space. Cafés mark specific sections of Dahiya as "happening" areas, contributing to rising real estate values and the "classing" of south Beirut's neighborhoods. This is particularly evident along Dahiya's northwestern and northeastern edges where reference to neighborhoods by name (e.g., Jnah and Bir Hassan) or prominent leisure sites within them (e.g., Fantasy World and Beirut Mall) illustrates their demarcation as separate from Dahiya in many people's perceptions. Sainte-Thérèse supplies another example. Several fashionable cafés line its main street, and waitstaff and patrons alike refer to the area with proud amusement as "New Dahiya" or "Gemmayzet al-Dahiya"—the Gemmayze of Dahiya, a reference to the trendy clubbing street in central Beirut.

As in much of the city, leisure has become a marker of inequality in south Beirut. While Beirut's spatial production is generally understood to relate to class variables, Dahiya's spatial production is often assumed to relate only to poverty and political-sectarianism.[34] The growth of Dahiya's moral leisure sector over the past decade begs otherwise, and demonstrates that it is also a classed space.

Not all area residents find the distinctions embedded in Dahiya's new cafés comforting. Because they are conceived for certain classes, these cafés generate new perceptions of social inequality. People favor or shun places in relation to their perceptions about social status and class, and some are quite critical of Dahiya's new businesses. For example, Zayn preferred working-class (sha'bi) cafés in Dahiya, such as the open-air ones located "under the bridge" (an overpass).

> There are places [other than the new cafés] that I like to go to, but maybe they're not pretty. The place we're in now [a new café], it's very traditional [in décor]; it is trying to make you think of your heritage, but I don't feel it. Maybe the quality of people, the social classes here, middle class and above, it bothers me. I don't like sitting with them. I prefer sitting with people from my own class. It has nothing to do with culture or education. I don't like to be surrounded by people of a higher class. It's going to impact me; maybe I would want to live like them. Working-class cafés create a social interaction, a social fabric, a familiarity, more than these places ruled by conspicuous consumption.

Zayn and his friends meet in places that function quite similarly to the male-dominated, working-class prewar coffee shops of Beirut's central district (Douaihy 2005). These mainly older men said they preferred such places because they strengthened social networks between different age groups, and enabled them to "interact with people from twenty to sixty years old, and talk politics and society."

Dahiya's moral leisure sector demonstrates how Beirut today is being reconfigured not only through the conceived spaces of the dominant powers in the city center but also through those in its so-called peripheries or suburbs. We would go so far as to suggest that the most interesting urban changes in the capital today are not located in its classic centers of downtown or Ras Beirut but rather in its new centers, established through political violence, wars, and displacements, and once stigmatized as peripheries. South Beirut is one of these new centers. Its cafés allow pious youths to spatially appropriate the city, and move away from family, religious, and political authorities, opening up interesting venues for change. At the same time, they consolidate Dahiya's political-sectarian entrenchment, class hierarchies, and socioeconomic inequalities. In our final chapter, we explore the ways that judgments about class, morality, and political-sectarianism emerge in ideas about taste and social hierarchy, and reconsider the question of whether moral leisure can lead to broader forms of change.

6

Good Taste, Leisure's Moral Spaces, and Sociopolitical Change in Lebanon

Shu dahiya, shu mish class [This is so Dahiya, so unclassy].

—AN EXPRESSION USED BY SOME BEIRUTIS

Thus far, we have seen how ideas about morality, space, and place come together to create specific forms of leisure for more or less pious Shiʿi Muslim residents of south Beirut. Choices about leisure activities and places are informed by different moral rubrics, as people negotiate social norms, religious tenets, and political loyalties. Pastimes and their settings are assessed according to ideas about where they are located and how their patrons behave—ideas built on assumptions about the relationship between morality and geography in the city. Yet how and where a person hangs out is also an expression of personal taste.

In this final chapter, we bring taste into the picture, and discuss how Dahiya's new leisure sites and practices are valued along with how judgments about class, morality, geography, and politics work together to produce ideas about taste and social hierarchy. We then conclude by thinking through the question of whether changing leisure practices and spaces can lead to broader social, political, and urban change.

CONTEXTUALIZING TASTE

Taste is about more than whether or not one happens to like a particular café and its various elements. In a now-classic quote, Pierre Bourdieu (1984, 6) stated,

> Taste classifies and it classifies the classifier. Social subjects, classified by their classifications, distinguish themselves by the distinctions they make, between the beautiful and the ugly, the distinguished and the vulgar, in which their position in the objective classifications is expressed or betrayed.

In other words, taste is more than personal preference. It both marks class and produces class boundaries. It especially does so because it is assumed to be a natural tendency; indeed, Bourdieu's suggestion that taste comes from one's position in a complex system of class hierarchy is at core an argument against the naturalness of taste. How people consume—including how they consume leisure—indicates and produces social hierarchies.

Taste is also about more than a café's décor or menu, though those elements do play a role. Hage's (1997, 127–28) discussion of ideas about the "spatial hierarchy of taste and sophistication" in Sydney's multicultural ethnic restaurant scene illustrates a complexity similar to what we see in Dahiya:

> Many elements operate to create an effect of differentiation here: the food quality and mode of presentation, the mode of deploying "authenticity," the work of culture itself such as the "sophistication" of the cooks, the waiters and the waitresses, and the way all of those relate to the clientele, the clientele's mode of eating and dressing, the quality of the paper on which the menus are printed, the quality of the printed material, the restaurant's furniture and its layout, the service, the wine list and many more."

For pious Shiʻi Muslims, a café's environment is one of the most important of these elements—encompassing the music played, its street address, the people who fill its seats, and how those customers behave—in addition to its interior, menu, and services.

Morality is linked to taste because potential café goers have firm ideas about the behavior of other people and what that behavior says about an establishment's respectability. Is customers' behavior "in good taste" and in keeping with dominant ideas about appropriate moral behavior within a number of rubrics? Place is linked to both morality and taste through the area of the city where the café is located. Is it a "good area"—one that is known to be both classy and safe for pious Shiʻi Muslims and their assumed political affiliations? Place is also linked to taste through café interiors; café styles are not incidental.[1] The somber spaces of formal dining-style interiors convey propriety and status, combining local values of hospitality with the European cosmopolitanism associated with the formal dining room. Heritage and nature-garden spaces counter assumptions about the moral corruption of the city, and encourage customers to identify with village and nation, and with village as nation—and thus with good moral values. Contemporary interiors highlight a more recent form of global citizenship—one linked to virtual communication networks and transnational corporate consumption.

The choice of leisure place and activity is a vehicle through which Dahiya dwellers and others express taste, with all its accompanying meanings, and through which social distinctions—including among people who can afford an argileh, an espresso, or a meal outside the home—are produced.[2] In south Beirut, café styles, ideas about morality, and notions about geography work together to produce distinctions of class disguised as distinctions of taste.

In *Distinction*, Bourdieu links taste to both economic and social capital, breaking the latter category into educational capital and ideas about social origin. Class emerges in the relationships between different forms of capital and the ways that those related clusters of differential capital affect people's behaviors through their habitus. To understand how forms of capital construct a middle class in south Beirut, it is critical to bring ideas about morality and geography to bear on understandings of class. Both morality and space here are also tied inextricably to sect, and sect and class in Lebanon cannot be understood in isolation from one another.[3] Nor can one understand class and sect in Beirut without considering different understandings of the city's geographies as well as moral behavior. In this context, the social distinctions produced by taste in leisure places and activities extend loudly to distinctions of sect and politics.

TASTE AND THE CLASS-SECT NEXUS IN LEBANON

As we have seen, south Beirut is associated with Shi'i Muslims, and residents and nonresidents alike make assumptions about the people and behavior in places in Dahiya based on the class-sect nexus that is so critical to Lebanese identity. Nonresidents often describe cafés in the area as having a "Dahiya quality"—a quality that connotes a negative valuation. The label also may be used pejoratively to qualify certain cafés elsewhere in the city, including Hamra, as "too Dahiya" or "for Dahiya people." Even some wealthier south Beirut dwellers, especially those who strive to disassociate themselves from the area, talk about a Dahiya quality that they think "devalues" their neighborhoods and local cafés. In all these cases, the term Dahiya is used to differentiate places as having lesser value and quality. By the standards of many residents of Hamra, no matter how wealthy a Dahiya neighborhood may be, it remains "not quite middle class." Class mobility is limited by ideas about sect, politics, and religiosity, in a hierarchy in which Shi'i Muslims rank below Sunni Muslims and Christians, the Hizbullah-led March 8 political coalition ranks below the Hariri-led

March 14 one, and visible Muslim religiosity ranks below Christian religiosity, invisible religiosity, and nonreligiosity. Exclaiming "this place is so Dahiya!" marks a person as belonging elsewhere, as being a tourist in south Beirut, and raises the status of the speaker in this social hierarchy.

Dahiya Style

One of the features that frequently prompted labeling a café as Dahiya was the aesthetics of its décor. As with any discussion of taste or aesthetics from an ethnographic perspective, we have tried to describe and situate café styles without judgment, to divorce ourselves from our (rather different) aesthetic sensibilities and tastes. In her discussion of Egyptian contemporary art and artists, Jessica Winegar (2006, 13) notes that "it is how these aesthetic understandings were constructed and mobilized that is important to analyze, not some essential aesthetic that we imagine Egyptian artists might share that is different from our own." This is how we approached café styles and thought through the role of taste in reproducing constructions of this community as distinct from others in Lebanon. At the same time, we were of course not immune to having personal responses to cafés, including sometimes a "this is so Dahiya" response.

In trying to capture what, if anything, was stylistically different about Dahiya's cafés, we constantly returned to eclecticism—whether in the diversity of patrons, organization of seating arrangements and services provided, menu offerings, or décor itself. As we argued in chapter 3, eclecticism reflects the diversity of the transnational and local experiences of Dahiya's residents in an increasingly globalized world. This eclecticism is viewed as less sophisticated by Beirut's elite in part because it is associated with Dahiya, but also because it is often compared to standards of urban sophistication cultivated in Lebanon over the past century that privilege a Eurocentric aesthetic model. Yet the move away from a Eurocentric—and more specifically Parisian—ideal for sophistication also signals the rise of both US and global-corporate aesthetic models, exemplified in chains like Starbucks as well as notions of ethnic chic. Dahiya's leisure sector emerged at a time when mixing and matching in a postmodernist pastiche had become the mark of a particular form of global sophistication, and the area's eclectic style can be read in that vein. Despite the restrictions of corporate capitalism, a transnational US stylistic model is far more flexible than a bourgeois French one, and more amenable to interpretation because it has less history and therefore fewer long-standing conventions.[4] Ironically, in a reckoning of cosmopolitanism that takes this broader geographic view and moves beyond Europe as the cultural center of the world, municipal Beirut's cosmopolitan elite represents the more provincial perspective and Dahiya's cosmopolitan elite represents the avant-garde.

For Beirut's elite, Dahiya cafés' Arabic and Islamic features, referents, and menu offerings are a key indicator of their departure from a Eurocentric ideal. While displays of heritage artifacts, Qur'ans, and paintings of religious scenes or mosques could be viewed within a transnational corporate model as examples of ethnic chic, this is not the perspective of Eurocentric elite Lebanese who denigrate these qualities. Their assumption that Arabic elements reflect lower-class status is reinforced by the tendency of Dahiya's waitstaff, for the most part, to speak Arabic rather than French or English with customers, and the numerous spelling mistakes in the English-language menus that were available.[5] Ideas about appropriate café activities also influence presumptions about the relationship between "Arab" or "Islamic" and class. If a café does not serve alcohol, it is assumed to be "Hizbullah related" by outsiders, with all the connotations that carries. Accompanying that assumption is the idea that because there is no alcohol, there will be more argileh. While argileh smoking is a primary activity in most Dahiya cafés, establishing such a causal link is difficult, especially because argileh smoking has become a popular trend among youths across Lebanon as well as transnationally. Despite that trend, however, many older residents of Beirut disdain youths' obsession with argileh, despise the practice as "too Arab" and "lower class," and see it as the resurgence of a bad habit that had been abandoned when Lebanon became "cosmopolitan," meaning European.

Dahiya Quality

The label "so Dahiya" also connotes the idea that both the service and material surroundings in south Beirut cafés are of "lesser quality" or "cheaper."[6] A range of service and material elements conveyed this sensibility, including poorly designed menus, cleaning supplies or water hoses visible in café corners, tiny and poorly designed bathrooms that were often missing details like soap dispensers, and low-quality building materials. Of course there are cafés and restaurants across Lebanon with these characteristics, but they share an association with a lower class of clientele. The fact that these features provoke the specific descriptor Dahiya reinforces a strong link between the area and a particular class position. Via the political-sectarian logic of space in the country, this association extends beyond place to include people and behavior; not only places, but also people and acts can be labeled Dahiya to indicate their lower-class position. This assumption persists despite the fact that customers in Dahiya's cafés share many characteristics of middle-class status with customers in cafés that are viewed as "better" in other urban neighborhoods—characteristics including levels of wealth, education, and consumption. In our café customer survey, when we compared place of residence with how people rated various café features, similar patterns emerged. People who lived in Beirut tended to rate the food in Dahiya cafés higher than Dahiya residents did, perhaps reflecting lingering notions that Dahiya is closer to the village, and therefore closer to fresher and more authentic food. On the other hand, Beirut residents rated décor, cleanliness, and service lower than people who lived in Dahiya. All these ratings reflect a combination of stereotypes about Dahiya and tastes shaped by different class/sect/geographic positions in Lebanon's social hierarchies.

In that survey, we also found that residents of Dahiya generally thought that their neighborhood cafés were more expensive than residents of Beirut found them to be, possibly reflecting different points of comparison. Are Dahiya's cafés in fact less expensive than those in other parts of the city? Overall they are, though one can find cafés and restaurants at varying price levels across Beirut's neighborhoods. South Beirut does not have the steeply priced restaurants one finds in Gemmayze or Zaytouneh Bay, and with the exception of al-Saha, an espresso or argileh is cheaper in Dahiya than in Hamra. At the same time, the clientele for Dahiya's cafés includes people who can afford Hamra's espresso, at least to the same extent that many Hamra residents can. And Dahiya's cafés are priced out of range for poor people.[7] They deliberately cultivate middle-class customers. Economic capital here clashes with what we might call spatial capital, as location in Dahiya itself works to lower prices.

Some café owners consciously contest the association of Dahiya with lower quality and "cheapness." For instance, the owner of Coda Café takes great pride in the fact that he hired a manager who previously worked at Starbucks for six years and a chef who had never been to Dahiya before his job interview. According to the owner, the chef assumed that the salary would be too low for him because of his stereotypes about the area, and was happily surprised by both his salary and the "fine dining establishment" that Coda proved itself to be. Coda's owner also charges slightly higher prices than other Dahiya cafés, insisting that this reflects the quality of his ingredients. He does this in part to deliberately cultivate a higher-class clientele. As he put it:

> I have preserved the quality of the customers. It is not acceptable [for], pardon my language, a street scum con artist [z'a'eh shalamasteh] to come here to drink coffee.[8] He'll tell you, "I don't have to pay three thousand lira [two US dollars] for a cup of coffee," so he goes and drinks it for five hundred lira in another café. Do you understand? I mean even the coffee that I am using is Agostino, a fancy Italian brand.

Not only does Coda's owner assume that a customer who can afford more expensive coffee will be of higher quality but he also suggests that a certain type of customer will appreciate the Agostino coffee his café serves and will understand that it is worth the price. This brings us to another meaning that people connote when they describe a café or restaurant as being so Dahiya: the lack of knowledge about leisure displayed by Dahiya's resident café customers.

LEISURE KNOWLEDGE

The notion that Dahiya means poor quality in cafés is fueled by the idea that south Beirut dwellers "don't know better," and will accept bad coffee, shabby building materials or furniture, and badly constructed restrooms. We heard this idea most frequently from waitstaff and café managers from Dahiya who had either trained at one of Beirut's hospitality schools or worked in the service industry outside south Beirut at some point in their careers. Sometimes waiters who worked elsewhere moved to a Dahiya café because it was closer to home, lessening their commute or providing a politically safer employment environment. Other ambitious young service industry professionals moved from Dahiya's cafés to more expensive restaurants in other Beirut neighborhoods. Regardless of the order of their experience outside Dahiya, these waiters sometimes complained that their Dahiya customers didn't know "international restaurant etiquette." They gave examples of this ignorance, such as the annoyed response of a male guest when a waiter handed his female dining companion a menu first. By telling us these sorts of stories, waiters positioned themselves as more knowledgeable than their customers, establishing their own social status against their clientele, even though in all likelihood they were wealthier than the waitstaff.

Café goers sometimes voiced similar complaints about the cafés. Some of our interviewees criticized the quality of service in south Beirut's cafés, comparing them negatively to those outside the area. Others suggested that their neighborhood cafés did not provide adequate customer service training for their staff. The complaints we heard included service being too slow and waiters not smiling enough or being overly absorbed in their own conversations.

The idea that Dahiya dwellers had to be "taught" leisure—or as one waiter put it, that they "need time to learn leisure"—also surfaced in relation to Hizbullah's projects of "culture," especially concerts and theater productions. Shaykh Ali spoke with great pride when he explained to us that one of their comedic plays was so popular that it had to be extended for an additional ten performances. For him, this was not merely about the party's popularity. More important, it showed that its constituents had begun to appreciate theater and other cultural performances in new ways—an appreciation that marked the newfound middle-class status of the community. At the same time, Hizbullah-sponsored performances are generally free to the public, indicating that they are not only filling a need for particular forms of entertainment but actually *cultivating* that need as well. Party officials talk about "developing culture" in relation to teaching particular tastes, as part of an ongoing project to develop their community and construct a middle-class constituency. In Shaykh Ali's words, as he described the party's orchestral concert series, "We are trying to develop the level of taste among people. This is our responsibility. We need to reset society's ears."

Other stakeholders use the new leisure sector to demonstrate that they are "like all Lebanese" in a retort to stereotypes linking Dahiya to a lack of leisure knowledge and possibilities. Hajj Jamal Makki, al-Saha's architect, for example, argued that al-Saha shows that "we can participate in leisure too! We can provide [Lebanese] heritage too! We used to be servants in places of leisure, now we can be served too!" His assertion extends beyond a desire to be associated with Lebanese heritage to a desire to be associated with a Lebanese leisure class—one that is served rather than supplying much of the labor for the service industry.[9]

In the end, judgments about the style and quality of south Beirut cafés along with their customers are intertwined with assumptions about both Dahiya and its pious Shi'i Muslim residents. In the assessments of most people outside south Beirut as well as many of its own residents, the area's lower status is not only related to ideas about economic class but also to assumptions about its residents' poor taste plus lack of cultural and urban knowledge. Those assumptions are related to sect and religiosity, as other Lebanese often presume that Shi'i Muslims are more religious than they are. They are also related to politics, as Shi'i Muslims are assumed to support Hizbullah and its March 8 coalition. As various forms of social distinction come together and are inscribed through taste, assessments of cafés and restaurants in Dahiya represent the entanglements of morality, geography, sect, class, and politics. Dahiya is viewed as the ugly, kitschy, or hyperauthentic poor cousin of Beirut's arrogant, bourgeois, or hyper-European haunts.

Similar judgments make Dahiya appealing for certain Beirutis. Young leftists sometimes make a point of preferring cafés that appear more Eastern—a political statement that also reveals the relationship between class, taste, and politics, where anti-imperialist stances are linked with specific tastes. These young leftists may make a point of traveling to Dahiya in a public display of an antisectarianism stance. In this sense, to be Dahiya has a particular allure, weaving together ideas about a space of resistance to Western imperialism with notions about authenticity in Eastern or Arab style. Dahiya is assumed to be less corrupted by colonial European and US global-corporate cultural forms—an assumption belied by the desires of the area's new middle class for KFC and café spaces modeled on a transnational pastiche, and that underestimates the complex tastes of south Beirut residents, especially youths.

"GOOD TASTE," OR CHOOSING "WHAT IS GOOD FOR YOU"

Young more or less pious Shi'i Muslims choose from a marketplace of moral, geographic, and aesthetic options for their leisure. They make these choices within a framework of taste and consumption that reproduces entanglements of class, sect, and politics. They also make these choices with conscious and conscientious reflection about their options in relation to multiple moral rubrics as well as different urban spaces. As Rabi' phrased it in the epigraph to chapter 4, "All we need to do is select. When you go to a store, you select what is good/appropriate for you."

The expectation that a person will select the option that is appropriate for them rests on two assumptions: that there are multiple options available, and that a person has the capacity to make the right choice from among those options. What is appropriate for a person can indicate personal preference, with all the contextual apparatus that carries. It can also point toward a moral choice, selecting the option that represents good in one or more of the moral rubrics within which the person making the choice lives. And it can suggest a choice related to one's personal sociospatial mapping of leisure geographies. By using the metaphor of a store, Rabi' draws parallels between making choices that reflect good taste, in all its meanings, and consumption. Consumerism in this context is both related to and quite different from the "semiotically crowded environment" that Gregory Starrett (1995, 51) describes in Egypt—where globally circulating commercial pop culture commodities and globally circulated religious commodities share shelf space along with attention. In Dahiya, neither religious consciousness nor consumerist sensibility is particularly new. Islamic religious commodities—books, wall hangings, and key chains—accompanied the Shi'i Islamic movement from its beginnings, whether as politically oriented commodities like Hizbullah paraphernalia or religiously oriented ones like miniature Qur'ans. And a consumerist sensibility has arguably imbued Lebanon's hyperprivatized economy for decades, where a pervasive link between commodities and identity means that marking status with name brands and consumer items may take precedence over basic needs.

Vanguard generation pious Shi'i Muslims have long critiqued this "focus on surface appearances," even as they may subtly display a name brand on the edge of a scarf. Tensions exist between modesty as a moral value and the emergence of the community en masse into the middle class. Patrick Haenni (2009, 328) has depicted "a Muslim consumerist society" whose constitutive factors include the emergence of a middle class that prioritized "market-friendly, individualistic beliefs." This market-related individualism produces a tension between hedonism and reinvigorated religiosity, and from that tension we see the emergence of multiple lifestyles within Muslim societies, expressed and produced through consumption (Haenni 2009).[10] Similarly, the tensions between modesty and middle-class consumption in Dahiya are leading to new leisure lifestyles. Indeed, youths we have spoken with and observed do not seem to experience this as a tension at all, and have embraced the notion that identity is displayed not by choosing whether or not to consume but rather by choosing what to consume and where. As good consumers in this context, young more or less pious Muslims expect to be able to choose leisure places and activities from within a set of moral and geographic options. The context of south Beirut facilitates such flexibility through the existence of multiple moral authorities, rubrics, and places for leisure as well as the quiet dominance of ideas about individualism. In this context, youths are able to produce numerous possibilities for moral leisure, creating a pastiche of behaviors, places, and ideas that are shaped by the contingencies of the situation—"situated moral action" (Schielke 2009b, S29) made more complex by debates about the very rules and spaces of fun. The question remains, What sorts of broader changes, if any, do these shifts—in leisure practices and geographies within and beyond south Beirut as well as its residents' changing ideas about how and where to have fun—signify or predict?

CAN LEISURE CATALYZE SOCIAL AND POLITICAL CHANGE?

Social change related to leisure practices and geographies is clearly taking place in south Beirut, but what does that social change mean? What are its potentials and limits? Might it lead to political change in Dahiya? Is what we have described easily dismissed as the shifting consumption habits of a new middle class, or the capitalist co-optation of Shi'i Islamist politics and Hizbullah's constituents? Or is there potential in these leisure dynamics for something more? Is south Beirut's new leisure sector a natural extension of the Islamic milieu and an example of the disciplining of desires for leisure in line with dominant ideas about morality? Or does it open up new political possibilities—potentially subversive ones?

Bourdieu's framework for understanding the relationship between taste, consumption, and class provides a coherent diagnosis for how taste and class are entangled. People, in this view, are strongly shaped by their locations in a complex social context and usually act in predictable ways. The changes we have portrayed fit fairly neatly into a model that foregrounds the construction of a Shi'i middle class through leisure choices and the continued shaping of those leisure choices by that consolidated class position. This may not necessarily forecast Hizbullah's dilution or downfall at the hands of capitalism as its constituents happily embrace a consumerist way of life. But the radical revolutionaries who were once the party's foundation have given way to more typically Lebanese politicians—not only as a result of Hizbullah's greater investments in national politics since 1992, but also in the wake of class mobility. Middle-class and youth desires for cafés that represent as well as enable a specific moral position can also be read as an outcome of the naturalization of Muslim mores in Dahiya to the degree that the absence of alcohol in a café is taken for granted by many of the area's residents.

To glimpse greater hope that the relationship between taste, class, and morality in Dahiya can be shaken in unexpectedly radical ways, we look to Jacques Ranciere, whose work allows for people's capacity to appreciate what is assumed to be outside the possibilities of taste (or knowledge) for their class position. In *The Emancipated Spectator*, Ranciere (2009, 10) applies the idea of "intellectual emancipation"—"the verification of the equality of intelligence," or the radical ideal that everyone has the same capacity to learn as everyone else—to theater.[11] He suggests that the oppositions between cultural producers and the audience, oppositions like knowing/viewing or activity/passivity, "specifically define a distribution of the sensible, an *a priori* distribution of the positions and capacities and incapacities attached to these positions. They are embodied allegories of inequality" (ibid., 12). These oppositional terms are therefore structural, indicating which person has a certain capacity based on their position in a social hierarchy—a determinism that can be extended to having specific tastes based on class position. Emancipation happens when that structural opposition between social positions is challenged, "when we understand that the self-evident facts that structure the relations between saying, seeing and doing themselves belong to the structure of domination and subjection" (ibid., 13). Applying this to leisure, taste is not owned by anyone in particular, and the meanings of café styles, activities, and locations are open to imaginative interpretive possibilities that go beyond the limitations of class position.[12] This is not a view that minimizes material and symbolic inequalities like those of the class-sect nexus in Lebanon. This is a perspective that insists that despite those inequalities, there is a *radical equality* of intellectual capacity among people. We see in that radical equality the possibility for tastes—including those related to moral leisure places—to be shaped outside the limitations of class position. In other words, new leisure practices in Dahiya always contain within them the potential to upend existing assumptions and norms related to morality, geography, and politics in Lebanon.

We conclude by thinking through some of the possibilities and limitations of new leisure in south Beirut—for Hizbullah, leisure and Islam, and morality and the city—keeping in mind both the power of the class-sect nexus in Lebanon and a hopeful possibility for change rooted in the idea of a radical equality of intellectual capacity.

Leisure in south Beirut is part of a broader phenomenon of urban change that is not only influenced by Hizbullah's efforts to shape it but is also affecting the party. This presents a major challenge, as the party is learning that it is unable to control its constituents, or the spaces where they live, work, and have fun. While capitalist consumption does to a certain extent depoliticize Hizbullah's young constituents, regular demonstrations of the real dangers facing the party and community—whether in the form of an Israeli attack or Lebanese sectarian political machinations—resolidify Shi'i youths' loyalties. One well-placed party official explained that Hizbullah understands that its circle of supporters has grown, and that this growth "naturally" leads to blurrier boundaries between pious and nonpious constituents. Unlike in Iran, where the moral disciplining of bodies and spaces is seen as a prerequisite to an Islamic state, in Dahiya, Fadlallah's views on individual moral responsibility are more common. Much is left up to the individual, and most people do not believe in forcing others to behave in particular ways, in part because the authenticity of intention behind behavior matters. Sayyid Ja'far took this concern further, criticizing those who would enforce moral norms, whether around dress or musical preference, by noting that forcing religious rules on someone will drive that person further away from morality.

Moreover, despite perceptions of south Beirut as a self-sufficient enclave, it is part of a state where diverse religious groups have the equal constitutional right to practice their faith in public, and establish faith-based or sectarian institutions. Dahiya's pious residents interact regularly with people who have different lifestyles and ideas. They may confront, on a daily basis, situations that are not faced by similarly pious Muslims in other cities like Riyadh, Jeddah, Doha, Kuwait, or Abu-Dhabi. In addition, Dahiya's demographics are changing. Greater numbers of refugees from Iraq and, more recently, Syria are moving to neighborhoods in the area where affordable housing is available. And the new Shi'i middle classes are beginning to move out to more affluent, less dense neighborhoods like Ramlet el-Bayda and Hadath.

Hizbullah today also has far bigger problems than the moral regulation of Dahiya dwellers' entertainment. The Israeli threat remains ever present. The party's stance supporting the Syrian regime in the face of uprisings that have led to civil war is an unpopular one, even among some of its constituents. Its opponents within Lebanon grow louder. And managing from within the government rather than the party's preferred stance of opposition poses new political challenges. The party has bigger "morality" problems as well, exposed in its media campaigns aimed to teach south Beirut's residents various moral lessons. These range from family values campaigns meant to combat rising divorce rates to civil order campaigns emphasizing the importance of obeying traffic signals, disposing of trash properly, and paying for electricity usage. Coupled with increasing reports of and residents' concerns about daily petty crime, crime-related violence, and rising drug use and abuse among Dahiya's youths—in keeping with high rates across Lebanon—the party simply cannot spare the energy and resources to set stricter moral limitations on café behavior.

The relationship between leisure and Islam will continue to shift in south Beirut. Consumerism will likely continue to dilute the ideological aspects of the Islamic milieu. At the same time, it may simultaneously consolidate the milieu by providing a market of pious people who want to spend time and money in ways that do not violate the religious rubric of morality. Even that rubric may change with time, as people, especially youths, navigate the tensions between religious and social moral rubrics, and as the interpretation and reinterpretation of various religious tenets continues. This is Islam as a living and constantly changing discursive tradition, or what Talal Asad (1986, 14–15) described as

> a tradition of Muslim discourse that addresses itself to conceptions of the Islamic past and future, with reference to a particular Islamic practice in the present. . . . It will be the practitioners' conceptions of what is apt performance, and of how the past is related to present practices, that will be crucial for tradition, not the apparent repetition of an old form.

Apt performance may be extended beyond practices like prayer to encompass the many ways that a pious Muslim strives to live a moral life. Through conversations and choices about leisure, a generation of young Shi'i Muslims in Dahiya is participating in this discursive tradition by striving to formulate norms that are commensurate with desires for both pleasure and morality. In the process, this generation is prompting changes within its community, including the reshaping of moral norms and the city's geographies.

New cafés and restaurants in Dahiya are both symptoms of changing ideas in the community and dynamic forces facilitating ongoing social change. Thus far these cafés have not been disruptive in the sense of a public sphere where political uprisings are debated and planned—the stereotype associated with Hamra's Modca or Café de Paris in the 1960s. Nor is Lebanon a part of the "Arab Spring," as people across the region rise up against dictatorial rule. In other Middle East contexts, especially Cairo, much has been made of the gender changes precipitated by new coffee shops because they have created new public spaces where women can socialize while maintaining their respectability (M. Peterson 2011; de Koning 2006). Dahiya's new cafés have certainly created spaces where men and women alike can hang out in lieu of the male-only spaces of traditional coffee shops or Internet gaming shops. The overall sense of gendered change is less than in those other contexts, however, because Lebanon has a longer history of mixed-gender interaction in public space. Instead, the new cafés' creation of possibilities for meeting members of the opposite sex and dating constitutes a far more significant change—one that impacts both young women and young men.

Another potential for change lies in the new geographies created by moral leisure sites across the city. "The spatial has *both* an element of order *and* an element of chaos," writes Doreen Massey (1993a, 156).[13] It is within the element of chaos and temporality of space that Massey finds the possibility for the political. New cafés have substantive potential for disruption in relation to the contours of morality and urban geography in both Dahiya and Beirut. They push Beirut to be more inclusive of the specific moral concerns of the more or less pious, as they push Dahiya to be more inclusive of people who do not share those concerns. Moral leisure is reconfiguring the entire city to be more inclusive of pious youths. It is also encouraging pious Beirutis to experience Dahiya and people who live at Dahiya's edges to venture deeper into its neighborhoods via the familiar settings of leisure.

The duality inherent in moral leisure places complicates their political potential. Cafés have the ability to "materialize and reproduce social contradictions while simultaneously producing the appropriate context to challenge them" (Graiouid 2007, 538). On the one hand, they can be interpreted as consolidating Dahiya as a Shi'i enclave for its pious residents, facilitating their self-sufficiency, cordoning them off from the rest of the city, and foreclosing possibilities for exchange and interaction. Moral leisure therefore reinforces the political economy and leadership of the Islamic milieu. On the other hand, we contend that a more complex reading is possible. The expansion of the moral leisure industry can be viewed as generating new possibilities for both Dahiya and Beirut. It is altering moral and spatial practices along with experiences of and in the city, and enabling people to contest the established boundaries of the Islamic milieu and dominant interactions between Dahiya and Beirut.

As going to the café becomes a habit for many south Beirut residents, especially youths, new patterns of daily spatial practices develop. These practices may lead to new forms of urban citizenship. If we understand urban citizenship to mean belonging to an urban community that is based

on shared recognition of a city's ways of life rather than on rights and re-
sponsibilities, it may lead to broader social and political change.[14] In this
way, without necessarily dismantling the established moral, political-
sectarian, and spatial orders in Dahiya or Beirut, cafés may encourage the
reimagination of those orders.

Beirut and Lebanon are ever-changing canvases. We have no doubt that
young people in south Beirut will continue to navigate moral and spatial
boundaries in relation to leisure in both predictable and surprisingly creative ways, as they bring their own interpretations, tastes, and desires to
the Islamic milieu.

Appendix: Quoted Figures and Characters

(Note that this list does not include everyone we interviewed, only those whom we quote directly in this book.)

POLITICAL AND RELIGIOUS FIGURES

Ali Fayyad: faculty member at Lebanese University, former director of a research center with close ties to Hizbullah, and elected a Hizbullah member of Parliament in 2009

Hajj Abbas: pseudonym for a Hizbullah official who works in media

Hajj Abu Saʿid: Mohammad Saʿid al-Khansa, Hizbullah founding member, politburo member, and mayor of Ghobeyri, a municipality in Dahiya

Hajj Adham: Adham Tabaja, CEO of the Inmaaʾ Group

Hajj Amin: Amin Chirri, Hizbullah former member of Parliament

Jamal Makki: architect, CEO of al-Sanabel, the architecture firm of al-Mabarrat

Sayyid Jaʿfar: Sayyid Muhammad Hussein Fadlallah's son and representative

Shaykh Ali: Ali Daher, director of Hizbullah's Lebanese Art Association

Shaykh Muhammad: representative for Sayyid Khamenei in Lebanon

CAFÉ OWNERS AND MANAGERS (PSEUDONYMS)

Fady: Dahiya café owner, return emigrant who used to own a restaurant in the United States

Hussam: Dahiya café owner, also a return emigrant from the United States

Maher: Dahiya café manager

Nayla: Dahiya café owner
Riyad: twenty-something-year-old café manager, used to work in
    Dahiya, now works in Hamra
Walid: Dahiya café manager

YOUTHS UNDER THIRTY (PSEUDONYMS)

(Note that not all youths shared their university/work affiliations or
majors.)

Abbas: engineering student in his early twenties
Ali: student in his early twenties
Alia: computer science student in her mid-twenties and married
Amer: engineering student in his early twenties
Amina: student in her late teens
Amira: student at Islamic University in her early twenties
Batoul: psychology student at Beirut Arab University in her early
    twenties
Danya: in her mid-twenties, works in media, has a college degree in engi-
    neering, and married
Diala: student at the Lebanese University in her early twenties
Dima: student in her early twenties
Fatima: student in her early twenties
Ghenwa: student in social sciences at the Lebanese University in her
    early twenties and married to Bilal
Hadi: in his mid-twenties and works in business
Hasan: student in his early twenties
Hasna: premed student in her late teens and engaged
Hussein: student in his early twenties
Ja'far: student in his early twenties
Jihad: engineering student at the American University of Beirut in his
    early twenties and engaged to Zayna
Lamia: in her mid-twenties, works in media, has college degree in educa-
    tion from the Lebanese University, and married
Layla: in her mid-twenties, works at a bank, and has college degree from
    Université Saint-Joseph
Lina: physics student in her late teens
Maisa: in her early twenties and a salesgirl at the Beirut Mall in the "alco-
    hol room"
Mariam: MBA student in her early twenties
Muhammad: student in his early twenties

Muhannad: student at the Lebanese American University in his early
   twenties
Nada: social sciences student at the Lebanese University in her
   mid-twenties
Tala: in her mid-twenties and works as an administrative assistant
Qasim: engineering student in his early twenties
Rabiʻ: in his late twenties, works at a radio station, and has a college de-
   gree in English
Rami: engineering student in his early twenties
Rana: Red Cross volunteer in her late twenties
Rima: Red Cross volunteer in her late twenties
Rola: student in her early twenties
Sahar: biochemistry student at the Lebanese University in her late teens
Soha: student in her early twenties
Yusef: engineering student in his early twenties
Zahra: business student in her late teens
Zayna: American University of Beirut student in her early twenties and
   engaged to Jihad
Zaynab: student in her early twenties

ADULTS OVER THIRTY/VANGUARD
GENERATION (PSEUDONYMS)

Abdallah: in his early forties, works in media, and married
Amani: in her late thirties, works in business, and married
Aziza: in her late thirties and owns her own business
Bilal: in his mid-thirties, works in media, has a degree from a technical
   school in electric work, and married to Ghenwa
Firas: in his mid-thirties, teaches Arabic at a local high school, has a col-
   lege degree in Arabic literature, and married
Hanady: in her late thirties, works at a bank, has a college degree from
   the Beirut Arab University, and married
Hajjeh Um Jaʻfar: in her early sixties and a volunteer at a charitable
   association
Mahmoud: in his mid-thirties, works at a radio station, and has a college
   degree in business
Saʻid: in his early forties, works in information technologies, has a degree
   from the American University in Beirut in computer science, and
   married
Samir: in his late thirties, works as an engineer, and married
Zayn: in his early forties, works in media, has a college degree in philosophy, and married

Notes

———

INTRODUCTION. Exploring Leisure, Morality, and Geography in South Beirut

1. This vignette is a reconstruction based on field notes taken by both authors as well as our research assistant Douaa Sheet.

2. We and our interlocutors all consistently used the French term décor to refer to café interiors, no matter what language we were primarily speaking. To capture that linguistic nuance, we retain the French spelling in this book.

3. We use the phrase "of the opposite sex" advisedly, because it reflects the way that our interlocutors in this book understand their social interactions and concerns about male-female interactions. The notions that sex is not binary and cisgender is not the only possibility are not part of their understandings of the world in which they live. Unless we are quoting an interviewee, however, we use the phrase "mixed-gender interaction" in lieu of "mixed-sex interaction," in order to underscore that moral assessments about those interactions are based on external signifiers related to gender identity as much as to sex.

4. We use the phrases southern suburb of Beirut and south Beirut interchangeably to emphasize that this area is in fact *part of* the capital city.

5. To be halal, food must be devoid of pork, blood, carrion, and alcohol. Animals must be slaughtered in God's name in "a clean kill" with a single fatal cut across the throat, and the blood must be drained as much as possible. Of course, assessing whether or not something is halal depends on context and interpretation, as one cannot tell simply by looking at food.

6. We capitalize Resistance when it refers specifically to Hizbullah's Islamic Resistance and otherwise leave the term lowercase.

7. For a thorough discussion of Ottoman coffeehouse culture, see Karababa and Ger 2011. References to coffeehouses date to Mecca and Cairo in the early fourteenth century.

8. These terms are often used interchangeably. Qahwa (again, ahweh) literally means "coffee" in Arabic. Maqha is derived from the same root.

9. Those in alleys had an especially notorious reputation for gambling and prostitution.

10. Graiouid's (2007, 541) discussion of contemporary Moroccan cafés highlights similar functions, as "[Moroccan] peasants find in café culture an emotional support which helps them integrate and adapt to city life."

11. For an in-depth analysis of Hamra's social and urban structure during that time, and particularly those new lifestyles, see Khalaf and Kongstadt 1973.

12. We use leisure and entertainment interchangeably. In Arabic, our interlocutors sometimes referred to leisure as *siyaha* (tourism). They occasionally used the word *tarfih*, and more frequently used a variety of terms implying relaxation and comfort (*riyaha*), changing atmosphere and de-stressing (*taghyir jaw*), and entertainment (*tasliyeh* and *bast*). We rarely encountered the word *lahu*, which both incorporates the playful component of leisure and is a more formal term.

13. There is a growing body of literature on consumption in the Muslim world, though usually centered on the consumption of products (Pink 2009; Fischer 2008; Abaza 2006; Meneley 2007; Salamandra 2004; Taraki 2008; Fealy 2008; Jones 2007).

14. Michel Foucault's (2005) genealogical approach to the concepts reveals ethics as the apparatus of correct self-formation in ancient Greece, later displaced by a moral apparatus during early Christianity. Both ethics and morality here are about a way of being right or wrong, but ethics is more specific, having to do with concrete pragmatic choices in every aspect of life, and morality with a normative framework against which what is good is judged.

15. For a thorough overview of the study of moralities in anthropology—not usually in those terms—as well as the slipperiness of the concept in the first place, see Howell 1996.

16. Joel Robbins (2007, 204) suggests that this "conflation of morality and culture" has led to the underdevelopment of the anthropology of morality.

17. See also Pandolfo (2007, 331), which notes that "in their attempt to restitute legibility," these works of Talal Asad and Mahmood "postulate the inherent rationality and coherence of religious discipline and practice, and turn away from exploring the complexity and singularity of lifeworlds."

18. See, for example, Dahlgren 2010; Deeb 2006; Masquelier 2007; Marsden 2005; Schielke 2009a, 2009b.

19. A similar focus on situational ethics is also seen in Dahlgren 2010; Masquelier 2007; Peterson 2010. Charles Hirschkind's (2006, 69) ethnography also provides glimpses of such complexity, as in the example of a man who smokes while listening to sermons and says that he knows it's wrong, but does it anyway.

20. On the one hand, Shi'i jurisprudence is often considered a special case because of the system of hierarchy for jurists and idea that the "door of interpretation" remains open in privileged ways in Shi'i thought. On the other hand, this represents a common distinction that Shi'i Muslims draw between themselves and Sunni Islam, and it is not in fact the case that in Sunni Islam, the door of interpretation was closed. See Hallaq 1984.

21. Compare Masquelier 2010. In Dahiya, these axes of increasing piety and morality are not necessarily linked to age or attaining adulthood.

22. Katherine Ewing (1990, 268) describes such oscillations as typical of the social human condition: "The same individual may shift frames of reference from one context to another, even from one moment to the next, and may tolerate considerable inconsistency in his or her own beliefs and opinions, often without realizing it," even as that individual may maintain the sense of an overall whole and cohesive identity.

23. Compare this to Dahlgren's (2010) discussion of manners/propriety concerning gender relations in a context of multiple moral frameworks in Yemen.

24. Robbins (2007) builds on a Dumontian notion of values as the hierarchically ranked elements of a culture, but modifies it in order to highlight the ways that a system of cultural value is compatible with cultural change.

25. In the Lebanese context, politics and sectarianism are inextricably intertwined, and political-sectarianism is integral to the constitution and distribution of power at all levels of the state and society.

26. In contrast to many of the older people in this community and Deeb's (2006) interlocutors for her earlier project, only three of our young interlocutors felt that helping the poor and a commitment to the community were important parts of their piety and morality. Many of the women interviewed as part of that earlier project continue to demonstrate a commitment to community work, suggesting a generational difference in ideas about the relationship between community commitment and piety.

27. *Mu'amalat* are acts unrelated to worship; they involve social interactions in this world. For an eloquent discussion of changing ideas about the relationship between religiosity and appropriate sociality, see Limbert 2010. In that Omani case, youths are more likely to suggest, in contrast to their elders, that sociality is *not* a necessary aspect of piety and in fact may interfere with it.

28. The earliest record we have seen of this view is in Fadlallah 2001.

29. See Deeb 2010. This example also underscores the variable relationship of social and religious moral rubrics to one another such that counterintuitively, society may in fact appear as the more conservative of the two. In the Lebanese Shi'i community, this actually may be the case most frequently when it comes to matters related to sexuality. In relation to reproductive technologies, Morgan Clarke (2009) also found that there were procedures that were allowed by religious authorities, but remained unacceptable to people—another instance of how society may be more conservative than religion.

30. Although the BCD did not succeed in embedding new neighborhoods into Beirut's urban fabric, it did offer some city dwellers places to meet, interact, and enjoy leisure time across sectarian though not class lines.

31. We capitalize the term Liberation to indicate the specific event of Israeli withdrawal from the South in May 2000, known in Lebanon as *al-Tahrir*.

32. See Fawaz, Harb, and Gharbieh 2012. These variables include the ability to negotiate with security guards, which may facilitate or delay access through checkpoints and barricades, and is related to age, income, race, and sect. This is not to say

that mobility was entirely foreclosed. See Kristen Monroe's (2009) recent disserta-
tion for an exploration of mobility *across* political, sectarian, and classed space in
Beirut that troubles the rigidity of these often-invoked categories of identity and
space in Lebanon.

33. See Lefebvre (1974) 1991; Massey 1993a. Lefebvre ([1974] 1991, 11–12)
theorized space as integrating the physical (nature and cosmos), mental (formal
abstractions about space), and social (the space occupied by "sensory phenomena"). This triadic "spatiology" allows researchers to "*expose* space, *decode* space,
and *read* space" (Merrifield 1993, 523; emphasis in original)—in other words, to
reveal the process by which space is produced. More specifically, Lefebvre posited
three dialectical components: representations of space, representational space, and
spatial practice. Representations of space (*le conçu*, or "conceived" space) are associated with power and relations of production, hegemonic abstract space tied to
capital and the dominant order, with its associated technocrats, bureaucrats, and
planning professionals. Representational spaces (*le vécu*, or "lived" space) embody
more or less coherent symbolic meanings and codes, and indicate the passively
experienced space of the imagination, the "alive" space of everyday life that conceived space invariably tries to control. Spatial practices "secrete" society's space
and are closely associated with perceived space (*le perçu*). They are generated from
people's perceptions as they map their routes between home, work, and leisure.

34. See, for example, Smith 2007; Curry 1999; Sack 1997, 2003.

35. These classifications are contested, opening the boundaries of what is right
and wrong to negotiation and reconfiguration. Most of the moral geographies literature focuses on specific social behavior, especially attitudes vis-à-vis people considered "deviant," including youths, queer people, the poor, and the homeless. For
instance, in the US context, Don Mitchell (2003) explores how public places lose
moral worth through the practices of marginalized groups—an analysis also made
in the European context by James Proctor and Michael Smith (1999) and Smith
(2000).

36. Henri Lefebvre ([1974] 1991, 86) uses the phrase social space to refer to his
triadic conception of space, noting that "social spaces interpenetrate one another
and/or superimpose themselves upon another." Pierre Bourdieu's (1989, 19–20)
conceptualization of social space also informs our analyses in later chapters of how
people classify spaces as moral, as social space operates as a symbolic space of distinction, "a space of lifestyles and status groups characterized by different lifestyles." For our discussion here of how spaces are dialectically produced in relation
to moral rubrics, we find Lefebvre's concept more useful.

37. Here, following Andrew Merrifield (1993, 521–22; emphasis in original),
the phrase practiced space is the nexus where Lefebvre's three spatial components
come together: "Place [is] a specific *form* emergent from an apparent stopping of
. . . the dynamics of capitalist social space. . . . The process of capital circulation
must take place as a thing somewhere so as to combine with other 'things' (such as
labour-power and means of production). . . . [Thus] flows do take on a thing form

in place and hence are always vulnerable in that place. . . . It follows here that place is not merely abstract space: it is the terrain where basic social practices—consumption, enjoyment, tradition, self-identification, solidarity, social support and social reproduction, etc.—are lived out. . . . [P]lace is where everyday life is *situated*. And as such, place can be taken as *practiced* space. . . . Consequently, spatial contradictions—that is, political conflicts between socio-economic interests and forces—express themselves in place."

38. There is a strong emergent urban studies literature centered on cities in the Arab world, including "the Cairo School of Urban Studies" (El-Sheshtawy 2009; Elyachar 2005; de Koning 2009; Sawalha 2010; Singerman and Amar 2006, Singerman and Amar 2009), though these works rarely theorize space productively in relation to Lefebvre. Our work builds more directly on the analyses of Farha Ghannam (2002) for Cairo, Mona Fawaz (2009) for Beirut, and Ahmed Kanna (2011) for Dubai—all of whom theorize the city relationally as a sociospatial product.

39. A *semsar* is a broker who facilitates a variety of land and property transactions, from selling and buying to renting land and/or apartments.

40. In keeping with feminist convention in writing in English, we use the phrase young women to mean young women of any marital status, under thirty years old. When directly quoting interlocutors, when we use young women, it is a translation for *sabaya*. When we use the term guys, it is a translation for *shabab* (sometimes translated as youths, depending on whether it is a gender-neutral term in the context of the sentence or not). When we use the word girls, we are translating our interlocutors' use of *banat* (literally, "girls") to refer to unmarried young women.

41. Many of these youths were students when we interviewed them, or simultaneously studying and working into their mid-twenties. It is relatively common in Lebanon for undergraduates to take longer than three (with the baccalaureate) or four years to complete their degrees. Some degrees require more years of study, and sometimes students work at the same time, taking fewer courses per year.

42. The few exceptions who tried to avoid the Internet included Mariam, who doesn't chat because she is scared of people who "make stuff up" to trick young women; Yusef, who was worried about "bad girls" from whom young men need to protect themselves; Abbas, who expressed serious concerns about Internet privacy; and Amira, who feels guilty about chatting because she thinks she could use that time more productively, whether in study or prayer. In two group interviews, young people who use the Internet highlighted the importance of one's intentions and purposes, noting that as long as moral boundaries are maintained, there is nothing wrong with chatting. This implicitly reflects Fadlallah's views, which are that there is no inherent problem with chatting as long as one focuses on "serious" topics and is cautious about not allowing chatting to lead to immoral behavior. Magazine articles in *Baqiyat Allah*, which presents Khamenei's perspectives, take a much more alarmist stance, suggesting precautions such as avoiding photographs or voice conversations in online communication, and asserting parental control

over Internet activity via online filtering programs that block chat rooms. He also suggests that youths who do chat should utilize personal and spiritual restraint in order to avoid wrongdoing online.

43. Lokman Slim is the son of a prominent lawyer and 1960s' member of Parliament, Mohsen Slim, from Ghobeyri, one of Dahiya's main neighborhoods. In the Shi'i community, Mohsen Slim is considered part of a bourgeoisie with strong ties to Christian elites. During the civil war, he moved his law practice to Paris, though he remained a major landowner in Ghobeyri, including among his holdings the family mansion. In 2004, Lokman Slim opened the Hangar, a space that houses the activities of UMAM, a nongovernmental organization that he founded with his German wife, Monika Borgmann (see http://www.umam-dr.org/). UMAM organizes a variety of cultural events including exhibitions, lectures, and film screenings that attract a primarily Beiruti intellectual audience to Dahiya. It prides itself on offering an open platform for debate as well as providing alcohol on site in direct defiance of both Hizbullah and the dominant local moral climate. Lokman Slim has also regularly attacked Hizbullah in various media outlets, especially since the 2006 war. For all these reasons, our interlocutors in this book are not part of UMAM's small circle of constituents.

44. See Wilkins 2008. There are a number of striking similarities between our young interlocutors and the US youths that Amy Wilkins features, especially the young Christians she interviewed.

45. On Cairo, see Abaza 2006; de Koning 2006; M. Peterson 2011. On Istanbul, see Houston 2001.

46. Fadlallah, for example, does not believe in enforcing sex segregation in social or work spaces other than schools and libraries, where his rationale for sex segregation is not based on morality but rather on "distraction"—akin to arguments for single-sex education in the United States. While this book was in production, the first women-only café opened in Dahiya. It remains to be seen how popular it well be and what effects it will have on the leisure scene in the area.

CHAPTER 1. New Leisure in South Beirut

1. There is a good deal of scholarship on the Shi'i community in Lebanon. We do not rehearse a comprehensive history of the community here but instead limit ourselves only to information important for a nonspecialist reader to follow the remainder of this book. For more in-depth treatments of the history of Shi'i Muslims in Lebanon, see AbuKhalil 1988; Abisaab 1999; Weiss 2010; Cobban 1985; Picard 1997.

2. *Hala* means "state of being" or "condition," and *saha* ranges in meaning from the literal "courtyard" to the figurative "arena" or "field." Together with the adjective *islamiyya*, the phrases translate as "Islamic state of being" or "Islamic arena," understood as specifically Shi'i in relation to this community in Lebanon. Often, islamiyya is not appended, indicating internalized assumptions about the nature of

the arena or state of being in question. Joseph Alagha describes a different usage of these phrases among the leadership of the community, including Fadlallah. Alagha (2011, 178) notes that al-hala al-islamiyya, which he translates as the "Islamic religious-political sphere," has given way to al-saha al-islamiyya, translated as the "Islamic cultural sphere." The use of these phrases ranges widely, and their meanings are in flux. Yet Alagha's point about the transition from a focus on the religious-political to the cultural is an important one, and is in keeping with our arguments.

3. Compare this to Amal Boubekeur's (2007, 76n4) use of the phrase *Islamic society of spectacle*, which she defines as "an ensemble of 'staging' supports used by Islamic elites to predicate, to affiliate, and to diffuse norms and values." Our understanding of the Islamic milieu includes this society of spectacle as one constitutive component. It also incorporates the notion of an "Islamic lifestyle" from Nilufar Gole's (1996) discussion of body politics, culture, and taste as processes of social distinction among Islamic elites in Istanbul.

4. The term infitah has a deep political history in the Middle East, and carries with it ideas of economic opening to capitalism as well as the accompanying potential for cultural change through increased consumerism.

5. For more on this mobilization, see Deeb 2006, 69–92; Halawi 1992; Norton 1987.

6. The Lebanese civil war (1975–90) involved over twenty-five militias along with several state armies and operatives, including those of Israel, Syria, Iraq, Iran, and the United States. On the civil war, see Fisk 1990; Picard 1996; Hanf 1993.

7. The Amal Movement is not involved in the leisure sector that we are examining. It is worth noting nonetheless that in regions that are under its control, such as the city of Tyre in South Lebanon, Amal does not prevent alcohol consumption.

8. See Kapeliouk 1982; MacBride 1984; Siegel 2001; report of the Kahan Commission (1983).

9. For more on Hizbullah's origins, history, relations with Iran and Syria, military and political activities, social and economic institutions, and discourses, see AbuKhalil 1991; Alagha 2011; Hamzeh 2000a, 2000b; Harb 2010a; Harik 2004; Mervin 2010; Norton 2007; Qassem 2005; Saad-Ghorayeb 2002.

10. For instance, Hizbullah participated with Amal and former prime minister Rafic Hariri's party on the board of the public agency Elyssar, which was set up in 1996 to replan the western coastal sections of Dahiya, an area of informal settlements with myriad unsettled property rights issues. Hizbullah "convinced" residents to accept Elyssar's financial compensation and leave their homes in order to facilitate the highways needed to complete Hariri's reconstruction of downtown Beirut. The party here clearly prioritized national political maneuverings and alliances over its constituents' rights. For more on this, see Harb 2001.

11. Compare this to Lisa Taraki's (2008) discussion of the rapid development of new urban commercial spaces for play in Ramallah catering to an emergent middleclass as well as youths in the wake of the first intifada and Oslo Accords.

12. Lebanon and Syria assert that the farms are Lebanese land, while Israel and the United Nations have declared the area part of the Golan Heights, and therefore, Syrian territory that is occupied by Israel. Asher Kaufman (2002, 593–94) argues that the dispute's origin lies in the inaccurate delineation of the Syrian-Lebanese border by French mandate authorities along the watershed of Mount Hermon rather than on property lines.

13. During the Syrian occupation, Hizbullah was assured of protection for its military Resistance and its leaders regularly asserted their disinterest in joining the quagmire of Lebanese politics, preferring to operate through parliamentary legislative reforms.

14. In keeping with this pattern, Hizbullah won 13 seats in the 2009 parliamentary election.

15. This learning curve began as early as 1996 when Hizbullah was forced by Syria to ally with Amal for the legislative elections, despite conflicts between the two groups. In 1998, for the municipal elections, Hizbullah was allowed to run against Amal and won most of the seats. Since then, like all Lebanese political parties, Hizbullah adjusts its political choices and alliances according to a range of variables, including national and local stakes, geography, and political circumstances.

16. For more on Hizbullah's military activity and the rules of the game governing cross-border conflict, see Norton 2000; Sobelman 2004.

17. Prior prisoner exchanges between Hizbullah and Israel set the precedent for Hizbullah's capture of Israeli soldiers to use in future exchanges.

18. Much has been written about why the July 12 operation led to a massive Israeli assault on Lebanon rather than the limited response called for by the "rules." Most analysts point to a combination of internal Israeli political dynamics with the relationship of the attack to the US "war on terror" and designs on Iran. Seymour Hersh (2006) documented a long-standing Israeli plan for the offensive with US advance collusion. See also Makdisi 2011.

19. The official figure of the Lebanese government is 1,191, while Human Rights Watch's (2007) report says "more than 1,125."

20. See Human Rights Watch 2007.

21. For more on the July 2006 war, see *MIT Electronic Journal of Middle East Studies* 2006; Hovsepian 2007.

22. Transcript of news conference held by Secretary Condoleeza Rice on Friday, July 21, 2006, http://www.washingtonpost.com/wp-dyn/content/article/2006/07/21/AR2006072100889.html (accessed November 29, 2012).

23. Hizbullah reimbursed those who had already paid for the reconstruction of their homes and provided twelve thousand US dollars to families whose homes were badly damaged or destroyed (Nasrallah called this its "housing policy" [*iwaaʾ*]). The sum was calculated to provide a year of rent, and was renewable annually until people were able to move back into their homes, which happened in fall 2012 for Haret Hreik residents.

24. For more on the post-2006 war reconstruction, see Al-Harithy 2010; Harb and Fawaz 2010.

25. Outspoken anti-Syria journalists Samir Kassir and Gibran Tueni were killed in 2005, and the following two years saw the assassinations of March 14 political leaders Pierre Gemayel, Walid Eido, and Antoine Ghanem.

26. On the construction of sectarianism in Lebanon, see Beydoun 1999; Corm 1987; Kassir 1994; Makdisi 2000. On the construction of a specifically Shi'i sectarian community, see Weiss 2010. Donald Donham's (2011) analysis of a violent conflict that was constructed as "ethnic" in South Africa can serve as a productive model for understanding the construction of violence as "sectarian."

27. While she overstates the control that Iran has today over the party, Roschanack Shaery-Eisenlohr (2009) provides a good discussion of the historical complexity of the relationship of Hizbullah and Lebanese Shi'a more broadly to Iran as well as the roots of accusations of being "Iranian" in Lebanon, relevant to contemporary political machinations.

28. Lebanese political parties have appropriated many of the colors of the rainbow—for example, orange signifies Aoun's Free Patriotic Movement while blue represents Hariri's Future Movement.

29. The economic reform plan included the privatization of state-owned utilities, raising value-added taxes, and reducing public sector pay rates and employment while neglecting to discuss unemployment, corruption, or nepotism. Lebanese labor unions mobilized against it with March 8 support, though March 8 failed to produce its own economic platform.

30. Three reasons seem to explain the disjuncture between Lebanon's real estate market and the global market: developers in Lebanon borrow minimally, and instead sell plots and apartments in advance of a project to fund it; apartment buyers generally are not engaged in speculative "flipping," and tend to be Lebanese residents or expat Lebanese and other Arabs who want a Beirut apartment; and the Lebanese banking sector has been relatively isolated from the global crash because its banks were restricted from purchasing large amounts of derivatives like CDOs (subprime mortgage derivative structures), and because when the global crisis struck, Lebanese moved their money from international and regional banks into local ones, increasing their foreign currency liquidity.

31. These included senior member Mustafa Badreddine, the brother-in-law of famous Hizbullah Resistance leader Imad Mughniyyeh.

32. For a thorough review of the history of planning policies in Lebanon, see Verdeil 2011. For an in-depth analysis of the southern suburbs during the 1960s, see Khuri 1975.

33. For more on the politics of naming Dahiya, see Harb 2003.

34. Amal remains active in some Dahiya neighborhoods, such as Ghobeyri and Bourj el-Barajneh, where it administers social service institutions and scout troops. Its authority in South Lebanon has lessened over time. For more on Amal's sociopolitical history, see Norton 1987.

35. For more details on the political background of these elections along with an analysis of local governments in Lebanon, see Favier 2001; Lebanese Center for Policy Studies 1999.

36. Following anthropological convention and with their permission, we have not changed the names of party officials and other public figures. After their initial introduction, we follow Lebanese conventions for respectful address, which generally means using a title plus first name—in this case, Hajj Abu Sa'id.

37. Anja Peleikis's (2000) case study of Zrariyeh, a village in South Lebanon, and its translocal connections to the Ivory Coast showed how remittances contribute to increased social status as well as wealth through investments in real estate.

38. In 2011, the World Bank Migration and Remittances Fact Book stated that Lebanon's inward remittances flow amounted to more than 8.17 billion US dollars (doubling the 2003 figure of 4.3 billion US dollars). This is about 15 percent of the Lebanese gross domestic product. Lebanese emigrants are more or less equally distributed among different sectarian groups: "Between 1975 and 2001, 23.2% of the total number of the Greek Orthodox community emigrated . . . followed by the Armenian Orthodox and the Greek Catholics 23.1% each, the Sunnis 22.2%, the Shiites 21% and the Maronites 20.9%. The Druze . . . emigrated least . . . with 14.7%" (Hourani 2003, 12).

39. As Mark Liechty (2003, 30) notes, "Class and consumption have to be seen as mutually constitutive cultural processes."

40. Here we follow Sherry Ortner (2003, 11): "I take it as fundamental that class is not some natural object lying around in the world but is culturally or discursively constructed." We take this to mean that material difference is deployed and understood in contextual ways. See also Mark Liechty's (2003) excellent review of the theoretical difficulties posed by defining the "middle class," and of course Bourdieu (1984) on cultural and other forms of capital.

41. The Birmingham school of cultural studies popularized a notion of youth as actively constructing subcultures through commodity forms (Hebdige 1979; Hall and Jefferson 1975). Several anthropologists have noted that the consequences of the subsequent focus on "youth culture" as a universally applicable concept has been fetishizations of youth as a category of resistance. For useful reviews of recent anthropology of youth literature, see Bucholtz 2002; Wulff 1995. For work on youth in cultural geography, see Skelton and Valentine 1998.

42. Examples include Borneman 1992; Cole and Durham 2007; Comaroff and Comaroff 2000; Christiansen, Utas, and Vigh 2006; Rofel 1999; Vigh 2006; Winegar 2006.

43. Our understanding of generations is also inspired by Lisa Rofel's (1999, 21–22) focus on different cohorts, or "visibly divided political generations" of Chinese women, in order to emphasize temporality and historical change, and highlight how "coming of age at particular moments creates telling fault lines through which meaning is transformed."

44. The exception is one woman who became committed at age nine against the wishes of her parents, but in keeping with the practices of her older siblings.

45. The pious Shiʻi interlocutors of Lara's first project exemplify the vanguard generation (Deeb 2006).

46. For details on this public piety based on authenticated forms of Islam, and its emergence as well as importance in the community, see Deeb 2006.

47. There is a gray area of people born between 1970 and 1978, although if we think about generational change as a gradual process linked to social and political transformations, those born during that period represent that process of change. Because our research was primarily conducted in 2008, people in this biological age bracket did not meet the criteria we set for our interviews with youths. Similarly, we did not interview people born after 1990, but speculate that at least for now, the trends we have seen that set pious youths apart from the Islamic vanguard generation are continuing.

48. Our project is not a study of youth culture or Muslim youth culture per se. For an excellent or thoughtful overview of scholarship on Muslim youths, see Bayat and Herrera 2010. See also Herrera 2009; Adely 2009; Swedenburg 2007.

49. In addition to denoting young men or people (depending on the context) in their late teens and twenties, shabab is also used as the opposite of ʻaʼilat, or "families," in some restaurants in the Arab world in order to segregate space or limit clientele. In this usage, shabab indicates groups of single young men, who are assumed to behave "badly," and therefore need to be isolated from families and young women. Such gendered age segregation is extremely rare in Lebanon, including Dahiya.

50. Men's dress was also the subject of conversation, though far less frequently. Muhammad, a pious young man in his early twenties who had completed the hajj, told us that friends sometimes harassed him for wearing shorts while playing football. "People were like, 'Oh, you're a hajj, how can you wear shorts!' " He continued incredulously, "It's not like there is a problem. I'm playing football."

51. Compare Carla Jones's (2007, 213) observation that "among middle-class young women in urban Java, and in Indonesia more broadly, expressions of Islamic piety have moved from explicitly anti-fashion frugal and moral critiques of an older generation to more commodified and explicitly fashionable expressions." This suggests a transnational dimension to this generational change.

52. In a survey by the Lebanese Ministry of Social Affairs conducted in 2006, the average age of marriage for women is 28.8 years nationally and 30.2 years in Beirut, while men's average age of marriage is 32.8 years.

53. Jad Melki's (2010) survey of Arab youths confirmed high rates of media consumption. In a recent survey of 583 Lebanese youths, Maud Stephan-Hachem and Azza Beydoun (2011) found that 94 percent have access to the Internet and 72 percent have a Facebook account. In his survey of 1,200 Lebanese youths, Charles Harb (2010, 13) found that 49.7 percent go online daily. See also Bayat and Herrera

2010; Newcomb 2006. Because the radically different social world of pious youths in Lebanon was built by the vanguard and not imposed through sudden globalization, there is an internal consistency that suggests that our interlocutors may be less "unbounded" than the Nepali youths described by Liechty (1995).

54. This includes a pious fashion industry (Moors and Tarlo 2007; Balasescu 2003), faith-based travel and pilgrimage (Pinto 2007; al-Hamarneh and Steiner 2004), "Islamic tourism" (Harb 2009; Hazbun 2008), religious commodities (Starrett 1995), and media (Eickelman 2000).

55. Ala al-Hamarneh and Christian Steiner (2004) and Waleed Hazbun (2008) note the post-9/11 shift of Arab Gulf tourists away from Europe and North America toward Arab destinations in order to avoid security hassles and increasing Islamophobia. As of 2012, this began to change due to restrictions on Gulf travel to Lebanon imposed by those states to punish Lebanon for its official stance in relation to the Syrian uprising. At the same time, North American tourism to Beirut has increased, as reflected in a series of *New York Times* travel articles highlighting the city in 2009–10.

56. See, for example, Graiouid 2007; Houston 2001; Khosravi 2007; Newcomb 2006; M. Peterson 2011; Salamandra 2004. A transnational Muslim youth "culture" may extend to Europe and North America as well, similar to Amel Boubekeur's (2007, 75) description of Muslim youths in France as seeking "the ambience of a 'cool' Islam, freed from the stigma of the 'old' Islamist rhetorics." To a certain extent, this rings true of our young interlocutors too, and the generational commonalities between her European Muslim interlocutors and our Lebanese Muslim ones may account for a greater similarity than one might expect, especially in relation to their understandings of and desires for incorporation into global culture.

57. This is confirmed by the International Crisis Group (2007, 19), which noted that the ongoing political division between the March 8 and March 14 alliances in Lebanon has "added another reason for religious moderation: because Hizbollah depends more heavily on the Shiite community, it must reach out to and reassure all Shiites, including those (such as the exiled bourgeoisie whose financial support it needs) who do not espouse a militant or religious view."

58. After 2006, the party-affiliated Lebanese Association for the Arts also began offering monthly talks by a wide range of Lebanese and Arab artists, occasionally involving universities as well, as part of deliberate efforts toward what it describes as "communication" and "discussion" in Lebanon.

59. On the capacity of Hizbullah to adjust to different stakes at the political and urban levels, legitimize these shifts in position and their associated paradoxes, and sustain its power for the past three decades, see Harb 2010a, 233–49.

60. Since 2011, we have also heard residents of Dahiya share these perceptions and express their concerns that Hizbullah is no longer able to control crime in the area. These fears were confirmed in August 2012 when members of the Meqdad clan—a large Shi'i family based in the Bekaa with a strong presence in Dahiya—

kidnapped twenty Syrians and one Turkish citizen. For more on that incident and its resolution, see Harb and Deeb 2012.

61. Cooperation with the internal security forces began in 2008, and in 2009 state traffic police were brought into Dahiya.

62. For discussions of the ways that social change and identity are frequently marked by, or assumed to be marked by, women's dress and especially the headscarf, see Abu-Lughod 2002; Deeb 2009.

CHAPTER 2. Producing Islamic Fun:
Hizbullah, Fadlallah, and the Entrepreneurs

1. For more on the party's earlier forms of cultural production, see Deeb 2008; Maasri 2012.

2. In 2009 or 2010, the LAA was divided into two associations that share leadership, but are responsible for different sectors of cultural production. Ressalat is now the organization responsible for media campaigns, while the Association for Reviving Resistance Heritage (jam'iyyat ihya' turath al-muqawama) is responsible for building large-scale structures, including Khiam, Mleeta, the Maroun al-Rass garden, and the memorial for Sayyid Abbas Musawi in the Bekaa village of Nabi Sheet, along with the perpetually being planned Resistance museum for Dahiya. For more on this museum, see Deeb 2008. See also the organization's Web site: http://www.ressalat.org.

3. Mleeta is a Resistance museum that opened in May 2010 in the hills above Saida. See Harb and Deeb 2011; http://www.mleeta.org. Maroun al-Rass is a village on the southern frontier overlooking Israeli settlements. After the 2006 war, Iran funded a LAA-designed public garden there, including children's playgrounds, landscaped areas, barbecue pits, and a mosque. The garden has become a destination for neighboring villagers and visitors from other parts of Lebanon who come to experience the "border." Resistance sites in the South and Bekaa Valley are simply marked with a billboard indicating the operation's name and date, with details of the attack, resulting military and human losses on the Israeli side, and accompanying illustrations. Often these roadside billboards are illegible to someone driving by; one needs to park and approach the billboard to actually be able to read its small fonts. The LAA director told us that these are still amateur and ultimately need to be reorganized to form a well-designed "Resistance trail" through South Lebanon.

4. Tarnikh is a made-up word using the root "ra kh wa" to suggest being floppy, and tanbaleh implies someone who lies around all day doing nothing. Also, as mentioned in the "Note on Language" at the start of this book, when interviewees inserted English words into mainly Arabic statements, those English terms are indicated with underlining.

5. The LAA has an orchestra and has recently branched into theater. Musical

and theatrical performances, including comedy shows, happen regularly, and as of 2010 are free and open to the public. These forms of cultural production are directed at youths in an explicit effort to provide morally and politically acceptable forms of entertainment—entertainment that is not viewed as "Western," corrupt, immoral, or otherwise compromised. Compare Hirschkind's (2006, 128) observation that the recent increase in various forms of "Islamically suitable" cultural production in Egypt, including songs, theater, and literature, are "part of the revival's attempt to create an ethically sustaining lifeworld."

6. Hizbullah controls much of the available entertainment for younger children (up to sixteen years old) in the Islamic milieu through its scouting and sports activities, including summer camps—activities that are professionally organized by its Youth Mobilization Unit. See also Le Thomas 2012. As these young people become more independent, they tend to grow less keen on Hizbullah-provided leisure, and begin exploring the new cafés in their neighborhoods or municipal Beirut.

7. He backs up his claims with references to statistical studies conducted by the party's research center, al-Markaz al-Istishari, and studies conducted by Lebanese University students. Despite his views about the influences of the Internet, Shaykh Ali keeps an active Facebook page, where he posts links to and photos of LAA-related events. In July 2011, this included a photo album celebrating the ride of eighty Harley-Davidson bikers to Mleeta.

8. Hizbullah's understanding of order is interesting. Shaykh Ali mentioned the private use of public space as one form of "disorder," and noted that a fatwa was issued to establish infringing on public space as haram. It appears that Hizbullah is increasingly becoming the "protector" of middle-class rights—protecting order for the more affluent and securing their assets. The party has been cooperating with the Lebanese internal police force to crack down on illegal activities in Dahiya, ranging from hashish smoking to major drug and prostitution rings, which have become more visible following the 2006 war.

9. We also appreciate the comment of one of our anonymous reviewers, noting that he has heard Shi'i gamers complain that these games aren't very good.

10. This is described by Hanin Ghaddar in her *Foreign Policy* article "Hezbollah's Extreme Makeover," March 17, 2010, http://www.foreignpolicy.com/articles/2010/03/17/hezbollah_s_extreme_makeover?page=0,1 (accessed July 27, 2011). Paintball has become a trendy pastime for young men throughout Greater Beirut, and most paintball places carry military names—not surprising given the nature of the activity.

11. Assaf is a prominent Lebanese director, actor, and playright who converted to Shi'i Islam; he is known for his avant-garde approach to theater. Abi-Saab is an eloquent cultural critic, currently editing the cultural section of *Al-Akhbar*, a newspaper perceived as having a relatively sympathetic stance toward Hizbullah.

12. See Maasri 2012. We thank Zeina Maasri for generously discussing her research with us; she explained that Abedini radically modernized Iranian art through typographic aesthetics that desacralized calligraphy. Some of the media campaigns

designed by the LAA are available at http://www.moqawama.org/monasabat/index.html? (accessed July 22, 2011). See, in particular, the campaign from January 1, 2011 titled Mawkab al-Ahzan.

13. South Beirut's municipalities are Ghobeyri, Bourj el-Barajneh, Haret Hreik, and Mrayjeh. The latter two were majority Maronite areas before the civil war, with Maronite mayors plus a mixed Maronite and Shi'i municipal council. Maronites were displaced by the war, and afterward most people who still owned property sold it and did not return. Municipal elections for Haret Hreik and Mrayjeh were delayed until a political consensus was reached between Hizbullah and the original Maronite residents who were registered to vote in the area. It was agreed that the mayor would be Maronite, but that decision-making power would remain in the hands of a Hizbullah majority. In Ghobeyri and Bourj el-Barajneh, Hizbullah won municipal elections in 1998, 2004, and 2010, with Hajj Abu Sa'id as mayor in Ghobeyri. Hajj Abu Sa'id has successfully led development there, partnering with international donors, the private sector, and nongovernmental organizations to improve circulation and infrastructure, establish public gardens, and build educational and cultural facilities. For more on this, see Harb 2009.

14. This is striking because of the Shi'i-Sunni tensions that emerged in the mid-2000s in Lebanon.

15. Augustus Richard Norton (2007, 104n1) notes that Hajj Abu Sa'id tolerated the sale of alcohol in Monoprix (now TSC), and quoted him as saying that "many of the Shi'a who had worked in West Africa 'drank like fish.' With a laugh he said, 'That's their choice.' "

16. The Arabic term ikhtilat literally translates as "mixing," but is closer in meaning to the French *mixité*, which refers specifically to mixed-gender social interaction or a lack of gender segregation.

17. We were told by a waiter at the only café where the owner refused to be interviewed that he (the owner) was "in the party" and therefore suspicious of our interest in his business. A longtime friend in Dahiya added that this person owned more than one café, was related to an important Hizbullah member, and tended to avoid the spotlight. Apart from this anecdotal information, we have no substantive evidence of Hizbullah's direct involvement in the leisure sector in Dahiya.

18. This well-known phrase occurs several times in the Qur'an and is considered a duty for Muslims.

19. The use of economic pressure to prevent the selling of alcohol takes place outside Dahiya as well and is not necessarily party organized. One of our vanguard interlocutors told us that he had walked out of his Beirut neighborhood's minimarket after discovering that it sold alcohol and had explained his actions to its owner, and that shortly thereafter, the owner called him into the store as he passed by and told him that he had stopped carrying alcohol due to pressure from a number of area residents.

20. In Lebanon, it is common for a distributor to subscribe to several different satellite networks (e.g., Orbit and Nile Sat) and then provide access to mixed pack-

ages of channels to local customers via cable for a small monthly fee—less than the cost of an actual direct subscription to the satellite network itself.

21. This is an ironic parallel to Talal Asad's (1993) critique of "religion" as an anthropological concept divorced from the workings of power.

22. This is not a new project, and party efforts to control every aspect of its constituents' lives have diminished significantly and had waning success over the past two decades. Several longtime Dahiya residents reported attempts by the party in the late 1980s and early 1990s to institute various "rules" ranging from dress codes to quiet hours at night. As one person told us, "People rebelled, started talking about it, saying how much they hated it, and word got back to the party, and they lightened up. They had no choice, or they would have lost their popular support."

23. Writing about the 1980s, prior to the formal existence of Hizbullah, Hala Jaber (1997, 53) suggests that businesses selling alcohol were "sent a warning in the form of a few sticks of dynamite hurled at their front doors" or "raided by unknown militiamen who took to smashing bottles of alcohol on display after lecturing the owners on the vices of their commodities." Since summer 2011, there have been reports that stores selling alcohol in villages and towns in South Lebanon affiliated with Amal or the Communist Party have been forced to close, and one store was dynamited in Tyre. Anti-Hizbullah media sources in Lebanon have accused the party of being behind these events, which Hizbullah denies.

24. This is not to say that Hizbullah's control is perceived negatively. It is also considered a source of protection and security, especially in times of political uncertainty. For instance, in Dahiya's neighborhood adjacent to the Christian area of Hadath, a café manager told us appreciatively, "Some guys from Hizbullah visited the people who live here in Sainte-Therese who are not Shiʻa, and they gave them a card and a phone number, and told them, if anyone bothers you, call this number, we will protect you."

25. For more on the institution of the *marjaʻiyya*, see Walbridge 2001b; Momen 1985; Khalaji 2006.

26. There are three schools of thought among jurisprudents about the purity of human beings: Fadlallah's universalist view, the perspective that only Muslims are taher, and the view that only "people of the book" are, including Jews and Christians with Muslims. While the matter of the nationality of one's domestic worker may seem relatively unimportant, this particular fatwa has larger ramifications ranging from the acceptability of non-Muslims in sacred spaces like mosques to coexistence in Lebanon.

27. Despite his efforts, "even at the height of Khomeini's prestige, most Shiʻa followed Grand Ayatollah Abuʻl Qasim Khuʻi in Iraq" (Walbridge 2001b, 5). A marjaʻ is responsible for distributing part of the *khums* and *zakat*, religious taxes. Khums in particular is a Shiʻi-specific annual tithe of one-fifth of the increase in one's income minus living expenses. See Mervin 2007.

28. The leader of the official Shi'i institution in Lebanon, the Supreme Islamic Shi'i Council, is also considered a religious authority by some pious people, although he is not necessarily a marja'. The council's former leader, Shaykh Muhammad Mahdi Shamseddine, who died in 2001, was a source of religious knowledge for many, especially those Shi'i Muslims who were not Hizbullah supporters or did not strictly emulate a marja'. His successor, Shaykh Abdul-Amir Qabalan, has been unable to establish himself as a religious authority and is primarily viewed as an administrator of religious affairs. There are other established jurisprudential references in the world today—for example, Grand Ayatollah Muhammad Ishaq Fayadh and Grand Ayatollah Bashir Hussein al-Najafi. They do not have a significant presence in the Lebanese Shi'i community, however.

29. Fadlallah has produced copious volumes and written at least forty books. For more on Fadlallah, see Sankari 2005. Talib Aziz 2001 provides a good overview of Fadlallah's rise to marja' status, and Stephan Rosiny 2001 discusses the controversies surrounding him. For more on the dynamic process of becoming a marja' in general, see Khalaji 2006; Walbridge 2001a.

30. This poll, conducted and reported by Theodor Hanf, is cited in Norton 2011. For a good discussion of contemporary marja's, especially those related to Najaf, see Norton 2011.

31. On Sistani, see Khalaji 2006. He suggests that Sistani has the largest worldwide following and that his popularity began before the US invasion of Iraq—though that brought him new publicity.

32. This may be in the process of changing; Sistani opened a new building with a cultural center and library in addition to the representative's office in 2009, on a main road in Dahiya.

33. Technically, all three provide opinions on where practices fall on a religious scale of acceptability that includes haram/*muharram* ("prohibited"), *makruh* ("not favored"), *mubah* ("neutral"), *mustahabb* ("commendable"), and *wajib* ("obligatory"). Nevertheless, most people in Dahiya including youths simply think of things as haram or halal (permissible), and jurisprudents seem to mirror that language in their advice.

34. Personal communication, May 2007.

35. *Dunya al-Shabab* (Fadlallah 1995), translated into English in 1998 as *World of Our Youth*, explicitly treats youth as a life stage during which people need guidance, and calls for communication and friendship between parents and youths along with efforts to understand youth perspectives, needs, and desires. Much of the book is in a question-and-answer format, covering themes ranging from marriage to education to the permissibility of playing dominos. It graced the bookshelves of many vanguard generation parents. Fadlallah's juristic office receives at least forty questions about and from youths per day, and frequently over one hundred questions daily. These questions arrive from around the world, and are asked via the Web site, by telephone, and in person. The typical turnaround time for

questions in 2010 was twenty-four to thirty-six hours (and indeed, we found this to be the case for the questions we asked via the Web site).

36. The earliest record we have seen of this view is in Fadlallah 2001.

37. When we noted how open to interpretation this seemed, Sayyid Ja'far acknowledged the inherent flexibility built into this statement, saying, "The interpretation is in the analysis of the situation: is she mature or not? She may see herself as mature."

38. Temporary marriage (*zawaj mu'aqqat*), also known as "pleasure marriage" *zawaj mut'a* or *sigheh* in Iran, has become much more visible among youths in Lebanon, and is increasingly used as a means to date and be intimate without committing a sin. This is a contracted relationship between a man and woman, without any witnesses, limited to a specified period of time and in accordance with a specified dowry, either symbolic or substantial, provided for the woman at the contract's end. For more on the practice in Iran, see Haeri 1989, 2004. For more on the practice among Lebanese youths today, see Deeb and Harb 2007. For more on Fadlallah's views on the practice, see Deeb 2010.

39. Some view this idea as existing in constant tension with the practice of following a jurisprudent to begin with.

40. In his work on Islamic jurisprudence about reproductive technologies in Lebanon, Clarke (2009, 71) notes, "Indeed, it is not always easy to tie down exactly what a given authority thinks. . . . [T]hey change their mind, an answer given in one context may not exactly match that given in another, intermediaries may relay a somewhat different version, and of course much depends on the rigour of the question." For more on fatwas as unenforced yet authoritative opinions, see Messick 1986; Agrama 2010. On the production of authoritative knowledge in jurisprudence through social and textual relations, including query-answer formations, see Messick 1996. On the effects of the Internet on these processes, see Clarke 2010. On cyber fatwas, see Wynn 2007.

41. For example, Sistani's opinion is that nail polish prevents water from passing over the skin and nail, and must be removed completely prior to ablutions (Moh'd Taki al-Hakim 2004, 104).

42. We have not been able to locate a written source confirming this. Lara heard a cleric from Fadlallah's office give this answer to a question on a radio call-in show in Beirut in July 2008, and in interviews and conversations, many women who followed Fadlallah understood this to be his view (and several had painted only four fingers and toes on each hand and foot).

43. Information Department of the Office of Sayyed Muhammad Hussein Fadlullah, "A Second Statement Issued by the Juristic Office of the Renovating Jurisprudent His Eminence, Sayyed Muhammad Hussein Fadlullah (ra) on the Issue of Emulation," in *Bayynat*, http://english.bayynat.org.lb/news/bayan_09072010.htm (accessed August 15, 2010).

44. Within Lebanon, Fadlallah was the most important jurisprudent standing against the idea of *wilayat al-faqih*, the political system of jurisprudential guidance

that underlies the Islamic Republic in Iran. He has also been a voice for intersectarian coexistence and dialogue in Lebanon since the 1990s.

45. While Fadlallah has two sons who are clerics (Sayyid Ali and Sayyid Ja'far), neither is of the age, stature, or religious rank to be a marja'. Furthermore, there is a great deal of debate in Shi'i Islam as to the appropriateness of sons playing a role in succession. Linda Walbridge (2001b) discusses the complexities of the roles of sons and sons-in-law in relation to the marja'iyya, noting that although they often play important supporting roles for their fathers, they do not "inherit" the mantle.

46. See http://www.assaha.info/en/about.php (accessed July 22, 2011).

47. Compare to Clarke 2010.

48. The reason that it is preferable to avoid eating seafood without scales is that there is no evidence to rule either way on such food, so avoiding it is precautionary but not necessary. In keeping with his tendency to forbid anything about which the ruling is unclear, Sistani instead states that only fish with scales that have been taken out of the water while alive or died within a fishing net may be eaten (Moh'd Taki al-Hakim 2004, 152).

49. Many Lebanese refer to all amusement parks as Luna Parks in the way that vacuum cleaners are referred to as Hoovers. We don't know how the Beirut Luna Park was named, although we speculate that it was named after the famous Coney Island Luna Park.

50. In another example of a failed café business, the owner of a florist shop that was destroyed during the 2006 war reopened it as a café after the war as a—short lived—way to "ride the wave of the era."

51. Mona's conversations with executives at the two major Islamic banks in Dahiya, Beit al-Mal and Bank al-Baraka, confirmed that neither of these institutions have provided loans for cafés or restaurants in Dahiya.

52. It is also possible that café owners in Dahiya have difficulty hiring people with experience in the service industry because of the associations others have of the area as poor or dangerous. One café owner complained about his difficulties hiring chefs for these reasons.

53. A few of our interlocutors who were frequent café customers complained about this lack of professionalism in cafés as well. As customers ourselves, we also sensed it in some of the cafés we visited in Dahiya, especially in relation to service. We are fully aware, however, that this is related to our own class positions and social trajectories.

54. Since our conversation with him, Riyad has left this restaurant in Dahiya and is now the senior manager at a major restaurant on Hamra Street. When we saw him there one evening, he told us that he was much happier with his new job.

55. This idea of "family entertainment" shares several characteristics with notions of family entertainment in the United States, including the idea of providing activities for multiple age groups and the importance of maintaining a morally appropriate environment.

56. There were several successful gyms in Dahiya's Haret Hreik neighborhood that were destroyed during the July 2006 war. This encouraged the Inmaa' group to build Family House near Haret Hreik in 2007.

57. Due to major technical and political problems, most areas of Lebanon experience regular daily electricity cuts.

58. Some owners seem to take this responsibility quite seriously. While conducting the customer survey, our research assistant had to wait for one owner to "check" the completed customer survey cards she had distributed before he would allow her to see them. She noticed he was erasing information from some cards. When he gave them to her, he explained that he was erasing writings some male customers had addressed to her (in obvious attempts to meet her) and apologized for their "bad behavior."

CHAPTER 3. Mapping Leisure and Café Styles

1. This is based on a survey of customers we conducted at different times of day in six cafés: 5.7 percent of them were under eighteen years of age, 42.7 percent were eighteen to twenty-five; 38.9 percent were twenty-six to thirty-five, and 12.7 percent were over thirty-five; 54.3 percent were male, and 45.7 percent female; and 67.1 percent were employed, 23.8 percent were students, 6 percent were housewives, and 2.8 percent were unemployed. Note that this does not preclude people from being both students and employed.

2. We sampled places according to their geographic distribution, trying to account for diversity of location, and tabulated and mapped the data. Information collected included: opening date, number of seats and floors, owner name(s), functions or services besides food, menu language and offerings, prices for three common items (coffee, argileh, and chicken sandwich), the availability of Internet access, a separate "families-only" room, and a prayer room. Families-only rooms are a way that some cafés in the Middle East segregate young single men from women on their own, or men who are with their spouses and children. In other words, it is a form, rare in Lebanon but more common elsewhere in the region, of sex and age segregation related to ideas about morality.

3. Figure 3.5 is based on interviews with three land brokers in Dahiya in 2010 who provided the range of prices in US dollars per square meter for specific areas. The "middle" category indicates land prices between fifteen hundred and two thousand US dollars, "middle to high" indicates twenty-five hundred to three thousand US dollars, "high" indicates three to five thousand US dollars, and "very high" indicates over five thousand US dollars. For benchmarking, 2010 land prices in high-end neighborhoods of municipal Beirut, such as Verdun, range between five and seven thousand US dollars per square meter. In Beirut's downtown, the price exceeded ten thousand US dollars. The map also includes the informal settlements and Palestinian refugee camps—lower-income neighborhoods of south Beirut. We

thank Mona Fawaz for sharing those data. The map is indicative, and neighborhood boundaries do not accurately reflect urban reality, which is not as homogeneously demarcated as represented.

4. Another neighborhood in Dahiya where sociospatial differences are striking is Jnah, home to Fantasy World, Coda Café, and other cafés. Jnah abuts the Horch el-Qatil informal settlement, but because Horch el-Qatil is topographically lower than the streets through which one accesses these entertainment sites, it is easily dismissed from the urban landscape.

5. Compare Said Graiouid's (2007, 538) description of the architectural structure of modern cafés in Morocco, which often include an upstairs section "appropriated by couples and students who use it as a romance or study area," because it "provides a protective shield from the public eye and generates a feeling of privacy and intimacy which is not found [elsewhere in the café]."

6. This is based on Pearson chi-squares with anything less than 0.05 being significant. This is a statistical method that compares expected and observed outcomes, and tells us if they are significantly different from one another. If they are, then there is a relationship (unspecified) between the two variables.

7. Bab al-Hara's bath was the brainchild of the interior designer for many of Dahiya's cafés, who we were told did his final project for college on a Turkish bath. The owner liked the idea of men bringing their families to the café to hang out while they went to the bath. Our many efforts to interview this designer failed; this was explained to us as due to his general reclusiveness.

8. It is worth noting that Internet access is quite expensive in Lebanon.

9. Television in Dahiya's cafés is a background element that generally does not interfere with café life (with the exception of televised World Cup or Eurocup football games and major speeches by Nasrallah). This differs from the impact of television on café practices in Morocco, where "audiences [decode] and [reconstruct] television texts and [inscribe] meta-narratives in their margins" (Graiouid 2007, 543–44).

10. In Lebanon, the coffee traditionally made at home by boiling ground coffee in water and then letting the grounds settle to the bottom of the cups after serving is called either Arabic or Turkish coffee, though some Lebanese prefer Arabic in a nod to their Armenian compatriots. Elsewhere—for instance, in Jordan—this coffee is called Turkish coffee and is distinct from Arabic coffee, which is a bitter brew of lightly roasted ground coffee served from a brass pot (*dalleh*) in handleless cups. Turkish coffee has its own set of drinking rituals linked to hospitality, and one is never supposed to charge for it. It is rarely seen in Lebanese restaurants at the end of a meal.

11. We surveyed the prices of the same three items at cafés in Hamra and at Rawda Café (also called Ahweh Chatila)—a seaside café off the Corniche, long frequented by working-class people, students, and leftists. Rawda's prices were comparable to those at al-Saha and Bay Rock in Dahiya. Prices differed drastically at cafés in Hamra where argileh could cost up to US$10.00 or 15,000 LBP and Ara-

bic/Turkish coffee up to US$3.30 or 5,000 LBP, while the latter averaged US$1.50 or 2,250 LBP in Dahiya, occasionally reaching US$2.00 or 3,000 LBP.

12. This differs from the naming of prewar cafés in Beirut, which were usually named after their owners (or managers) or location (Douaihy 2005). Morocco's contemporary cafés tend to be named after the owners' children or grandchildren in "a desire to 'home' [the café's] public space" (Graiouid 2007, 539).

13. Charles Harb's (2010, 12) survey of Lebanese youths across the country found that 41.4 percent had college degrees, as compared to 24 percent of the US population.

14. Elaine Chun and Keith Walters (2010) discuss this transliteration system as "Arabizi," citing a 2010 conference paper by Amy Johnson (Johnson 2010). For more on new forms of transliteration prompted by the Internet and text messaging, see also Abdulla 2008.

15. Mona Abaza (2006) notes a similar shift to English as the most common second language in Cairo.

16. For the past decade, the French Embassy's cultural center in Lebanon has been expanding its services in Shi'i-majority regions of the country, establishing libraries with French books and media, providing information about pursuing higher education in France, and offering French language courses. These efforts suggest that French authorities are trying to influence Shi'i ideas about culture, especially ideas among youths.

17. We prefer to think of this as eclecticism rather than hybridity, following Jessica Winegar's (2006) astute observation that the idea of a hybrid suggests a duality that does not adequately convey the complexity of multiple processes of cultural translations involving several different locales. This section draws on our fieldwork experiences and conversations as well as a photographic survey of eight café interiors.

18. As opposed to the negative sense, which involves all sorts of traditions that need to be left behind for the sake of progress.

19. According to Robert Saliba (2004, 26–27), the triple arch is a feature of the "central hall house" (along with red tiles and wrought iron balustrades), an architectural form celebrated as a "national icon, the source of [Lebanese] architectural identity, and . . . traditional building type par excellence." He adds that these features were adapted by different social groups according to owners' wealth, social status, and lifestyle, and that they have been used and abused across sect and class, and have become part of Lebanese contemporary popular culture's symbols.

20. In 2005, al-Saha was awarded an architectural prize by the Arab Cities Association for its "daring design and its contribution to traditional architecture."

21. He also told Mona that he had accumulated hundreds of antique objects from years of travel to Malaysia, Syria, and Turkey, and that al-Saha was the ideal space to exhibit this collection.

22. The museum is reminiscent of Qasr Moussa, a famous wax museum in the Chouf dedicated to showing village activities in a similar fortress-like building. Al-Saha's museum has become a destination for school field trips.

23. See Christa Salamandra's (2004) work on the recent re-creations of "old Damascus" in new cultural forms, including restaurants and cafés. See also Khosravi 2008; Houston 2001.

24. See, for example, Shahram Khosravi's (2008) analysis of a teahouse in Tehran that is built and decorated to resemble a rural village house.

25. And indeed, older people often associated rising drug use and divorce rates across Beirut, including in Dahiya, with the city, idealizing the rural as a space of moral order.

26. In keeping with this, sociologist Talal Atrissi told us that in his work on Hizbullah anthems, he has noticed an increase, as compared to the 1980s and early 1990s, in lyrics paying homage to the Lebanese village and natural landscape.

27. Empty lots are rare in Dahiya, and are more likely to be used for housing or commercial projects, especially along main roads, than for cafés or restaurants.

28. This trend is sometimes found in homes in Dahiya and Beirut where people grow herbs and vegetables on their balconies or roofs. This is especially the case for those who experienced the city in the 1950s, a time when urban agriculture was a common practice because more people lived in buildings with gardens. See Makhzoumi 2008.

29. Fiori's design changed when Nayla sold it one year later.

30. Many in Ras Beirut's cosmopolitan middle and upper classes considered argileh smoking an uncivilized practice, associating it with the poorer classes and Eastern rather than European cultural practices. On the popularity of "shisha cafés" in France and their relationship to Orientalist marketing, see Pages–El Karoui 2010.

31. Similarly, the relatively new Beirut Mall in Ghobeyri or City Mall in Dora are comparable to a US or global-corporate mall, in contrast to the older ABC shopping centers in Lebanon, which more closely resemble a European model. This illustrates the importance of timing to style. Abaza (2006) notes a similar shift from Europe, especially France, to the United States (in the guise of "the global") as a reference point for Cairo's cosmopolitan elite and upwardly mobile.

32. For example, on June 26, 2010, there was an Arabic language festival in Hamra that used art, photography, and performances to call on Lebanese to use Arabic. Lebanese code switching is also lauded—sometimes sarcastically—as a national trait, such as on T-shirts that proclaim "hi, kifak, ça va?"—a stereotypical greeting used to connote Lebanese multilinguality.

33. Compare M. Peterson's (2011, 159) discussion of new coffee shops in Cairo that are "simultaneously at least three spaces: a global space that derives its meaning from its indexical connections to the global coffee commodity chain, a translocal space that signifies by its iconicity with similar sites around the world, and a local space that signifies by its contrasts with other local spaces, particularly the ahwa [sic] [traditional coffee shop]."

34. This is also seen across Lebanon in the appearance of multiple food stations at weddings, with each representing a different ethnic cuisine.

35. Few cafés were professionally designed.

36. In one café, we were struck by the geometric forms used in the gypsum ceiling and were told by the manager that they were designed by a gypsum skilled worker, a Syrian migrant laborer.

CHAPTER 4. Flexible Morality, Respectful Choices, Smaller Transgressions

1. During Ramadan or Ashura, for instance, people who might frequent restaurants with alcohol on the menu during other months may cease to do so temporarily. For an eloquent analysis of Ramadan as a time of "exceptional morality," see Schielke 2009b.

2. With the exception of the dabkeh, a Lebanese folk dance, which we discuss further below.

3. Consistent with how our interlocutors use these terms, we use haram throughout this book to indicate something that is considered religiously forbidden, and halal to refer to religiously permissible.

4. For more on the morality of various forms of music and singing among Muslim jurisprudents, see al-Faruqi 1985.

5. Email communication, August 3, 2010.

6. This reflects Sistani's general adherence to the principle of "necessary avoidance" of anything that could potentially lead to activities that are haram. *Lahu* is the term jurisprudents often use when noting that certain forms of entertainment are haram; it connotes pleasure, amusement, and fun, but seems to be used to highlight the unimportance or wastefulness of certain pastimes, and their potential to lead people into haram activities. Notably, while the representatives of Khamenei and Sistani both used the word to explain what was halal and haram to us, Fadlallah's representative did not.

7. On this matter Hizbullah has parted ways with its formal *marja'*, as an article in the December 2002 issue of *Baqiyat Allah* suggests that only musical instruments used by the Prophet are permissible because the use of other instruments will promote immoral practices.

8. As of 2010, these performances only included male musicians and the occasional small group of female singers. Shaykh Ali's explanation for this highlighted social over religious reasons, and used Iran as an example where there are female musicians in orchestras. There remain in his view, however, limitations on female performance, including a prohibition on women singing alone such that their voices may be recognized. The concerts are for mixed audiences, with both single-sex and mixed-seating areas so that audience members can choose to sit wherever they are most comfortable. For a nuanced discussion of debates about the permissibility of young women singing nationalist songs in a school context in Jordan, see Adely 2007.

9. He also claimed that they are working, through party-supported songs and

music videos (on YouTube and Al-Manar television), to provide an alternative for youths. "We don't know if this alternative will compete with the market because there are thousands of opportunities for people to go and listen to any type of music. We cannot compete . . . but we can fill a small hole in this field."

10. For Sistani, this includes anthems sung or performed in groups that might in any way approximate lahu.

11. For discussions of moral conflict and negotiation related to music in other Islamic contexts, see Adely 2007; Marsden 2007; Gazzah 2008; Peterson 2010.

12. Most jurists use the concept of a *kabira* or "great sin" (plural, *kaba'ir*) to refer to a few serious acts, including murder and usury, and not to transgressions like drinking alcohol. Unlike in many Christian theologies, in Islam sin is a deed, not a state of being. Most of our interlocutors believed that on Judgment Day, one's good and bad deeds would be weighed against each other, and that sincere repentance could erase an act of sin from this record. Some of them used words like *ma'siya* (disobedience or rebellion) and *khit'* (mistake or lapse) to describe a deed that transgressed God's will and violated the religious rubric for morality. Others just used phrases like "do haram." These terms are often translated as the word sin, including on Fadlallah's Web site, where sin is used in English to refer to a range of transgressions. See, for example, http://english.bayynat.org.lb/FridaySpeeches/ke_17092010.htm (accessed July 23, 2012).

13. See, for example, Hirschkind's (2006) discussion of ethical modes of listening to sermons. Hirschkind (ibid., 35) also notes "music's ability to bypass the faculty of rational judgment and directly affect the senses of the listener" as a matter of concern for jurisprudents.

14. Fairuz is an iconic Lebanese singer, and Umm Kulthum was an iconic Egyptian singer; both women are revered and loved throughout the Arab world.

15. Araq is an anise-flavored alcoholic drink common in the Levant.

16. Several verses in the Qur'an are frequently cited in relation to the prohibition of alcohol, including one saying that Muslims cannot pray while intoxicated, and another calling on people to abstain from fermented beverages and gambling because they make one forget God. While there is a general consensus among Muslims that alcohol is at best strongly discouraged, if not altogether prohibited, debate exists in relation to specific terms used. For example, *sukara* is used for intoxicated without specifying a substance in one verse, and *al-khamr* is used in others, which is the noun derived from the verbal root "to ferment," often translated as "wine" and extended to all forms of alcohol.

17. On this matter, Fadlallah and Sistani share the view is that it is haram to sit at a table that includes alcohol, but it is acceptable to go to a place where alcohol is served provided that one is not encouraging the "work of the restaurant" and is not sitting at a table with alcohol on it (email communication with Fadlallah's juristic office on May 29, 2012; Moh'd al-Hakim 2004, 154–55).

18. Only two of the young people we spoke with said that they would absolutely stop being friends with someone who drank.

19. On intersectarian networks in Lebanon, see Joseph 1975. On the production of sectarianism through historical processes in Lebanon, see Makdisi 2000. On these processes specifically in the Shi'i community, see Weiss 2010.

20. This comment also highlights how decisions are constrained by Dahiya's urban features—its density, pollution, distance from natural landscapes, and lack of public spaces.

21. There is a plethora of literature theorizing the relationship between women's bodies and ideas about identity and morality. A few examples related specifically to the headscarf include Abu-Lughod 1998; Ahmed 1992; Deeb 2006; Gole 1996; Secor 2002.

22. A mawlid is a celebration of the Prophet's birth, or in Shi'i Islam, the birth of one of the Twelve Imams. Mawlids often involve music and dancing.

23. Few Lebanese women wear the 'abaya, and most who do are related to major religious or political figures in the community. This form of dress is more commonly associated with Iran and Iraq.

24. The youths that Miriam Gazzah (2008) interviewed also highlight the importance of their individualized decision making in relation to music and Islam. She follows Olivier Roy in connecting this individualism to the postmigration context of Europe. Roy (2004) points to the lack of consensus on religious issues in the European context and Muslims' minority status as factors leading to this heightened individualism.

25. It is common for young men to refer to the more overtly pious among them as shaykhs. This can be said with varying tones to convey respect, derision, or description.

26. Compare Adeline Masquelier's (2010) discussion of life trajectories in Niger, where young men expect to become more "serious" and religious with age.

27. As Dorothea Schulz (2003) argues, new circulations of knowledge through technology transform ideas about individual responsibility so that as access to religious knowledge increases, people make new claims for responsibility and emphasize their individual opinions about religious interpretations.

28. Contrast Mahmood's (2005) discussion of how through practice, one cultivates pious or virtuous dispositions.

29. It was more common for vanguard generation activists and Hizbullah members to find this conviction-first perspective troubling. Noha, for example, a prominent Hizbullah member, told Lara in 2000 that girls should wear the headscarf at age nine and then work on themselves to bring their piety in line with their actions, and that the scarf would help them do so.

30. On Cairo, see M. Peterson 2011. On Morocco, see Graiouid 2007. Rachel Newcomb (2006) highlights the more complex negotiations of gender that accompany the presence of women in public spaces in Fes, a context where the public presence of women remains fraught. In Lebanon, constraints remain on women's employment in cafés, although several Dahiya cafés hire young women, some of whom wear the headscarf and some of whom who do not.

31. Based on a quick Google search, the phrase "emo hijab" seems common in Muslim American communities as well as in the Middle East. Emo here is short for "emotion" and traces to "emo-core," an epithet directed at certain bands in Washington, DC's hard-core movement in the mid-1980s (Greenwald 2003). It eventually slipped—via 1990s' alternative rock—into mainstream US music, with its defining feature continuing to be the hyperemotionality of its (usually androcentric) lyrics.

32. The subculture style associated with emo includes elements like black clothing, black leather wristbands, studded belts and collars, and hair that is dyed black, sometimes with streaks of bright pink, blue, or other colors. Associated hairstyle trends were created with fabrics, as young women combined bright underscarves with lacy-black coverings tied in complex ways.

33. On the recent transnational popularity of argileh (referred to elsewhere as hookah, shisha, and nargile) among youths, see Abaza 2006; Bowman 2009; Peterson 2010; Pages–El Karoui 2010.

34. Email communication, August 3, 2010.

35. His opinion is that *mu'assal* (flavored tobacco) is better than *'ajami* (plain, dried tobacco), because one is "burning sugar," which is "a natural thing." This idea contradicts general agreement that smoking tobacco soaked in flavoring and glycerine is far worse for one's health.

36. In August 2011, Parliament passed a law banning smoking in public spaces. The law has been implemented in stages, and went into effect for the hospitality sector (restaurants, cafés, and pubs) in September 2012. As of December 2012, authorities were largely able to enforce this law. Most cafés, especially the larger ones, have reorganized their seating areas to allow argileh smoking in enclosed sections and/or outdoors. Smaller cafés and pubs in isolated streets, however, have been transgressing the law.

37. For a discussion of the gendered social effects of this sense of being under others' scrutiny, see Naber 2012.

38. Barbara Drieskens (n.d.) also notes the importance of reputation in relation to where young women will behave in what ways. Spaces outside one's neighborhood are safer for flirting, for instance, because even if people are seen, those seeing them can more easily turn a blind eye.

39. Lebanese, especially youths, often use the word ya'ni the way that youths in the United States use the term like.

40. In addition, two young men and one young woman said they avoid being around people who are playing cards or pool because people playing those games often curse loudly. Fadlallah has "legalized games involving gambling as long as no money was exchanged" (Aziz 2001, 211).

41. Although religious opinions use a five-category scale of acceptability, most people in Dahiya simply think of things as haram or halal.

42. As a result of the constraints on young women's behavior, the most insight-

ful discussions we have had with young women about dating have been one-on-one informal conversations, as opposed to the group interviews that were possible with young men. In group contexts, young women freely told stories about other people they knew or stories about their refusals of male advances, emphasizing their compliance with ideals of female social propriety. This points to both the methodological difficulties of research on sexuality as well as the continued stigma associated with nonmarital heterosexual relationships in Lebanon.

43. While some young women who have had temporary marriages inform their future husbands about these relationships, others depend on hymen reconstruction surgeries—which Fadlallah has allowed within particular circumstances—to avoid having to justify or reveal them.

44. Compare Schielke's (2009a) discussion of contradictory ideas and practices around sexuality and romantic love among young Egyptian men.

45. According to the UN Development Program's (1998, 98) *Human Development Report*, the ratio of single males aged thirty to thirty-four to single females aged twenty-five to twenty-nine in Lebanon was less than seven to ten in 1996. We could not locate updated numbers, but these 1996 figures continue to be used in other studies as a reference: http://www.dailystar.com.lb/Business/Lebanon/Feb/23/Brain-drain-or-brain-gain-A-Lebanese-perspective.ashx#axzz20FnPyYNe.

46. See, for example, Mahdavi 2008.

CHAPTER 5. Comforting Territory, New Urban Experiences, and the Moral City

1. For example, a trendy guidebook to Beirut—*Beyroutes*—includes an insert called "How to Survive in Dahiya" (Chahine 2010) that provides flippant advice for navigating the area that both implicitly and explicitly highlights stereotypes about Dahiya and its residents as poor, chaotic, dirty, and low class. Ironically, many of these stereotypes describe characteristics of most Beirut neighborhoods (e.g., intermittent electricity and street vendors). The overall effect is to define Dahiya as different—a place where Beirutis and visitors can go as tourists to gawk at people, religious practice, and poverty, or as bargain-hunting consumers venturing into the ghetto for cheap goods.

2. There are of course many people with social, kin, and economic relationships that cross the Dahiya-Beirut divide as well as residents of both areas who have built genuine relationships of political solidarity beyond these divisions. Here we are describing the stereotypical understandings of the other that dominate public discourse and seep into daily conversations. Going "to see" Dahiya was common in the post-2006 war period when dozens of people who had never set foot in the area ventured there on "disaster tourism" trips, coming to see the destruction and photographing people desperately looking for the remains of their personal possessions in the rubble. Spencer Platt's 2006 World Press Photo of the Year captured a telling

image of this phenomenon, http://www.archive.worldpressphoto.org/search/lay out/result/indeling/detailwpp/form/wpp/q/ishoofdafbeelding/true/trefwoord/ year/2006 (accessed December 2, 2012).

3. For an earlier discussion of martyr images in Dahiya, see Deeb 2006, 42–66. After hanging in the sun and dust for months, these images fade, losing their color and the captions celebrating the individual martyrs. Hizballah's media office replaces them with new photos annually on Martyrs' Day, although this is not done systematically or on all streets. During election seasons, the media office refurbishes and repaints the metal frames used to hang the images.

4. When asked where they spent their free time, many of our interlocutors mentioned the Corniche, describing a need to go to the sea to walk, breathe fresh air, enjoy the view of an open horizon, relax and forget their worries, play, and laugh. They contrasted the sea with Dahiya's density, traffic, and pollution, and saw it as an escape from the stress of urban life.

5. In her classes, Mona regularly shows photos of neighborhoods in Dahiya without naming them and asks students to guess their location. Her students' answers invariably indicate the working-class neighborhoods in Beirut with which they are familiar (e.g., Tariq al-Jadidah and Basta), and students are often startled when she tells them that these photos are of Dahiya, as they imagine the place to look like a slum. Similarly, when Mona takes her students on field visits to Dahiya, they are surprised at the similarity of the urban fabric with that of the rest of Beirut.

6. Indeed, all these areas should be associated with municipal Beirut in a new administrative unit coordinating the urban affairs of the entire agglomeration. Their current separation into different municipalities and governorates generates major urban management and planning problems, the most obvious of which is at the level of traffic and infrastructure—but this is beyond the scope of this book.

7. According to the land brokers we interviewed in 2010, the most expensive real estate in Dahiya at the time was five thousand US dollars per square meter. In municipal Beirut in 2010, the price of a square meter ranged from five to ten thousand US dollars.

8. These sectarian, political, and moral geographies are not static. They have been shaped by Lebanon's recent history, and continue to shift in response to local, national, and geopolitical events and trends.

9. Entre-soi is a French word referring to the preference of social groups to stay with their own, leading to social and spatial segregation along with the formation of ghettos. See Maurin 2004.

10. Hage builds on Bourdieu's notion of habitus and posits that familiarity is produced in spaces where implicit knowledge allows a person to feel secure. Feeling at home is then "a feeling of shared symbolic forms, shared morality, shared values and most importantly perhaps, shared language" (Hage 1997, 103). See also Ben Malbon's (1998, 269) discussion of clubs as spaces where one feels at ease if one has "this desire to be in accord with the group rather than to be exposed amongst

strangers, to feel an affinity with a place and the people within it, though not necessarily a sense of unity."

11. Raouche and Manara are neighborhoods in west Beirut, and Broummana is
a Christian-majority mountain town that serves as a resort area in summer.

12. For a detailed discussion of how Hizbullah has worked to intensify the
interaction between spatiality and religiosity in south Beirut over the past three
decades, see Harb 2010b.

13. For a more nuanced view of Tariq al-Jadidah in light of recent violence in
the neighborhood, see http://www.jadaliyya.com/pages/index/5627/about-last
-night (accessed July 28, 2012).

14. As of 2012, tourism to Syria has been curtailed due to violence.

15. Not everyone agrees that prices in Dahiya are the same as those in Beirut.
Many youths mentioned that the reason they do not go to Beirut for leisure is that
they cannot afford a coffee or argileh there. We take this up further below.

16. Walid Jumblatt, the political leader of the Druze community, repeatedly
used the term taqawqu' specifically to refer to the sociospatial isolation of Hizbullah in Dahiya during the intense May 2008 conflict between the March 8 and March
14 political alliances. Nasrallah then appropriated the word in his speeches, distancing the party from it. It is unlikely that Jihad is using taqawqu' in Jumblatt's politicized sense; he is more likely referring to its spatial dimension.

17. Agnes Deboulet and Isabelle Berry-Chickhaoui (2000) use competences to
refer to the resources that citizens' utilize to think, use, appropriate, and transform
private and public urban spaces, especially in the context of rapidly changing built
environments.

18. In her work on the local knowledge that young people use to navigate urban
public spaces (and private places like shopping malls), Caitlin Cahill refers to
guidelines as "rules" that determine "street literacy." Cahill (2000, 268) argues that
these rules are "socially mediated directives for behavior bounded by invisible but
implicit social understandings of what is acceptable." We use this notion of rules
with an added caveat. While many of our interlocutors may view their personal
rules as directives, we instead understand them more as guidelines for behavior.

19. Since this interview was conducted, the moral leisure scene in Beirut has
grown to include more cafés that do not serve alcohol, though songs are played in
the background.

20. Compare Heiko Henkel's (2007) work on how pious people in Istanbul
"foreground" selected symbols, places, and neighborhoods, and infuse domestic,
work, and leisurely sociospatial practices with Muslim values in order to "inhabit"
the city in a Muslim way.

21. Compare Catherine Robinson's (2000) discussion of how the differentiation
of space into positive and negative areas, routes, and locations generated safe, comfortable, reliable, and stabilizing routines for youths in Australia.

22. This negative stereotyping that criticizes spatial practices at the Corniche
and dreads their spread to Horch Beirut is echoed by a Lebanese blogger: "You

might be surprised, but I'm actually with keeping people away from this [Horch Beirut] park until they really deserve it. I mean look at all the public spaces in Beirut, are we treating them good? The corniche at Ain El-Mrayseh, for example, looks like one big shisha cafe now! Young boys come in their 1990 BMW and Golf cars, turn up their radios to Ali El-Deek [popular Syrian male singer] songs, set their shisha, and start dancing Dabke! wala anawran min heik [you "can't get more vulgar than this"] [sic]." Available at http://www.plus961.com/2012/02/horsh -beirut (accessed August 20, 2012).

23. Several activist groups have been mobilizing against the municipality, and lobbying to open the park and enhance public spaces in the city. These include At the Edge of the City, Nahnoo, and Dictaphone Group. See http://attheedgeofthe city.wordpress.com, http://www.nahnoo.org, and http://www.dictaphonegroup .org, respectively.

24. Based on the post–civil war power-sharing formula among different sectarian groups, Beirut's mayor is a Sunni Muslim affiliated with the Hariri camp, while Beirut's governor is a Greek Orthodox Christian chosen by the Maronite Christian president of the republic. Political bickering between the two often leads to deadlock in the governance of the Lebanese capital.

25. Leisure sites are also proliferating in the northeastern parts of Greater Beirut. These cafés serve alcohol and play songs, and thus do not abide by the moral norms of Dahiya's cafés. They do resemble them, however, in their eclectic design and the prevalence of argileh.

26. Compare Graiouid's (2007) discussion of Moroccan cafés as social spaces of informal collective practices that generate congeniality among customers through a wide range of communicative practices including humor, solidarity, and play.

27. See Tom Hall, Amanda Coffey, and Howard Williamson's (1995, 510) analysis of casual talk, including gossip and jokes, as "low-level identity work" through which "a flow and exchange of information in which local knowledge, common sense understandings and individual perspectives are variously affirmed, contested, and negotiated over."

28. Jane Jacobs (1961) deemed these among the fundamental aspects of city life.

29. People are moving events out of their homes, and instead into cafés and restaurants, in part because more women are working outside the home and have little time to prepare meals for large groups, and in part due to socioeconomic mobility, as more of Dahiya's residents can afford to invite groups out for meals.

30. The use of café spaces for events that formerly would have been hosted at home, especially by women, calls into question the borderline between public and private spheres by allowing what Graiouid (2007, 536–37) described as the "domestication" of the café into a family space.

31. The owner of the café in Sainte-Thérèse who chooses what kind of music to play based on the appearance of her customers is a case in point. The geographic location of her café facilitates that practice, which would be more difficult in areas closer to Dahiya's center.

32. For example, as we go to press a major Kuwaiti investor is conducting a feasibility study for a mall on the airport road. Additionally, less than ten years after the French-owned Monoprix supermarket and BHV mall opened in 1998–99, the Kuwaiti-owned TSC supermarket replaced them. They reopened in an adjacent location in 2011.

33. Middle-class Lebanese often seek to organize their environment in ordered and hygienic ways (e.g., trimmed landscaping and tidiness) that they believe separate them from what they view as the messy and informal sociospatial practices of lower-class people, who are stigmatized as dirty and disorderly. Hizbullah's Values campaign was aligned with these techniques of disciplining spaces and bodies in favor of the party's middle-class constituents. On how middle-class groups order suburban space, see Ayata 2006. On Calcutta, see Kaviraj 1997.

34. Monroe (2011) stresses the extent to which this phenomenon is underresearched.

CHAPTER 6. Good Taste, Leisure's Moral Spaces, and Sociopolitical Change in Lebanon

1. As Corinne Kratz (2011, 22, 25) notes in her analysis of museum exhibitions, the ways in which design elements are brought together create what she calls "rhetorics of value," "powerful persuasions that draw on and synthesize an array of sensory and communicative resources and media," which highlight "the ways evaluation and valorization combine with and are effected through persuasive form and practice" to construct identities as well as values.

2. For instance, while Aziza's mother is happy to occasionally spend time and money in many of Dahiya's new cafés and restaurants with a few family members, when she wanted to throw a party at one of the larger places for a hundred guests, she quickly discovered that the cost would be prohibitive.

3. For Bourdieu, resources other than economic ones become capital when they have value related to how a person establishes oneself in relation to others in a hierarchical society. In that sense, we can speak here of moral and spatial capital.

4. Examples of these conventions include particular models of outdoor terrace seating and leather and wood interiors in addition to specific menu items. Café de Flore represents the classic archetype; see http://www.cafédeflore.fr/ (accessed July 25, 2012). See also Haine 1996.

5. Note that these characteristics are not unique to Dahiya, and there are cafés in other parts of the city—including Gemmayze, an area assumed to be more Eurocentric—that share them.

6. There are also quality distinctions within Dahiya. Al-Saha, for example, is viewed as a higher-status and more expensive restaurant than other places (which it is), and among cafés, various hierarchies also exist.

7. We rarely heard complaints about café prices in the area, and most were from

older individuals and those who were especially pious. The latter were usually uncomfortable with consumption in general, and found spending money in cafés "when there are poor people to feed" to be a symptom of societal waste and immorality.

8. Z'a'eh is a derogatory term for the urban poor derived from the word for "alley" [*zuqaq*] with additional connotations of criminality, and shalamasteh is slang for a hustler or charlatan.

9. He is referring to the Shi'i community's history of filling low-wage service sector jobs in Beirut.

10. Greg Fealy (2008, 28) suggests that contemporary believers of all faiths are seeking moral guidance in new ways, in a "largely individualized process with the 'consuming self' at its center."

11. Intellectual emancipation is an idea that Ranciere excavates from French philosopher Joseph Jacotet in Ranciere's earlier work *The Ignorant Schoolmaster*.

12. Compare to Ortner's (2003, 13) suggestion that "imagination, at both the level of the individual and the level of public culture, can always exceed the limits of any given [class] position."

13. Spatial form is organized and socially produced, leading to coherence manifested in geographic elements like location and distribution. But because the spatial location of physical objects in relation to one another might not be directly caused and emerges from "the independent operation of separate dominations" (Massey 1993a, 159), an element of chaos is also intrinsic to the spatial.

14. For an elaboration of this notion of urban citizenship, see Holston and Appadurai 1996, 192.

Glossary

'adi: normal
'ayb: shameful
ahweh or *qahwa*: coffee or coffee shop
akhlaq: morals
al-hala al-islamiyya: the Islamic milieu
argileh: hookah
banat: literally "girls"; used in Lebanon to refer to unmarried young
    women
barra: literally "outside;" connotes outdoors, external, foreign; used by
    many of our interlocutors to refer to places outside Dahiya
dabkeh: traditional Lebanese folk dance
diwaniyyeh (plural, *diwaniyyat*): Arabic-style seating area with low
    couches
ghara'iz: sexual instincts, lust
ghayyir jaw: literally "change atmosphere," often used to mean
    "de-stress"
halal: religiously permissible
haram: religiously prohibited
hijab: headscarf
ikhtilat: literally "mixing," but closer in meaning to the French *mixité*,
    which refers specifically to mixed-gender social interaction or a lack of
    gender segregation
ihtiram: respect
iltizam: religious commitment
infitah: opening up
kabira (plural, *kaba'ir*): great sin
katb kitab: signing of the marriage contract
lahu: amusement, pleasure, fun
maqha: coffee shop
marja' al-taqlid: jurisprudential reference; religious scholar emulated
    with regard to religious practice; literally "source for imitation"

mu'amalat: maintaining good social relations, Islamic value
muhafiz: conservative
muhajjaba: a woman who wears the Islamic headscarf
multazim/a: religiously committed person
munasib: appropriate
qiyam: values
sabaya: young women, gals
sha'bi: working class, "of the people," popular (in the Marxist sense of
    class, not trend)
shabab: guys, youths
shar'i: religiously legitimate, based on the shari'a
shari'a: Islamic law, really a set of interpretations that vary historically
    and geographically
sharqi or *shar'i*: Eastern
shawq: longing, desire
thaqafa: culture
turath: heritage
zawaj mu'aqqat: temporary marriage
zo': taste

References

Abaza, Mona. 2006. *Changing Consumer Cultures of Modern Egypt: Cairo's Urban Reshaping*. Leiden: Brill.

Abdulla, Rasha A. 2008. "Arabic Language Use and Content on the Internet." In *Access to Knowledge Toolkit I*, ed. Hala Essalmawi, 124–41. Alexandrina, Egypt: Bibliotheca Alexandrina.

Abisaab, Rula. 1999. "Shi'ite Beginnings and Scholastic Tradition in Jabal 'Amil in Lebanon." *Muslim World* 89:1–21.

AbuKhalil, As'ad. 1988. "The Palestinian-Shiite War in Lebanon: An Examination of Its Origins." *Third World Affairs* 10 (1): 77–89.

———. 1991. "Ideology and Practice of Hizballah in Lebanon: Islamization of Leninist Organizational Principles." *Middle Eastern Studies* 27:390–403.

Abu-Lughod, Lila. 1998. "Introduction: Feminist Longings and Postcolonial Conditions." In *Remaking Women, Feminism, and Modernity in the Middle East*, 3–31. Princeton, NJ: Princeton University Press.

———. 2002. "Do Muslim Women Really Need Saving? Anthropological Reflections on Cultural Relativism and Its Others." *American Anthropologist* 104 (3): 783–90.

Adely, Fida. 2007. "Is Music Haram? Jordanian Girls Educating Each Other about Nation, Faith, and Gender in School." *Teachers College Record* 109 (7): 1663–81.

———. 2009. "Everyday Youth Places: Youth in Educational Spaces." *International Journal of Middle East Studies* 41:372–73.

Agrama, Hussein Ali. 2010. "Ethics, Tradition, Authority: Toward an Anthropology of the Fatwa." *American Ethnologist* 37 (1): 2–18.

Ahmed, Leila. 1992. *Women and Gender in Islam: Historical Roots of a Modern Debate*. New Haven, CT: Yale University Press.

Alagha, Joseph. 2011. *Hizbullah's Identity Construction*. Amsterdam: Amsterdam University Press.

Al-Faruqi, Lois Ibsen. 1985. "Music, Musicians, and Muslim Law." *Asian Music* 17 (1): 3–37.

al-Hamarneh, Ala, and Christian Steiner. 2004. "Islamic Tourism: Rethinking the Strategies of Tourism Development in the Arab World after September 11, 2001." *Comparative Studies of South Asia, Africa, and the Middle East* 24:173–82.

Al-Harithy, Howayda, ed. 2010. *Lessons in Post-War Reconstruction: Case Studies from Lebanon after the July 2006 War*. London: Routledge.

Asad, Talal. 1986. "The Idea of an Anthropology of Islam." Occasional papers series, Center for Contemporary Arab Studies, Georgetown University, Washington, DC.

———. 1993. *Genealogies of Religion: Discipline and Reasons of Power in Christianity and Islam*. Baltimore: Johns Hopkins University Press.

Atrissi, Talal. 2008. "Chants de la résistance et libanisation du Hezbollah." In *Hezbollah: Etat des lieux*, ed. Sabrina Mervin, 247–51. Paris: Actes Sud.

Ayata, Sencer. 2002. "The New Middle-Class and the Joys of Suburbia." In *Fragments of Culture*, ed. Deniz Kandiyoti and Saktanber Ayse, 25–42. London: IB Tauris.

Aziz, Talib. 2001. "Fadlallah and the Making of the Marja'iyya." In *The Most Learned of the Shi'a: The Institution of the Marja' Taqlid*, ed. Linda Walbridge, 3–13. Oxford: Oxford University Press.

Balasescu, Alex. 2003. "Islamic Headscarves, Fashion Designers, and New Geographies of Modernity." *Fashion Theory: The Journal of Dress, Body, and Culture* 7 (1): 39–56.

Bayat, Asef. 2007. "Islamism and the Politics of Fun." *Public Culture* 19 (3): 433–59.

———. 2010a. *Life as Politics: How Ordinary People Change the Middle East*. Stanford, CA: Stanford University Press.

———. 2010b. "Muslim Youth and the Claim of Youthfulness." In *Being Young and Muslim: New Cultural Politics in the Global South and North*, ed. Linda Herrera and Asef Bayat, 26–47. Oxford: Oxford University Press.

Beydoun, Ahmad. 1999. *Al-Jumhuriyya al-mutaqatti'a: Masa'ir al-sigha al-lubnaniyya ba'd ittifaq al-Taef*. Beirut: Dar An-Nahar.

Borneman, John. 1992. *Belonging in the Two Berlins: Kin, State, Nation*. Cambridge: Cambridge University Press.

Boubekeur, Amel. 2007. "Post-Islamist Culture: A New Form of Mobilization?" *History of Religions* 47 (1): 75–94.

Bourdieu, Pierre. 1984. *Distinction: A Social Critique of the Judgment of Taste*. Translated by Richard Nice. Cambridge, MA: Harvard University Press.

———. 1989. "Social Space and Symbolic Power." *Sociological Theory* 7 (1): 14–25.

Bowman, Jim. 2009. "Time to Smell the Sweet Smoke: Fantasy Themes and Rhetorical Vision in Nargile Cultures." *Journal of Popular Culture* 42 (3): 442–57.

Bucholtz, Mary. 2002. "Youth and Cultural Practice." *Annual Review of Anthropology* 31:525–52.

Cahill, Caitlin. 2000. "Street Literacy: Urban Teenagers' Strategies for Negotiating Their Neighborhood." *Journal of Youth Studies* 3 (3): 251–77.

Chahine, Zinab. 2010. "How to Survive in Dahiya." In *Beyroutes: A Guide to Beirut.* Beirut: ARCHIS.

Christiansen, Catrine, Mats Utas, and Henrik E. Vigh. 2006. "Introduction: Navigating Youth, Generating Adulthood." In *Navigating Youth, Generating Adulthood,* ed. Catrine Christiansen, Mats Utas, and Henrik E. Vigh, 9–30. Uppsala, Sweden: Nordic Africa Institute.

Chun, Elaine, and Keith Walters. 2011. "Orienting to Arab Orientalisms: Language, Race, and Humor in a YouTube Video." In *Digital Discourse: Language in the New Media,* ed. Crispin Thurlow and Kristine Mroczeck, 251–76. New York: Oxford University Press.

Clarke, Morgan. 2009. *Islam and New Kinship: Reproductive Technology and the Shariah in Lebanon.* London: Berghahn Books.

———. 2010. "Neo-Calligraphy: Religious Authority and Media Technology in Contemporary Shiite Islam." *Contemporary Studies in Society and History* 52 (2): 351–83.

Cobban, Helena. 1985. *The Making of Modern Lebanon.* London: Hutchinson.

Cole, Jennifer, and Deborah Durham. 2007. "Introduction: Age, Regeneration, and the Intimate Politics of Globalization." In *Generations and Globalization,* ed. Jennifer Cole and Deborah Durham, 1–28. Bloomington: Indiana University Press.

Comaroff, Jean, and John L. Comaroff. 2000. "Millennial Capitalism: First Thoughts on a Second Coming." *Public Culture* 12 (2): 291–343.

Corm, George. 1987. "Le système institutionnel libanais." In *Liban: Espoir et réalités,* ed. Basma Kodmani-Darwish, 17–26. Paris: Institut français des relations internationals.

Curry, Michael. 1999. "'Hereness' and the Normativity of Place." In *Geography and Ethics: Journeys in a Moral Terrain,* ed. James D. Proctor and David M. Smith, 95–105. London: Routledge.

Dahlgren, Susanne. 2010. *Contesting Realities: The Public Sphere and Morality in Southern Yemen.* Syracuse, NY: Syracuse University Press.

Deboulet, Agnes, and Isabelle Berry-Chikhaoui. 2000. *Les compétences des citadins dans le Monde Arabe. Penser, Faire et Transformer la Ville.* Paris: Karthala.

Deeb, Lara. 2006. *An Enchanted Modern: Gender and Public Piety in Shi'i Lebanon.* Princeton, NJ: Princeton University Press.

———. 2008. "Exhibiting the 'Just-Lived Past': Hizbullah's Nationalist Narratives in Transnational Political Context." *Contemporary Studies in Society and History* 50 (2): 369–99.

———. 2009. "Piety Politics and the Role of a Transnational Feminist Analysis." *Journal of the Royal Anthropological Institute* 15 (1): 112–26.

———. 2010. "Sayyid Muhammad Husayn Fadlallah and Lebanese Shi'i Youth." *Journal of Shi'a Islamic Studies* 3 (4): 405–26.

Deeb, Lara, and Mona Harb. 2007. "Sanctioned Pleasures: Youth, Piety, and Leisure in Beirut." *Middle East Report* 245:12–19.

Dehghan, Saeed Kamali. 2010. "Music Fails to Chime with Islamic Values, Says Iran's Supreme Leader. *Guardian*, August 2. http://www.guardian.co.uk/world/2010/aug/02/iran-supreme-leader-music-islam (accessed October 11, 2010).

de Koning, Anouk. 2006. "Café Latte and Caesar Salad: Cosmopolitan Belonging in Cairo's Coffee Shops." In *Cairo Cosmopolitan: Politics, Culture, and Urban Space in the New Globalized Middle East*, ed. Diane Singerman and Paul Amar, 221–34. Cairo: American University in Cairo Press.

———. 2009. *Global Dreams: Class, Gender, and Public Space in Cosmopolitan Cairo*. Cairo: American University of Cairo Press.

Donham, Donald L. 2011. *Violence in a Time of Liberation: Murder and Ethnicity at a South African Gold Mine, 1994*. Durham, NC: Duke University Press.

Douaihy, Chawqi. 2005. *Maqahi Bayrut al-sha'biyya, 1950–1990*. Beirut: Dar an-Nahar.

Drieskens, Barbara. n.d. "Spaces of Seduction." Unpublished manuscript.

Durkheim, Emile. 1965. *The Elementary Forms of Religious Life*. Translated by Joseph Ward Swain. New York: Free Press.

Dumont, Louis. 1977. *From Mandeville to Marx: The Genesis and Triumph of Economic Ideology*. Chicago: University of Chicago Press.

Eickelman, Dale F. 2000. "Islam and the Languages of Modernity." *Daedalus* 129:119–35.

Elsheshtawy, Yasser. 2009. *Dubai: Behind an Urban Spectacle*. London: Routledge.

Elyachar, Julia. 2005. *Markets of Dispossession: NGOS, Economic Development, and the State in Cairo*. Durham, NC: Duke University Press.

Ewing, Catherine. 1990. "The Illusion of Wholeness: Culture, Self, and the Experience of Inconsistency." *Ethos* 18:251–78.

Fadlallah, Ayatollah al-Uzma Sayyid Muhammad Hussein. 1998. *World of Our Youth*. Translated by Khaleel Mohammed. Montreal: Organization for the Advancement of Islamic Knowledge and Humanitarian Services.

———. 2001. *Al-Masa'il al-Fiqhiyyeh*. Beirut: Dar al-Malak.

Favier, Agnes, ed. 2001. *Municipalités et pouvoirs locaux au Liban*. Beirut: Centre d'Etudes et de Recherches sur le Moyen-Orient.

Fawaz, Mona. 2009. "Neo-liberal Urbanity and the Right to the City: A View from Beirut's Periphery." *Development and Change* 40 (5): 827–52.

Fawaz, Mona, Mona Harb, and Ahmad Gharbieh. 2012. "Living Beirut's Security Zones: An Investigation of the Modalities and Practices of Urban Security." *City and Society* 24 (2): 173–95.

Fealy, Greg. 2008. "Consuming Islam: Commodified Religion and Aspirational Pietism in Contemporary Indonesia." In *Expressing Islam: Religious Life and Politics in Indonesia*, ed. Greg Fealy and Sally White, 15–39. Singapore: Institute of Southeast Asia Studies Publishing.

Fischer, Johan. 2008. *Proper Islamic Consumption: Shopping among the Malays in Modern Malaysia*. Copenhagen: NIAS Press.

Fisk, Robert. 1990. *Pity the Nation: The Abduction of Lebanon*. New York: Simon and Schuster.

Foucault, Michel. 2005. *The Hermeneutics of the Subject: Lectures at the Collège de France, 1981–1982*. Translated by Graham Burchell. New York: Picador.

Gazzah, Miriam. 2008. *Rhythms and Rhymes of Life: Music and Identification Processes of Dutch-Moroccan Youth*. Amsterdam: Amsterdam University Press.

Ghaddar, Hanin. 2010. Hezbollah's Extreme Makeover. Foreign Policy, March 17. http://www.foreignpolicy.com/articles/2010/03/17/hezbollah_s_extreme _makeover?page=0,1.

Ghannam, Farha. 2002. *Remaking the Modern: Relocation and the Politics of Identity in a Global Cairo*. Berkeley: University of California Press.

Gole, Nilufar. 1996. *The Forbidden Modern: Civilization and Veiling*. Ann Arbor: University of Michigan Press.

Graiouid, Said. 2007. "A Place on the Terrace: Café Culture and the Public Sphere in Morocco." *Journal of North African Studies* 12 (4): 531–50.

Greenwald, Andy. 2003. *Nothing Feels Good: Punk Rock, Teenagers, and Emo*. New York: St. Martin's Press.

Haenni, Patrick. 2009. "The Economic Politics of Muslim Consumption." In *Muslim Societies in the Age of Mass Consumption: Politics, Culture, and Identity between the Local and the Global*, ed. Johanna Pink, 327–42. Cambridge, UK: Cambridge Scholars Publishing.

Haeri, Shahla. 1989. *Law of Desire: Temporary Marriage in Shiʻi Iran*. Syracuse, NY: Syracuse University Press.

———. 2004. "Mutʻa: Regulating Sexuality and Gender Relations in Postrevolutionary Iran." In *Islamic Legal Interpretation: Muftis and their Fatwas*, ed. Muhammad Khalid Masud, Brinkley Messick, and David S. Powers, 251–61. Cambridge, MA: Harvard University Press.

Hage, Ghassan. 1996. "The Spatial Imaginary of National Practices: Dwelling-Domesticating/Being-Exterminating." *Environment and Planning* 14:463–85.

———. 1997. "At Home in the Entrails of the West: Multiculturalism, 'Ethnic Food,' and Migrant Home-Building." In *Home/World: Space, Community, and Marginality in Sydney's West*, ed. Helen Grace, Ghassan Hage, Lesley Johnson, Julie Langsworth, and Michael Symonds, 99–153. Sydney: Pluto Press.

Haine, W. Scott. 1998. *The World of the Paris Café: Sociability among the French Working Class, 1789–1914*. Baltimore, MD: Johns Hopkins University Press.

Halawi, Majed. 1992. *A Lebanon Defied: Musa al-Sadr and the Shiʻa Community*. Boulder, CO: Westview Press.

Hall, Stuart, and Tony Jefferson, eds. 1975. *Resistance through Rituals: Youth Subcultures in Post-War Britain*. London: Hutchinson.

Hall, Tom, Amanda Coffey, and Howard Williamson. 1999. "Self, Space, and Place:

Youth Identities and Citizenship." *British Journal of Sociology of Education* 20 (4): 501–13.

Hallaq, Wael B. 1984. "Was the Gate of Ijtihad Closed?" *International Journal of Middle East Studies* 16 (1): 3–41.

Hamzeh, A. Nazar. 2000a. "Lebanon's Islamists and Local Politics: A New Reality." *Third World Quarterly* 21:739–59.

———. 2000b. "Myth and Reality." *Index on Censorship* 29:128–30.

Hanf, Theodore. 1993. *Coexistence in Wartime Lebanon: Decline of a State and Rise of a Nation*. London: I. B. Tauris.

Harb, Charles. 2010. "Describing the Lebanese Youth: A National and Psycho-Social Survey." Youth in the Arab World working paper series, Issam Fares Institute for Public Policy and International Affairs, American University of Beirut.

Harb, Mona. 2001. "Urban Governance in Post-War Beirut: Resources, Negotiations, and Contestations in the Elyssar Project." In *Capital Cities: Ethnographies of Urban Governance in the Middle East*, ed. Seteney Shami, 111–33. Toronto: Toronto University Press.

———. 2003. "La Dahiye de Beyrouth: Parcours d'une stigmatisation urbaine, consolidation d'un territoire politique." *Genèses* 51:70–91.

———. 2009. "La gestion du local par les municipalités du Hezbollah." *Critique Internationale* 42:57–72.

———. 2010a. *Le Hezbollah à Beyrouth (1985–2005): De la Banlieue à la Ville*. Paris: IFPO-Karthala.

———. 2010b. "On Religiosity and Spatiality: Lessons from Hezbollah in Beirut." In *The Fundamentalist City? Religiosity and the Remaking of Urban Space*, ed. Nezar AlSayyad and Mejgan Massoumi, 125–41. London: Routledge.

Harb, Mona, and Lara Deeb. 2011. "Culture and History and Landscape: Hizbullah's Efforts to Shape the Islamic Milieu in Lebanon." *Arab Studies Journal* 14 (2): 10–41.

———. 2012. "Fissures in Hizballah's Edifice of Control." *Middle East Report Online*, October 31. http://www.merip.org (accessed December 1, 2012).

Harb, Mona, and Mona Fawaz. 2010. "Influencing the Politics of Post-War Reconstruction in Haret-Hreik." In *Lessons in Post- War Reconstruction: Case Studies from Lebanon after the July 2006 War*, ed. Howayda Al-Harithy, 21–45. London: Routledge.

Harik, Judith Palmer. 2004. *Hezbollah: The Changing Face of Terrorism*. London: I. B. Tauris.

Hattox, Ralph S. 1985. *Coffee and Coffeehouses: The Origins of a Social Beverage in the Medieval Near East*. Seattle: University of Washington Press.

Haugbolle, Sune. 2010. *War and Memory in Lebanon*. Cambridge: Cambridge University Press.

Hazbun, Waleed. 2008. *Beaches, Ruins, Resorts: The Politics of Tourism in the Arab World*. Minneapolis: University of Minnesota Press.

Hebdige, Dick. 1979. *Subculture: The Meaning of Style*. London: Methuen.

Henkel, Heiko. 2007. "The Location of Islam: Inhabiting Istanbul in a Muslim Way." *American Ethnologist* 34 (1): 57–70.

Herrera, Linda. 2009. "Youth and Generational Renewal in the Middle East." *International Journal of Middle East Studies* 41 (3): 268–371.

Herrera, Linda, and Asef Bayat, eds. 2010. *Being Young and Muslim: New Cultural Politics in the Global South and North*. Oxford: Oxford University Press.

Hersh, Seymour. 2006. "Watching Lebanon: Washington's Interests in Israel's War." *New Yorker*, August 21. http://www.newyorker.com/archive/2006/08/21/060821fa_fact (accessed December 1, 2012).

Hirschkind, Charles. 2006. *The Ethical Soundscape: Cassette Sermons and Islamic Counterpublics*. New York: Columbia University Press.

Holston, James, and Arjun Appadurai. 1999. "Introduction: Cities and Citizenships." In *Cities and Citizenships*, ed. James Holston, 1–20. Durham, NC: Duke University Press.

Hourani, Guita. 2003. "Emigration, Transnational Family Networks, and Remittances: Overview of the Situation in Lebanon." Paper presented at the Mediterranean Forum on Migrations, Institute for Mediterranean Studies, University of Lugano, Switzerland.

Houston, Christopher. 2001. "The Brewing of Islamist Modernity: Tea Gardens and Public Space in Istanbul." *Theory, Culture, and Society* 18 (6): 77–97.

Hovsepian, Nubar, ed. 2008. *The War on Lebanon: A Reader*. Northampton, MA: Interlink Publishers.

Howell, Signe. 1996. Introduction to *Ethnography of Moralities*. Edited by Signe Howell. London: Routledge.

Human Rights Watch. 2007. "Why They Died: Civilian Casualties in Lebanon during the 2006 War." September 5. http://www.hrw.org/reports/2007/09/05/why-they-died (accessed December 1, 2012).

International Crisis Group. 2007. "Hizbollah and the Lebanese Crisis." Middle East report no. 69, October 10.

Jaber, Hala. 1997. *Hezbollah: Born with a Vengeance*. New York: Columbia University Press.

Jacobs, Jane. 1961. *The Death and Life of Great American Cities*. New York: Modern Library Edition.

Johnson, Amy. 2010. "il7mdella good ;) : Code Choice and Arabizi in a Meebo Chatroom." Paper presented at Georgetown University, Washington, DC.

Jones, Carla. 2007. "Fashion and Faith in Urban Indonesia." *Fashion Theory* 11 (2–3): 211–32.

Joseph, Suad. 1975. "The Politicization of Religious Sects in Borj Hammoud, Lebanon." PhD diss., Columbia University.

Kahan Commission. 1983. "Report of the Commission of Kahan Inquiry into the Events at the Refugee Camps in Beirut." http://www.mfa.gov.il/MFA/Foreign%20Relations/Israels%20Foreign%20Relations%20since%201947/

1982-1984/104%20Report%20of%20the%20Commission%20of%20Inquiry %20into%20the%20e (accessed December 1, 2012).

Kanna, Ahmed. 2011. *Dubai: The City as Corporation*. Minneapolis: University of Minnesota Press.

Kapeliouk, Amnon. 1982. *Sabra and Shatila: Inquiry into a Massacre*. Belmont, MA: Association of Arab-American University Graduates Press.

Karababa, Eminegul, and Ger Gullz. 2011. "Early Modern Ottoman Coffeehouse Culture and the Formation of the Consumer Subject." *Journal of Consumer Research* 37 (5): 737–60.

Kassir, Samir. 1994. *La guerre au Liban: De la dissension nationale au conflit régional*. Paris: Karthala.

Kaufman, Asher. 2002. "Who Owns the Shebaa Farms? Chronicle of a Territorial Dispute." *Middle East Journal* 56 (4): 576–95.

Kaviraj, Sudipta. 1997. "Filth and the Public Sphere: Concepts and Practices about Space in Calcutta." *Public Culture* 10 (1): 83–113.

Keith, Michael, and Steve Pile. 1993. "The Place of Politics." In *Place and the Politics of Identity*, ed. Keith Michael and Pile Steve, 22–40. New York: Routledge.

Khalaf, Samir, and Per Kongstadt. 1973. *Hamra of Beirut: A Case of Rapid Urbanization*. Leiden: Brill.

Khalaji, Mehdi. 2006. "The Last Marja: Sistani and the End of Traditional Religious Authority in Shiism." Policy Focus no. 59, Washington Institute for Near East Policy, Washington, DC.

Khosravi, Shahram. 2007. *Young and Defiant in Tehran*. Philadelphia: University of Pennsylvania Press.

Khuri, Fuad. 1975. *From Village to Suburb: Order and Change in Greater Beirut*. Chicago: University of Illinois Press.

Kirli, Cengiz. 2004. "Coffeehouse: Public Opinion in the Nineteenth-Century Ottoman Empire." In *Public Islam and the Common Good*, ed. Armando Salvatore and Dale Eickelman, 75–98. Leiden: Brill.

Kratz, Corinne A. 2011. "Rhetorics of Value: Constituting Worth and Meaning through Cultural Display." *Visual Anthropology Review* 27 (1): 21–48.

Lambek, Michael. 2000. "The Anthropology of Religion, and the Quarrel between Poetry and Philosophy." *Current Anthropology* 41 (3): 309–20.

Lebanese Center for Policy Studies. 1999. *Al-intikhabat al-baladiyya fi Lubnan 1998, makhad al-dimukratiyya fil mujtama'at al-mahaliyya*. Beirut: Lebanese Center for Policy Studies.

Lefebvre, Henri. (1974) 1991. *The Production of Space*. Translated by Donald Nicholson-Smith. Oxford: Blackwell.

Le Thomas, Catherine. 2012. *Les ecoles chiites au Liban. Construction communautaire et mobilization politique*. Paris: Karthala-IFPO.

Liechty, Mark. 1995. "Media, Markets, and Modernization: Youth Identities and the Experience of Modernity in Kathmandu, Nepal." In *Youth Cultures: A Cross-Cultural Perspective*, ed. Vered Amit-Talia and Helena Wulff, 166–201. London: Routledge.

———. 2003. *Suitably Modern: Making Middle-Class Culture in a New Consumer Society*. Princeton, NJ: Princeton University Press.

Limbert, Mandana E. 2010. *In the Time of Oil: Piety, Memory, and Social Life in an Omani Town*. Stanford, CA: Stanford University Press.

Maasri, Zeina. 2012. "The Aesthetics of Belonging: Transformations in Hizbullah's Political Posters (1985–2006)." *Middle East Journal of Culture and Communication* 5:149–89.

MacBride, Sean. 1984. *Israel in Lebanon: The Report of the International Commission*. Ithaca, NY.

Mahdavi, Pardis. 2009. *Passionate Uprisings: Iran's Sexual Revolution*. Stanford, CA: Stanford University Press.

Mahmood, Saba. 2005. *Politics of Piety: The Islamic Revival and the Feminist Subject*. Princeton, NJ: Princeton University Press.

Makdisi, Karim. 2011. "Constructing Security Council Resolution 1701 for Lebanon in the Shadow of the 'War on Terror.'" *International Peacekeeping* 18 (1): 4–20.

Makdisi, Ussama. 2000. *The Culture of Sectarianism Community, History, and Violence in Nineteenth-Century Ottoman Lebanon*. Berkeley: University of California Press.

Makhzoumi, Jala. 2008. "Interrogating the Hakura Tradition: Lebanese Garden as Product and Production." *International Association for the Study of Traditional Dwellings and Settlements* 200:50–60.

Malbon, Ben. 1998. "Clubbing: Consumption, Identity, and the Spatial Practices of Every-Night Life." In *Cool Places*, ed. Tracey Skelton and Gill Valentine, 266–86. London: Routledge.

Mannheim, Karl. 1952. "The Problem of Generations." In *Essays on the Sociology of Knowledge*, ed. Paul Kecskemeti, 276–320. New York: Oxford University Press.

Marsden, Magnus. 2005. *Living Islam: Muslim Religious Experience in Pakistan's North-West Frontier*. Cambridge: Cambridge University Press.

———. 2007. "All-Male Sonic Gatherings, Islamic Reform, and Masculinity in Northern Pakistan." *American Ethnologist* 34 (3): 473–90.

Martin, William H., and Sandra Mason. 2004. "Leisure in an Islamic Context." *World Leisure Journal* 46 (1): 4–13.

Masquelier, Adeline. 2007. "Negotiating Futures: Islam, Youth, and the State in Niger." In *Islam and Muslim Politics in Africa*, ed. Benjamin F. Soares and Rene Otayek, 243–62. New York: Palgrave Macmillan.

———. 2010. "Securing Futures: Youth, Generation, and Muslim Identities in Niger." In *Being Young and Muslim: New Cultural Politics in the Global South and North*, ed. Linda Herrera and Asef Bayat, 226–39. Oxford: Oxford University Press.

Massey, Doreen. 1993a. "Politics and Space/Time." In *Place and the Politics of Identity*, ed. Keith Michael and Pile Steve, 141–61. New York: Routledge.

———. 1993b. "Power-Geometry and a Progressive Sense of Place." In *Mapping the Futures: Local Cultures, Global Change*, ed. John Bird, Barry Curtis, Tim Putnam, and Lisa Tickner, 59–69. London: Routledge.

Maurin, E. 2004. *Le Ghetto Français. Enquête sur le Séparatisme Français*. Paris: Seuil.

Melki, Jad. 2010. "Media Habits of MENA Youth: A Three-Country Survey." Youth in the Arab World working paper series, Issam Fares Institute for Public Policy and International Affairs, American University of Beirut.

Meneley, Anne. 1996. *Tournaments of Value: Sociability and Hierarchy in a Yemeni Town*. Toronto: University of Toronto Press.

———. 2007. "Fashions and Fundamentalisms in Fin de siècle Temen: Chador Barbie and Islamic Socks." *Cultural Anthropology* 22 (2): 214–43.

Merrifield, Andrew. 1993. "Place and Space: A Lefebvrian Reconciliation." *Transactions of the British Institute of Geographers* 18:516–31.

Mervin, Sabrina, ed. 2007. *Les mondes chiites et l'Iran*. Paris: Karthala-IFPO.

Messick, Brinkley. 1986. *The Calligraphic State: Textual Domination and History in a Muslim Society*. Berkeley: University of California Press.

Miller, Daniel, ed. 1995. *Worlds Apart: Modernity Through the Prism of the Local*. London: Routledge.

Mitchell, Don. 2003. *The Right to the City: Social Justice the Fight for Public Space*. New York: Guilford Press.

MIT Electronic Journal of Middle East Studies. 2006. Special issue on the July 2006 war 6 (Summer).http://home.medewerker.uva.nl/r.e.c.leenders/bestanden/MITEJMES_Vol_6_Summer-pp%20188-.204.pdf (accessed December 1, 2012).

Moh'd Taki al-Hakim, Abdel-Hadi al-Sayyid. 2004. *Al-Fiqh lil Mughtaribin wifq fatawa samahutallah al-uzma, al-sayyid Ali al-Sistani*. Beirut: Dar al-Muarrikh al-Arabi.

Momen, Moojan. 1985. *An introduction to Shi'i Islam: The History and Doctrines of Twelver Shi'ism*. New Haven, CT: Yale University Press.

Moors, Annelise, and Emma Tarlo. 2007. "Introduction: Muslim Fashion." *Fashion Theory* 11 (2–3): 133–41.

Monroe, Kristin. 2009. "Civic Cartographies: Space, Power, and Public Culture in Beirut." PhD diss., Stanford University.

———. 2011. "Being Mobile in Beirut." *City and Society* 23 (1): 91–111.

Naber, Nadine. 2012. *Arab America: Gender, Cultural Politics, and Activism*. New York: New York University Press.

Nasr, Salim. 2003. "The New Social Map." In *Lebanon in Limbo: Postwar Society and State in an Uncertain Regional Environment*, ed. Theodore Hanf and Nasr Salam, 143–58. Baden-Baden: Nomos Verlagsgesellschaft.

Newcomb, Rachel. 2006. "Gendering the City, Gendering the Nation: Contesting Urban Space in Fes, Morocco." *City and Society* 18 (2): 288–311.

Norton, Augustus Richard. 1987. *Amal and the Shi'a: Struggle for the Soul of Lebanon*. Austin: University of Texas Press.

———. 2000. "Hizballah and the Israeli Withdrawal from Lebanon." *Journal of Palestine Studies* 30 (1): 22–35.

———. 2007. *Hizbullah*. Princeton, NJ: Princeton University Press.

———. 2011. "Al-Najaf: Its Resurgence as a Religious and University Center." *Middle East Policy* 18:132–45.

Ortner, Sherry B. 1998. "Identities: The Hidden Life of Class." *Journal of Anthropological Research* 54:1–17.

———. 2003. *New Jersey Dreaming: Capital, Culture, and the Class of '58*. Durham, NC: Duke University Press.

Pages–El Karoui, Delphine. 2010. "Shisha Cafés in France: Reinventing the Oriental Dream, from Exoticism to Beurs Integration." *Die Erde* 141 (1–2): 31–63.

Pandolfo, Stefania. 2007. "'The Burning': Finitude and the Politico-Theological Imagination of Illegal Migration." *Anthropological Theory* 7 (September): 329–63.

Peleikis, Anja. 2000. "The Emergence of a Translocal Community: The Case of a South Lebanese Village and Its Migrant Connections to Ivory Coast." *Cahiers d'études sur la Méditerranée orientale et le monde turco-iranien* 30:297–317.

Peterson, Jennifer. 2010. "Al-shabab al-masriyun wa aghani al-mulid." *Bahithat: Cultural Practices of Arab Youth* 24:62–80.

Peterson, Mark Allen. 2011. *Connected in Cairo: Growing up Cosmopolitan in the Modern Middle East*. Bloomington: Indiana University Press.

Picard, Elizabeth. 1996. *Lebanon, a Shattered Country: Myths and Realities of the Wars in Lebanon*. New York: Holmes and Meier.

———. 1997. "The Lebanese Shi'a and Political Violence in Lebanon." In *The Legitimization of Violence*, ed. David E. Apter, 189–233. New York: New York University Press.

———. 2000. "The Political Economy of Civil War in Lebanon." In *War, Institutions, and Social Change in the Middle East*, ed. Steven Heydemann, 292–324. Berkeley: University of California Press.

Pink, Johanna, ed. 2009. *Muslim Societies in the Age of Mass Consumption: Politics, Culture, and Identity between the Local and the Global*. Cambridge: Cambridge Scholars Publishing.

Pinto, Paulo G. 2007. "Pilgrimage, Commodities, and Religious Objectification: The Making of Transnational Shiism between Iran and Syria." *Comparative Studies of South Asia, Africa, and the Middle East* 27 (1): 109–25.

Proctor, James D., and David M. Smith, eds. 1999. *Geography and Ethics: Journeys in a Moral Terrain*. London: Routledge.

Qassem, Naim. 2005. *Hizbullah: The Story from Within*. Translated by Dalia Khalil. London: Saki.

Ranciere, Jacques. 2009. *The Emancipated Spectator*. Translated by Gregory Elliott. London: Verso.

Robbins, Joel. 2007. "Between Reproduction and Freedom: Morality, Value, and Radical Cultural Change." *Ethnos* 72 (3): 293–314.

Robinson, Catherine. 2000. "Creating Space, Creating Self: Street-Frequenting Youth in the City and Suburbs." *Journal of Youth Studies* 3–4:429–43.

Rofel, Lisa. 1999. *Other Modernities: Gendered Yearnings in China after Socialism*. Berkeley: University of California Press.

Rosiny, Stephan. 2001. "The Tragedy of Fatima al-Zahra." In *The Twelver Shi'a in Modern Times*, ed. Rainer Brunner and Werner Ende, 207–19. Leiden: Brill.

Roy, Olivier. 2004. *Globalized Islam: The Search for a New Ummah*. New York: Columbia University Press.

Saad-Ghorayeb, Amal. 2002. *Hizb'ullah: Politics and Religion*. London: Pluto Press.

Salamandra, Christa. 2004. *A New Old Damascus: Authenticity and Distinction in Urban Syria*. Bloomington: Indiana University Press.

Saliba, Robert. 2004. "The Genesis of Modern Architecture in Beirut, 1840–1940." In *Architecture Reintroduced: New Projects in Societies in Change*, ed. Jamal Abed, 23–34. Geneva: Aga Khan Institute for Architecture.

Sankari, Jamal. 2005. *Fadlallah: The Making of a Radical Shi'ite Leader*. London: Saki.

Sawalha, Aseel. 2010. *Reconstructing Beirut: Memory and Space in a Postwar Arab City*. Austin: University of Texas Press.

Schielke, Samuli. 2009a. "Ambivalent Commitments: Troubles of Morality, Religiosity, and Aspiration among Young Egyptians." *Journal of Religion in Africa* 39:158–85.

———. 2009b. "Being Good in Ramadan: Ambivalence, Fragmentation, and the Moral Self in the Lives of Young Egyptians." *Journal of the Royal Anthropological Institute*, n.s.:S24–240.

Schulz, Dorothea E. 2003. "Charisma and Brotherhood Revisited: Mass-Mediated Forms of Spirituality in Urban Mali." *Journal of Religion in Africa* 33 (2): 146–71.

Secor, Anna. 2002. "Veil and Urban Space in Istanbul." *Gender, Place, and Culture* 9 (1): 221–53.

Shaery-Eisenlohr, Roschanack. 2009. "Territorializing Piety: Genealogy, Transnationalism, and Shi'ite Politics in Modern Lebanon." *Comparative Studies in Society and History* 51 (3): 533–62.

Siegel, Ellen. 2001. "After Nineteen Years: Sabra and Shatila Remembered." *Middle East Policy* 8. http://www.mafhoum.com/press2/79P9.htm (accessed December 1, 2012).

Simone, Abdou Maliq. 2010. "Reaching a Larger World: Muslim Youth and Expanding Circuits of Operation." In *Being Young and Muslim*, ed. Linda Herrera and Asef Bayat, 145–60. Oxford: Oxford University Press.

Singerman, Diane, and Paul Amar, eds. 2006. *Cairo Cosmopolitan: Politics, Culture, and Urban Space in the New Globalized Middle East*. Cairo: American University in Cairo Press.

———, eds. 2009. *Cairo Contested: Governance, Urban Space, and Global Modernity*. Cairo: American University in Cairo Press.

Skelton, Tracey, and Gill Valentine, eds. 1998. *Cool Places: Geographies of Youth Culture*. London: Routledge.

Smith, David M. 2000. *Moral Geographies: Ethics in a World of Difference*. Edinburgh: Edinburgh University Press.

———. 2007. "The Moral Aspects of Place." *Planning Theory* 6 (1): 7–15.

Sobelman, Daniel. 2004. "New Rules of the Game: Israel and Hezbollah after the Withdrawal from Lebanon." Memorandum no. 69, Jaffee Center for Strategic Studies, Tel Aviv, January.

Starrett, Gregory. 1995. "The Political Economy of Religious Commodities in Cairo." *American Anthropologist* 97 (1): 51–68.

Stephan-Hachem, Maud, and Azza Charara-Beydoun. 2011. "Bayn al-lahu wal jadd: Al-mumarasat al-thaqafiyya lil shabab al-lubnani (dirasa maydaniyya)." *Idafat* 13:47–80.

Stone, Christopher. 2008. *Popular Culture and Nationalism in Lebanon: The Fairouz and Rahbani Nation*. London: Routledge.

Swedenburg, Ted. 2007. "Imagined Youths." *Middle East Report* 245:4–11.

Taraki, Lisa. 2008. "Urban Modernity on the Periphery: A New Middle Class Reinvents the Palestinian City." *Social Text* 26 (2): 61–81.

UNDP. 1998. "Youth and Development." National Human Development Report for Lebanon.

Varzi, Roxanne. 2006. *Warring Souls: Youth, Media, and Martyrdom in Post-Revolution Iran*. Durham, NC: Duke University Press.

Veblen, Thorstein. (1899) 1994. *The Theory of the Leisure Class: An Economic Study of Institutions*. London: Dover Publications.

Verdeil, Eric. 2011. *Beyrouth et ses urbanistes. Une ville en plans (1946–1975)*. Beirut: Institut Français du Proche-Orient.

Vigh, Henrik E. 2006. "Social Death and Violent Life Chances." In *Navigating Youth, Generating Adulthood: Social Becoming in an African Context*, ed. Catrine Christiansen, Mats Utas, and Henrik E. Vigh, 31–60. Uppsala, Sweden: Nordic Africa Institute.

Walbridge, Linda S. 2001a. "The Counterreformation: Becoming a Marja' in the Modern World." In *The Most Learned of the Shi'a: The Institution of the Marja' Taqlid*, 230–46. Oxford: Oxford University Press.

———. 2001b. "Introduction: Shi'ism and Authority." In *The Most Learned of the Shi'a: The Institution of the Marja' Taqlid*, 3–13. Oxford: Oxford University Press.

Weiss, Max. 2010. *The Shadow of Sectarianism: Law, Shi'ism, and the Making of Modern Lebanon*. Cambridge, MA: Harvard University Press.

Wilkins, Amy C. 2008. *Wannabes, Goths, and Christians: The Boundaries of Sex, Style, and Status.* Chicago: University of Chicago Press.

Winegar, Jessica. 2006. *Creative Reckonings: The Politics of Art and Culture in Contemporary Egypt.* Stanford, CA: Stanford University Press.

Wulff, Helena. 1995. "Introducing Youth Culture in Its Own Right: The State of the Art and New Possibilities." In *Youth Cultures: A Cross-Cultural Perspective*, ed. Vered Amit-Talai and Helena Wulff, 1–18. London and New York: Routledge.

Wynn, Lisa. 2007. "Reproductive Health Technologies and Cyber Fatwas." Paper presented at the annual meeting of the American Anthropological Association, Washington, DC, November 30.

Index

———

Note: Page numbers in italics indicate figures.

'abaya, 152, 252n23
Abaza, Mona, 118
Abedini, Reza, 69–70, 240n12
Abou-Saab, Pierre, 69, 240n11
Abu Sa'id al-Khansa. *See* al-Khansa, Abu Sa'id
Aghadir, 123, *124*
Ain el-Mreisseh neighborhood, 205
Ain el-Rummaneh neighborhood, 178
alcohol, 7–8, 94–95, 212; morality of, 18, 20, 66, 142–44, 251n12, 251nn16–17; sales of in cafés, 71, 75, 112, 144, 241n19, 242n23, 256n19; social negotiations on, 144–51, 159
Amal, 39, 233n7, 242n24; founding of, 38; political participation of, 233n10, 234n15; social services network of, 50–51, 235n34
American University of Beirut, 31, 60, 205
Aoun, Michel, 6, 7, 41, 44, 61, 235n28
Arabic coffee, 247n10
Arabic language, 112–13, 128, 212, 248n12, 248nn14–16, 249n32
Arab Spring, 32, 33–34, 220–21
argileh, 2, 5, 13–14, 212; flavored tobacco for, 7, 112, 253n35; legal bans on, 253n36; morality of, 50, 64, 68, 161–63; popularity of, 126, 161, 248n30; price of, 112, 247n11
Aristotelian thought, 16
Asad, Talal, 220, 228n17, 242n21
al-Asadi, Hazar, 28
al-Assad, Bashar, 49
Assaf, Roger, 69, 240n11
Assaha International Group, 85

Association for Reviving Resistance Heritage, 239n2
Atrissi, Talal, 63, 248n26
authenticated belief and practice, 157
'ayb, 21, 162–63

Baalbek Festival, 128
Bab al-Hara café, 1–10, 112; décor of, 116, *126,* 127; gym and bath facilities of, 5–6, 111, 247n7; manager of, 4; owner of, 3
Bab al-Hara television series, 116
Badaro neighborhood, 24
Badreddine, Mustafa, 235n31
Baqiyat Allah magazine, 29, 81, 137, 231n42
Bayat, Asef, 14, 32
Bay Rock restaurants, 71, 103, 247n11
beer, 94–95
behavior. *See* moral flexibility
Beirut, 178–80, 255nn5–6; Central District (BCD) of, 24, 229n30; Corniche of, 197–98; Eurocentric aesthetic model in, 211–12, 258n5; French-style café culture in, 12–13, 33, 126–27, 189, 213, 220, 247n11, 258n5; as immoral space, 181–88; power-sharing governance of, 198, 257n24; rights to moral leisure in, 202–7, 257n25. *See also* Dahiya; geography of leisure
Beirut Mall, 54–55, 71, 76, 248n31
Bekaa Valley, 42, 50–51
Berri, Nabih, 45
Berry-Chickhaoui, Isabelle, 256n17
Beydoun, Azza, 237n53
Bint Jbeil, 42–43
Bir Hassan neighborhood, 206

Bluetoth technology, 172–74
border crossing, 144
Bou-Assi, Wissam, 28
Boubekeur, Amel, 233n3, 238n56
Bourdieu, Pierre, 208–10, 217–18, 230n36,
  236n40, 255n10, 258n3
Bourj el-Barajneh neighborhood, 241n13
Bourj Hammoud neighborhood, 178
Broummana, 184, 256n11

Café 33, 112
Café de Flore, 258n4
Café de Paris, 13, 220
cafés in Dahiya, 1–15, 32–33, 199–207,
  257n27; blurred boundaries of public
  and private in, 200, 257n30; customer
  demographics of, 29, 111, 246n1; expansion of, 103, 105; female employees of,
  252n30; geographic distribution of, 28,
  103–9; Islamic legitimacy of, 7–11;
  middle-class owners of, 54; mixed-
  gender interaction in, 33, 65, 72, 76, 109,
  200–202, 227n3, 232n46, 241n16; moral
  policing in, 93–100; music in, 142,
  257n31; rapid spread of, 89–90; sociospatial dynamics of, 26–28; as spaces for
  leisure, 10–15, 64, 99–100; stylistic diversity of, 109–12; survey of, 28–29,
  102–13
Café.Yet, 102–3, 112, 127–28, 130, 142, 177
Café Younes, 13
Cahill, Caitlin, 256n17
Cairo School of Urban Studies, 231n38
Caracalla Folk Dancers, 128–29
Caribou, 13
change, 217–22
Chirri, Amin, 71–72
Chun, Elaine, 248n14
civil war, 13, 38–39, 64, 233nn6–7; sectarian
  population displacements of, 24, 47–48,
  241n13; Taif agreement ending, 48
Clarke, Morgan, 229n29, 244n40
class distinctions. See social class
Coda Café, 109–11, 124–25, 142, 213–14,
  247n4
Coffee Bean and Tea Leaf, 13
coffeehouses. See cafés in Dahiya; tradi-
  tional coffeehouses
coffee preparation, 247n10
Coffey, Amanda, 257n27

Communist Party, 242n24
consumer development projects, 54
consumption of leisure, 13–15, 62–63, 216–
  17, 220
contemporary style cafés, 124–27, 209–10,
  248n31
Corniche, 178, 197–98, 255n4, 256n22
Crepaway, 13
customer demographics, 29, 111, 246n1
customer service, 214–15

dabkeh (dance), 20, 140–41, 152–55, 250n2
Dagher, Diala, 29
Daher, Ali, 63, 68–69, 121, 138, 214–15,
  240nn7–8, 250nn8–9
Dahiya (South Beirut), 7, 25–26, 227n4,
  241n13; crime and social challenges in,
  63–64, 240n8, 248n25, 248–49nn60–61;
  demographics of, 7–8, 219; history of,
  46–50; Hizbullah's domination of, 48–
  49; informal settlements in, 108, 122,
  247n4; Islamic milieu of, 37–38,
  232–33nn2–3; July 2006 war on, 42–43,
  49–50, 187, 234n18, 234n23; leisure opportunities in, 35–38, 40, 55–56, 61–65,
  149, 199–207, 252n20; maps of, 104–6,
  108, 110; municipal councils of, 70–71;
  political participation of, 51; Resistance
  museum planned for, 239n2; returning
  emigrants to, 53, 62, 63, 66, 71–72, 117;
  Shi'i middle class in, 50–55, 210–16; stereotypes of, 176–80, 185–87, 210–12,
  254–55nn1–3, 256n22; transnational development investment in, 205, 258n32;
  urban development in, 51. See also cafés
  in Dahiya
dancing, 20, 140–41, 152–55, 250n2
Deboulet, Agnes, 256n17
Deeb, Lara, 157
disaster tourism, 177, 254n2
Distinction (Bourdieu), 210
diversity, 130–31. See also style of cafés
Diwan, 111
diwaniyyat seating, 115, 130
Doha agreement of 2008, 44, 45
Dora neighborhood, 178
Douaihy, Chawqi, 13
downtown Beirut (Central District), 24,
  229n30
Druze, 44, 184

eclectic styles, 127–34, 211–12, 248n17, 248n33
Egypt, 31–33, 118, 128, 161, 221, 248n33
Eido, Walid, 235n25
Elyssar, 233n10
The Emancipated Spectator (Ranciere), 218–19
al-Emdad Foundation, 1, 130–31, *177*
emigrants, 148–49; goodbye parties for, 149; return of to Lebanon, 53, 62, 63, 66, 71–72, 117
emo hijabis, 31, 158–59, 253nn31–32
engagement, 169
English language use, 112–13, 128, 188, 212
entrepreneurs. *See* private sector entrepreneurs
Everyday Café, 103
Ewing, Katherine, 229n22
Ezzedine, Salah, 54

Fadlallah, Grand Ayatollah Sayyid Muhammad Hussein, 1, 29, 38–39, 242n26, 244n41; advice office of, 78, 243n35; on alcohol, 251n17; on argileh, 23, 161–62; on chatting, 231n42; on displays of wealth, 14–15; on domestic workers, 76, 242n26; on hymen reconstruction surgery, 254n43; on individual responsibility and choice, 18, 82–83, 98–99, 156–57, 219; on morality and leisure, 79–80; on music and songs, 137–38, 140, 141; on permission to marry, 22–23, 81–82, 244n37; popularity of, 76–77, 80–84, 243n35; on sin, 251n12; social service work of, 1, 50, 81, 85–87; on *wilayat al-faqih*, 244n44; writings of, 243n29, 243n35
Fadlallah, Sayyid Ali, 245n45
Fadlallah, Sayyid Ja'far, 78–79, 245n45; on argileh smoking, 161–62; on individual responsibility and choice, 81–83, 98–99, 219; on music and songs, 137–38
Fairuz (singer), 140, 142, 251n14
Family House, 92, 103, 112, 246n46
Fantasy World, 35–36, 53–54, 61, 65, 247n4; family focus of, 92–93, 102–3, 193; formal style of, 123, 130; Hizbullah's facilitation of, 71–72; as positive example, 87–89; private spaces at, 76
Farah Park, 88, 92

Fawaz, Mona, 231n38
Fayadh, Grand Ayatollah Muhammad Ishaq, 243n28
Fayyad, Ali, 63, 98
Fealy, Greg, 259n10
Fiori, 111, 112, 125–26, 142, 248n29
flexibility. *See* moral flexibility
flirtation, 11, 136, 168–75, 253n38
folk culture, 128–29
formal style cafés, 122–24, 209
Foucault, Michel, 228n14
France/French: café culture of, 12–13, 33, 126–27, 247n11; Horsh Beirut park reconstruction aid from, 198; language use of, 112–13, 128, 212, 248n16; as Lebanese aesthetic model, 211–12; mandate of in Lebanon, 12
Frangieh, Sleiman, 44
Free Patriotic Movement, 7, 44, 46, 235n28
Freiha, Anis, 116, 118
fun. *See* leisure
Furn el-Chebbak neighborhood, 178
Future Movement, 41, 42, 233n10, 235n28

Gazzah, Miriam, 252n24
Gemayel, Pierre, 235n25
Gemmayze neighborhood, 13, 258n4
gender contexts, 8, 11, 20; of argileh use, 161–63; binary nature of, 227n2; under French influence, 12; of geography of leisure, 193–94; of moral flexibility, 150–51, 158–64; of moral policing, 95–100; of music and songs, 139–40; of pools and gyms, 72–73; of respectful behavior, 21, 165, 197; of virginity, 169–70, 254n43; of weddings, 152–55. *See also* mixed-gender interaction
general strike of 2007, 44–45
generational differences, 20–21, 56–61. *See also* Islamic vanguard generation
geography, 7–11, 27–28, 30; moral production of spaces in, 26–28, 230nn33–37; of the political-sectarian rubric, 24–26, 179–80, 183–85, 229n32. *See also* spatial practices
geography of leisure, 176–207, 221; in Beirut, 178–80; class contexts of, 103–9; confinement in Dahiya in, 188–90; in Dahiya, 199–207, 257n27; expansion of moral leisure in, 202–7; individual

geography of leisure (*cont.*)
guidelines in, 192–94; mapping of moral
sites in, 195–98; neighborhood street life
and, 199–200, 257nn27–30; piety and,
181–82; pilgrimage trips in, 189;
political-sectarian comfort zone in, 180–
88, 202–7, 255nn8–9; pride and belonging in, 185–88; urban competences in,
190–92, 256nn17–18
Ghanem, Antoine, 235n25
Ghannam, Farha, 231n38
Gharbieh, Ahmad, 28
al-Ghazali, Imam, 137
Ghobeyri Cultural Center, 73
Ghobeyri neighborhood, 51, 53, 198,
241n13. *See also* al-Khansa, Abu Sa'id
globalization: corporate aesthetic models
of, 211, 258n4; diversity of styles of,
130–31
Gloria Jeans, 13
Golan Heights, 234n12
goodbye parties, 149
good taste. *See* taste
gossip, 163–64
Graiouid, Said, 247n5, 257n26, 257n30
Grapes of Wrath attack, 40
Greater Beirut. *See* Beirut; Dahiya
Green Line, 24

habitus, 255n10
Hadath neighborhood, 107, 219, 242n24
Hadi Nasrallah highway, 177
Haenni, Patrick, 217
Hage, Ghassan, 182, 209, 255n10
halal, 8, 71, 86–87, 112, 227n5, 243n33
Hall, Tom, 257n27
al-Hamarneh, Ala, 238n55
Hamra Café, 13, 118
Hamra neighborhood: pious cafés in, 205;
traditional café culture in, 12–13, 33,
126–27, 213, 220, 247n11, 258n5
Hangar, 31, 232n43
haraja (embarrassment), 146–47
Harakat al-Mahrumin, 38
haram, 21, 243n33, 250n3, 253n41; alcohol
as, 7–8, 18, 20, 66, 71, 75, 94–95, 112,
142–44, 241n19, 242n23, 251n16; food
as, 8, 71, 86–87, 112, 227n5, 245n48;
music/songs as, 66, 78, 99–100, 136–44,
152–55, 250n2; principle of necessary
avoidance of, 81, 138, 250n6

Harb, Charles, 237n53
Haret Hreik neighborhood, 42–43, 107,
179, 234n23, 241n13
Hariri, Rafic: assassination of, 13, 25, 41,
43–44, 49, 229n32; indictments for death
of, 45–46, 183–84, 235n31; rebuilding of
Beirut by, 44, 48–49
Hariri, Saad, 41; Future Movement political
party of, 233n10, 235n28; March 14 coalition of, 41–45, 50, 210–11, 235n25,
238n57
al-Hariri, Bahiyya, 41
Haugbolle, Sune, 118
Hay el-Sellom informal settlement, 107–9
Hazbun, Waleed, 238n55
headscarf. *See hijab*
Henkel, Heiko, 256n20
heritage style cafés, 114–19, 209, 248n19–20
Hersh, Seymour, 234n18
hijab, 19–20, 25, 30, 151; diverse forms of,
65, 152, 252n23; "emo" style of, 31,
158–59, 252–53nn30–31; as personal
choice, 59–60, 237n44; respectfulness
for, 158, 159, 163; shifting meaning of,
22–23, 57, 59, 158–61, 237n51
hijab hypocrisy, 59
Hizbullah, 7, 19, 66–76; children's activities
of, 240n6; civil order campaign of, 220;
control of Dahiya by, 48–49, 241n17;
control of leisure by, 10–11, 97–101,
143, 219–20, 242n24; cultural production by, 67–70, 74–75, 138, 214–15;
Emdad Foundation of, 1, 130–31, *177*;
facilitation of private investment by, 70–
73, 88; history of, 38–46; indictments for
Hariri's assassination of, 45–46, 183–84,
235n31; *infitah* (opening up) of, 38, 62–
65, 100–101, 233n4, 238nn56–57; March
8 coalition of, 41, 43–45, 49–50, 210–11,
235n29, 238n57; on material consumption, 15; media network of, 1, 6, 40, 67,
91; moral rubric in support for, 23; on
music, 137–38, 250–51nn7–10; neighborhoods friendly to, 9; neighborhood
watch groups of, 73–74, 241n18, 242n22;
political participation of, 39–41, 43–46,
48, 51, 218, 233n10, 234nn14–15,
241n13; popularity and growth of, 25,
44, 46, 170, 219, 238n57; Ras Beirut action by, 45, 50; research arm of, 240n7;
social welfare network of, 40, 43, 50–51,

63, 234n23; spiritual leadership of, 77; on Syrian revolution, 34. *See also* Lebanese Association for the Arts; the Resistance

Horch el-Qatil settlement, 247n4

Horsh Beirut park, 198, 256–57nn22–23

Houston, Christopher, 122

hybrid styles, 248n17

hymen reconstruction surgery, 254n43

Il Ponte, 112, 120, *131–33*, 131–34

Inmaa' Group, 71–72, 87–89, 92–93, 103. *See also* Fantasy World

intellectual emancipation, 218–19, 259n11

Internet, 7, 60–61, 102; Hizbullah's efforts to control, 74–75; social networking on, 30, 172–74, 192; Wi-Fi availability for, 111, 125, 247n8

inverted Orientalism, 134

Iran, 31–32; desacralized calligraphy of, 240n12; female musical performance in, 250n8; Islamic Revolution of, 39; religious jurisprudence in, 137, 244n44; Shi'i alignment with, 44, 235n27; Tehran's contemporary urbanity in, 62; temporary marriage in, 244n38

Islam: café culture in, 11–15; leisure in, 11, 14; as living and changing tradition, 220; modesty as value of, 14–24. *See also* religious jurisprudence

Islamic milieu of Dahiya, 37–38, 232–33nn2–3; control of, 97–101; at al-Saha Traditional Village, 85–87

Islamic vanguard generation, 56–59, 237n47; on café courtship, 171; on individual moral choices, 252n29; on moral leisure, 68–69, 155; on respect for *hijab*, 158, 159

Isma' ya Rida (Freiha), 116

Israel: July 2006 war of, 42–44, 49–50, 187, 234n18, 234n23; Lebanese prisoners in, 41; Liberation from, 25, 35, 37, 40, 49, 229n31; occupations of Lebanon by, 35, 39–40, 49, 234n12; ongoing armed conflict with, 41–42, 219–20

Jaber, Hala, 242n23

Jeita Country Club, 134

Jihad al-Binaa', 43

Jnah neighborhood, 206, 247n4

Jones, Carla, 237n51

Jordan, 116–17

Jumblatt, Walid, 256n16

Ka3kaya, 13, 205

Kanana, 102

Kanna, Ahmed, 231n38

Kassir, Samir, 235n25

Kaufman, Asher, 234n12

Kfouri, Wael, 139–40

Khadra, Sami, 77, 239n2

Khamenei, Grand Ayatollah Sayyid Ali Hosseini, 29, 76–80, 84, 231n42; on argileh smoking, 161–62; on individual responsibility and choice, 82–83; on music, 137–38, 250n7; on permission to marry, 82; on youth culture, 81

al-Khansa, Abu Sa'id, 51, 53–54, 56, 88; on censorship, 75; facilitation of private investment by, 71–73, 241n13, 241n15

Khiam tourism, 67

Khomeyni, Grand Ayatollah Ruhollah, 76–77

Khu'i, Grand Ayatollah Abu' Qasim, 76–78, 242n27

knowledge about leisure, 214–16

Koumeyha, Fatima, 28

Kratz, Corinne, 258n1

LAA. *See* Lebanese Association for the Arts

Lahoud, Emile, 45

language use, 112–13, 128, 188, 212, 248n12, 248nn14–16

"Laylit Hubb" (Umm Kulthum), 140

Laziz, 13

Lebanese American University, 205

Lebanese Association for the Arts (LAA), 67–70, 73, 239n2; cultural production by, 239nn2–3, 239n5, 240n8; Family Values and Order campaigns of, 69–70, 97–99, 220, 258n33; Sun of Freedom Orchestra of, 138, 250n8; teaching of leisure by, 214–15

Lebanese University, 50, 60, 107

Lefebvre, Henri, 26–27, 204–5, 230n33, 230–31nn36–38

leisure: cafés as spaces for, 10–15, 64, 228n12; as catalyst for change, 217–22; commercial consumption in, 13–15, 62–63, 216–17, 220; Hizbullah's *infitah* and, 38, 62–65, 100–101, 233n4, 238nn56–57;

leisure (cont.)
  Islamic jurisprudence on, 11; as marker
    of class status, 14–15, 27; sociospatial
    dynamics of, 26–28. *See also* cafés in Da-
    hiya; geography of leisure; moral flexi-
    bility; production of leisure
Le Marché, 112
Les Amis, 112
Liberation (*al-Tahrir*), 25, 35, 37, 40, 49,
    229n31
Liechty, Mark, 236nn39–40
Luna Park, 88, 245n49

Al-Mabarrat Association, 1, 50, 81, 85–87
Mahmood, Saba, 16–18, 228n17
Makki, Jamal, 115–16, 119, 215, 247n21
Malbon, Ben, 255n10
Manara neighborhood, 184, 256n11
al-Manar TV, 1, 6, 91
Mannheim, Karl, 56
maqha cafés, 12, 227nn8–9
Marada party, 44
March 8 movement, 41, 43–45, 49–50, 210–
    11, 235n29, 238n57
March 14 coalition, 41–45, 50, 238n57; class
    context of, 210–11; political leaders of,
    235n25
al-Markaz al-Ishtishari, 240n7
Mar Mikhail neighborhood, 107
Maroun el-Rass tourism, 67, 239nn2–3
marriage: average age of, 61, 237n51; court-
    ship and dating for, 168–75; engagement
    period before, 169; sectarianism and,
    168, 174; temporary form of, 167, 169,
    244n38, 254n43
martyr images, 177, 255n3
Massey, Doreen, 221
material consumption, 14–15, 62–63, 216–
    17, 220
Melki, Jad, 237n53
Melody television, 142
Meneley, Anne, 22
Meqdad clan, 248n60
Merrifield, Andrew, 230n37
middle classes, 236n40; expanded moral lei-
    sure of, 205–7, 258n33; expanding Shi'i
    membership in, 50–55, 61–62, 188, 205–
    6, 210–16, 218, 246n3; expansion of
    cafés among, 107–9; formal household
    décor of, 123–24; weddings among,
    51–52

Miqati, Nijab, 46
Miqdad, Shaykh Muhammad, 78–79, 82–83,
    162–63
Mitchell, Don, 230n35
mixed-gender interaction, 33, 65, 72, 76,
    109, 200–202, 221, 227n3, 232n46,
    241n16; moral policing of, 95–100; at
    weddings, 152–55; women's *hijab* and,
    158–61
Mleeta, 67–68, 121, 122, 239nn2–3
Modca, 13, 220
moral flexibility, 11, 29–30, 32, 60, 135–75,
    217, 229n22; on alcohol, 142–44,
    251nn16–17; in flirtation and courtship,
    11, 136, 168–75, 253n41; gender con-
    texts of, 150–51, 155–61, 158–61; on
    great sins, 139, 251n12; individual
    choice in, 155–58, 192–94, 219, 252n29;
    on public *vs.* private spaces, 139, 150–
    51, 161, 163, 165–67, 200, 257n30; reli-
    gious jurisprudence on, 17–24, 228n20,
    244n37, 244n40; respectful behavior
    and, 11, 164–67, 197; social negotiation
    and compromise in, 144–55, 201–2; on
    songs, 66, 78, 100, 136–44; of the youth
    generation, 60, 62, 138–42, 244n38,
    244n40
morality, 7–11, 15–24, 27–28, 30; café polic-
    ing of, 93–100; configuration in space of,
    26–28; definition of, 15–16, 228n14; as
    gendered, 11, 227n2; in geography of
    leisure, 195–98; individual responsibility
    and choice in, 18, 82–83, 98–99, 136,
    155–58; as Islamic value, 14–15; multiple
    rubrics of, 18–26, 179–80; scholarly lit-
    erature on, 16–17, 228nn14–19; sources
    of community authority on, 60; state
    regulation of, 31–32; taste of in con-
    sumption, 209–10, 216–17, 220; transna-
    tional market for, 62–63. *See also* reli-
    gious jurisprudence; rubrics of morality
Mrayjeh neighborhood, 241n13
MTV, 142
multilingual code-switching. *See* language
    use
multisectarian culture, 128–29, 148
Municipality Federation, 71
Musawi, Sayyid Abbas, 239n2
music/songs, 66, 78, 100, 136–44, 152–55,
    250n2
mutaqawqa'in, 190, 256n16

Nabi Sheet tourism, 239n2
nail polish, 83–84, 244nn41–42
al-Najafi, Grand Ayatollah Hashir Hussein, 243n28
Nasamat café, 119–21
Nasrallah, Sayyid Hassan, 6–7, 42–43, 45, 138, 256n16
nature-garden style cafés, 119–22, 209, 248n28
neoliberal capitalism, 27; economic reforms of, 45, 235n29; transnational market-place of, 62–63
Newcomb, Rachel, 252n30
Norton, Augustus Richard, 241n15
nostalgia, 118–19
Noureddine, Ayat, 76
al-Nour radio, 91

Ortner, Sherry, 55, 236n40, 259n12
O TV, 6

Palestine/Palestinians, 33–34; refugee camps of, 107, 108; Sabra and Shatila massacres of, 39
Pandolfo, Stefania, 228n17
patron demographics, 29, 111, 246n1
Peleikis, Anja, 236n37
Peterson, Mark, 248n33
piety, 14; among youth, 56–62, 98, 236n41, 237n50; class context of, 210–11; geo-graphic comfort zone of, 181–82; of the Islamic vanguard generation, 57–59, 145; men's clothing and, 237n50; noncon-formist exceptions to, 30–31, 232n43; normative practices of, 22–23, 30, 32, 58–59, 65, 229nn26–27, 231n42; rela-tionship of to morality, 15–18, 20, 151, 228nn21–22. See also hijab; morality
pilgrimage, 189
place. See geography; spatial practices
political-sectarian rubric of morality, 19, 23, 33–34, 229n25; geography of, 24–26, 179–80, 183–85, 229n32, 255n8; in gov-ernment power-sharing formula, 198, 257n24; intersection with class and taste of, 210–16, 258n3; Sunni-Shi'i polariza-tion in, 43–46, 63, 184–85
Politics of Piety (Mahmood), 16–18
pop music, 134–42
private sector entrepreneurs, 87–97; family focus of, 92–100, 245nn55–56; Hizbul-lah's facilitation of, 70–73, 88; Inmaa' Group as, 71–72, 87–89; unbusinesslike tendencies of, 89–92, 245nn50–53
"The Problem of Generations" (Mannheim), 56
production of leisure, 66–101; Hizbullah's facilitation of, 66–76, 88, 100–101, 143, 240nn6–8, 241n17, 242n22; moral polic-ing in, 92–100; multiplicity of possibili-ties in, 66–67; private sector entrepre-neurs in, 87–97; religious jurisprudence on, 76–87, 98–99, 242n26, 243n33; re-turning emigrants in, 66, 71–72, 89–90, 117

Qabalan, Shaykh Abdul-Amir, 243n28
Qana massacre, 40, 41
Qaradawi, Shaykh Yusef, 137
Qasr Moussa, 247n22
queer (LGBT) community, 31
Qur'an and hadith, 14. See also religious jurisprudence

Rahbani brothers performances, 118, 128
Ramlet el-Bayda neighborhood, 219
Ranciere, Jacques, 218–19, 259n11
Raouche neighborhood, 184, 203, 256n11
Ras Beirut neighborhood, 24, 31, 248n30; March 8 attack on, 45, 50; middle class of, 55
Ras el-Nabeh neighborhood, 24, 107
Rawda Café, 247n11
real estate, 45, 178, 205, 235n30, 255n7
regional context, 31–34
religiosity. See piety
religious jurisprudence, 76–87, 242n26, 243n28, 243n33; al-Saha Traditional Vil-lage and, 85–87; Fadlallah's role in, 77–78, 80–85, 219, 244n44; principle of nec-essary avoidance in, 81, 138, 250n6; succession in, 245n45; tradition of flexi-bility in, 17–24, 228n20, 244n37, 244n40. See also moral flexibility
religious rubric of morality, 19–21, 58, 60, 148–50, 179–80, 229n27
research process: interviews and interlocu-tors in, 29–31, 60, 150, 231nn39–42; par-ticipant observation fieldwork in, 28–29
the Resistance, 9, 19, 33–34, 39–40, 227n6; LAA's narration of, 67–68; planned museum on, 239n2; popularity of, 170;

the Resistance (*cont.*)
 visual reminders of, 177–78. *See also*
   Hizbullah
respectfulness, 11, 136, 164–67, 197
Resselat, 239n2
Rice, Condoleezza, 42
Ristretto, 13
Robbins, Joel, 18–19, 228n16, 229n24
Robinson, Catherine, 256n21
Rofel, Lisa, 236n43
rubrics of morality, 18–24, 26; overlap in,
   21–23; political-sectarian sphere of, 19,
   23–26, 179–80, 183–85, 229n25; religious
   sphere of, 19–21, 58, 60, 229n27; social
   sphere of, 19, 21–22, 229n27; taste and,
   216–17

Sabra and Shatila massacres, 39
al-Sadr, Musa, 38
al-Saha Traditional Village, 35–36, 61, 65,
   85–87, 102–3, 177; heritage style of,
   115–16, 119, 247nn20–22; prices at,
   247n11, 258n6; service variety at, 111;
   weddings at, 154
Sainte-Thérèse neighborhood, 107, 142,
   206, 257n31
Saliba, Robert, 248n19
satellite television, 61, 74–75, 100, 111,
   241n20, 247n9
Schielke, Samuli, 16–17, 18, 32
Schulz, Dorothea, 252n29
seafood, 87, 245n48
sectarianism, 43–44, 49–50; civil war population displacements and, 24, 47–48; geography of leisure and, 179–80, 183–85;
   ghettoization in, 190, 256n16; in-group
   marriage and, 168, 174; intersection of
   with class, 55; in rubrics of morality, 19,
   23, 24–26, 229n25; Sunni-Shi'i polarization as, 43–46, 63, 184–85
semsar (land brokers), 29, 231n39
sexuality, 229n29; moral policing of, 95–
   100; public displays of, 165–67; queer
   (LGBT) community and, 31; virginity
   and, 169–70, 254n43. *See also* gender
   contexts
Shaery-Eisenlohr, Roschanack, 235n27
Shamseddine, Shaykh Muhammad Mahdi,
   243n28
shar'i (as term), 8
Shebaa Farms, 41–42, 234n12

Sheet, Douaa, 28–29, 227n1
al-Sheikh, Na'eem, 140
Shi'i community, 7–11; alignment of with
   Iran and Syria, 44, 219–20, 235n27; diaspora of, 51, 52; as exotic other, 134, 176–
   77; expanding middle class of, 50–55,
   61–62, 107, *108*, 205–6, 210–16, 218,
   246n3; leisure spaces of, 11; marginalization of in Lebanon, 39, 43–44, 48; moral
   flexibility in, 11, 17–24, 29–30, 32, 60,
   228n20, 229n22, 244n37, 244n40; service
   sector jobs of, 259n9; sources of moral
   authority in, 60; stereotypes of, 25, 44,
   176–80, 185–87, 210–12, 254–55nn1–3,
   256n22; vanguard generation of, 56–59,
   145; village ties of, 119, 120, 181. *See
   also* Hizbullah; rubrics of morality
Siniora, Fuad, 42, 43
Sistani, Grand Ayatollah Sayyid Ali al-
   Husayni, 29, 77–80, 84, 243nn31–32; on
   alcohol, 251n17; on music, 137–38,
   251n10; on nail polish, 244n41; principle
   of necessary avoidance of, 81, 138,
   250n6; on seafood, 245n48
sit-in of 2008, 44, 49–50
Slim, Lokman, 31, 232n43
smoking. *See* argileh
Sobh wa Masa, 112
social class: expanded moral leisure and,
   205–7, 258n33; expanding Shi'i middle
   class, 50–55, 61–62, 107–9, 188, 205–6,
   218, 246n3; intersection of with sect, 55;
   leisure as marker of, 14–15, 27; of marginalized Shi'i, 44, 48; taste as marker of,
   208–16, 258n1; of wealthy Shi'i, 53–54.
   See also middle classes
social networking, 30, 172–74, 192, 231n42
social rubric of morality, 19, 21–22, 179–80,
   229n27; mapping a geography of leisure
   in, 195–98; negotiations and compromise in, 148–50, 201–2; respectfulness
   in, 11, 136, 164–67, 197
social spaces. *See* spatial practices
Solidere, 48–49
Souq al-Hamadiyya, 189
South Beirut. *See* Dahiya
Southern Lebanese Army, 39–40
southern suburb of Beirut. *See* Dahiya
spatial practices, 26–28, 99–100, 221–22,
   230n35, 259n13; in Dahiya's new cafés,
   199–207, 257n27; intersection of with

class and sect, 55–56, 208–16; Lefebvre's triadic model of, 26–27, 204–5, 230–31nn36–38, 230n33; practicing morality and, 195–98; in public *vs.* private spaces, 139, 150–51, 161, 163, 165–67, 200, 257n30; in urban studies literature, 231n38. *See also* geography of leisure
sports, 111
Starbucks, 13, 211, 213
Starrett, Gregory, 216
Steiner, Christian, 238n55
Stephan-Hachem, Maud, 237n53
Stone, Christopher, 118
style of cafés, 113–34, 209–16, 258n4; contemporary style of, 124–27, 248n31; eclecticism and diversity in, 127–34, 211–12, 248n17, 248n33; formal style of, 122–24; heritage style of, 114–19, 248n19–22; nature-garden style of, 119–22, 248n28; nostalgia in, 118–19
Suleiman, Michel, 45–46
Supreme Islamic Shi'i Council, 38, 78, 243n28
survey of Dahiya's cafés, 28–29, 102–13, 246n2; on age of customers, 29, 111, 246n1; on gender preferences, 109–11, 247n6; on menu options, 112, 247n10; on music and television, 111, 247n9; on naming and language use, 112–13, 212, 248n12, 248n14; on prices, *110*, 112, 212–13, 247n11, 258nn6–7; on quality, 212–14; on service variety, *110*, 111–12; on size, *110*; on style and décor, 113–34, 211–12, 248n17
Sweet Café, 53, 103, 109–11, 112, 114, 117
Swiss Time, 121, 122–23, 134
Syria: Golan Heights of, 234n12; heritage-style restaurants in, 116–17; occupation of Lebanon by, 41, 48, 234n13; revolution in, 34; Shi'i community alignment with, 44, 219–20; tourism to, 189, 256n14

Tabaja, Adham, 88–89, 92–97, 98
Tariq al-Jadidah neighborhood, 198
taste, 11, 208–16, 258n1, 258n3; as catalyst for change, 218–22; Dahiya quality and, 212–14, 258n4, 258nn6–8; Dahiya style and, 211–12; in moral consumption, 216–17, 220; in teaching of leisure, 214–16

taxis, 139, 141
temporary marriage, 167, 169, 244n38, 254n43
Terrace, 111, 112, 116–17, 127, *128*, 193
tobacco, 112
tourism, 62, 238n55; LAA's jihad tourism, 68–69; for pilgrimages, 189; at al-Saha Traditional Village, 85–87; in Syria, 189, 256n14
traditional coffeehouses, 11–15, 33, 107–9, 227nn8–9
transliteration, 248n14
transnational marketplace: family networks in, 51, 52, 62–63, 236nn37–38; of morality, 62–63; of youth culture, 238n56
Tueni, Gibran, 235n25
Turkey, 31–32, 33
Turkish coffee, 247n10

UMAM, 95, 232n43
Umm Kulthum, 140, 251n14
UN Interim Force in Lebanon, 42
United States: alliance of with Israel, 42, 234n18; alliance of with Saudi Arabia, 44; global corporate aesthetics of, 211, 258n4; products associated with, 9, 76; war of on terror, 78, 234n18
urban citizenship, 221–22
urban competences, 190–92, 256nn17–18

vanguard generation. *See* Islamic vanguard generation
Veblen, Thorston, 14
village style cafés, 114–19, 209, 248n19–22

Wahhab, Wi'am, 44
Walbridge, Linda, 245n45
Walters, Keith, 248n14
weddings, 152–55
Wehbe, Haifa, 141
Williamson, Howard, 257n27
Winegar, Jessica, 211
World of Our Youth (Fadlallah), 243n35

X5 café, 112

youth generation (*shabab* and *sabaya*), 56–61, 215–17, 236n41, 236n43, 237nn47–49; on alcohol, 143–44; argileh use of, 161–63, 212; average age of marriage of, 61, 237n51; Fadlallah's influence on,

youth generation (*cont.*)
  83–84, 243n35; Fadlallah's views on, 81–
  84, 244n37; flirtation and courtship of,
  11, 136, 168–75, 253n41; geography of
  leisure of, 180, 195–98; *hijab* and appearance of, 158–61, 170; on individual
  choice, 136, 155–58; media consumption
  of, 61, 75, 237n53; mixed-gender interaction of, 95–97; moral flexibility of, 60,
  62, 217, 244n38, 244n40; music and
  songs of, 138–42; piety of, 56–62, 98,
  236n41, 237n50; on respectful behavior,
  164–67; sedentary habits of, 67–68; on
  social negotiations and compromise,
  144–55; spaces of for leisure, 99–100;
  transnational culture of, 238n56; urban
  competences of, 190–92, 256nn17–18
Youth Mobilization Unit, 240n6